THE PUBLIC SPEAKER'S

TREASURE CHEST

The
Public Speaker's
Treasure Chest

*A Compendium of
Source Material to
Make Your Speech
Sparkle*

by

Herbert V. Prochnow

A. Thomas & Co.

BLACKPOOL

First British edition, July 1954

PRINTED IN GREAT BRITAIN BY
MORRISON AND GIBB LIMITED, LONDON AND EDINBURGH

PREFACE

This book has been written for two groups of persons—the many men and women who must occasionally make an address, introduce a speaker, or preside at a meeting; and the large number of persons who would like to improve their conversation.

At the beginning of the book there are two chapters which show how to prepare a speech and how to make a speech sparkle. It is hoped that the reader will be able by a study of these chapters to grasp the essential steps in the preparation of any speech. Many illustrations have been included to be helpful.

To make the book also a compendium of source material that may be used on many occasions in speeches and conversation, there are included over 4000 humorous stories, epigrams, similes, amusing definitions, quotations from literature, interesting incidents from famous lives, and unusual phrases. These materials are the practical tools by which speeches and conversation are made fascinating and colorful. Books have been published which contained humorous stories; other books have presented similes or quotations. In this book, however, an effort is made to show in a single volume not only how to write a good speech, but also to present an abundance of material which will assist in the preparation of speeches and the improvement of conversation. The range is from the simplest humorous story to the more difficult tools of effective speech. The public speaker has here instantly available a treasure chest of all types of speech materials.

The most commonly used method of making speeches and conversation more interesting is humor. There are times when a joke, well told, will strikingly illustrate a point, or definitely relieve a tense moment in discussion or argument. At other times a short, barbed epigram, subtly introduced, is helpful. Sometimes a good humorous definition is of assistance. But humor must never be dragged in or consist merely of a series of irrelevant jokes. It must be to the point, clearly told, and without any "that reminds me" introduction.

Quotations from the Bible and from literature are important speech materials because they frequently represent the most unusual, thoughtful and classic expressions great men have made on significant subjects.

The simile is used by far too few men and women. Yet it is a simple and serviceable tool of speech. An occasional simile adds distinct character to utterance and to writing.

There are also the infinite number of interesting incidents which may be obtained from the stories of famous lives. In them one finds illustrations of achievement, tragedy, patience, adversity, persistence and all the experiences of human life. The wider one's reading in this field, the richer one's conversation and speech. Finally, by careful reading one acquires the knowledge which permits unusual phrases, such as those in Chapter IX, to be made a part of daily conversation and prepared or extemporaneous speeches. Eloquence may be one of the products of wise use of the increased knowledge which comes from reading good books. Repeated study and daily use of the source materials in this book will return rich rewards.

This book has grown in part out of the practical experience of addressing hundreds of business and banking conventions, associations of commerce, Rotary, Kiwanis, Lions and Optimists clubs, high school and college commencements, professional societies and other organizations. To the extent that it serves to make speeches and conversation more effective and interesting, it will have served its purpose.

H. V. P.

CONTENTS

PREFACE   v

I. HOW TO PREPARE YOUR SPEECH   1

II. HOW TO MAKE YOUR SPEECH SPARKLE   36

III. PUBLIC SPEAKING IN A NUTSHELL   58

IV. JOKES AND JESTS   62

V. WISE CRACKS AND EPIGRAMS   190

VI. AMUSING DEFINITIONS   222

VII. INTERESTING LIVES AND INTERESTING FACTS   235

VIII. SIMILES   254

IX. COLORFUL PHRASES FOR SPARKLING SPEECH   269

X. BIBLICAL QUOTATIONS   286

XI. A RICH TREASURE HOUSE OF SELECTED QUOTATIONS   302

THE PUBLIC SPEAKER'S

TREASURE CHEST

Chapter I

HOW TO PREPARE YOUR SPEECH

::

Epictetus, the Stoic philosopher, once said, "No great thing is created suddenly, any more than a bunch of grapes or a fig. If you tell me that you desire a fig, I answer you that there must be time. Let it first blossom, then bear fruit, then ripen."

One may say with equal truth that no great speech is created suddenly. The ideas it contains almost invariably grow out of years of experience. And the actual preparation of the speech itself generally requires many hours of concentrated thought and hard work, if it is to be a significant contribution on any subject. The unpardonable sin in public speaking is the sin of inadequate preparation. However, the experienced speaker understands how to organize and prepare an effective address. He uses a number of relatively simple tools of speech which greatly assist him, and which anyone may readily learn and use.

1* Cicero said there were five essentials in public speaking: (a) determining exactly what one should say; (b) arranging the material in the proper order and with good judgment; (c) clothing the speech in well-chosen words and carefully phrased sentences; (d) fixing the speech in mind; (e) delivering it with dignity and grace. It will be helpful to each of us always to keep in mind these five essential steps which embrace the whole subject of public speaking.

2 When we proceed to the actual preparation of the speech itself, we find there are three simple divisions in almost every speech: the introduction; the body or the discussion; and the conclusion or summary. The introduction should clearly state the subject to be discussed so that the audience may thoroughly understand it. The body of the speech or the discussion should be a carefully prepared, logically arranged statement of the ideas

---

* The numbers which appear in consecutive order at the left-hand margin throughout the book refer to the index (see page 383). The use of the index will make it possible to refer instantly to related ideas and source material throughout the book.

which the speaker wishes to convey. It is advisable to divide the main body of the speech into several parts, perhaps two, three or four. Each of these parts should make a complete unit in itself so the audience will find it easier to keep the essential ideas of the speech clearly in mind. Finally, in the conclusion, the speaker usually should summarize in a few brief sentences the two, three or four ideas he presented in the main body of the speech. This plan of dividing a speech into an introduction, body, and conclusion is the most desirable form for most occasions, and for most speakers, and any deviation from it should come only after one has gained considerable experience in speaking.

Having taken what may be called a panoramic view of a speech, we are ready to present in considerably more detail the exact steps necessary for its preparation. Not all persons prepare speeches with the same thoroughness and exacting attention. Consequently, not all persons give equally good speeches.

3   The steps here outlined as necessary in preparing a speech are designed to be comprehensive and of assistance both to the beginner and to the more polished public speaker. With experience, some of the steps may perhaps be eliminated or modified, but finished public speaking is a high art, and it requires something more than slipshod and careless preparation.

4   Senator Arthur H. Vandenberg, an able speaker, has advised us that in his opinion "scrupulous and painstaking preparation is indispensable. When brilliance and force are extemporaneous in a public address, they are the exception that proves the rule." Every conscientious speaker is acutely and sensitively aware of the serious nature of his responsibilities. Therefore, many speakers will spend from a half hour to as much as one or two hours in preparation for each minute they expect to speak. A fifteen minute speech would mean a minimum of seven and one-half hours of preparation.

When one addresses an audience of one hundred people for thirty minutes, it is the equivalent of taking 3,000 minutes of one person's time. That means fifty hours, or more than six days of eight hours each. It would be little short of criminal deliberately to waste one person's time for six **working** days. Yet that is precisely what happens when a speaker without complete and thorough preparation takes the time of an audience of one hundred persons. If the audience is larger, the waste of time is proportionately greater. Should a person receive an invitation to address a meeting **and know** that he will not have time to make proper preparation for the occasion, he should decline the invitation. To accept it would be unfair to the audience and harmful to himself and the institution or business he represents.

An invitation to speak is a distinct honor. It may mean that a group of persons believe the speaker has exceptional knowledge in a field, or command of some phase of a subject, superior to that of many others who would like to receive his ideas. It may mean that others believe he has the ability to analyze and interpret a subject to the enlightenment of his audience. And in some instances it may mean that the speaker has the extraordinary ability to inspire others to greater achievement in life. No speaker who seriously contemplates these possibilities and the responsibilities they carry will ever appear before any audience poorly prepared. He will strive earnestly to fill each address with constructive ideas, logically arranged and eloquently presented. Too many speakers are unpardonably casual about the preparation of their speeches. To paraphrase Ben Jonson, any fool may talk, but only a wise man, thoroughly prepared, can give a great speech.

The outline which follows presents in a rather definitive form the steps almost every speaker will find it helpful to take in preparing a speech:

5   STEPS IN PREPARING A SPEECH

I. Determine the exact subject of the speech so that the objective is distinct in the mind of the speaker. If the speaker himself has a hazy conception of the nature of his subject, if his mind is foggy or fuzzy, and if he does not see clearly the outlines and limitations of his topic, how can he expect to leave his audience other than confused?

II. Think through the whole subject to be certain that he has formulated his own ideas and conclusions. In most cases, these ideas and conclusions will be predicated upon his own study, observation and experience.

III. Read exhaustively all the speeches, pamphlets and books on the subject of his speech. It may be necessary to take some notes. This work is not as difficult as it may appear. No wise person will ordinarily agree to speak in a field about which he knows nothing. Nor will an intelligent chairman of a program committee invite a speaker who is ignorant of his subject. Consequently, in preparing his address, the speaker will already be intimately acquainted with much of the material available on the topic. But he must be certain that he has a comprehensive understanding of the entire subject and is familiar with the most recent studies in that field. A superficial or shallow understanding of the subject may lead to disaster before an intelligent audience.

IV. Outline the speech into its three principal divisions and any minor subdivisions as follows:

A. Introduction.
B. Main body of the speech or discussion, perhaps divided into two, three, or four subdivisions.
C. The conclusion or summary.

V. Write out the speech after it has been fully outlined. Long experienced speakers may find it possible simply to outline an address and speak from the outline. But the person who is striving for perfection should in the beginning at least write out each speech in its entirety. Otherwise there is almost certain to be looseness in the structure of the speech. A Virginia mother who was criticizing an inadequately prepared speech of her own son said, "Jim, you may call that a speech, but I call it simply running off at the mouth." The failure of beginners particularly to write out a speech results in sloppiness of expression. Writing a speech tends to give preciseness and exactness in wording. Most persons may find it easier to write a speech longhand and then have it typed.
6 Senator Robert A. Taft has advised us that he prepares his addresses by the following method:

I jot down a number of ideas. Then I arrange those ideas and work them out in greater detail, so that the notes may cover as much as two foolscap pages. Then I dictate the address. Then I correct the first draft and have it written. Sometimes there is a second correction.
I should judge that it may take me eight hours to prepare a thirty-minute address, assuming that I do not have any extensive reading or research.
Of course sometimes it is not possible to prepare an address fully, but it is much better to do so even if you intend to speak extemporaneously.

7 Dr. Harry Emerson Fosdick has given us the following instructive and interesting explanation of the procedure he uses in preparing his sermons:

I always write out my sermons in full in advance. To the best of my recollection, after nearly forty years of preaching, I have never preached a sermon that was not written out fully. I do not see how any one can keep his substance serious, and his style flexible and varied unless he writes in full. At any rate, for myself there is no other method that is conceivable.
As for delivery, that I handle in varied ways; sometimes having the manuscript before me and reading freely; and sometimes drawing an outline from it and speaking from the notes.
With regard to the time spent on an average sermon it is very difficult to reckon that. How can one reckon the long period during which a sermon matures, oftentimes unconsciously germinating from some seed of an idea planted long before? All that I can do is to deal with the actual writing process, and not at all with the hours spent on the theme that contributed the substantial material to the sermon, and that there is no way of clocking. I would estimate that I spend a half hour in writing for each minute of the sermon.

No one can read the statements of these two eminent men without being impressed with the seriousness with which they assume the responsibility of speaking to an audience and the thoroughness with which they prepare their addresses.

8   WRITING THE INTRODUCTION

The two parts of an address most difficult to prepare are the introduction and the conclusion. Both must be relatively short. Both must be worked out with the greatest care. Senator Robert F. Reynolds has informed us that he arranges his "speech for a point in the program following the addresses of others." Then "I can listen very carefully to what the speakers before me have to say." In that way the Senator obtains points from other addresses which he can turn over in his mind for development. "I have found," advises Senator Reynolds, "that this has always given me a good start, and that is a lot to take into consideration in addressing an audience, whether your speech is a prepared one or an extemporaneous one. If you can get the ears of your listeners at the outset, then there is not much difficulty in keeping their attention."

In the introduction, the proposition to be discussed must be trimmed to its precise proportions. Sometimes, with experience, the introduction may be eliminated, particularly if the title clearly conveys the nature of the topic. However, it is almost always necessary to use an introduction, and eight possible methods of beginning an address are presented below with illustrations:

9   A. *Announce the subject directly in the first sentence or paragraph.*

ILLUSTRATIONS

Henry J. Allen, former Governor of Kansas and United States Senator, used the following concise introductory statement:

I aim to talk to you tonight about the Pan-American Conference at Lima. Most of you have heard the statement of Will Rogers that "the United States never lost a war nor won a conference." That appraisal is out of date since the Pan-American Conference. We won that conference.

George F. Barrett, Attorney General of Illinois, addressing the National Association of Attorneys General—

My subject—"The Future of Our States and Cities in Our Governmental Structure," is one of great importance to us as Attorneys General. But it is of even greater importance to the citizens of our states. It is vitally important to all citizens of the United States, not because of its academic significance, but for the reason that out of it may come the answer to the problem which is bothering so many of us, the problem which is our prime concern in these days

of world-wide uncertainty. That problem tersely stated is—Which Way
America?

George E. Sokolsky began one of his addresses with this brief introduction—

What I want to talk to you about tonight is the American way of life. Of
course there are men who say that there is no such thing as an American way
of life; there is not anything like a European way of life or an Asiatic way of
life; that people live as they do largely because of natural resources or man
power, or machinery; that they are what they are purely because of external
conditions; that nothing else matters.

In one short paragraph, in fact, in one short sentence of only a few
words the speaker was into his subject.

10 B. *Tell a story of human interest, "paint a picture" or give an illustration.*

Each one of the examples which follow is different, but each one intro-
duces the subject with an interesting word picture.

ILLUSTRATIONS

11 Albert Edward Wiggam speaking on "Pack Up Your Worries" over
the National Broadcasting Company Blue Network from America's Town
Meeting of the Air—

The other evening I was lying on the sofa listening to a symphony and
thinking what a grand and glorious world this is with nothing to worry about
when, as it closed, some bull-voiced gentleman began to shout that Niagara
Falls was about to be destroyed by the power companies. In two minutes he
had my nerves on edge and my hair on end, aghast at the frightful catastrophe.
According to his picture of it, the Falls will soon be a mere trickle, and the
rapids below a brook so stagnant it will breed mosquitoes. As a honeymoon
resort it will be a total loss, and as a result the marriage rate will go down,
the birth rate will drop, and the American people will soon be a vanished
breed, on their way to join the ichthyosaurus and the dodo.

I said to Mrs. Wiggam, I thought I had enough to worry about—taxes,
unbalanced budgets, increased bald-headedness, both inside and out—and now
I've got to sit up nights worrying about Niagara Falls. I tell you these reformers
and setters-of-things-to-rights are giving us the national jitters.

12 Dr. Arthur H. Compton, one of the world's greatest scientists and
Nobel Prize Winner, beginning an address on "Truth Makes Us Free"—

You probably have wondered what a scientist would be like, and by way
of introduction perhaps I can tell you a story my sister told me a few years ago.
It happens that my sister lives in India. Her husband is Principal of a
Mission College in Allahabad, and as they moved to Allahabad they had to
move into a house that was one of these old mission houses with high ceilings,

hard to heat when it got a little cool, but very good for keeping the hot air stirring.

But this house had been standing there so long that it was in bad repair and she needed to have some things looked after. She got a Hindu carpenter to come in to look after the windows, and she pointed out a window that needed to have the windowsill fixed. It had to be put right in a number of different ways.

She drew a little sketch as to how it was to be done, and then she was busy elsewhere around the house for several hours. When she came back, she found that the carpenter had made a pretty bad mess of the thing. It was going to be difficult ever to make it look like a proper window again, and she was, naturally, exasperated.

When he explained that he had tried to follow instructions she said: "But why didn't you use your common sense?" And this little Hindu, my sister said, pulled himself up to his full height and said: "But common sense, madam, common sense is a gift of God; I have technical knowledge only."

So when you come to have a person representing science talk to you, what would you expect to get? Technical knowledge, I suppose, is one of those things that one takes for granted; it is a part of one's job; but life is something more than that. Each of us has to be, before he is a carpenter or a painter or a butcher or a baker, he has to be a man. He has to be a citizen of his country. He has to be a human being to live with his fellow human beings, and it is that which requires common sense.

Channing Pollock, speaking on "I Am a Reactionary"—

When I was a youngster, oh, say twenty years ago, Broadway at 42nd Street in New York was perhaps the most remarkable thoroughfare in the world. Within a few blocks there were forty or fifty theaters, all dignified buildings, and many of them, like the New Amsterdam, really magnificent. After a matinee, culture, wealth, fashion and beauty ran like a river between its banks. First nights attracted first families and almost everybody noted in literature and the arts.

It was long afterward that first-night audiences in New York City came to consist mainly of wine agents, movie scouts, and ladies who regularly changed their hair and their husbands.

Today Broadway is devoted to flea circuses, burlesque houses, and orange-juice stands. Barkers and hawkers litter the sidewalks, along which flow the scum of humanity. The classic façades of the New Amsterdam and Times Square have been covered with enough signs and architectural eye-catchers to make a Hollywood holiday.

Broadway is the Bowery. And so is the world. What has happened to Broadway has happened to the world. It has become a vulgar world, a pushing, shoving, selfish and pitiless world.

Now, if anyone came along, another builder of Rockefeller Centers, let us say, and proposed restoring Broadway to its pristine dignity and glory, would you call him a reactionary? Probably not, and yet that word is commonly used for any man or woman who wants to restore anything.

Frank T. Bell in a speech on "Fish and Their Management" presented an interesting illustration in terms the audience could understand.

Nearly 3,000,000,000 pounds of fish make up our annual catch. If all these fish were landed at one port, it would require ten full-size freight trains moving every day in the year to haul them to the market. These fish bring a total income of over $60,000,000 to 117,000 fishermen. When we include manufacturing and distribution connected with the fisheries, we find that we have a billion dollar industry.

Merle Thorpe, speaking on "The Business of Government"—

As I work at my desk I can look out of my office window and see the west wings of the White House. There the general manager of this one-hundred-billion-dollar corporation, of which you and I are the stockholders, calls together his ten "vice presidents" to discuss recommendations that go to our board of directors on Capitol Hill.

13   Robert H. Jackson as Attorney General of the United States addressed the Eastern Association of College Deans and Advisers of Men on "Why a College Education?" His opening paragraph was a story of interest to every one of his listeners because it was related directly to their field. He said:

Perhaps you have heard about the College Executives who were discussing what they wanted to do after retirement age. One hoped to run a prison or school of correction so the alumni would never come back to visit. Another chose to manage an orphan asylum so he would not be plagued with advice from parents.

14   Daniel M. Eisenberg in a speech on "I Bring 'Em Back" broadcast over the Columbia Network—

In sixteen years I have located about 165,000 missing men, women and children. My organization is the only commercial one of its kind. It is designed primarily for people who don't want to go to the police or to the Traveler's Aid.

The most popular disappearance act I call "The Case of the Missing Husband." In sixteen years I've been asked to trace more than 75,000 husbands who have done the Arabian-tent-folding stunt. And, this will probably startle you: I've been asked to locate only twelve wives in that same period! There's a fairly simple explanation for that. Most women are not equipped to earn a living. They are accustomed to the social protection of a home and family, and very few of them have any money of their own with which to start on a flight into the unknown.

It's not the young husbands who run away from their wives. Just the opposite. My figures show that out of 100,000 husbands who disappear, close to eighty-five per cent are men past the age of forty.

15   C. *Use a statement that excites attention, arouses curiosity, surprises the audience, or is particularly informative.*

16 Dr. Hans Christian Adamson talking on "Don't Tread on Me" arouses curiosity in his introduction.

Ever since they made their appearance in the Garden of Eden snakes have probably been libeled more than any other creatures on earth. Popular fable has them stealing milk, rolling like hoops, using their tails as whips and stingers, and tripping up people by coiling around their legs. They are accused of being slimy and of having the hypnotic eye. They are said to be wise, to have the speed of "chained lightning" and never to die until sundown. All of which is perfect nonsense.

Alfred M. Landon speaking in October, 1941, on "The Contribution of the Republican Party to National Defense" opened with this short and striking sentence: "Here we are tonight, just American citizens, facing a situation growing worse each hour."

17 Mark Sullivan in an address on "What is Liberalism?"—

Up until the year 1917, there were two types of government in the world. One type consisted of democracies; the other of monarchies with varying modifications. At that time, preceding 1917, all the conflict about government that took place in the world was a conflict between these two types, between monarchy and democracy.

Of the democracies, the United States was the outstanding example. We were the outstanding example of it, and we were, in practical effect, the inventor of it. From the time we set it up, from the time we adopted our Constitution, in 1789, we had been a model for the rest of mankind. For 128 years, every change of government that had taken place anywhere (that was important or lasting) had been a departure from monarchy, or a limitation of it; followed by an adoption or extension of democratic forms.

The world seemed to share with us the conviction that the American model was the latest and best. Complacently we assumed—and by imitation other nations confirmed our complacency—that the last word in government had been said. In that confident complacency America rested for 128 years. We were sure we had the latest and best model of government—we took it as much for granted as we took the days of the week.

18 Dr. Edgar De Witt Jones speaking on the subject "Adventures Among Great Americans"—

I am a great believer in American history, and if I had the ear of the young people of America today, I would say, "Open the history of your country and live again with those mighty spirits that gave verve and substance and glory to the making of the Republic." Our country is opulent in the great characters it has produced. Whoever ventures into a study of American history ventures into a veritable field of the cloth of gold. It would seem that when the American Revolution was in the offing, and during that period and immediately afterwards, we had men to match the mountains. Think of it!

In those stirring times in Maryland was Luther Martin, in New York was John Jay and that brilliant statesman, Alexander Hamilton. In Pennsylvania was wise old Ben Franklin and Albert Gallatin, and in Massachusetts were the Adamses, John and John Quincy, and their great radical cousin, Samuel Adams.

But it is in Virginia that we find the galaxy of American greatness in that period. The tongue of the Revolution, Patrick Henry, was a Virginian. The pen of the Revolution, Thomas Jefferson, was a Virginian. The sword of the Revolution, George Washington, was a Virginian. The father of the Constitution, James Madison, was a Virginian. The author of the Monroe Doctrine, James Monroe, was a Virginian. The greatest of all the great Chief Justices of the United States, John Marshall, was a Virginian.

19 Dr. Ruth Alexander in an address on "Religion as a Force in Government"—

The alarm clock of history is wound up in periods of world crises and proceeds to run down between times. Today's days are lived at the high tension of alarm. Catastrophe confronts us, and with superficial inquiry as to its cause, we seek to correct it. Many of us pronounce the cure to lie in a vague "Liberalism," without realizing that liberalism has strayed far from its adherence to Liberty. Liberalism, as preached and practiced today, is coincident with security—the polar opposite of Liberty. It is, in fact, but an alibi for socialism and centralized power. The bait of man as his brother's keeper attracts many of our noblest spirits, but the poisonous hook lies hidden in man's power over his brother. Interference, even on another's behalf, is incompatible with freedom, and history has shown it to lead irrevocably to final relinquishment of democratic institutions.

I am here to challenge politico-economic maladjustment as the cause of world unrest. I am here to attribute it primarily to paralysis of religion as the supreme historic force in the government of human relations.

20 A particularly informative opening for a speech on "America's Conquest of Suffering and Disease" by a Chicago businessman, stated:

Since the early days of the pioneers when, in six months, pestilence and starvation reduced the first Virginia colony from 500 people to 60 and the Plymouth colony buried half its membership, America has poured into its warfare on poverty, starvation, disease and pestilence all those relentless energies which other nations too often express in warfare. In 1663 the first hospital was built; in 1934, 6,334 hospitals were registered by the American Medical Association. In that span of 271 years, American medical science drew the fangs of small pox, typhoid fever, yellow fever, rickets, diphtheria, tuberculosis and countless other devastating diseases.

In this progress there is no inclination to rest on the oars. With thousands of trained scientists carrying the battle to the enemy at every point, it is evident to all that we are on the threshold of even greater developments.

21 D. *Tell a humorous story that is definitely related to the subject or to the situation under which the speaker is addressing the audience.*

No story must be used simply to introduce humor. However, a good humorous story, well told and relevant, may provide an excellent introduction. If a speaker can tell a humorous story on himself, the audience enjoys it especially. Observe how frequently this device is used by actors entertaining over the radio. Over 1,000 humorous stories of all kinds and suitable for many occasions are presented in Chapter IV.

ILLUSTRATIONS

22 Dr. Allen A. Stockdale opening a series of public addresses to be given at Barrington, Illinois, on fourteen consecutive nights by outstanding leaders of American thought—

You people are going to meet together for a good many nights here in this Barrington Town-Warming, and in this glorious community.

There was an old Methodist preacher one time, a remarkable old fellow possessing a wonderful dry wit. He was conducting a revival meeting, and one fellow who was converted regularly every winter came up to the altar again. There he was right on scheduled time. He was praying: "Oh, Lord, fill me full, fill me full." This dear old Methodist preacher said: "Lord, don't do it, he leaks."

Well, I hope you folks won't get into that trouble here with all of this glorious menu that is in store for you.

I feel the responsibility of opening this program. It looks like a pretty big task. There was a man one time who was very successful, living in New York, who went back to the little town where he was born to see if he could find anybody he knew when he was a boy.

Finally he came upon an old town character, Old Hezekiah. There he was, just the same as when this New Yorker was a boy. He walked over to him and said: "Hello, Hezekiah, you still here?" Hezekiah said: "Yep, I'm still around." He said: "What are you doing, Hezekiah?" "Oh, jest about the same as usual." He said: "Now look here, Hezekiah, are you still going up to the little church?" "Yep, I still go up to the little church." "Tell me, do you still pump the organ up at the little church?" "Yep, I still pump the organ up at the little church, and say, by heck, last Sunday they had a new organist, and I pumped a piece he couldn't play."

I don't know if somebody is pumping a piece I can't play, but here I am anyway, ready to help you get started on this glorious something that we call a town-warming.

23 H. V. Kaltenborn, radio news broadcaster, speaking on "Looking at Europe From Here"—

Mr. Chairman, when you were saying those nice things about me it really made me feel good because, you know, the audience that listened to my speeches during the crisis did not have quite as good an opinion of what I did as you do. I kept getting telegrams almost from the first hour. This is the way they came. Here is one addressed to Columbia: "If you take that self-styled propaganda minister off the air, Europe might have a chance to solve her problems."

Here is a back-handed compliment for Columbia: "Your foreign broadcasts are very fine, but can't you put Kaltenborn on the kiddies' program?"

And here is another dig: "Deeply appreciate Kaltenborn but in crisis long to hear Boake Carter."

After I had said that I met Adolf Hitler and had several interviews with Benito Mussolini, and tried to tell what kind of chap Mussolini was in contrast with Hitler, and then, after I said I had talked with Daladier and Chamberlain and Beneš, along comes this: "Kaltenborn seemed to be clubby with every personage famous or infamous in this turbulent world. I have been waiting patiently to hear of his having a private conference with the Almighty."

And he goes on: "I am confidently expecting him to tell us one of these days that he has told the Angel Gabriel not to blow his horn before 10:00 A.M. Eastern Standard Time."

Of course, it is not only when you talk about a foreign crisis that you get into trouble, but just say something of national politics and see what happens to you—if you're a commentator. I ventured the other day to say something I thought was harmless. I said I felt poverty could never be completely eradicated, that, comparatively speaking, we would always have a certain amount of poverty with us, and this is one of the answers I got to that: "Just because you are too damn dumb to settle poverty, don't think Roosevelt can't, you small-town stuff."

Every now and then you get one letter that makes up for a hundred of the other kind. Here is one from a charming lady. I know she is charming because of what she said.

"Dear Mr. Kaltenborn, you are the most wonderful thing on the air. When I hear your manly voice it is as though you stood by the side of my bed and held my hand and talked just to me."

What pleased me most, because it included within itself so much of the exemplary quality of good English, force, elegance, ease, and brevity, was the comment sent to me on a postcard that just had three words, each one doubly underlined, and it said, "Nuts to you."

24 Channing Pollock, playwright, author and lecturer—

I have had a delightful afternoon here reaching its consummation in that most charming introduction. But an introduction like that makes me think of a story told me a great many years ago by a very dear friend of mine, named Charles Klein, who wrote a play called *The Lion and the Mouse*, which all of you little boys and girls are too young to remember.

Mr. Klein also wrote a play called *The Ne'er Do Well*, which didn't. And he told me that when the curtain fell on the last act of *The Ne'er Do Well* in New York a young woman sitting behind him touched him on the shoulder and said: "Are you Mr. Klein?" He said: "Yes." She said: "Before the curtain rose on your play I took the liberty of cutting off a lock of your hair, and now I would like to give it back."

After an introduction like that I am never sure that you may not want to give back my lock of hair. I can use it, you see.

Now, I have one more reason for being a little bit alarmed about introductions.

About four weeks ago I went to see *Victoria Regina* in New York. I was coming out of the theater, when I met my old friend, Mr. James T. Powers, who used to be the star of *The Geisha*. That also was when you were all in the cradle. But I had not seen Jim for about twenty years.

He came over to me and he said: "Have you five minutes? I would like you to meet my wife. There is nobody in the world admires you the way my wife does. She thinks you are the greatest author in America. She reads every line you write. She thinks you are the greatest speaker in the world, and she once went 150 miles to hear you speak."

So he took me over to his wife and said: "Dear, I want you to know Heywood Broun." Do you wonder that I am frightened at introductions? You know I thought Mrs. Higgins was going to finish up by saying: "Ladies and gentlemen, I present Mr. Heywood Broun."

The late Knute Rockne, famous football coach of Notre Dame University—

It is rather awe-inspiring to me to see so many of you here this noon. I did not know there were so many executives in my home town.

In addressing you, I feel very much like a certain Irishman said he felt when it came to playing football. This chap said he was not much good until he got warmed up and sweaty, and then just as soon as he got to sweating good he was all in.

25 Not all speakers can introduce humor at the beginning of an address as spontaneously as George Bernard Shaw did when he appeared before a London audience which had applauded him vociferously. He stepped to the front of the platform ready to give his speech. The crowd was calling wildly for him. As the roar subsided, and in that tense moment of silence, just before he began, a voice from the balcony cried "Blah!" That would have finished many speakers. But not Shaw. He looked up and said calmly, "Brother, I agree with you fully, but what can two of us do against so many?"

26 E. *Use a chart, table, map or some other form of exhibit.*

This is a rather unusual introduction, but may be very successful. Claude Stout, Deputy Commissioner of Banking of Colorado, addressing the Colorado Bankers Association, effectively used a chart which showed in striking figures the losses which banks might eliminate and the additional income they might earn by proper service charges.

27 F. *Ask a challenging question.*

A thought-provoking question, directly to the point of the address, focuses the attention of an audience immediately upon the subject.

28 Dr. Henry Noble McCracken speaking on "Study What You Like"—

Why in every other field of human activity is the goal of utility stressed while in education it seems to be held in contempt? Why should a student be called not a student because he chooses to study what seems to be of advantage to him? Just why is there all this nonsense about vocational studies?

29 Albert J. Beveridge talking on "Work and Habits"—

Every man's problem is how to be effective. Consciously or unconsciously, the question you are asking yourself is, "How shall I make my strength count for most in this world of effort?" And this is the question which every one of us ought to ask himself. But not for the purpose of mere selfish gain: not to get money for the sake of money, or fame for the sake of fame, but for the sake of usefulness in the world; for the sake of helpfulness to those we love and of all humanity. Selfishness poisons all it touches, and makes all achievement dead-sea fruit which turns to ashes on the lips.

So the great question, "How shall I make the most of myself?" which every worker in the world is asking, must be nobly asked, and therefore unselfishly asked if you would have it wisely answered. There are two words that solve this query of your destiny, and those two words are work and habits.

30 Dr. Donald B. Armstrong, Vice President of the Metropolitan Insurance Company, broadcasting an address over the Columbia Network on "Magic Bullets."

Have you ever thought how great is man's love of magic; how persistently through all history he has sought magic short-cuts to the attainment of his ends, or to escape his ills or the penalty of his errors? In no field is this more true than in that of medicine. Man has long searched for "magic bullets" that might be shot into his system, so to speak, and that would go directly to the affected part, attack the trouble-making influence, and eliminate or destroy it without injuring the body itself.

Professor Walter Miles of Yale University began an address on "Mental Longevity" with this interesting question: "Are old folks as bright as the young ones?" Both the old and the young would like to know the answer to that question.

31 G. *State facts which show the importance of the subject to the welfare of the audience.*

32 The following introduction for an address on "Edison's Frontiers" before representatives of the electric industry shows the importance of the subject to the growth of the electric industry:

Electricity means light, power, measurement, therapy, amusement, perhaps transmutation. Have all its frontiers been explored and pre-empted? Obviously not.

In the ten years 1923-1933, four new farms came on high-line for every one so supplied with electric current previously. In 1934, there were over one million electrified farms, including some 260,000 with individual lighting plants. But 84 per cent or over five million farms are still without electricity and its genii. Compared to the Gold Rush of '49, here is opportunity to the nth power. Balance the farmer's earning power, run a high-line past his gate, and you swing the door upon frontiers of business to the tune of 5,000,000 new refrigerators, 5,000,000 washing machines, 5,000,000 vacuum cleaners, 5,000,000 flatirons and countless ironing machines, electric clocks, radios, toasters, lamps, bulbs, motors, movies, television sets.

33 Dr. S. Bernard Wortis, Chief Neurologist of New York University Clinic, broadcasting an address on "The 'Stress Periods' of Life" over the Columbia Network in collaboration with the New York Academy of Medicine—

If every man and woman knew more about the periods in life when the stresses and strains were greater—and could learn to manage and adapt to these periods, we would have less nervous and mental illness in this country. The problem of caring for the mentally ill is yearly becoming a greater communal and national burden. Let me give you an idea of the magnitude of the problem.

More than half of the hospital beds of this country are filled with persons mentally ill. There are over 500,000 insane patients in the United States, and an additional 150,000 hospital beds are occupied by persons mentally defective or epileptic. Each year about 100,000 new mentally ill persons are admitted to our hospitals.

The cost of caring for the mentally ill is colossal; for the entire country it amounts to 225 million dollars yearly. Since 1923, New York State alone has spent over 100 million dollars for new and urgently needed mental hospital buildings. The cost and maintenance of such buildings and personnel, through the New York State Department of Mental Hygiene, is over 35 million dollars per year in New York State alone!

34 H. *Begin by a significant quotation or idea from some other person.*

ILLUSTRATIONS

35 Newell Dwight Hillis speaking on "Character: Its Materials and External Teachers"—

Dying, Horace Greeley exclaimed: "Fame is a vapor, popularity an accident, riches take wings, those who cheer today will curse tomorrow, only one thing endures—character!" These weighty words bid all remember that life's one task is the making of manhood. Our world is a college, events are teachers, happiness is the graduating point, character is the diploma God gives man.

36 On another occasion Newell Dwight Hillis stated in an introduction to an address on "Conscience and Character," "Von Humboldt said that every man, however good, has a yet better man within him. When the outer man is unfaithful to his deeper convictions, the hidden man whispers a protest. The name of this whisper in the soul is conscience."

37 Abbott Lawrence Lowell began the inaugural address when he became president of Harvard University with these words:

Among his other wise sayings, Aristotle remarked that man is by nature a social animal; and it is in order to develop his powers as a social being that American colleges exist. The object of the undergraduate department is not to produce hermits, each imprisoned in the cell of his own intellectual pursuits, but men fitted to take their places in the community and live in contact with their fellow men.

38 The question is often asked, "Should you ever apologize in opening a speech?" The answer is "No! never, never apologize in opening a speech." Do not say, "I did not have time to prepare." The audience is the best judge of that condition. Why should you tell your audience they are not worth the time it would take you to prepare a speech? Why should you tell them that this occasion did not mean enough to you to consider serious preparation? Do not say either, "I don't know how to talk," or "I have nothing to say." If not, why did you accept? Surely you would not willingly bore an audience. Moreover, these statements are a reflection upon the judgment of the program committee which invited you to speak. What the audience wants is not apologies. They want the best speech—and not even the second best speech—you can possibly give with thorough preparation.

There are some introductions which seem to be in the nature of apologies, which, however, are not apologies of the kind we have described. They may be statements indicating that the speaker feels himself humble in the face of his responsibilities. They may even be sincere compliments to the audience. The listeners do not object to that kind of introduction. It is one thing actually to be unprepared and quite a different matter to be fully prepared, but humble when you contemplate the responsibilities of giving a good address. Introductions of this character follow:

A business executive addressing the Erie, Pennsylvania, Association of Commerce on "The Problems of Management"—"I should be much less than frank if I did not tell you that I know there are men in this audience eminently better qualified to speak on this subject than I am, men who could bring to this discussion far richer experience, infinitely greater wisdom and more mature reflection." The gray-headed business executives in that audience liked that statement. The speaker was not posing as a know-all. By his sincerity, they knew he proposed to give them the best thinking on the subject at his command.

The late Dr. Glenn Frank, former president of the University of Wisconsin, speaking on "The Statesmanship of Business and the Business of Statesmanship"—

Of one thing I am sure, and that is that you did not invite me here under any delusion that I am a businessman, or that I know anything you do not know about the mystical secrets of office procedure, or high finance. It would, therefore, be a sterile presumption on my part to try to discuss with you any of the technical aspects of business organization or financial procedure. You do not, I am sure, expect me to do that. And I have no desire to assume the glib omniscience of the after-dinner speaker who can solve everybody's problem but his own within the limits of thirty minutes.

39 The classic example of a speaker who seemed to deprecate his ability was Mark Antony when he said,

> I am no orator, as Brutus is,
> But, as you know me all, a plain blunt man,
>
> .   .   .   .
>
> For I have neither wit, nor worth, nor words,
> Action, nor utterance, nor the power of speech
> To stir men's blood; I only speak right on.

40   WRITING THE BODY OF THE SPEECH

The body is the substance of the speech. Fill it with facts and figures. They speak in a singularly convincing fashion. In addition, the facts and figures presented consecutively throughout the body of the address must march directly to the conclusion the speaker hopes to establish. The listeners should never have to say, "What in the world did the remarks the speaker made on (this or that subject) have to do with his conclusion?"

The listener must receive something definite that he can carry away with him. What a pitiful spectacle a speaker makes when he becomes mired through an entire address in generalities and abstractions. Let us assume that the speaker has taken for his subject the hazards of operating a retail business. He says, "The retailer is engaged in a very hazardous business. His profits are small and his future is uncertain." Those are generalities. He might have said, "The retailer is engaged in a very hazardous business. The best studies available by the mercantile credit agencies indicate that the average retail store lives sixty-six months. In one middle western city, for example, there are 1,200 retail stores. Thirty of these stores go out of business every month—three hundred sixty stores die yearly. Thirty-two new stores are established monthly—many of them to lose their capital in a few months." Every audience likes the speaker who digs out new facts, new figures, new material relating to their interests. No matter how skillful he may be with words, no speaker can satisfactorily paint and prop up a speech lacking substance. The speaker who will make a reasonable effort to build substance into his address is certain to be acclaimed by his audience. Out of every ten speakers, seven are almost certain to fail to make a serious effort to get worth while facts for an audience, two will do a fair job, and one will make a comprehensive and exhaustive study of the subject. Even a little effort will place a speaker among the first three out of ten. A little more effort will leave him just one real competitor out of ten speakers on the average two-day convention program.

Specifically, what guiding principles can be set down for the preparation of the body of the speech? There are at least five as follows:

41 A. *Know the subject thoroughly.*

Strange as it may seem, few men are masters of their fields. The author has made a number of studies in the field of selling. With the assistance of college students of business administration, he has made tests of the knowledge which sales persons in various lines possess relative to the goods they sell. Certainly one would assume that a hat salesman, a shirt salesman, a hardware salesman, would have considerable knowledge of the field in which each of them sells. However, these tests in a number of lines reveal that out of ten sales persons, six or seven know practically nothing about the goods they sell, two or three know a little and one person is well informed. And yet these persons are supposed to make convincing sales speeches. Enthusiasm in selling and in speaking grows out of knowledge. A person who does not know his subject has nothing about which to enthuse. Unfortunately, not a few speakers are compelled to play around in the suburbs of their subject because they are ignorant of it.

ILLUSTRATIONS

42 Frank T. Bell speaking on "Fish and Their Management" knows fish and gives some interesting facts about them.

It often happens that indirect methods and an elaborate technique are required to discover apparently simple facts about the lives of fish. It may be necessary to study the prevailing drifts of ocean currents by releasing thousands of drift bottles, and to collect in two nets hundreds of samples of the eggs and larvae present in the surface water, in order to discover the location and the extent of the spawning ground, how far the young fish are carried by the currents, and at what age a fish reaches maturity.

Take for example the mackerel. Studies of Atlantic coastal waters have revealed that the spawning grounds of the mackerel are in the area off New York Harbor between Cape May, New Jersey, and Montauk, Long Island. The migration of these and other important species is only now beginning to be understood.

We can tag fish, much as identifying bands are attached to ducks and other migratory birds. A numbered disc of celluloid or a metal clip is fastened to the fish and it is then released; a small reward is offered for a record of its recapture. We have tagged over 60,000 cod and many thousands of salmon, haddock, weakfish, scup, flounders and other species.

43 William Allen White, Editor of the *Emporia Gazette*, is probably the best informed person in the United States on the functions and operations of a country town newspaper. Note how vividly he analyzes the foundation of the country town newspaper in this excerpt from an address broadcast over the Columbia Network.

The American country town paper rests entirely upon the theory of the dignity of the human spirit. It is democracy embodied. It emphasizes the individual. For instance, here is an item: "John Jones is in town today with the first load of hay from the third cutting of alfalfa." That item is the alpha and omega of small town journalism. It dignifies John Jones. It dignifies labor. It dignifies small business. And now, Mrs. Jones has the first forsythia out in her Emporia garden—that's a news item. We're glorifying Mrs. Jones. We're glorifying the human spirit, making the Joneses proud to be Joneses, to cut themselves hay; to have a beautiful individual garden. Upon that glorification rests the American country newspaper, and, incidentally, the American democracy.

44 A businessman describing a pair of pliers—

These pliers are hand-forged and hand-finished. They are made of high-carbon steel. If I could break one of those handles, I could show you a grain of steel as fine as the grain of a file. Ordinary pliers work loose at the pivot. The pivot wears, and after it's worn it jams. That's because the holes are punched. The holes in these pliers aren't punched, they're drilled. Take a good firm grip on the handles. Notice how they fit your hand—how they stick? See those little button-like things on the handles, with the little holes in the center? That's the suction-grip idea. When you're working around your car with those pliers and the handles become greasy, they won't slip. Notice the finish. Ordinary pliers rust. The nickel plating chips off. The nickel on those pliers will stick; and that's because they are made perfectly smooth and clean, and then plated. Those pliers will last a lifetime. They're guaranteed.

Competitively, what chance has an ordinary salesman who does not know the product against this businessman who does? Simply no chance!

In speaking, knowledge brings confidence and confidence brings enthusiasm.

45 B. *Use facts, figures and illustrations.*

It is worth repeating again and again that illustrative matter filled with illuminating facts and figures is the most persuasive and interesting material for the body of speeches. Figures frequently have an eloquence that cannot be captured in phrases.

ILLUSTRATIONS

46 Arthur M. Hyde, former Governor of Missouri and Secretary of Agriculture under President Hoover, gives a splendid illustration of what opportunity under liberty means.

In a clearing of the forests of Kentucky stands a crude log cabin. It is bare within and forbidding without. It speaks of the deepest poverty. Stretched upon the bare earth floor in the cabin lies a ragged untaught boy, poring, by the flickering light of the fireplace, over a borrowed book. He lifts his eyes to gaze upon the burdened form of his pioneer mother, and I hear him say:

"Life is hard. The future seems hopeless.

"My fathers fought in the American Revolution. They helped adopt the Constitution of America. They gave allegiance to a government, not by men but by laws which should be of equal application to all.

"Clad in the skins of animals, they penetrated the wilderness. With rifle nearby, they hewed logs for their cabins, cleared lands for their fields, and built homes for their children. Their eyes held a constant vision in which all men should be free to work out their own destiny, to plan their own lives in their own way, to possess the fruits of their own toil, and to stand or fall by their own efforts.

"Poor and humble though I am, I have a chance. In my country no doors are barred to me because I am poor. I can work. Be the reward much or little, it will be mine. I can learn; the knowledge will give me power. Thank God, I have a chance."

And the ragged boy rose to become the railsplitter, the country store keeper, the small town lawyer, the advocate of a great cause, the exemplar of individual liberty under the law, the great American President, the emancipator of a race, the defender and preserver of the American Union.

This is the triumph, in the life of one man, of a human soul given equal opportunity under liberty.

This illustration in Mr. Hyde's address gave warmth to the abstract subject of liberty. It made the idea live.

47 Dr. Clarence M. Hincks speaking on "Mental Disability—Last of the Taboos" begins the body of his address with an extraordinarily vivid illustration of the problem he is to discuss.

The frequency of mental disease is such as to challenge the attention of all thinking men. Mental ailments are much more prevalent than most of us realize. Do you know that occupied beds in our mental institutions outnumber those in all other hospitals combined? At this moment over 400,000 of our fellow citizens are being treated for crippling forms of mental disease in mental hospitals throughout the country. Indeed, at the present rate of new admissions, it can be predicted that four children out of every hundred born in the United States will, in the absence of effective preventive measures, become the victims of major psychoses or so-called insanity, and will have to enter mental institutions at some time during their lives. This constitutes almost as large a proportion of children as will eventually graduate from our colleges and universities.

48 Herbert Hoover speaking on "Can Europe's Children Be Saved?"—

A survey of Belgium three months ago by the leading physicians and health authorities showed the march of the tragedy we had tried to prevent. The report reaffirms that strong adults can survive for awhile on a meager ration of bread and potatoes of late mostly furnished by the Germans. The shortage in meats, fats and milk is crucifying the children. This report showed that the people are devoting practically all their meager fats and milk to the children under three years of age. Yet with all this sacrifice there is a deficiency in food for even the little ones. The report continues that the worst effects of starvation show among the children from three years upwards. They say that 47 per cent of the children in the kindergartens, 63 per cent of primary schools, and 42 per cent in the higher schools were in a definitely weak condition. They inform us that many children were unable to come to school at all.

Mr. Hoover might have spoken generally of the starvation of children, but his talk was in specific terms of meats, fats, milk and the number of children who were in weak condition.

49 Dr. Haven Emerson speaking on "Let's Reshuffle our Doctors" talks with facts and figures.

Of the 1,100,000 persons engaged in all varieties of medical care in its broadest sense, 120,000 are physicians in private practice, and 20,000 more work in a multitude of institutions. Hence, there is about one doctor of medicine for each 900 people in the United States.

If such a ratio of doctors to people everywhere prevailed equally in all states, and in farm and rural areas and cities, no one would be inconvenienced except by the unavoidable delays in transportation of the doctor to patients in mountain, prairie, forest, and coastal regions. As a matter of fact there is one physician to each 245 persons in the District of Columbia, obviously because of the large number and size of federal services requiring medical participation or direction. There is one physician to 1,351 persons in Missouri. There are six states where there are less than 700 persons for each physician and there are two states, Colorado and California, where there are approximately 500 persons per physician.

There are 10 states with more than 1,000 persons per physician and three with more than 1,300 persons per physician.

Average incomes in Alabama are $321 a year; in Mississippi $328; in North

Carolina $367 and in South Carolina $390; while that of the United States as a whole is $614, and it is in just these low income states that there are the lowest ratios of doctors to people. In the states with a high ratio of doctors to population, such as California, Colorado, New York, Illinois, Massachusetts, and Maryland, the average income is well above that of the people of the United States as a whole.

Thus a major job facing our society is to provide conditions which will tempt competent physicians to distribute themselves proportionately among the population.

50 George Barton Cutten, President of Colgate University, speaking on "The Bugaboo of Communism" to the students of that university illustrated his address by references to subjects near to the daily thinking and experience of his audience. President Cutten said:

A communist is a socialist without a sense of humor. Russia was supposed by those who did not live there, and a few who did, to be communistic. It certainly qualified in lacking humor, but practically, while professing to be communistic, it has always been ruled by a bureaucracy or a dictator, and in recent years has leaned so increasingly toward the latter form that it is now almost wholly that. As an iridescent dream communism ranks high, but as a working society it has never reached Class B. Perhaps because it is purely theoretical, it is supposed to have almost arrived at full term in the minds of many college professors. I am sometimes asked if we have any communists on our college faculty, and I have to reply that I have occasionally heard rumors of such, but careful investigation does not reveal that any of them are sharing their salaries, and until they do I am not worried. In our climate, with the thermometer 50 degrees below zero, ideological flights get a rude shock from an impending coal bill. With all apologies to the coal dealers, let me say that that brings you down to solid rock.

51 Dr. Edgar Mayer talking on "Genius and Tuberculosis" did not confine his remarks to generalities. In the body of his speech he gave a vivid picture of genius struggling with tuberculosis.

One most widely acclaimed, a gigantic figure in the literary world, so well called the apostle of cheerfulness, was Robert Louis Stevenson. If illness be regarded as a calamity, his genius provided a compensation to himself and the world. Robert Louis Stevenson spent years crippled with only his imagination to give him sustenance. Nevertheless, to the last, he retained a delightful philosophy, wrote beautiful prayers, poems, narratives and ever-interesting letters, despite a life of illness. Coming of a race of renowned engineers who had built lighthouses on almost every dangerous coast in Scotland, he too— had he been a rugged, healthy boy—might have followed this life work. Tuberculosis early marked him for its own. His appearance betrayed the so-called phthisical habitus. He was described as being "badly set up, long, lean, spidery, with sunken chest, oval brow, soft brown eyes, haunting smile, and lankness of cheek, giving the impression of a tuberculous countenance."

Imagine him as a young boy, bedfast with fever and racking cough, unable to be comforted except by the magic carpet of his mind, which took him out of the prison of his counterpane to rugged adventure—to *Treasure Island* and the thrills of being *Kidnapped*—to London fog and the home of *Dr. Jekyll and Mr. Hyde* Perhaps because of the endless days and nights in bed, Robert Louis Stevenson could understand more than most men the whimsicality and tenderness of childhood, and produce some of the most beautiful children's verse in the English language.

Disease, however, did not darken his view of life and only on rare occasion did he adopt the invalid point of view. In the essay, *Ordered South,* he writes: "To me the medicine bottles on my chimney and the blood in my handkerchief are accidents. They do not color my view of life and I should think myself a trifler and in bad taste if I introduced to the world these unimportant trifles."

52 Geoffrey Crowther, British publicist and economic writer, speaking on "The Vanishing Briton" clearly portrays the problem of declining population which faces many nations.

The year in which the record number of children was born in England—omitting the wholly abnormal post-war year 1920—was 1903, when there were just short of a million births. Thirty years—one generation—later, in 1933, there were only about 700,000 births. The number of births has fallen by about a quarter in one generation. This is all the more striking when you reflect that the parents of the 1933 babies were, broadly speaking, the 1903 babies. One million English men and women born in 1903 were producing only 700,000 babies thirty years later. The present race of Englishmen is not reproducing itself.

When you come to think of it, this is an alarming state of affairs. For, if one million 1903 children only produce 700,000 1933 babies, what will the size of the next generation be? When the 1933 babies are themselves 30 years old, how many children will they have? If they follow the example of their parents, they will only have about 500,000. And the next generation of babies will only be 350,000 in number, the next 240,000, and so on. Indeed, those who have studied the subject closely have predicted that if we go on as we have been going in recent decades, the population of England will have fallen from 40 millions to 5 millions within a hundred years from now. . . .

It is not merely the English who are vanishing. I think I am right in saying that there is not a single white race of which we have adequate statistics which is not showing the same phenomenon of falling births.

53 C. *If the audience is to be convinced of some proposition, begin with subject matter with which there is agreement.*

This is the old principle of proceeding from the known, and agreed upon, to the unknown. There must be agreement between the speaker and the audience at the beginning. Read and reread the speech Shakespeare gave Mark Antony as his oration over the dead body of Caesar. Mark Antony began "For Brutus is an honorable man. So are they all honorable men." Thus he called the conspirators honorable men. But gradually as he presented the facts, he turned the mob on Brutus and his conspira-

B

tors. Before that address had been completed those Roman citizens were crying, "We'll burn the house of Brutus. Away, then! Come, seek the conspirators." Antony began by agreement with the hostile listeners, but finally he led them to his viewpoint.

54 D. *Do not argue, but explain.*

No audience likes the speaker who states at the outset that he is going to convince them of his viewpoint or change their ideas. The immediate reaction is "I don't believe it" or skeptically, "Well, let's hear what you have to say." Again, give the audience facts, information and figures. Explain your story. Let the facts change the viewpoint of the audience. The proper attitude is one of "Come, let us reason together." The object of public speaking is to present truth convincingly.

55 A business executive who recently spoke on "Tests of Management" at the annual dinner of the Chamber of Commerce of Fremont, Nebraska, did not argue on the general merit of accurate cost accounting. He told a simple story to his audience, many of whom were retailers. "In a little Middle Western town," he said, "there is a very successful hardware retailer. Several years ago he determined to know more about the turn-over of each class of goods in his store. He found over one hundred classes of goods—paint, stoves, cutlery, nails and many others. He discovered that some goods sold much less readily than other merchandise. In fact, some articles stayed in the store four, ten and sixteen times as long as other goods. Consequently, the capital invested and the space in the store were used four, ten and sixteen times longer for these slower-moving items. Therefore, the interest cost and the rent were much higher on these items. Then he started to reduce his inventory on the slower-moving, less profitable items. An example of what this merchant accomplished after he knew the turnover and cost of each class of goods is enlightening. On one counter he reduced the space occupied by slow-moving goods 66 per cent. In the vacant space he placed faster-moving items with the result that in one year his sales on that one counter increased $7,000. He followed the same policy over his entire store, reducing the inventory of slow-moving items and increasing his sales and net profits."

No amount of argument could have been as influential as that one illustration of what another retailer had done with problems identical to those of the men in the audience.

56 Frederick L. Schuman, noted author and educator, broadcasting an address, "And There Is No Peace," over the Columbia Network one year before World War II began, described the confusion in Europe and

Asia. In pointing out the need, as he saw it, for action by the Western powers, he explained his viewpoint by a simple reference to Shakespeare's *Hamlet*.

I would suggest to you that the source of this confusion is quite simple. It is as simple and as bitter in its implications as Shakespeare's tragedy of *Hamlet*. In that drama you will recall that the Gloomy Prince of Denmark asks himself whether " 'tis nobler in the mind to suffer the slings and arrows of outrageous fortune or to take up arms against a sea of troubles and by opposing end them." He is hesitant and irresolute and confesses that his "native hue of resolution is all sicklied o'er with the pale casts of thought." He shrinks from action and prefers empty words. He does nothing and thus plunges himself and his family and his people into disaster.

Hamlet's question is the question which for seven long years has faced those peoples and governments of the world which are committed to peace and are fearful of war.

57 E. *State briefly and clearly either at the beginning of the body of the speech or better, one by one, as the main part of the address unfolds, the two, three or four points to be discussed.*

ILLUSTRATIONS

58 Dr. S. Bernard Wortis, broadcasting an address on "The 'Stress Periods' of Life" over the Columbia Network had pointed out in his introduction the alarming fact that one out of every twenty persons goes to a mental hospital sooner or later through life. Then he stated briefly at the beginning of the body of his address the specific points he would discuss.

Obviously, a problem of such great importance to the national health and welfare requires careful study, especially since much of such mental illness can be avoided by a little knowledge of the simple methods of prevention.

There are certain periods in life when each person is subjected in greater degree to the experience of "growing up." All depends on the health of the individual and his or her ability to adjust to these trying episodes. Where in life do these "stress periods" occur, and what are the common problems of such periods?

They may be roughly grouped as (1) the time of childhood, (2) the time of adolescence, (3) the time of marriage and the experiences of raising a family, (4) the time of the physiological change of life, the menopause in women and men, and (5) the time of old age. These are the five important periods of one's life. Each of these experiences is full of possibilities for better health, if properly managed, or for physical or mental illness, if improperly managed.

Let us consider the problems of childhood first, etc.

George F. Barrett, Attorney General of Illinois, talking on "The Future of Our States and Cities in Our Governmental Structure" before the National Association of Attorneys General—

You and I are attorneys general of separate states comprising a great union. Our duty as attorneys general is that of pleading the cause of the people of our respective states before the courts and tribunals which are the custodians of their liberty. But the final court—the last tribunal of appeal in America—is the people themselves. Therefore, it is our duty, as attorneys for the people, to speak plainly and candidly to those who are the judges of their own cause upon the important issues which bear upon the future of their own country.

I shall attempt today to do just that.

The choice then that our people have is between three general types of governmental structure. One—a decentralized government; two—a government based on a distribution and balance of powers; and three—a centralized or autocratic government.

59   WRITING THE CONCLUSION

The ability to prepare an address so that it gradually becomes more intensified in its thought from the beginning to the end is one of the highest achievements in public speaking. It enables the speaker to hold an audience increasingly in suspense as he proceeds with his speech. The audience is aware that the speech is becoming stronger and stronger in its argument and in its eloquence. Whenever a speech begins with a climax and descends in its interest, it is certain to be a failure. After an introduction which obtains the attention of the audience, the first point in the body of the speech should be good, but each succeeding one should be better until the speech reaches a grand climax.

60   Almost every American adult is familiar with the great climax of the address which won for William Jennings Bryan the nomination for the Presidency of the United States when he said:

Having behind us the producing masses of this nation and the world, supported by the commercial interests, the laboring interests, and the toilers everywhere, we will answer their demand for a gold standard by saying to them: You shall not press down upon the brow of labor this crown of thorns; you shall not crucify mankind upon a cross of gold.

61   Abraham Lincoln's Second Inaugural Address had one of the most magnificent endings of any speech in history.

Fondly do we hope, fervently do we pray, that this mighty scourge of war may speedily pass away. Yet if God wills that it continue until all the wealth piled by the bondsman's two hundred and fifty years of unrequited toil shall be sunk, and until every drop of blood drawn with the lash shall be paid by another drawn with the sword, as was said three thousand years ago, so still it must be said that "the judgments of the Lord are true and righteous altogether."

With malice toward none; with charity for all; with firmness in the right, as God gives us to see the right, let us strive on to finish the work we are in; to bind up the nation's wounds; to care for him who shall have borne the battle, and for his widow and his orphan—to do all which may achieve and cherish a just and lasting peace among ourselves, and with all nations.

62 The closing sentence of Webster's "First Bunker Hill Monument Oration" are also majestic in their sweep.

And let the sacred obligations which have devolved on this generation, and on us, sink deep into our hearts. Those who established our liberty and our government are daily dropping from among us. The great trust now descends to new hands. Let us apply ourselves to that which is presented to us, as our appropriate object. We can win no laurels in a war for independence. Earlier and worthier hands have gathered them all. Nor are there places for us by the side of Solon, and Alfred, and other founders of states. Our fathers have filled them. But there remains to us a great duty of defense and preservation; and there is opened to us, also, a noble pursuit, to which the spirit of the times strongly invites us. Our proper business is improvement. Let our age be the age of improvement. In a day of peace, let us advance the arts of peace and the works of peace. Let us develop the resources of our land, call forth its powers, build up its institutions, promote all its great interests, and see whether we also, in our day and generation, may not perform something worthy to be remembered. Let us cultivate a true spirit of union and harmony. In pursuing the great objects which our condition points out to us, let us act under a settled conviction, and an habitual feeling, that these twenty-four States are one country. Let our conceptions be enlarged to the circle of our duties. Let us extend our ideas over the whole of the vast field in which we are called to act. Let our object be, *our country, our whole country, and nothing but our country.* And, by the blessing of God, may that country itself become a vast and splendid monument, not of oppression and terror, but of wisdom, of peace, and of liberty, upon which the world may gaze with admiration forever!

No speech should be left "hanging in the air" without a conclusion. The words at the end of the speech are generally remembered the longest by the audience. Therefore, the speaker must take the greatest possible advantage of the opportunity the conclusion affords to re-emphasize his message. The following methods for closing a speech are practical, and they are helpful to most speakers; it is suggested that you choose the method which is best suited for each of your speeches:

63 A. *Outline concisely the major points you have made in the body of the speech.*

This is the method which will be most helpful on most occasions, as it serves to place special emphasis upon the points which the speaker has tried to establish. It summarizes the entire speech in a few words.

Dr. S. Bernard Wortis, to whose address on "The 'Stress Periods' of Life" reference has already been made, closed his discussion of the five "stress periods" of life with this very concise restatement: "The recognition and treatment of nervous and mental illness has come into a new era. The physician not only helps those obviously mentally ill, but he also can help guide the normal person through the five difficult stages of childhood, adolescence, marriage, change of life and old age."

A banker addressing a convocation at the one hundred and twenty-fifth anniversary of Allegheny College on the subject, "The Banker's Stewardship," had discussed in the body of the address four essential requirements of that stewardship. In his conclusion, he summarized and repeated slowly and with emphasis the four points of that address as follows:

These are but meager and insufficient outlines of the banker's stewardship, but they indicate four major requirements of his stewardship:
  1. A knowledge of the development of the American banking system;
  2. A knowledge of his bank;
  3. A knowledge of the operation of the American economic order and of the importance of thrift in our economy; and finally
  4. A knowledge of world banking and financial problems.

64 B. *Use a quotation from the Bible or literature.*

An appropriate quotation is one of the most effective means of concluding a speech. It tends to lift the conclusion to a particularly high level because it adds style, dignity and beauty. Chapter X with almost 300 quotations from the Bible and Chapter XI with over 1200 quotations from the world's great literature and from various other sources will be distinctly helpful to you.

ILLUSTRATIONS

65 Arthur M. Hyde speaking on liberty and the American form of government closed his address with a significant Biblical illustration and a suitable quotation from literature.

When the Master of Men trod the earth, He said, "Ye shall know the truth, and the truth shall make you free." The dictators of His day nailed Him to a cross. But the truth He brought has overturned every throne, uprooted every dictator of His time. The cycles of truth are long, but they roll down the centuries with certainty and power.

We may be very sure that if America abandons liberty to follow the swamp-lights of either Fascism or Collectivism out into the bogs of Communism, future generations of America must climb slowly and painfully back out of that foul morass to fight again and to die to regain the liberties which this generation so thoughtlessly tossed away.

"The truth shall make you free." Free—not rich. Freedom was the promise. Since that promise was made, the centuries have waxed and waned, economic tides have risen and fallen, but humanity has never ceased its struggle to be free. Autocrats have enslaved men, dictators have regimented them, tyrants have ground them down. But 1800 years after that old promise, there was set up in America a system of government based upon the dignity and inviolability of the individual soul, declaring that all men have God-given, inalienable rights to life, liberty and the pursuit of happiness. In the 150 years since that happy event, this old world, released from tyranny, watered by individual liberty, revivified by the initiative of millions of free men working in their own way for themselves and their children, has produced more of human happiness and has made greater progress in art, science, education and economic prosperity than in all the previous centuries of experimentation with the absolute state put together. "By their fruits ye shall know them."

> "The shouting and the tumult dies,
> The captains and the kings depart,
> Still stands thine ancient sacrifice
> An humble and a contrite heart,
> Lord God of Hosts, be with us yet,
> Lest we forget, lest we forget."

66 Mark Sullivan in a speech on "What is Liberalism?" in which he had contrasted authoritarian government with liberal democratic government, and individualism with collectivism, concluded his address forcefully as follows:

What I have said tonight, I have said before. I have said it over and over. I have been saying it, in print and in addresses, ever since America was faced by this conflict between two contrasting forms of society, and two contrasting forms of government. I expect to continue saying it, until America makes her choice. I shall keep my stand on the side of liberal government, individualist society. If, on occasion, I and this cause suffer set-back, I shall take comfort in four lines of an old Scotch ballad:

> "I am hurt," Sir Andrew Barton said,
> "I am hurt, but I am not slain;
> I'll lie me down and bleed a while,
> And then I'll fight again."

67 Dr. Arthur H. Compton, distinguished American scientist, ended an address in which he had dwelt upon man's responsibility with a very appropriate quotation.

Fortunately for us, as we see the rather terrible mess we make of a good many things, we can be only too thankful that our Creator has kept in His hands the major part of responsibility. But more and more that responsibility is being laid upon our shoulders.

It means that man is sharing with his God the responsibility for making this world the best of all possible worlds. And one finds that he is faced with a challenge, a challenge and an opportunity of working with his Creator to make of this world of ours the kind of world that we would have it; by learning to understand what the world is like, by learning to understand our own natures so that we can discipline our lives and make the most of them.

Learn the truth that we may be freer to develop ourselves in the best possible ways. Learn the need for good will among men that we may co-operate. Learn the means of co-operation. Those are the great problems, and that is the great opportunity we have to do our part in making that world a more effective world.

> "Ye prate of patterns and the web of doom.
> Is God then tangled in a warp and woof?
> Is not the Weaver at the Weaver's place?
> Go seat you at the loom.
> Create the goodness that is heaven's proof.
> Work with God if ye would see His face."

68 Dr. Edgar De Witt Jones talking on great Americans of the past—Washington, Jefferson, Webster, Clay, Lincoln, Cleveland and Bryan—

And as for these great characters that I have presented tonight, and the still larger company of which there is a glorious galaxy, let me say in the noble words of Tennyson:

> "They are gone who seem'd so great.—
> Gone; but nothing can bereave them
> Of the force they made their own
> Being here, and we believe them
> Something far advanced in State,
> And that they wear a truer crown
> Than any wreath that man can weave them.

> "Speak no more of their renown,
> Lay your earthly fancies down,
> And in the vast cathedral leave them,
> God accept them, Christ receive them."

69 William Allen White speaking at the celebration of the fiftieth anniversary of Riis House on the material progress of mankind, and calling attention particularly to the part better housing might play in relieving injustice and creating happiness—

What is it, this indefinable urge of humanity toward what we call the pursuit of happiness? We can measure units of mechanical force, calories, kilowatts and the subatomic tendencies of the ether. But who can weigh this ancient, eternal impulse of man, more powerful than the material spirits man has called from the vasty deep of nature? Through the incarnation in a human identity with which we have endowed man's eternal quest and its tragic story—whether the story of the incarnation of the spirit of justice is myth or a quickening spirit—what beauty, what truth, what glowing power of human love abides with us—even in this cruel world! It is a new thing on the planet since men came here. We marvel at it. We shrink before this spirit of justice. Wars rage around its manifestations, its aspirations, and, alas, man who is its implement, the generations which are its machinery—man still is ignorant of its source. Still, even in his yearning, man is fearful of its power.

How strange it is that we hear across the ages the heart-break of that voice: "Have I been so long a time with you and yet thou has not known me?"

70 C. *Bring the speech to a grand climax.*

The difficulty of bringing a speech to a grand climax has already been discussed. However, after experience and practice a speaker may use this form of conclusion.

ILLUSTRATIONS

71 Franklin D. Roosevelt, speaking on International Affairs at Chautauqua, New York—

We seek to dominate no other nation. We ask no territorial expansion. We oppose imperialism. We desire reduction in world armaments.

We believe in democracy; we believe in freedom; we believe in peace. We offer to every nation of the world the handclasp of the good neighbor. Let those who wish our friendship look us in the eye and take our hand.

72 Carle C. Conway, Chairman of the Board of Directors of the Continental Can Company, speaking on "Business Must Go Ahead" before the Real Estate Board and the Chamber of Commerce of Kansas City, pointed out the great achievements of American businessmen, and closed with the following challenge as the climax of the address:

It is time we lifted up our heads! It is time we appreciated our strength and serviceability and power. But our job is only beginning, and a thrilling job it is. We have the opportunity, the responsibility, yes, the sacred duty of proving for all time that under the American system of free enterprise, American businessmen, doing things the American way, can accomplish more than any other system on earth.

73 D. *Compliment the audience or leave a note of encouragement or optimism.*

A sincere compliment or expression of hope for the future pleases an audience.

ILLUSTRATIONS

74 Franklin D. Roosevelt, addressing a conference of the International Labor Organization on November 6, 1941, closed with the following paragraphs in which he emphasized the significant part that organization would play in the future:

There must be no place in the post-war world for special privilege for either individuals or nations. And again in the words of the Atlantic Charter: "All States, great and small, victor or vanquished" must have "access, on equal

B

terms, to the trade and to the raw materials of the world which are needed for their economic prosperity."

In the planning of such international action the International Labor Organization, with its representation of labor and management, its technical knowledge and experience, will be an invaluable instrument for peace. Your organization will have an essential part to play in building up a stable international system of social justice for all peoples everywhere. As part of your great world organization, the people of the United States are determined to respond fully to the opportunity and the challenge of this historic responsibility, so well exemplified at this historic meeting in this historic home of an ancient democracy.

75 Leon Henderson speaking to the American Association of Advertising Agencies and the Association of National Advertisers in November, 1941, discussed some of the problems advertising organizations face in a period of national emergency, but closed with a compliment and with a note of encouragement.

So far as advertising is concerned, I repeat that it must survive as a thriving dynamic force. Not only does it deserve to continue because of its contributions to our way of life but it has a job to do now. And I can visualize an even greater use of the technique when peace comes and a vast surplus of men, materials and productive capacity calls for the vision and leadership to translate these resources from production for war to production for peace. When that time comes it is my judgment that if we are intelligent and resourceful, new and vast horizons will open for us all. Our job now is to hasten that day.

76 E. *Describe a dramatic scene, a great moment in history, science or business, or give a brief biographical story.*

ILLUSTRATIONS

77 Dr. Allen A. Stockdale in an address on "Making Spiritual Power" pointed out some of the great forces, including the spiritual, which made America. Then he concluded with the following fascinating story:

No place under the shining sun would one rather live than in the United States of America today.

Here it is, and it is yours. I say it is worth fighting for. It is worth living for. It is worth doing the things that are truly great.

When Bishop Hughes was president of DePauw University, there came into DePauw one of the awkwardest looking greenhorns that ever came to college. He had about three acres of hands and legs that he did not know what to do with. He had continued to grow until he was six feet three, but his shiny pea-green Sunday-best suit had not grown as he did, and he had grown right out of it.

This awkward lad came to college. He had a good father and a good mother that wanted him to succeed but they could not give him money. They lived on a slanting farm somewhere in the west. One evening they were sitting at the table and the boy said to the father: "I fell off the farm three times today." That was the kind of a farm it was. How could they get ahead on a farm like that? They could not, but this fellow was going to have an education.

So he came to DePauw University and he soon found what a hot iron and a damp cloth could do to his breeches, and he got a crease in his trousers. Nowadays all he would have to do would be to throw away his garters and let his socks fall, and he would be a typical college boy.

But he got a crease in his trousers, and it was not long before the girls discovered him. He soon had enough dates to pass them around to the other boys. Then they discovered that he had what it takes on the gridiron, and in the classroom. And this awkward greenhorn became a cultured college gentleman.

He was chosen as the honored speaker on Commencement Day. Early Monday morning of Commencement Week, when the train stopped at the depot, two of the funniest folks you ever saw got off. The old man had an accordion suitcase. He would just put everything in it and never would get the blooming thing full. And the dear old lady had on an old-fashioned dress. But this boy did not care. They were his father and his mother.

He picked the little lady up in his arms and he kissed both her cheeks, and he took them up and introduced them to Bishop Hughes, and to all of his fraternity brothers and girl friends. That was his father and his mother. They had been the creators of his very life. They had given him his heart and soul and spirit and inspiration, and he was not ashamed of them, no matter how they looked or the way they were dressed.

And then came that great address on graduation day, and he held that audience spell-bound, and in the silence that fell over them when he was through, as the people were sort of taking a new breath, a man sitting behind the strange old couple saw this boy's father lean over to the dear old lady and then heard him say: "Well, mother, I guess that is about the best crop we ever raised."

That is your America, and whenever this country becomes so contacted with subversive and destructive doctrines of a misguided chaotic world that it cannot see the center, the heart and soul, of this spiritual source of power, when we fail to make personalities that can be trusted, we fail to make an America.

78 Bob Trout, CBS news commentator, broadcasting a speech on "Cardinal of Charity" at the time of the death of Patrick Cardinal Hayes, Archbishop of New York—

In the dim soft light, George Cardinal Mundelein stood high above the body of the 71-year-old Cardinal and sang the solemn Mass. With holy water and incense, the final blessing was given, while outside in the sunshine, listening through loudspeakers, men knelt in the streets and women wept and forgot to dry their tears.

Sabers flashed, and white gloves snapped to salute when a bugle sounded taps, and the flags were dipped one last time. And the words of the prayer were all around, louder than the muffled drums, louder than the tolling bells:

"Eternal rest grant unto him, Oh Lord,
And let perpetual light shine upon him."

Thus, in shadowy cathedral and in city streets, did New York say farewell to a dear and great friend, His Eminence, Patrick Cardinal Hayes, Prince of the Church, Cardinal of Charity.

79 F. *Ask the audience to take some form of action or to adopt a certain viewpoint on some matter.*

80 Linton Wells, journalist and author, broadcasting an address on Columbia's Lecture Hall on the subject "We Need Another Canal"—

On another occasion, President Somoza of Nicaragua said to me in all sincerity:

"Through me, Nicaragua offers the United States her most sincere cooperation in the maintenance of peace, in the defense of this continent, and in the promotion of mutual trade and commerce.

"I am a most devoted friend and admirer of the United States. And even if I were not, I believe firmly that all of us should help and work with the United States. Because, as long as it exists as a free and powerful nation, these small countries of ours especially will be free and independent. While if the United States should some day lose her power by our lack of understanding and good will, we would be converted into European or Asiatic colonies. God forbid that such a thing should ever happen."

Yes; God forbid that such a thing should ever happen. But it can and may happen unless we get busy and take appropriate action to fulfill our destiny as the sole protector of this hemisphere. And one of those measures is to undertake the immediate construction of an inter-oceanic canal across Nicaragua. An investment of $722,000,000 in such a project—a monetary drop in the defense bucket these days—would one day pay fabulous dividends.

81 Dr. Preston Bradley closed one of his addresses with a challenge to the audience to adopt the viewpoint of sacrifice, and not greed, if America is to stand as a great example to the world.

Let us, ladies and gentlemen, settle down to the task of making this thing called democracy work, and when we make it work in America, and in our hearts, God will see to it that it finally works in all the world. And this world will become the kingdom of our God and the brotherhood of man, a reality, because of the Fatherhood of God.

And the challenge to you, and the challenge to me, is that before we are Democrats, or Republicans, before we are any of the things that separate us, let us, above all, and in all, and through all, let us upon the altar of our country place a sacrifice and stop treating that altar as a crib out of which to feed.

82 A Middle Western banker closed an address before the Oregon Bankers Association with the following summary and appeal:

These are the issues that confront us. These are the problems. They demand three things:

    First—Cooperation with our competitors to promote the best principles of bank operation.

    Second—Strict observance of sound management principles by every banker in the operation of his bank.

Third—Banking leadership that meets its present problems courageously and frankly.

If we could read the human story back of every savings and commercial passbook; if we could see the home, the work, the business trials, and the hopes each passbook represents; if we could clearly visualize the problems of each depositor, the education of his children, the care of dependents, the hope, after years of work, for a competence in old age; if we could really evaluate the significant role the banker plays in the economic advancement of a nation; I believe we would approach our daily work tomorrow with a new sense of its great importance. No other responsibility in our business life transcends it. Let us bring to it thorough knowledge, broad experience, and outstanding management ability.

83 G. *Tell a humorous story or give a suitable witty comment.*

Humor that definitely relates itself to the speech makes a splendid conclusion. Chapter IV with more than 1000 carefully chosen humorous stories, Chapter V with over 500 epigrams and witty comments, and Chapter VI with 200 humorous definitions will provide an almost inexhaustible source of materials for this purpose.

ILLUSTRATION

84 An Eastern business executive has used a humorous letter very successfully in his conclusion. When he has completed the body of his address and has summarized in a few words the conclusion, he adds, "Now if there are any of you who are a little discouraged in the operation of your businesses, I should like to have you take home with you some of the cheer that a father expressed to his daughter in a letter which I have here. (Holds up copy of sheet with letter.) The daughter is coming home with her husband and children to live with father. Will you note particularly the last paragraph as I come to it." Then the speaker reads this letter:

Dear Daughter:

I note from your letter that you are coming home with Wilfred and the children to live with us because Wilfred received an "adjustment" in his salary, which was an insult to him. Wilfred, of course, never could endure insults.

As you know, your brother Frank came home with his wife about a month ago after his salary had been unfavorably "reconsidered." Your sister Elsie, who has been a secretary to an officer of a corporation, recently had to take a position as a typist. She resigned because she refused to be reduced to the level of a common typist, so we are expecting her any day.

(Speaker: Here is the last paragraph.)

You ask about my own business. It is coming along fine. It was sold on the court house steps last Friday, but there were no bidders, so the sheriff let me keep it. That makes the best month I have had since the upturn.

Your loving father

That conclusion invariably brings an excellent response from the audience.

Chapter 2

HOW TO MAKE YOUR SPEECH SPARKLE

....

After the first written draft or outline of a speech is prepared, it should be painstakingly revised and refined. Each sentence must be written and rewritten until every unnecessary word is eliminated. However, great care must be exercised that the revisions and polishing do not remove the freshness, naturalness and vigor that may have been in the first draft.

In seeking to give style and effectiveness to the wording and phrasing of a speech, one must never forget that clearness of expression is the first imperative. Everything in style must yield to clarity.

85 The effort that eloquent speakers make to obtain style and effectiveness of expression is well illustrated by the comment of Phyllis Moir writing of Winston Churchill in *I Was Winston Churchill's Private Secretary.*

I can see him now, pacing slowly up and down the room, his hands clasped behind his back, his shoulders hunched, his head sunk forward in deep thought, slowly and haltingly dictating the beginning of a speech or an article. I wait, my pencil poised in midair, as he whispers phrases to himself, carefully weighing each word and striving to make his thoughts balance. Nothing may be put down until it has been tested aloud and found satisfactory. A happy choice brings a glint of triumph to his eye; a poor one is instantly discarded. He will continue the search until every detail—of sound, rhythm and harmony—is to his liking. Sometimes there are long halts, during which he patiently sounds out a phrase a dozen times, this way and that, making the cigar in his hand serve as a baton to punctuate the rhythm of his words.[1]

From this statement it is evident that Winston Churchill's eloquence does not just happen. It isn't accidental. It is the most carefully studied effort of a great mind that has struggled word by word and phrase by phrase for the brilliant expression of ideas that will move nations.

86 There are a number of tools of effective speech which enable one to

[1] Phyllis, Moir, *I Was Winston Churchill's Private Secretary,* pp. 154-155, New York: Wilfred Funk, Inc., 1941.

refine and perfect expression. They enable even the most inexperienced speaker to give a speech a sparkling quality. The order in which they are presented is not one of their relative importance, because these speech tools may be used on different occasions and for different purposes. Keep these effective speech tools definitely in mind as you revise your speeches to make them sparkle.

87 I. *Insert suitable humorous stories, epigrams and amusing definitions.*

Study the written draft or outline of your speech thoughtfully to determine exactly where a humorous comment would be appropriate, if the speech permits humor. Chapter IV contains over one thousand humorous stories suitable for introducing a speaker, beginning an address, making statistical or other dry material interesting, lightening a speech that has necessarily been long or has dwelt on many subjects, expressing appreciation for attention, and generally assisting a speaker to give just the right touch of humor needed to make a speech successful. Speeches on particularly serious occasions may not permit of humor. However, for the great majority of addresses, and also in daily conversation, no tool of speech is more generally helpful than good humor. Abraham Lincoln's political speeches and conversation with their generous use of humor are excellent illustrations.

The humorous stories in Chapter IV have been chosen from many thousands. Each story may be successfully adapted to a large number of different types of situations. For example, consider the following story: A professor in a western university taught mathematics and statistics. One day he was standing, dressed in his bathing suit, at the edge of a swimming pool on the university campus when a beautiful coed accidentally dropped her camera into the deep end of the pool. She called to the elderly professor for help. He said he would be glad to dive after the camera, but first wanted to know why she happened to choose him when there were so many young men within easy reach to do the job. She answered, "Professor, you have apparently forgotten me, but I am in your large statistics class. I have found that you can go *down deeper, stay down longer, and come up drier* than anyone I know."

The speaker can use this story in almost any address containing statistics or facts which may be essential to the address, but a bit dry. He may add that in explaining his statistics he does not propose to go down too deep, stay down too long, or come up too dry. The story may also be used in connection with the relationships of professors and students, and with topics dealing with education.

The speaker should select generally those humorous stories which are definitely appropriate to the subject matter and which illustrate points he wishes to emphasize. The humor should not all come at one point, but should be spaced at intervals through the speech. However, never use a humorous story which is entirely irrelevant and is merely inserted to wake up a drowsy audience in the hope that its members will listen to a dull speech. The way to wake up a drowsy audience is to wake up the speaker. The humor must always relate itself directly to the discussion.

88 Sometimes another tool—an epigram or witty comment—is more effective than a humorous story. Subtly introduced, the epigram may serve fully as well as a comparatively long humorous story. Moreover, it conserves time. A speaker before the Grand Rapids Association of Credit Men discussed at length America's progress and the inventive genius of her industrial scientists. He said, "These scientists are remarkably resourceful." Then, almost before the audience was aware of it, he added, "They couldn't open our day-coach train windows, so they air-conditioned our trains." The change from a serious statement to a witty comment was so rapid it surprised the listeners, and as they caught the full significance of the humor, they laughed heartily. It takes but a moment to give a witty comment, and the speaker goes on immediately. The humor provides "the pause that refreshes" for the audience.

89 Dr. Will Durant, the distinguished philosopher, was giving an address before the Rotary Club of Chicago in which he was discussing for a few minutes the philosophy of Friedrich Nietzsche. Remember that Dr. Durant has for many years been a university professor. Commenting on Nietzsche, Dr. Durant said—

in 1870 . . . Friedrich Nietzsche walked out of a hospital. He had been rejected from military service. He had weak ribs. He had poor eyes. He was flat-footed. He was a professor.

The last sentence caught the audience by surprise, but in a moment the laughter spread over that large audience. It was a terse, unexpected, humorous comment, and it was on the speaker, which made it twice as good.

90 A businessman was speaking of the necessity for work and thrift in any economic order, whether it be capitalistic or socialistic. "Of course," he added, "I know there are some men who would say that my philosophy is one of 'Work hard and save your money, and when you are old, you can have the things that only the young can enjoy.'" The audience liked that bit of humor which the speaker credited to his critics. Then he went on to prove his case.

Over five hundred epigrammatic comments from many sources and on many subjects are included in Chapter V. These short and pointed statements will be of great assistance in creating effective speeches. They also assist in making ordinary conversation sparkle. Almost every address requires at least one or two pertinent quotable epigrams.

91 Occasionally also a speaker may find an opportunity to use an amusing definition, and more than two hundred such definitions will be found in Chapter VI. With a little practice anyone can create such definitions out of humorous stories and jokes. They provide a different type of humor combining some of the qualities of jokes and epigrams. Dr. Joseph Jastrow, famous professor of psychology at the University of Wisconsin, began one of his addresses with this amusing definition: "The psychologist has been slanderously defined as a man who tells you what everybody knows in language nobody can understand." That definition made an attention-winning introduction.

92 Ed Wynn's definition of a parking space as the place "where you take your car to have those little dents put in the mudguards," and Fred Allen's definition of a gentleman as "any man who wouldn't hit a woman with his hat on," are typical, amusing definitions that tell a good story in one sentence.

93 II. *Use illustrations from biography, from plays, or from literature.*

If the speech is one of inspiration, perhaps to a body of students, a college graduating class, a church congregation, or an after-dinner audience, stories of achievement, persistence, courage, tact and patience from the lives of statesmen, scientists, industrialists, writers, musicians, artists and others whose lives have been of widespread interest, will help to illustrate the speech and make it entertaining and instructive. Few things in the world are more inspiring to an audience than the stories of lives lived significantly. Chapter VII includes a number of short stories of the character suggested.

ILLUSTRATIONS

94 The author has frequently outlined to audiences the life of the great scientist, Michael Pupin, in attempting to show some of the tests which determine whether men and businesses succeed or fail. His life is one of the most fascinating records of achievement in human history. Any speaker could hold an audience completely by a brief recital of this biography if the story logically could be made a part of the speech.

The story of Michael Pupin's life has generally been used at the conclusion of the address. It clearly illustrates such points in men's lives as (1) the simplicity to wonder, or inquisitiveness, (2) the determination to get the facts, (3) and the ability to apply practically what has been learned.

THE STORY OF MICHAEL PUPIN AS USED IN A SPEECH[2]

Only a little more than a half a century ago, Michael Pupin, a shepherd boy, guarded his flocks by night among the fields of Serbia. As the flocks ranged the open fields, grazing under the stars and trampling the meadows hard with their feet, thieves often lurked in the bordering cornfields awaiting an opportunity to make off with a part of the herd. This lad and hundreds of other Serbian boys were taught a method of signaling one another for warning and help. Each carried a knife with a long wooden handle. This he would thrust deep into the ground. Then, in case the cattle thieves approached, he would strike against the wooden handle and the sound would be transmitted through the ground to another boy some distance away. The other boy, with his ear pressed against the ground, could hear and interpret the message.

"Why is it," Michael Pupin asked his mother, "that we can signal this way? Why is it that the sound can be heard through the ground but not through the air? Why is it the signals can be heard in the pasture land so much better than in the plowed fields?"

But the boy's mother could not answer his questions, nor could the village teacher. However, having an eager mind and great determination, the boy decided to go to America where he might win an education and find out the answers to these strange and perplexing questions. I call your particular attention to the fact that hundreds of other boys under the same circumstances and with the same set of conditions merely accepted these things without once questioning them just because they had always done them that way.

So it was that a penniless immigrant boy from Serbia, at the age of only fifteen, landed in New York in 1874; and, years later, having worked his way through Columbia University, concentrated the wonder and simplicity of his mind upon the problem of sound which had puzzled him as a shepherd boy in that Serbian field. The results of his thinking—what he accomplished for the long distance telephone and for radio communication by his inventions— are known the world over.

"If during the past twenty-two years this company had been compelled to do without one invention of Michael Pupin," an official of the American Telephone and Telegraph Company once said, "and yet give the same service it is giving today, the company would have had to spend at least $100,000,000 more than it has expended." Another official of the same company, when asked if he would care to sell a certain invention back to Professor Pupin, replied, "Yes, if he will buy the Telephone Company with it. Our whole plant has been adjusted to this invention, and when one goes, the other also must go."

And still these inventions in which millions of dollars of capital have been invested were the result of the thinking of a mere country lad who had the simplicity to wonder, the determination to know, and the power to apply what he learned.

95   Dr. Glenn Frank speaking on "If the Young Can But See," uses a dramatic illustration from a play.

I was a guest at the Chicago opening of Shaw's *Saint Joan* as her triumphant

[2] For the full story of his life read Pupin, Michael, *From Immigrant to Inventor*, New York: Charles Scribner's Sons, 1924.

spirit sang through the lips of Katharine Cornell . . . For me the high moment of the play came in the much abused Epilogue.

Here was the scene.

It was twenty-five years after the burning of the Maid. The curtain rose on the bed-chamber of King Charles the Seventh of France, who, at the opening of the play, was the none-too-bright Dauphin. The spirits of those who played a part in the trial and burning at the stake of Joan were entering the King's chamber. Among them was an old rector, formerly a chaplain to the Cardinal of Winchester, a little deaf and a little daft. He had gone somewhat crazy from brooding over the burning of Joan, but insisted that the sight of that burning had saved him.

"Well you see," he said, "I did a very cruel thing once because I did not know what cruelty was like. I had not seen it, you know. That is the great thing: you must see it. And then you are redeemed and saved."

"Were not the sufferings of our Lord Christ enough for you?" asked the Bishop of Beauvais.

"No," said the old rector. "Oh no, not at all. I had seen them in pictures, and read of them in books, and been greatly moved by them, as I thought. But it was no use. It was not our Lord that redeemed me, but a young woman whom I saw actually burnt to death. It was dreadful. But it saved me. I have been a different man ever since."

Poor old priest, driven astray in his wits by the haunting memory of his youthful inability to see what cruelty is like without watching a maid burn slowly to death at the hands of her executioners, a man who had to wait for events to educate his judgments!

The Bishop of Beauvais looked at him pityingly and, with infinite pathos in his voice, cried out, "Must then a Christ perish in torment in every age to save those that have no imagination?"

I covet for you who are about to be graduated . . . the godlike gifts of insight and understanding. You will need them in the days ahead.

There are many such stories in literature. Wide reading in the field of biography is strongly recommended. Interesting facts and interesting incidents from interesting lives may make the difference between a dull and a worth-while and colorful speech. Searching until one finds this material pays rich rewards.

96 An official of the American Bankers Association addressed a convention of the American Institute of Banking which has as its members many thousands of young men in the banking business. He spoke of some of the practical aspects of bank operation, and then for the last half of his address, which was on the subject of, "The Challenge for Banking Leadership," he discussed the five qualities essential to leadership in banking. This part of his address is presented because it applies to leadership in every field. Note also the clarity with which the five points are developed and the use of biography at the end of the discussion.

Having presented some of the problems confronting us, let us consider the five qualities that are essential to leadership in the banking business today. How can the banker train himself to sound judgment and to decisive, courageous, and persistent action in line with his findings; how can he inspire that confidence and loyalty throughout his organization which makes his business a team instead of a rabble?

97   First of all, the banker of today and of the future must know—he must have knowledge. There are countless people who are crammed with information, but totally lacking in knowledge. In place of guesses, conjectures, and prejudices, we must substitute knowledge. The difference between knowledge and information, as I am thinking of it, is that knowledge is a clean-cut grasp of all the facts you need in order to solve your problem; while information is ill-assorted, encyclopedic, but not necessarily complete and pertinent. The well-known scientist, Professor Michelson, once answered a question regarding a certain study he was making as follows: "When I get through, I shall be able in nine days to measure a certain piece of land that otherwise would take nine weeks." When the banker of the future has gathered his facts and clarified his viewpoint, he will be able to cut through a new road to his objective that may turn weeks into days.

98   We come then to the second essential of a successful banker—imagination.
Perhaps something of the difference between knowledge and information depends upon the constructive imagination that is brought to bear upon the facts, for facts in themselves are not important except as their influence is projected and their destiny foretold.

The banking business, frankly, was for many years transacted between four stone walls. It is within the present generation that banking has very largely broken away from behind the four walls, and without sacrificing its ability to pass upon credits with cool judgment, it has given some rein to constructive imagination.

I believe that there are going to be further fundamental changes in our financial and economic life, before which tradition and prejudice will prove to be blind leadership. The banking leaders of the future must think, imagine, dream—and then work out the substance of their dreams. The characteristic of the great thinkers in any field has always been their freedom from tradition and their ability to give their imagination free rein. Originality always follows imagination. On imagination is dependent most of the great inventions and forward movements in our history. Imagination takes facts or materials and from countless unrelated parts combines a unit that produces or accomplishes something new in the world. Of course any of us can cite examples where imagination which has gone headlong in the pursuit of new ideas has suffered severe losses. But how much greater, immeasurably, have been the losses inflicted by frozen adherence to outworn methods.

All the elements that make up the radio were in existence before the radio was invented. These elements were combined by the imagination in a new way to develop something as new and as important in its day as the invention of printing. The Northwest had all of its resources before Jim Hill used his imagination and then brought into existence a great new empire of the North. The basic essentials of our Federal Reserve System were in existence before the act was passed, under which these forces were interrelated and placed in operation.

Imagination is the intangible, the spirit, the flame, the breath of life that animates common clay. Nothing is more essential to leadership than imagination; yet it must be controlled, constructive, balanced. The leader must tread the high ground that lies between iron-bound tradition and unbridled dreaming.

99 And so we arrive at the third essential quality of the young bank executive —sound thinking. The balancing quality that must be linked with imagination is sound thinking. The dreamer dreams himself a castle in the air. The man with imagination and ability to think consecutively dreams a castle and delves into the earth, plans a foundation able to bear the crushing weights above it, actually erects his beams and arches, and builds up solidly to the very pinnacle of the structure.

Cultivate the thinking habit and the ability to think. We should not be carried away by the idea that in this day of rush and hurry there is something sacred about the snap judgment of the go-getter. Emerson once said that the hardest job in the world is to think. Perhaps that is why some bankers of the past seemingly chose to figure ten or twelve hours a day rather than to face a management problem and think through it to the point where they were able to lead an attack upon it. How many bankers are there who daily sit down alone, with the door shut against the deadly routine of detail, to think through independently upon some major problem in bank operation that confronts them? How many banks are there whose policies have been determined by the directors and officers through logical thinking based upon all the factors involved?

Some may feel that imagination and thinking are synonymous. I believe, however, that we have here three separate and distinct essentials of leadership —knowledge, imagination, thinking. Too many bankers have looked at the problem of declining profits as a hopeless one. They lacked the imagination to dream of a better day. Some have set up wrong standards and thus brought their institutions to grief. They lacked knowledge. Others have misinterpreted the figures and have arrived at conclusions that involved them in trouble. They lacked the ability to think straight.

100 The fourth essential of leadership is initiative. There are a surprising number of people who know how their business should be organized and operated, but who do nothing about it. There are intelligent thinkers who lack the impulse, the ambition, the initiative to put their ideas and convictions and dreams into practice.

Banking needs more self-starters. It needs more leaders who are convinced they are right and who are determined to see the matter through. There are plenty of bankers who have thought of setting up service charges, float charges, and other plans for leveling up the bank's profits; but they have failed to act. While some hesitate and question whether their conclusions are correct, while others procrastinate and wait for someone else to take the lead, while still others claim the time is not yet ripe, the true leader rallies his organization and carries the matter through.

One of the nation's leading bankers once said that the hardest task of his career was to get out of his overalls. Even when a person has all the essential qualifications for success, it may take great courage and initiative to shoulder responsibility and step to the head of the column. The greatest losses in history have been in the lives of the millions whose powers remained dormant all through their lives.

101 One other essential—hard work—sheer application, resolute, persevering, tough-fibered.

There has never been an army in which the rank and file did not picture the leaders as enjoying ease and luxury. But the great military leaders—Caesar, Napoleon, Grant, Pershing—were indefatigable workers. They had almost unbreakable health. They had bulldog tenaciousness. Early and late they were at their problems. They outdid other men in leadership, just as an engine that runs longer and faster will outdo the motor that slows down, that runs intermittently, that never produces in any twenty-four hours all the power that maximum operation would derive from it.

Business is full of the romance of youngsters whose chief characteristic was working hard and keeping at it.

102 There was a green farmer boy who decided he would rather stand behind a counter than follow a plow. He seemed so obviously lacking in sales ability that for a time no merchant would hire him. He failed in his first position, and in his second his salary was reduced. He even agreed that he was a misfit—but he stuck. Out of his first five stores, I believe, three failed. But he persisted and worked hard. And that boy, Frank W. Woolworth, became the greatest retail merchant in the world with a store in every city of eight thousand or more population in this country.

103 There was another lad who clerked in a grocery store sixteen hours a day and studied mathematics in his odd moments. He became interested in the doings of the steel plant whose employees traded at this store. He began to study steel and sought a position in the plant. He carried a surveyor's chain and drove stakes. At night he studied mathematics and engineering. He did not despair. He could not be diverted. He kept the pressure on for seven years. And that boy, Charles Schwab, mastered the iron industry and became one of the great industrial leaders in this country.

104 There was a young man named Cyrus McCormick who worked and waited eight harvest times for a chance to sell a queer new contraption.

Finally he sold a reaper—and the revolution of the agricultural industry began.

105 There was a lad who sold papers on a train. When he grew up, several million men and a score of billions of dollars of capital were given profitable employment through his inventions. Even in middle life, Thomas Edison continued to work twenty hours a day, if necessary, to accomplish his purpose.

106 Leadership is not play. Leadership in the banking of the future, as I have tried to visualize it, offers countless positions of varying opportunity, of which the highest pinnacles will carry almost unbearable responsibility in the new era that may lie just over the next hill. There will be men with the fire and iron to qualify even for these places. Such men must have had the very finest preparation and the most grueling tests which the banking profession knows. Their reward will be the attainment of these highest pinnacles of achievement, and the rendering of an immeasurable service to their times.

107 III. *Repeat some words or phrases to stamp them indelibly upon the minds of the listeners.*

108   A classic example of reiteration is found in one of the greatest
addresses of all time, the "Sermon on the Mount." In that address, as it
is recorded in St. Matthew, Chapter 7 and verses 24 to 27, the Master
says, "Therefore whosoever heareth these sayings of mine, and doeth
them, I will liken him unto a wise man, which built his house upon a
rock: And the rain descended, and the floods came, and the winds blew,
and beat upon that house; and it fell not: for it was founded upon a rock.
And everyone that heareth these sayings of mine, and doeth them not,
shall be likened unto a foolish man, which built his house upon the sand:
And the rain descended, and the floods came, and the winds blew, and
beat upon that house; and it fell: and great was the fall of it."

109   Again in St. Matthew, Chapter 5 and verses 29 and 30, we find the
Master saying, "And if thy right eye offend thee, pluck it out, and cast it
from thee: for it is profitable for thee that one of thy members should
perish, and not that thy whole body should be cast into hell. And if thy
right hand offend thee, cut it off, and cast it from thee: for it is profitable
for thee that one of thy members should perish, and not that thy whole
body should be cast into hell."

110   Dr. Glenn Frank speaking on "The Statesmanship of Business and
the Business of Statesmanship" uses repetition at the beginning only of
three sentences to re-emphasize the fact that the nation has changed.

So I suggest that sooner or later, as a nation, we shall have to face the
political implications of the following obvious facts:
We are no longer a small nation; we are a large nation.
We are no longer a simple civilization; we are an increasingly complex and
technical civilization.
We are no longer an agricultural nation alone; we are an industrial nation
as well.

111   In an address before a conference at the University of Illinois, one
of the speakers said, "Everywhere in the world today there is an uneasy
sense that we are in the midst of profound changes in our social, political
and economic life. The flow of events seems to be forcing men and nations
relentlessly to a choice between strikingly different and strongly com-
peting philosophies of national life." Then in the paragraph immediately
following, for emphasis, he repeated the same idea in slightly different
words. He wished clearly to portray a world in chaos. "Everywhere," he
continued, "men are struggling with new social forces, for the world is
economically and politically disheveled. It threatens to ride to its doom
in a powder cart, as nations engage in 'the co-operative suicide of war.'

There are some men who believe that the world's economic machine is rapidly running down, that its soundest business and financial traditions are being repudiated in various parts of the world, and that unless there be a release again of the great fountains of private and free enterprise, the progress of decades may be lost."

112   One of the best known and most striking illustrations of repetition is to be found in the following quotation from an address by Robert Ingersoll:

A little while ago, I stood by the grave of the old Napoleon—a magnificent tomb of gilt and gold, almost fit for a dead deity—and gazed upon the sarcophagus of black Egyptian marble, where rest the ashes of that restless man. I leaned over the balustrade and thought about the career of the greatest soldier of the modern world.

I saw him walking upon the banks of the Seine contemplating suicide. I saw him at Toulon; I saw him putting down the mob in the streets of Paris; I saw him at the head of the army in Italy; I saw him crossing the bridge of Lodi with the tricolor in his hand; I saw him in Egypt in the shadow of the Pyramids; I saw him conquer the Alps and mingle the eagles of France with the eagles of the crags; I saw him at Marengo, at Ulm, and Austerlitz; I saw him in Russia where the infantry of the snow and the cavalry of the wild blast scattered his legions like winter's withered leaves; I saw him at Leipzig in defeat and disaster—driven by a million bayonets back upon Paris—clutched like a wild beast—banished to Elba. I saw him escape and retake an empire by the force of his genius. I saw him upon the frightful field of Waterloo, where Chance and Fortune combined to wreck the fortunes of their former king, and I saw him at St. Helena, with his hands crossed behind him, gazing out upon the sad and solemn sea.

I thought of the orphans and widows he had made, of the tears that had been shed for his glory, and of the only woman he ever loved, pushed from his heart by the cold hand of ambition; and I said I would rather have been a French peasant and worn wooden shoes; I would rather have lived in a hut with a vine growing over the door and the grapes growing purple in the rays of the autumn sun; I would rather have been that poor peasant with my loving wife by my side, knitting as the day died out of the sky, with my children about my knee and their arms about me, I would rather have been that man and gone down to the tongueless silence of the dreamless dust than have been that imperial personification of force and murder.

Note also in the following short passage from Edmund Burke's address, "The Age of Chivalry Is Gone," how repetition aids the emphasis: "But the age of chivalry is gone. That of sophisters, economists, and calculators, has succeeded; and the glory of Europe is extinguished forever. Never, never more, shall we behold that generous loyalty to rank and sex, that proud submission, that dignified obedience, that subordination of the heart, which kept alive, even in servitude itself, the spirit of an exalted freedom. The unbought grace of life, the cheap defence of nations, the nurse of manly sentiment and heroic enterprise, is gone. It is gone, that sensibility of principle, that chastity of honour, which felt a stain like a wound, which inspired courage . . . which ennobled whatever it touched."

A simple but slightly different use of repetition in which a question is first asked, and is then followed by variations in the question, is illustrated in the following quotation from an address on the subject of a liberal education by Thomas Henry Huxley: "Let us ask ourselves, what is education? Above all things, what is our ideal of a thoroughly liberal education?—of that education which, if we could begin life again, we would give ourselves—of that education which, if we could mould the fates to our own will, we would give our children."

In a speech on "The Romance of Life," Dr. Preston Bradley, well-known Chicago minister, lecturer and author, said, "First, there must be within our democracy a revival, a renaissance, a new birth—call it what you will—there must be a new realization of the value of human personality. We must have a new birth of value as to human personality." Note in this quotation also the mastery of the art of repetition.

113   IV. *Intersperse short sentences with long ones.*

In baseball, this might be called changing the pace. It makes it easier for the listener to understand the speech, because he does not have continually to follow tedious, long sentences. It relieves the monotony that would accompany the repeated use of nothing but long sentences or the recurrent use of the staccato-like short sentence.

ILLUSTRATIONS

114   The late Dr. Glenn Frank giving a baccalaureate address at The University of Wisconsin—

I am not so old as to have lost my memory of what must be surging through the minds of you who are about to step from the sheltered life of the student into active participation in the life of your time. And unless I have forgotten the emotions that swept my mind, some twenty-five years ago, when I completed my university training and stood poised, as you are poised, for a plunge into the outer world, I know that all sorts of anxieties haunt your minds, anxieties about the first and further steps in your careers. And these normal anxieties that you would feel even if all skies were cloudless, have, I know, been trebled by the political and economic distraction through which your nation has been passing as you have pursued your training.

What shall you do with these anxieties?

I want to be honest with you. I do not want to minimize one whit the uncertainties that infest the economic affairs of your time. I do not want to raise in your minds a single hope that will be doomed to die unfulfilled. But I do want to stir in you, if I can, every hope that can be fulfilled.

What, then, shall I say?

With a full sense of my responsibility to be realistic with you, I beg you not to let anxiety rest too heavily upon your minds.

Life is still conquerable for your generation both in the field of public policy and in the field of personal achievement.

115 Dr. Will Durant speaking on "What Are the Lessons of History?"

Now we come to another lesson of history, which is a little more dangerous: That the concentration of wealth in the hands of a minority of the population is inevitable in any society. Why? Because men are naturally unequal. Some are clever; some are virtuous; some are strong; some are weak; some are healthy; some are sickly; some are brave; some are timid; and out of small natural differences that give you a headstart come the tremendous differences in the development of society such as you see growing rapidly in America from 1750 to 1940.

116 V. *Use a series of short, crisp sentences.*

The experienced speaker may not only intersperse occasional short sentences with longer ones, but he may also insert in his address one or two paragraphs of short, sharp and clean-cut sentences that introduce a certain briskness.

ILLUSTRATIONS

In one of his addresses, Arthur M. Hyde said, "Justice is not social, economic or political. It is all of them. Justice is justice, plain and unqualified. It cannot be qualified. If limited to a class, it is no longer justice. Every citizen, not merely a class, is entitled to justice."

Channing Pollock, eminent playwright, lecturer and author, in an address on "I Am a Reactionary," gave a good example of the use of crisp sentences. He said, "A hundred and fifty years ago a group of gentlemen got together and wrote a document called the Declaration of Independence. It set the world on fire. Suddenly the human being was free. Suddenly man ceased to be a pawn of the state. Suddenly he realized that he was the captain of his soul. And mankind made more material progress in the next 150 years than in the 5000 years that went before."

George E. Sokolsky, author and columnist, in an address on "The American Way of Life," said, "How can they talk about technological unemployment when we are so flexible? We have courage. We take risks. We readjust. We achieve because we are free and nobody can stop us from doing it. When we cease to be free, we will be stopped. Life will become stabilized. There will be no improvements."

117 The late Knute Rockne, famous football coach of Notre Dame, in talking on "Athletics and Leadership," gave an excellent example of the use of a series of terse comments. He said:

Some of you may say, this will to win is a bad thing. In what way is it a bad thing? Education is supposed to prepare a young man for life. Life is competition. Success in life goes only to the man who competes successfully. A successful lawyer is the man who goes out and wins—wins law cases. A successful physician is a man who goes out and wins—saves lives and restores men to health. A successful sales manager is a man who goes out and wins—sells the goods. The successful executive is the man who can make money and stay out of the bankruptcy court. There is no reward for the loser. There is nothing wrong with the will to win. The only penalty should be that the man who wins unfairly should be set down.

All of these illustrations indicate how the short, crisp sentence may be used to give a speech "punch."

118 VI. *Use similes occasionally.*

Webster's *Collegiate Dictionary* states that a simile is "a figure of speech by which one thing, action, or relation is likened or explicitly compared, often with *as* or *like*, to something of different kind or quality." The simile is one of the oldest forms of speech. The three hundred examples of similes in Chapter VIII are included to indicate their exact nature. These similes do not at all exhaust the field, for there are thousands of illustrations in speeches, literature, and newspaper and magazine articles. New similes are being created daily. The similes given are not to be memorized unless one wishes to learn them. With a little patience and practice each of us can create similes for his own use—similes fully as sparkling and fascinating. How much more interesting it is to say "the man went through things like a customs inspector" instead of "he examined everything." How much more colorful to state "the village was as desolate as a cemetery," instead of "the village was desolate." Make it a practice to use similes both in speeches and in conversation.

119 VII. *Avoid boresome repetition by the use of appropriate synonyms.*

The dictionary and a book of synonyms are necessary additions to your library if you wish to speak, write or converse well. They will enable you to find exactly the right word for a particular use.

A synonym is a word having the same or nearly the same essential meaning as another word. Synonyms enable the speaker to have some variation in his language when otherwise he might use the same word repeatedly. A well-known American executive repeats the word "tremendous" twenty-five or more times in one speech. In fact, he uses the word a *tremendous* number of times.

There are few perfect synonyms, that is, words with exactly the same meaning as other words, so the speaker must choose his synonyms with judgment. The word *weak*, for example, may suggest as possible synonyms—feeble, infirm, faint, sickly, exhausted, groggy, spent, wasted, powerless, helpless, impotent, spineless, frail, fragile, flimsy, enervated, languishing and debilitated. Examine a speech carefully, sentence by sentence, to see whether suitable synonyms may be chosen for words which have been used so often they have become monotonous.

120   VIII. *Use appropriate antonyms to create contrasts.*

An antonym is a word whose meaning is opposite that of another word. The choice of good antonyms is necessary to create strong contrasts. A possible choice, for example, of antonyms for *weak* or *weakness* might be strength, power, potency, energy, vigor, force, stamina, virility, vitality and puissance. Examine a speech critically to see whether words that are used to bring out contrasts do so with the greatest effectiveness; if not, replace them with words which do.

121   IX. *Use questions.*

A question often serves to challenge the attention of an audience and to give emphasis to a point. In Chapter I we called attention to the possibility of using questions in the introduction. However, questions are equally valuable in the body of the address.

ILLUSTRATIONS

122   John Sergeant speaking on "Militarism and Progress," said, "I would ask: What did Cromwell, with all his military genius, do for England? He overthrew the monarchy, and he established dictatorial power in his own person. And what happened next? Another soldier overthrew the dictatorship, and restored the monarchy. The sword effected both. Cromwell made one revolution, and Monk another. And what did the people of England gain by it? Nothing. Absolutely nothing."

Chief Justice Marshall speaking on the "Federal Constitution"—

What are the favorite maxims of democracy? A strict observance of justice and public faith and a steady adherence to virtue. These, sir, are the principles of a good government. No mischief, no misfortune, ought to deter us from a strict observance of justice and public faith. Would to heaven that these principles had been observed under the present government! Had this been the case the friends of liberty would not be so willing now to part with it. Can we boast that our government is founded on these maxims? Can we pretend to the enjoyment of political freedom or security when we are told that a man has been, by an act of Assembly, struck out of existence without a trial by jury, without examination, without being confronted with his accusers and witnesses, without the benefits of the law of the land? Where is our safety when we are told that this act was justifiable because the person was not a Socrates? What has become of the worthy member's maxims? Is this one of them? Shall it be a maxim that a man shall be deprived of his life without the benefit of law? Shall such a deprivation of life be justified by answering that a man's life was not taken *secundum artem*, because he was a bad man? Shall it be a maxim that government ought not to be empowered to protect virtue?

These questions are vital ones. They go directly to the heart of Marshall's discussion.

Walter D. Fuller in speaking on "Prosperity After the War" used an excellent combination of short questions with short answers.

Why does industrial management stand uncertain?

Is it because management does not want to make the materials of defense?

No. Even before this country was designated the "arsenal of democracy," American industry was conscious of—and was meeting—its responsibility for fulfilling the defense program. Never has it questioned its function. Industry will produce according to the specifications of whatever defense program the nation may adopt.

Is management uncertain because of dissatisfaction with defense profits?

No. It expects no considerable profits. It supported the adoption of excess profits taxes as an emergency policy.

What symptoms then does industry see now, to put it on the anxious seat?

Industry sees one control after another being established over our industrial system in the name of defense, with no assurance whatsoever that these controls will be only temporary.

Industry sees post-war planning by the National Resources Board that talks about utilizing to the utmost "our system of modified free enterprise," and it ponders uncertainly what "modification" means.

Industry wonders how important defense production is, when government sits blandly by while two groups of labor leaders make defense plants the battleground for jurisdictional warfare.

Mark Sullivan talking on "What is Liberalism?"—

There is another word of which I think there is much current misuse. "Democracy" is like "liberty," a word which commands affection from Americans. But lately I see many allusions to what is called "economic democracy."

Just what would that phrase mean, if it means anything? We know what political democracy means. Political democracy means political equality—one man, one vote. Would "economic democracy" mean "economic equality"—one man, one unit of property?

123 X. *Place ideas in contrast to each other.*

Placing ideas in contrast to one another is sometimes called antithesis. Occasionally one even finds antithesis within single sentences as in Burke's speech on "The Age of Chivalry" when he speaks of "All the pleasing allusions which made power gentle and obedience liberal." Note the contrast between power and gentle, obedience and liberal. In another place he says: "Never, never more shall we behold . . . that proud submission, that dignified obedience. . . ." Again note the contrast, particularly of proud and submission.

ILLUSTRATIONS

Demosthenes often used contrasts in his addresses, as illustrated in his speech "On the Crown."

Contrast now the circumstances of your life and mine, gently and with temper, Aeschines; and then ask these people whose fortune they would each of them prefer. You taught reading, I went to school: you performed initiations, I received them: you danced in the chorus, I furnished it: you were assembly-clerk, I was a speaker: you acted third parts, I heard you: you broke down, and I hissed: you have worked as a statesman for the enemy, I for my country. I pass by the rest; but this very day I am on my probation for a crown, and am acknowledged to be innocent of all offense; while you are already judged to be a pettifogger, and the question is, whether you shall continue that trade, or at once be silenced by not getting a fifth part of the votes. A happy fortune, do you see, you have enjoyed, that you should denounce mine as miserable!

John Haynes Holmes speaking on "Are We in the Hands of Fate?"—

Such is the fatalism into which we have been betrayed. Before 1914, an optimistic fatalism which assured us that we were floating on a quiet stream into a haven of perfect bliss! After that dreadful date, a pessimistic fatalism which assured us that we were caught in a maelstrom of disaster from which there is no escape!

The element of contrast is present also in these sentences of Dr. Glenn Frank's: (1) "A stage-coach citizenship may prove the undoing of an express-train world." (2) "And whether it be noble or ignoble, religious or irreligious, the able young man of today is not interested in the exclusive task of 'labeling men and women for transportation to a realm unknown' and sedulously avoiding straightforward consideration of that reconstruction of human society which Jesus of Nazareth had in mind when he talked of the Kingdom of God coming on earth."

124 XI. *Use colorful phrases and figures of speech.*

Chapter IX contains one hundred and seventy-three phrases and figures of speech which may be employed to give an address character and style. "Barkis is willin'," "Greeks bearing gifts," "a Jason's quest" are typical expressions which assist the speaker and writer to give more color to his ideas. A speaker who was describing the slow evolution of great ideas in industry, and in all fields of life, mentioned the gradual development of the automobile from the earliest models three decades ago to the stream-lined cars of the present day. "It is apparent," he said, "that this great industry did not develop overnight. It did not spring Minerva-like from the head of Jove."

125 Dr. Will Durant speaking on "What Are the Lessons of History?" said, "So I should say that civilizations begin with religion and stoicism;

they end with skepticism and unbelief, and the undisciplined pursuit of individual pleasure. A civilization is born stoic and dies epicurean." In that one last short sentence of only eight words, using two colorful words, "stoic" and "epicurean," Dr. Durant made a splendid summary of his viewpoint.

One of the reasons Hugh S. Johnson's language is picturesque is that he frequently uses figures of expression such as those in Chapter IX. Comprehensive reading will be helpful in adding many figures of speech to your vocabulary. The one hundred and seventy-three chosen for Chapter IX will make an excellent start.

126 XII. *Use suitable Biblical quotations.*

Biblical quotations may be used not only in the introduction and in the conclusion of many speeches, but they may also be used vividly to express ideas in the body of speeches. It is not possible to use a Biblical quotation in every speech, but where it can be done to emphasize a point, it makes a distinctly worth-while addition. The Bible is the richest source book of quotations in the world. The Presidents of the United States have often quoted from the Old and New Testaments to convey their messages to the people. A frequent study of the almost three hundred Biblical quotations in Chapter X will bring gratifying returns in the ability to express your ideas well.

ILLUSTRATIONS

127 Dr. Glenn Frank delivering a Baccalaureate Address on the subject, "If the Young Can But See"—

The dullard must wait for events to overtake him. He lacks the sensitive imagination and disciplined powers of analysis to enable him to anticipate and to discount events. He never knows that a policy is bad until it has worked havoc in his life or in the life of his time. He never knows that a policy is good until it has dropped the ripe fruits of its goodness in his lap. Thus he must go through life victimized by the tragic results of bad policies that wiser men would have forestalled and robbed of the benefits of good policies that more farseeing men would have brought into being. With all this, he may be technically a learned man, but, lacking insight and understanding, his learning becomes so much waste lumber.

Down the ages the capacity to anticipate and to discount bad ideas and the capacity to sense in advance and to appropriate good ideas, without waiting for events to indicate their badness or their goodness, has been considered the supreme achievement of man as a thinking animal.

When the Lord of Ancient Israel was searching for the most withering rebuke and the most devastating penalty he could lay upon a recreant people, he asked that they be robbed of the capacity to see and to understand.

"Make the heart of his people fat," he cried, "and make their ears heavy, and shut their eyes; lest they see with their eyes, and hear with their ears, and understand with their heart, and be healed."

And from Isaiah to Bernard Shaw this belief that insight and understanding are the godlike gifts has held.

128 President Daniel L. Marsh of Boston University addressing the National Council of Education—

I do not know of any finer expression of values, any better cataloguing of ideas to which our emotions might properly be attached, or any more adequate ideal as a stimulus to the will, than St. Paul gives in his letter to the Philippians: "Whatsoever things are true, whatsoever things are honorable, whatsoever things are just, whatsoever things are pure, whatsoever things are lovely, whatsoever things are of good report: if there be any virtue, and if there be any praise, think on these things."

That ideal is the touchstone of freedom. Examine your life and see if what I say is not true. "The unexamined life is not worthy of being lived by one who calls himself a man," said Socrates. "*Think* on these things," said Paul; take an inventory of these things, keep your mind upon them, set a value upon them; for thought precedes accomplishment. We grow like the things we think about. The good is positive, not negative.

129 XIII. *Use appropriate quotations from literature.*

Other than the Bible, perhaps the most frequently quoted sources are the writings of Shakespeare. Among the more than 1,200 quotations in Chapter XI, there are over 150 from Shakespeare. The 1,200 quotations have been carefully selected from the world's great literature, from addresses and from other sources. In almost every speech you will be able to use one or more quotations. Choose them carefully and they are certain to give style to your address.

ILLUSTRATIONS

130 An educator addressing a Wisconsin High School Commencement class on the great significance of decision in life said:

On the importance of decision we may say with James Russell Lowell:
"Once to every man and nation comes the moment to decide,
In the strife of Truth with Falsehood, for the good or evil side."

131 John Haynes Holmes speaking at Lehigh University on "Are We in the Hands of Fate?"—

There is no such thing as security any more. There is as little permanency in values as stability in institutions. For years the preachers of religion have proclaimed "the deceitfulness of riches," and the emptiness of all merely material possessions. Well, here they are—the prophecies come true! Now we know that the things of the spirit alone endure. In our time, as in times before, there has come the moment described by Prospero, in Shakespeare's play, *The Tempest*, when

> ". . . all which (we) inherit shall dissolve,
> And, like this insubstantial pageant faded,
> Leave not a rack behind."

132 Francis Biddle, Attorney General of the United States, speaking before the California State Bar Association—

For myself, I hold firmly to that faith in free institutions which is implicit in the theme of this convention. I am confident that the same vitality of free government which has brought our nation through one hundred fifty years to its present stature will enable it in the future as in the past to "meet with Triumph and Disaster and treat those two imposters just the same."

133 XIV. *Use words, phrases, clauses and sentences in groups of two or three occasionally.*

The use of words, phrases and sentences in groups of two or three gives rhythm and force to a speech. No attempt should be made to arrange these groups in every sentence or paragraph as it would lead to monotony. But most of us will not be guilty of the excessive use of this tool of speech.

ILLUSTRATIONS

134 In just three famous words, "Veni, vidi, vici," or, "I came, I saw, I conquered," Julius Caesar described his triumph over King Pharnaces of the Bosporus in 47 B.C. Those words, "having all the same cadence," said Plutarch, "carry with them a very suitable air of brevity" which brevity conforms to the swiftness and completeness of Caesar's victory. Cadence runs thought a close second in evoking the applause of an audience.

"Give me liberty, or give me death" was the expression of a great conviction. But it was even more. It was the brilliant expression of that conviction. Consider the sentence carefully. Two ideas are balanced on each side of the word "or." The ideas of liberty or death also are in contrast. Both clauses begin with the same words "give me," so that there is alliteration.

135 The eulogy delivered by General (Light Horse Harry) Henry Lee upon the death of George Washington contains a famous phrase illustrating the grouping of three phrases. Lee said upon that historic occasion, "To the memory of the man, first in war, first in peace, and first in the hearts of his countrymen."

Franklin D. Roosevelt concluded a radio address on September 11, 1941, with this climactic sentence:

And with that inner strength that comes to a free people conscious of their duty, conscious of the righteousness of what they do, they will—with divine

c

help and guidance—stand their ground against this latest assault upon their democracy, their sovereignty and their freedom.

Observe the rhythm and the power in the last eight words.

Walter D. Fuller, President of the Curtis Publishing Company, speaking before the Cleveland Advertising Club:

We must not lose sight of the fact that we can save democracy only with the tools of production and selling—we can save free enterprise only by utilizing free enterprise, we can save advertising and selling only by using more advertising and selling.

A banker speaking before the Nebraska Bankers Association said: "It would be gratifying if it were possible to suggest here a program of the banker's responsibility, so comprehensive in its plan, so complete in its parts, and so convincing in its presentation that it would challenge the thinking of this intelligent audience." This sentence not only illustrates the grouping of three phrases, but also the use of alliteration which follows in Point XV.

136 XV. *Alliteration.*

Webster's *Collegiate Dictionary*, Fifth Edition, defines alliteration as the "repetition of the same sound at the beginning of two or more consecutive words or of words near one another; specifically, recurrence of the same consonant sound or of vowel sounds initially in accented syllables of verse, as in 'in a somer seson when soft was the sonne.' (*Piers Plowman.*)"

Alliteration gives a speech sparkle because it adds harmony, swing and rhythm. It would become distinctly tiresome if used in every sentence, but employed occasionally in a speech it thrills an audience. The speaker who may hope that at least parts of his speeches will be quoted, or will live, will find (1) the arrangement of words, phrases, clauses, and sentences in groups of two or three, and (2) the use of alliteration to be two of the most effective speech tools to assist him.

137 Winston Churchill knows that alliteration fascinates an audience and makes speeches moving and forceful. He said, "We cannot *fail* or *falter.*" He commented of a certain person that he was "a man of *light* and *learning*"; in a great emergency he declared, "Let us to the task, to the battle and the toil."

Claude G. Bowers, distinguished American diplomat, talking to the Phi Beta Kappa chapter at Yale said, "The American Democracy is mobilized today to wage a war of extermination against privilege and pillage. We prime our guns against bureaucracy and plutocracy." "Privilege and pillage," "bureaucracy and plutocracy" are ringing phrases because of the alliteration.

138   The late Dr. Glenn Frank was one of the greatest masters of alliteration America has ever known, as indicated by the following examples chosen at random from his speeches and writings:

"They say that when the acid test was applied, the prophet turned politician, and the realist was lost in the rhetorician."

"We are convicted of plain bankruptcy of political intelligence."

"It is better that we frankly take our latitude and longitude in relation to our war-time ideals than that we attempt the perilous practice of self-delusion."

"The mind and the mood of the masses is the soil of the policy."

"We place our foreign affairs in the hands . . . of men who bring to the politics of a planet the vision of a parish."

"The most perilous disease in the world is not leprosy, but lopsidedness."

"Facts are not concerned with flattery."

"He became the partisan and pamphleteer of Christianity."

"It is not the analyses of the classroom, but the actualities of the marketplace."

"A nation's army is only the clenched fist of its factories and farms."

Alliteration enables one to give to a speech what Lynn Harold Hough called "the gracious loveliness of finely wrought phrases."

Chapter 3

PUBLIC SPEAKING IN A NUTSHELL

....

I. Determine the exact subject so that it is entirely clear in your mind. If you have a hazy conception of the precise limitations of your topic, the audience naturally will be confused.

II. Think through the whole subject and formulate your own ideas and conclusions.

III. Read exhaustively all important speeches, pamphlets and books on the subject with which you are not familiar. Take notes on significant points.

IV. Outline the subject as follows:
    A. Introduction.
    B. Body of the speech, subdivided generally into two, three or four parts.
    C. Conclusion.

V. Write out the speech fully. Experienced speakers may find it possible simply to outline an address and speak from the outline, but writing a speech eliminates wordiness and gives exactness to expression.
    A. The introduction must be short. It may be developed in one of the following eight ways:
        1. Announce the subject directly in the first sentence or paragraph.
        2. Tell a story of human interest, "paint a picture" or give an illustration.
        3. Use a statement that excites attention, arouses curiosity, surprises the audience, or is particularly informative.
        4. Tell a humorous story that is definitely related to the subject or to the situation under which you are addressing the audience.

5. Use a chart, table, map or some other form of exhibit.
6. Ask a challenging question.
7. State facts which show the importance of the subject to the welfare of the audience.
8. Begin by a significant quotation or idea from some other person.

B. The body is the substance of the speech. Fill it with facts and concrete illustrations, and not simply with generalities. The following ideas will be of assistance in writing this part of your speech.
1. Know the subject thoroughly.
2. Use facts, figures and illustrations.
3. If the audience is to be convinced of some proposition, begin with subject matter with which there is agreement.
4. Do not argue, but explain.
5. State briefly and clearly either at the beginning of the body of the speech or one by one, as the main part of the address unfolds, the two, three or four points to be discussed. To provide suspense, it is generally better to give the points, one by one, as the speech progresses.

C. The conclusion must ordinarily be short, and it is generally advisable to use it to re-emphasize the points developed in the body of a speech. The following seven methods may be used to conclude a speech:
1. Outline concisely the major points you have made in the body of the speech.
2. Use a quotation from the Bible or literature.
3. Bring the speech to a grand climax.
4. Compliment the audience or leave a note of encouragement or optimism.
5. Describe a dramatic scene, a great moment in history, science or business, or give a brief biographical story.
6. Ask the audience to take some form of action or to adopt a certain viewpoint on some matter.
7. Tell a humorous story or give a suitable witty comment.

140   HOW TO MAKE YOUR SPEECH SPARKLE

Rewrite and refine the speech until every unnecessary word is eliminated. The following fifteen effective speech tools will greatly assist you in the revision of your speech and will help to make it sparkle:

I. Insert suitable humorous stories, epigrams and amusing definitions.

II. Use illustrations from biography, from plays, or from literature.

III. Repeat some words or phrases to stamp them indelibly upon the minds of the listeners.

IV. Intersperse short sentences with long ones.

V. Use a series of short, crisp sentences.

VI. Use similes occasionally.

VII. Avoid boresome repetition by the use of appropriate synonyms.

VIII. Use appropriate antonyms to create contrasts.

IX. Use questions.

X. Place ideas in contrast to each other.

XI. Use colorful phrases and figures of speech.

XII. Use suitable Biblical quotations.

XIII. Use appropriate quotations from literature.

XIV. Use words, phrases, clauses and sentences in groups of two or three occasionally.

XV. Use alliteration.

141-142   WHEN YOU ARE BEFORE THE AUDIENCE

I. Open your mouth and speak distinctly and loudly enough to be heard by every person in the audience.

II. Don't worry about nervousness as you start speaking. It's a good sign. Almost every able speaker is nervous at the outset. It indicates he is "on edge" and ready. The time to worry is when you are not "keyed up" with nervous energy. If you have thoroughly prepared, you are the master of the situation.

III. Give your speech in one of the following ways:

1. Read it if you must, but read it so well it sounds as if you were speaking without a manuscript.

2. Have your manuscript before you, but refer to it only occasionally. This requires reading the manuscript over and over until you are thoroughly familiar with it.

3. Write out the address or outline it in detail. Then go over it repeatedly until you are entirely familiar with it. Speak only from notes.

4. Write out the speech or outline it in detail. Then go over it repeatedly until you are completely familiar with it. Speak without notes.

5. Write out the speech and memorize it. Be sure you speak naturally.

Follow whichever method is best for you. Try gradually to eliminate reading as much as you can. Whatever you do read, must be read well, or you will lose your audience at once. All important state addresses necessarily must be read to avoid even the slightest misstatement.

IV. Should you gesture? You may, but your gestures must come naturally. You never learn gestures solely from a book of rules. The following simple suggestions may help you:

1. Merely permit your hands to fall loosely to your sides. You may place your hands behind your back and even occasionally in your pockets if you wish.
2. If you must twiddle your fingers, do it behind your back.
3. Stand in one place, and do not pace up and down the platform like a caged lion. These nervous movements distract an audience.
4. Do not point your forefinger at the audience as if you were scolding the neighbor's children.
5. Generally avoid: repeated wide swings of the arms; numerous lightning-like movements of the forearms; and constant pounding on the table. Any frequently repeated gesture is tiresome.
6. It is better to err on the side of too few gestures than too many.
7. Above all, be natural.

V. Keep your speech within the limits of the time allotted to you.

143   WHAT PUBLIC SPEAKING REQUIRES

I. Sincere convictions earnestly expressed. You cannot convince others of what you do not believe.
II. Unquestioned knowledge of your subject. You cannot explain to others what you do not understand.
III. Painstaking preparation of every speech. You are deeply indebted to the audience for the privilege they have given you. A good speech is the best expression of your gratitude.
IV. Practice at home, but never before an audience.

SINCERITY, KNOWLEDGE, PREPARATION and PRACTICE—these are the four great requirements of public speaking.

Chapter 4

JOKES AND JESTS

....

144   Out the Window He Must Go

There are audiences and audiences. Some rank high in the scale of intelligence (like this one), and have a peculiar ability to disconcert a speaker. Even those low in the scale of intelligence provide their embarrassing moments. Henry Brown had a great desire to become a public speaker and accepted every invitation that came his way. One day the superintendent of the state insane asylum asked him to speak to an assembly of the inmates. The day came for the speech; Brown had hardly begun when a fellow in the back of the room said, "Rotten." Brown was nervous, but continued. The inmate yelled "Rotten" still louder. Brown considered the nature of his audience and decided to give his speech one more whirl. He began all over, but the fellow yelled "Rotten" again so loudly the whole audience was disturbed. Brown finally turned to the superintendent and said, "Steve, shall I go on, or shall I stop?" The superintendent said, "Henry, you go right ahead. We've had that fellow in here ten years, and this is the first time he ever showed any intelligence." (A speaker might add, "When a speaker can get in that position with an unintelligent audience, it is obvious that he faces real hazards in talking to an intelligent audience.")

145   Cramped in His Style

A speaker said that as he surveyed the breadth of his subject, he could not help but think of Bishop Jones who was invited to speak before a great convention. A telegram he received from the program committee read as follows: "We should like to have you address our convention on the subject, 'THE WORLD, THE WAR, AND THE CHURCH.'" He gave the matter some consideration and felt he would like to address the convention, but the magnitude of the subject bothered him considerably. So he wired them as follows: "Gentlemen, I should like to address your great convention. However, I should not like to be cramped in my style or restricted in my remarks by any such narrow subject as 'THE WORLD, THE WAR, AND THE CHURCH.' I should be glad to come if you will add to it, 'THE SUN, THE MOON, AND THE STARS.'" (A story suitable when one is given a very broad subject to discuss.)

146   Do It Over Right

Farmer (to new hired hand): "Where's that mule I told you to take out and have shod?"

New Hand: "Did you say 'shod'? I thought you said 'shot.' I've just been buryin' her."

147 START OVER

Customer: "I haven't come to any ham in this sandwich yet."
Waiter: "Try another bite."
Customer (taking huge mouthful): "Nope, none yet."
Waiter: "Dog-gone it! You must have gone right past it."

148 WHAT?

Teacher: "Now, Robert, what are you doing—learning something?"
Robert: "No, sir; I'm listening to you."

149 IT SHRINKS IN THE HEAT

"Is a ton of coal very much, papa?"
"That depends, my son, on whether you are shoveling or buying it."

150 THIS IS DISCIPLINE

Mrs. Shopalot: "Can you alter this dress to fit me?"
Salesman: "Certainly not. That isn't done any more. You will have to be altered to fit the dress."

151 A WEE BIT TOO PIOUS

A Scottish lady invited a gentleman to dinner on a particular day and he accepted with the reservation, "If I am spared."
"Weel, weel," replied she, "if ye're deid I'll no' expect ye."

152 A STATISTICS STORY

I never listen to a speaker launch out on one of those long discussions, filled with statistics of all kinds, or commit the same error myself, but that I think of the professor in a western university who taught mathematics and statistics. One day he was standing, dressed in his bathing suit, at the edge of a swimming pool on the university campus when a beautiful co-ed accidentally dropped her camera into the deep end of the pool. She called to the elderly professor for help. He said he would be glad to dive down after the camera, but first wanted to know why she happened to choose him when there were so many young men within easy reach to do the job. She answered, "Professor, you have apparently forgotten me, but I am in your large statistics class. I have found that you can *go down deeper—stay down longer—and come up drier*—than anyone I know."—I do not propose to go down too deep, stay down too long, or come up too dry with these statistics.

153 ANOTHER STATISTICS STORY

The old gentleman was buying a pair of shoes. He said he didn't think the leather was very good. The salesman said, "The leather in those shoes will last longer than you do." The elderly gentleman, who was 98, said, "Young man that's where you're wrong. Statistics show that fewer people die after 98 years of age than at any other age up to that time."

C*

154   It Made a Difference

Visitor: If your mother gave you two apples and told you to give one to your brother, would you give him the little one or the big one?

Johnny: Do you mean my little brother or my big one?

155   Getting Out of a Bad Fix

A business man who had been through several years of depression decided he needed a vacation. When he discussed the matter with his wife, she said that she wanted to go along with him on a trip which he was planning to take around the world. He agreed, and then she added that she would like to take her mother along. He was not certain that he wished to take his mother-in-law along with him on a trip around the world for his health. They argued about it for a while; the argument finally was compromised—and the three of them went on the trip. One day when they were in Central Africa, half way around the world, camping out in the open, they arose in the morning, and lo and behold! the mother-in-law was missing. They looked for her for several hours and finally found her standing in a cleared spot in a dense forest with a mountain lion ten feet away, roaring.

The wife cried: "John, John, what shall we do for mother?"

He looked the situation over carefully, meditated for a moment and said, "Mary, it looks to me as if the lion got himself into that fix. Let him get himself out the best way that he can." (A speaker might say, "Considering the controversial nature of this subject, I presume I ought to get myself out of this situation as quickly and with as little embarrassment as possible.")

156   You Put Him to Sleep

A man fell asleep in the congregation of a church. The preacher stopped and asked a young boy sitting beside the man to wake him up. The boy said, "Wake him up yourself—you put him to sleep." (Suitable if a speech is long.)

157   Concise

A waitress came to the tired traveler who had just seated himself in a small-town restaurant. The menu was a very short one. The waitress said, "Will you have roast beef for dinner?" He said, "No." She said, "In that case dinner's over." (A good illustration of conciseness.)

158   Proud Father

Two parsons were having lunch at a farm during the progress of certain anniversary celebrations. The farmer's wife cooked a couple of chickens, saying that the family could dine on the remains after the visitors had gone. But the hungry parsons wolfed the chickens bare.

Later the farmer was conducting his guests round the farm, when an old rooster commenced to crow ad lib. "Seems mighty proud of himself," said one of the guests.

"No wonder," growled the farmer, "he's got two sons in the ministry."

159   This Modern Age!

"Daddy, what is a bachelor?"

"A bachelor, my boy, is a man who didn't have a car when he was young."

160   GOT HIS GOAT

Angry Man: "Why did you tax me $8.00 for my goat?"

Tax Adjuster: "Well, keep him out of the street. The law says, 'For private possessions bounding and a-butting on public property, $2.00 a running foot.'"

161   VISITING CARD

Sandy joined a golf club and was told by the professional that if his name was on his golf balls and they were lost, they would be returned to him when found.

"Good," said the Scot. "Put my name on this ball."

The pro did so.

"Would you also put M.D. after it?" said the new member. "I'm a doctor."

The pro obeyed.

"There's just one more thing," went on the Scot. "Can ye squeeze 'Hours 10 to 3' on it as well?"

162   SPELLING

"How is Hennery gettin' along with school, Eph?"

"Not so well, Garge. They're learnin' him to spell taters with a 'p.'"

163   WHO WOULDN'T!

A candidate for the police force was being verbally examined. "If you were by yourself in a police car and were pursued by a desperate gang of criminals in another car doing forty miles an hour along a lonely road, what would you do?" The candidate looked puzzled for a moment. Then he replied: "Fifty.

164   NO LEISURE

A farmer who went to a large city to see the sights engaged a room at a hotel and before retiring asked the clerk about the hours for meals.

"We have breakfast from 7 to 11, dinner from 12 to 3, and supper from 6 to 8," explained the clerk.

"Look here," inquired the farmer in surprise, "what time am I going to see the town?"

165   NO HURRY

Meek voice over the telephone: "Doctor, this is Mr. Henpeck. My wife just dislocated her jaw. If you're out this way next week or the week after, you might drop in and see her."

166   FROM MISSOURI

"Aren't people funny?"

"Yes. If you tell a man that there are 270,678,934,341 stars in the universe, he'll believe you—but if a sign says 'Fresh Paint,' that same man has to make a personal investigation."

167   A FRIEND IN NEED

The midday whistle had blown when Murphy shouted, "Has anyone seen me vest?"

"Sure, Murphy," said Pat, "and ye've got it on."

"Right and I have," replied Murphy, gazing solemnly at his bosom, "and it's a good thing ye seen it or I'd have gone home without it."

168 STUMBLING-BLOCK

Prisoner: "Judge, I don't know what to do."

Judge: "Why, how's that?"

Prisoner: "I swore to tell the truth, but every time I try some lawyer objects."

169 COLOSSAL

"Well, Johnny," said the uncle who hadn't seen him for some time, "you are getting to be quite a big boy now, aren't you?"

"Yep," replied the kid, "pop says I'm growing like the public debt."

170 MIGHT BE WORSE

"What do you think of our two candidates for mayor?"

"Well, I'm glad only one can be elected."

171 NOT OVER-DEMANDING

Rexford: "I suppose you think I'm a perfect idiot?"

Roberts: "Oh, none of us is perfect."

172 IDENTIFICATION

First Lawyer: "You're a low-down cheat!"

Second Lawyer: "You're an unmitigated liar!"

Judge (rapping): "Now that the attorneys have identified each other we shall proceed with the case."

173 NO LAUGHING MATTER

Draper: "These are especially strong shirts, madam. They simply laugh at the laundry."

Customer: "I know that kind; I had some which came back with their sides split."

174 FILIAL LOVE

Dad: "Son, I'm spanking you because I love you."

Son: "I'd sure like to be big enough to return your love."

175 AIR-CONDITIONED

"Janitor, you could cool our apartment nicely if you would run ice-water through the radiators."

"Can't be done, madam."

"What did you have in them last winter?"

176 SUCCESS

"How is your doctor son getting on in his practice?"

"Excellently—he has made enough money so he can occasionally tell a patient there is nothing wrong with him."

177 PLENTY

"What would I get," inquired the man who had just insured his property against fire, "if this building should burn down tonight?" . . . "I would say," replied the insurance-agent, "about ten years."

178   ABOUT COMPLETE

"So you are building a new house, eh? How are you getting along with it?"

"Fine. I've got the roof and the mortgage on it, and I expect to have the furnace and the sheriff in before fall."

179   NO REGRETS

"I'm sorry—I quite forgot your party the other evening!"

"Oh, weren't you there?"

180   FAMILIAR

Guide: "This castle has stood for six hundred years. Not a stone has been touched, nothing altered, nothing replaced."

Visitor: "Um, they must have the same landlord we have."

181   CHIT-CHAT

Officer (to colored driver who has been whipping his horse): "Don't whip him, man—talk to him."

Driver (to horse, by way of opening the conversation): "Ah comes from N'Awleans. Where does youall come from?"

182   NO FAVORS

Son: "Say, Dad, that apple I just ate had a worm in it, and I ate that, too."

Parent: "What! Here, drink this water and wash it down."

But Junior shook his head. "Aw, let 'im walk down."

183   WITH A SPEEDY RECOVERY

Hewitt: "You don't seem to think much of him."

Jewell: "If he had his conscience taken out, it would be a minor operation."

184   ON THE SPOT

Office-Boy (nervously): "Please, sir, I think you're wanted on the 'phone."

Employer: "You think! What's the good of thinking?"

"Well, sir, the voice at the other end said, 'Hello, is that you, you old idiot?'"

185   A SYSTEM

"Are you saving any money since you started your budget system?"

"Sure. By the time we have balanced it up every evening, it's too late to go anywhere."

186   HE MADE SURE

Many are the stories told about the care Gen. Smedley D. Butler always took in looking after the welfare of the men in his command—especially as regarded their food. One relates that when he was in command of Camp Pontenazen, France, he met two soldiers carrying a large soup kettle from the kitchen.

"Here you," he ordered, "let me taste that."

"But, Gen ——"

"Don't give me any buts—get a spoon!"

"Yes, sir!" the soldier replied, and running back in the kitchen, brought a spoon.

The General took the desired taste, and gingerly spat it out. "You don't call that stuff soup, do you?" he shouted. "No, sir!" replied the soldier. "That's what I was trying to tell you—it's dishwater, sir!"

187   CLOSE SHAVE

Man (getting a shave): "Barber, will you please give me a glass of water?"
Barber: "What is the matter? Something in your throat?"
Man: "No—I want to see if my neck leaks."

188   TACT

Mikhail: "You look positively beautiful tonight."
Elsie: "Oh, you flatterer!"
Mikhail: "No, it's true. I had to look twice before I recognized you."

189   SLOW MOTION

A cameraman, working for the educational department of a film company, met an old farmer in town and said:
"I've just been taking some moving pictures of life out on your farm."
"Did you catch any of my men in motion?" asked the old farmer curiously.
"Sure I did."
The farmer shook his head reflectively, then commented: "Science is a wonderful thing."

190   A QUESTION OF TITLE

"After another season," said Farmer Corntassel, "I guess we'll have a chef for the summer boarders."
"What's a chef?" asked Mrs. Corntassel.
"A chef is a man with a big enough vocabulary to give the soup a different name every day."

191   ENTHUSIASTIC

Husband (after the theater): "But, dear, what did you object to?"
Wife: "Why, the idea of your bellowing 'Author! Author!' at a Shakespearean drama."

192   THAT'S TOO VAGUE

Heard in the tube: "How old should you say she is?"
"Oh, somewhere in the middle flirties!"

193   HANDY

"Can you serve company?" asked the housewife when she was hiring the servant.
"Yes, mum; both ways."
"What do you mean?" asked the puzzled one.
"So's they'll come again, or stay away."

194   BUT THAT WAS 'WAY BACK

Doctor: "What was the most you ever weighed?"
Patient: "154 pounds."
Doctor: "And what was the least you ever weighed?"
Patient: "8¼ pounds."

195   FINIS

"Am I g-g-going to d-d-die, doctor?"

"My dear Mr. Smith, that's the last thing you'll do!"

196   HEARD AT THE ZOO

A huge elephant and a tiny mouse were in the same cage at the zoo. The elephant was in a particularly ugly and truculent mood. Looking down at the mouse with disgust he trumpeted, "You're the puniest, the weakest, the most insignificant thing I've ever seen!" "Well," piped the mouse in a plaintive squeak, "don't forget, I've been sick."

197   EXCLUSIVE

"Yes," said the boastful young man, "my family can trace its ancestry back to William the Conqueror."

"I suppose," remarked his friend, "you'll be telling us that your ancestors were in the Ark with Noah?"

"Certainly not," said the other. "My people had a boat of their own."

198   STILL GREEN

Boss: "You are twenty minutes late again. Don't you know what time we start work at this factory?"

New Employee: "No, sir, they're always at it when I get here."

199   STAYING SAFE

In a small hotel in Kingston, Ontario, so a returning traveler reports, there is a yellowing sign tacked to the dingy wall behind the desk on which the proprietor proclaims his fixed inbred skepticism of all humanity. It reads: "No checks cashed. Not even good ones."

200   DODDERING

Lawyer: "Then your husband, I take it, is elderly?"

Client: "Elderly? Why, he's so old he gets winded playing chess."

201   BE CAREFUL

Father: "Why were you kept in at school?"

Mike: "I didn't know where the Azores were."

Father: "In the future, just remember where you put things."

202   PREFERRED

"Your fiance is a charming man. He has a certain something."

"Yes, but I would rather he had something certain."

203   MUSIC

Daughter: "Did you ever hear anything so wonderful?" (as the radio ground out the latest in swing).

Father: "Can't say I have, although I once heard a collision between a truck-load of milk cans and a car filled with ducks."

204   INSULTED

"What do you mean," roared the politician, "by publicly insulting me in your old rag of a paper? I will not stand for it, and I demand an immediate apology."

"Just a moment," answered the editor. "Didn't the news item appear exactly as you gave it to us, namely, that you had resigned as city treasurer?"

"It did, but where did you put it?—in the column under the heading 'Public Improvements.'"

205 HOLE-IN-ONE

Then there was the sweet young thing who was being initiated into the mysteries of golf by her boy friend. "And now tell me," she said coyly, "which club do I use to make a hole-in-one?"

206 THERE'S GOOD IN EVERYTHING

"Polygamy would never work in this country."

"Why not?"

"Think of getting several wives in a kitchenette at one time."

207 THE TOP

"What is the outstanding contribution that chemistry has given to the world."

Flo: "Blondes."

208 STILL ADVERTISING

A traveler seeking advertisements for a local paper called at the village grocer's. Upon presenting his card, he was surprised when the gray-haired proprietor said: "Nothing doing. Been established eighty years, and never advertised."

"Excuse me, sir, but what is that building on the hill?" asked the traveler.

"The village church," said the grocer.

"Been there long?" asked the other.

"About three hundred years."

"Well," was the reply, "they still ring the bell."

209 PUZZLER

The little girl was impressed by the sermon describing the attractions of heaven. Some time later she asked her mother:

"Do cats go to heaven?"

Her mother replied that since animals do not have souls they could hardly be expected to go to heaven.

"Then where do the angels get strings for their harps?"

210 ASSURANCE

A negro preacher had pestered his bishop so much with appeals for help that the bishop finally told him in a tone of finality that he didn't want to hear any more appeals from him.

The next week there came a letter from the preacher as follows: "Dear Bishop: I assure you this is not an appeal. I assure you it is a report. I have no pants."

211 STATISTICS

Chief Instructor: "Now remember, men, statistics don't lie. Now, for an example, if twelve men could build a house in one day, one man could build the same house in twelve days. Do you understand what I mean? Jeep, give me an example."

Jeep: "You mean that if one boat could cross the ocean in six days, six boats could cross the ocean in one day."

212 A DRY SPEAKER

Everything that could be done to make the great unemployed meeting a success had been accomplished. A large hall and a good speaker had been engaged. When the latter arrived, he seemed to be in a crabby frame of mind. Looking around he beckoned the chairman.

"I would like to have a glass of water on my table, if you please," he said.

"To drink?" was the chairman's idiotic question.

"Oh, no," was the sarcastic retort, "when I've been speaking a half hour, I do a high dive."

213 FROM THE INSIDE

"Look at that one—the one staring at us through the bars. Doesn't he look intelligent?"

"Yes. There is something uncanny about it."

"He looks as if he understood every word we're saying."

"Walks on his hind legs, too, and swings his arms."

"There! He's got a peanut. Let's see what he does with it."

"Well, what do you think about that! He knows enough to take the shell off before he eats it just like we do."

"That's a female alongside of him. Listen to her chatter at him. He doesn't seem to be paying much attention to her, though."

"She must be his mate."

"They look kind of sad, don't they?"

"Yes. I guess they wish they were in here with us monkeys."

214 BANKRUPT

"Dear folks: Please send four hundred dollars at once; the school is bankrupt and each student has to pay double tuition. Kindly make the check out to me. Your son, Elmer."

215 HE FOUND OUT

A colored man was caught trying to sell insurance without a license, and was hauled before the insurance commissioner.

"Don't you know," demanded the commissioner, "that you can't sell insurance in this town without a license?"

"Boss," said the colored one. "Dat splains de mattah. I done foun' out dat I couldn't sell none, but I didn't know whats de reezin wuz ontil you tole me."

216 EASY TO HIDE

Mister (hurrying to get dressed for a party)—"Ouch, I bumped my crazy bone."

Missus—"Well, just part your hair on the other side and it will never show."

217 LITERAL

Mother: "Sonny, go over and find out how old Mrs. Harris is this morning."

Sonny (on return): "She says today she's 73 years, six months and two days."

218   It Is, Dear

"You know, dear, John doesn't seem to be as well dressed as he was when you married him."

"That's funny. I'm sure it's the same suit."

219   Believes in Signs

Teacher (to tardy student)—"Why are you late?"

Bobby—"Well, a sign down here ——"

Teacher—"Well, what has a sign got to do with it?"

Bobby—"The sign said: 'School ahead; go slow.'"

220   Tsk Tsk!

"Is your Daddy home, sonny?"

"No, sir. He hasn't been home since mother caught Santa Claus kissing the maid."

221   If You Are Discouraged

If you are discouraged, compare your problems with those of the father who wrote this letter. Note particularly the last paragraph. The daughter wrote that she was coming home with her husband to live with father. Father wrote as follows:

"Dear Daughter:

I note from your letter that you are coming home with Wilfred and the children to live with us because Wilfred received an 'adjustment' in his salary, which was an insult to him. Wilfred, I assume, feels he can not endure the insult.

As you know, your brother Frank came home with his wife about a month ago after his salary had been 'reconsidered.' Your sister Elsie, who had been a secretary to an officer of a corporation, recently had to take a position as a stenographer. She resigned because she refused to be reduced to the level of a plain stenographer, so we are expecting her any day.

You ask about my own business. It is coming along fine. It was sold on the court house steps last Friday, but there were no bidders, so the sheriff let me keep it. That makes the best month I have had since the upturn.

                                        Your loving father"

222   Finished His Speech but Hasn't Stopped Talking

A man walked out of a hall where a speaker was addressing a meeting. Some one in the corridor asked him if the speaker had finished his speech. He said, "Yes, he finished his speech shortly after he started, but he hasn't stopped talking." (Suitable if a speech is long.)

223   Adaptation

In a physiology class the teacher said, "Johnnie, can you give a familiar example of the human body as it adapts itself to changed conditions?"

"Yes, ma'am," said Johnnie, "my aunt gained 50 pounds in a year, and her skin never cracked."

224   OVER THE LINE

Wifey: "Don't you think, dear, that a man has more sense after he is married?"

Hubby: "Yes, but it's too late then."

225   SUBTLE, INDEED

Little Georgie received a new drum for Christmas, and shortly thereafter, when father came home from work one evening, mother said: "I don't think that man upstairs likes to hear Georgie play his drum, but he's certainly subtle about it."

Father: "Why?"

Mother: "Well, this afternoon he gave Georgie a knife, and asked him if he knew what was inside the drum."

226   GOOD HUNTING

1st Hunter: "Hey, Bill."

2nd Hunter: "Yeah."

1st Hunter: "Are you all right?"

2nd Hunter: "Yeah."

1st Hunter: "Then I've shot a bear."

227   SELF-MADE MAN

A youngster stood gazing intently at his father's visitor, a homely man of large proportions. At length the portly one becoming a bit embarrassed, said: "Well, my boy, what are you looking at me for?"

"Why," replied the boy, "Daddy told Mother that you were a self-made man, and I want to see what you look like."

"Quite right," said the gratified guest. "I am a self-made man."

"But what did you make yourself like that for?" asked the boy, with considerable surprise.

228   THE GOOD OLD WAY

Judge: "Couldn't this case have been settled out of court?"

Defendant: "Yer honor, shure an' that is exactly what we wuz thryin' to do whin a couple av police butted in."

229   SOFT PEDAL

Amateur Singer: "When I sing, I get tears in my eyes. What can I do to stop that?"

Singing Teacher: "Try stuffing cotton in your ears."

230   FULL INFORMATION

He: "If you'll give me your telephone number, I'll call you up some time."

She: "It's in the book."

He: "Fine! And what's your name?"

She: "That's in the book, too!"

231   PUTTING ON THE RITZ

The newly rich woman was trying to make an impression: "I clean my diamonds with ammonia, my rubies with wine, my emeralds with brandy, and my sapphires with fresh milk."

"I don't clean mine," said the quiet woman sitting next to her; "when mine get dirty, I just throw them away."

232   WASTE OF MONEY

"Brutha Jones, is you-all goin' t' donate somethin' to fence in ouah cemetery?"

"Whaffer yo' want to fence a cemetery? Dem as is in can't git out, and dem as is out sho' don't want to git in."

233   DADDY

Officer (to man pacing sidewalk at 3 o'clock in the morning): "What are you doing here?"

Gentleman: "I forgot my key, officer, and I'm waiting for my children to come home and let me in."

234   LITTLE SHOT

A mountaineer took his son to a school to enroll him.

"My boy's arter larnin', what dya have?" he asked the teacher.

"We offer English, trigonometry, spelling, etc.," she replied.

"Well, give him some of that thar trigernometry; he's the worst shot in the family."

235   QUEER NAMES

Englishman: "Odd names your towns have. Hoboken, Weehawken, Oshkosh, Poughkeepsie."

American: "I suppose they do sound queer to English ears. Do you live in London all of the time?"

Englishman: "No indeed. I spend part of my time at Chipping Norton, and divide the rest between Bigglewade and Leighton Buzzard."

236   LIKELY

Mother (to son wandering around the room): "What are you looking for?"

Son: "Nothing."

Mother: "You'll find it in the box where the candy was."

237   FULL STOP

The genius of a local man had carried him to big success in business without much aid of education.

He was asked to distribute the prizes at a school, and made the usual speech of good counsel.

"Now, boys," he said, "always remember that education is a great thing. There's nothing like education. Take arithmetic. Through education we learn that twice two makes four, that twice six makes twelve, that seven sevens make— and then there's geography."

238   NO HURRY

A Scotch minister was walking through a street in a village one misty evening when he fell into a deep hole. There was no ladder by which he could make his escape and he began to shout for help. A passing laborer heard his cries and looking down, asked who he was. The minister told him, whereupon the laborer remarked: "Weel, weel, ye needna kick up sic' a noise. You'll no be needed afore Sawbath, an' this is only Wednesday nicht."

239 PRACTICALLY NONE
Albert: "What's the difference between a drama and a melodrama?"
Bernard: "Well in a drama the heroine merely throws the villain over. In a melodrama, she throws him over the cliff!"

240 MODEL?
Wife: "My husband has no bad habits whatsoever. He never drinks, and he spends all his evenings at home. Why he doesn't even belong to a club."
Friend: "Does he smoke?"
Wife: "Only in moderation. He likes a cigar after he has had a good dinner, but I don't suppose he smokes two cigars a month."

241 MISUNDERSTANDING
Salesman: "Sonny, is your mother at home?"
Small Boy: "Yes, sir."
Salesman (after knocking in vain): "I thought you said she was at home?"
Small Boy: "Yes, sir, but I don't live here."

242 A GOOD REASON
Little Betty was crying bitterly. Her mother asked what was the matter.
"Boo hoo! My new shoes hurt me!"
"Well, no wonder! You have them on the wrong feet," replied Mother.
Betty kept on crying and would not be comforted. "I haven't any other feet," she cried.

243 PENNY WISE
Mother: "Come here, Johnnie; I have some good news for you."
Johnnie (without enthusiasm): "Yes, I know; father is home again."
Mother: "Yes, but how did you know?"
Johnnie: "My bank won't rattle any more."

244 HIS EXAMPLE
Teacher: "Can you give me a good example of how heat expands things and cold contracts them?"
Pupil: "Well, the days are much longer in the summer."

245 TOO PRESUMPTUOUS
Hobo: "Lady, have youse got any old cast-off husband's clothing?"
Lady: "Why, no, we're still living together."

246 DIFFICULTIES
Joe: "What's become of the Hikers' Club?"
Jim: "Oh, it disbanded. It was getting too hard to persuade passing motorists to pick us up and give us a lift."

247 MISTAKEN IDENTITY
"I tell you I won't have this room," protested the old lady to the bell boy. "I ain't goin' to pay my good money for a pigsty with a measly little foldin' bed in it. You think jest because I'm from the country ——"

Disgusted, the boy cut her short. "Get in, mum. Get in. This ain't your room. This is the elevator."

248   No Change

"Looks like rain today," said the milkman as he poured the customary quart of milk. "It always does," replied the housewife, compressing her lips with cold significance.

249   Point Scored

Waiters, of course, are not in a position to snap back at ill-bred guests; but one English head waiter once made the perfect retort to an uncouth customer:

"My position, sir," he said, "does not allow me to argue with you; but if it ever came to a choice of weapons, I would choose grammar."

250   Appeal to Reason

Answer received by the credit department of a Chicago firm:

"I don't expect to beat you out of any money. But I am going to say one thing I am not working so I don't make anything and until I go to work I can't pay you anything so keep your shirt on and as soon as I start to work I will send some money. But if you don't keep it on, well just take it off and hold it until after Xmas."

251   Pilot

Smith: "My wife asked me to take our old cat off somewhere and lose it. So I put it in a basket and tramped out into the country for about eight miles."

Jones: "Did you lose the cat?"

Smith: "Lose it! If I hadn't followed it, I'd never have got back home."

252   Enterprise

"Almost every man can find work if he uses his brains," asserted the man who had traveled a good deal. "That is, if he has the ability to adapt himself like the piano-tuner I once met in the Far West.

"We were in a wild, unsettled country, and I said to him, 'Surely piano-tuning can't be very lucrative here. I should not imagine that pianos were very plentiful in this region.'

"'No, they're not,' said the piano-tuner, 'but I make a pretty fair income by tightening up barbed-wire fences.'"

253   Excuse It Please

Liza, the Negro cook, answered the telephone one morning and a cheerful voice inquired, "What number is this?"

Liza was in no mood for trifling and said with some asperity, "You-all ought to know. You done called it!"

254   Problem

Father: "Isn't it wonderful how little chicks get out of their shells?"

Son: "What get's me is how they get in."

255   Butcher

Barber: "How is the razor, sir? Does it go easy?"

Man: "Well, that depends on the operation. If you're shaving me, it goes hard, but if you're merely skinning me it goes tolerable easy."

256 H-M-M

"Weak eyes, have you? Well, how many lines can you read on that chart?"
"What chart?"

257 NATURALLY

Usher: "How far down do you wish to sit, sir?"
Patron: "All the way, of course."

258 NO MYSTERY

Jones: "How do you spend your income?"
Smith: "About 30 per cent for shelter, 30 per cent for clothing, 40 per cent for food and 20 per cent for amusement."
Jones: "But that adds up to 120 per cent."
Smith: "That's right."

259 DEPRESSION

"Those sausages you sent me were meat at one end and corn meal at the other."
"Yes, ma'am. In these hard times, it's difficult to make both ends meat."

260 FUTILE

Teacher Tourist: "This seems to be a very dangerous precipice. It's a wonder they don't put up a warning sign."
Native: "Yes, it is dangerous, but they kept a warning sign up for two years and no one fell over, so it was taken down."

261 STRIKE

Dentist: "Why this tooth has gold in it! I didn't know it had been filled."
Patient: "It hasn't. That's my back collar-button you've struck."

262 MATCH

Mike: "That's a queer pair of stockings you have on, Pat,—one red and the other green."
Pat: "Yes, and I've got another pair like it at home."

263 CALLED

The teacher was testing the knowledge of the kindergarten class. Slapping a half-dollar on the desk, she asked sharply, "What is that?" Instantly a voice from the back row said, "Tails!"

264 A GOOD REASON

The youngster was being chided for his low grades. As an alibi he said, "Well all of the boys at school got C's and D's, too."
"All of them?" he was cross questioned. "How about little Johnny Jones, who lives down the street?"
"Oh, he got high grades," the youngster admitted. "But you see, he's different. He has two bright parents."

265 PREDICAMENT

Q. "My lawn is full of weeds. I have tried weed-killer and digging them up, but they return. What should I do?"

A. "You must just learn to love them."

266 ALIBI

Gus Kahn overheard this repartee between two rabid Californians during a heavy rain-storm in Los Angeles. Both watched the downpour with embarrassed expressions . . . Finally, after a deep silence, one said to the other: "Boy, some terrible weather certainly blows in from Nevada, doesn't it?"

267 HORN

Repair-man: "Shall I install a loud or soft horn, sir?"

O'Leary: "Just one with a dirty sneer."

268 WHISKERS

Ernie: "My uncle can play the piano by ear."

Gurney: "That's nothing. My uncle fiddles with his whiskers."

269 PANTS PRESSED?

"Have you ever appeared as a witness before?"

"Yes, your honor."

"In what suit?"

"My blue serge."

270 SERVICE

Diner: "Have you any wild duck?"

Waiter: "No, sir, but we can take a tame one and irritate it for you."

271 STRATEGY

Officer: "Now tell me, what is your idea of strategy?"

Rookie: "It's when you're out of ammunition, but keep right on firing."

272 PROFESSOR'S WIFE

"Hello; is that the police station?"

"Yes, what's the matter?"

"I just wanted to tell you that you need not search for my husband. I found him myself. He had forgotten to take off his overcoat, and I hung him in the closet by mistake."

273 POLITE

A New York traffic expert says that the London drivers and chauffeurs enliven many occasions by their wit and sarcasm. One London driver drew up when he saw a pedestrian directly in his way, leaned over and very politely inquired:

"I say, sir, may I ask what are your plans?"

274 REST IN PEACE

A party of sailors were being shown over the cathedral by a guide.

"Behind the altar," he told them, "lies Richard the Second. In the churchyard outside lies Mary Queen of Scots; also Henry the Eighth. And who," he demanded, halting above an unmarked flagstone, "who do you think is a-lying 'ere?"

"Well," answered a salt, "I don't know for sure, but I have my suspicions."

275 BARGAIN

The decrepit old car drove up to the toll-bridge.

"Fifty cents," cried the gateman.

"Sold," replied the driver.

276 ACID TONGUE

Chemistry Professor: "Jones, what does HNO3 signify?"

Cadet Jones: "Well, ah, er'r—I've got it right on the tip of my tongue, sir."

Chemistry Professor: "Well, you'd better spit it out. It's nitric acid."

277 COLORED JOKE

Rastus: "Say, Sambo, what time in your life does yo' think yo' was scared the wust?"

Sambo: "Once when ah wuz callin' on a hen-house an' de farmer come in an' caught me. Boy, wuz ah scared."

Rastus: "How are yo' shuah dat wuz de worstest yo' evah been scared?"

Sambo: "Cause de farmer grab me by de shoulder an' say: 'White boy, whut yo' doin' heah?'"

278 TOO RESTLESS

Angler: "You've been watching me for three hours. Why don't you try fishing yourself?"

Onlooker: "I ain't got the patience."

279 INVENTIVE

"Why are you eating with your knife?"

"My fork leaks."

280 HIS DIFFICULTY

"Humph! I could write a story as good as this, if I had a mind to."

"Sure, but that's exactly what you lack."

281 THAT'S DIFFERENT

"You didn't take a vacation this year, did you?"

"No, I thought I needed a rest."

282 DELAY

"A nice sort of welcome!" said the father visiting his son at a boarding school. "I am hardly out of the train when you ask me for money."

"Well, dad, you must admit the train was twenty minutes late."

283 DOCTOR'S PRESCRIPTION

"Your doctor's out here with a flat tire."

"Diagnose the case as flatulency of the perimeter and charge him accordingly," ordered the garage man. "That's the way he does."

284   NOT WHOLLY DUMB

"Don't they teach you to salute in your company?" roared the Major to Patrick Malone, who had passed him without raising his hand.

"Yes, sir," replied Pat.

"Then why didn't you salute?"

"Well, sir," was the candid reply, "I didn't want to attract more attention than I had to, 'cause I ain't supposed to be out here without a pass."

285   MODERN

Visitor: "How old are you, sonny?"

Boston Boy: "That's hard to say, sir. According to my latest school tests, I have a psychological age of 11 and a moral age of 10. Anatomically, I'm 7; mentally I'm 9. But I suppose you refer to my chronological age. That's 8— but nobody pays any attention to that nowadays."

286   GENEROSITY

Marine: "Say, Pal, will you loan me a nickel. I want to call a friend."

Sailor: "Here's fifteen cents, call all your friends."

287   LUCKY

"Mr. Chairman," complained the speaker, "I have been on my feet for nearly ten minutes, but there is so much interruption I can hardly hear myself speak."

"Cheer up, my friend," came a voice from the rear, "you are not missin' much."

288   EXPERIENCED PARTY GOER

"Your friend Joe seemed to be the life of the party."

"Yes, he was the only one who could talk louder than the radio."

289   BIGOTED

"How do you like your new boss, Mayme?"

"Oh, he ain't so bad, Lil, only he's kinda bigoted."

"Whadda y'mean, bigoted?"

"Well, he thinks words can only be spelled one way."

290   HIS TURN

A club of eccentric young men had for one of their rules that on Tuesday evenings any man who asked in the clubroom a question which he was unable to answer himself should pay a fine of one dollar. One evening Tomkinson asked: "Why doesn't a ground squirrel leave any dirt around the top of his hole when he digs it?"

After some deliberation he was called upon to answer his own question. "That's easy," he said. "The squirrel starts at the bottom and digs up."

"All very nice," suggested a member, "but how does it get to the bottom?"

"That's your question," answered Tomkinson.

291   SILENCER

Betty: "Your new overcoat is pretty loud, isn't it?"

Billy: "Yeah, but I'm gonna buy a muffler to go with it."

292   MISAPPREHENSION

Rastus: "Da's some better now, honey. Ah don't like to see yo face all frowned up. Does yo smile mean yo fo'gives me?"

Mandy: "Stay away fum me, man. I'se jes' smiling to rest mah face."

293   STRETCHING THE POINT

A railroad agent in Africa had been "bawled out" for doing things without orders from headquarters. One day his boss received the following startling telegram:

"Tiger on platform eating conductor. Wire instructions."

294   EFFICIENCY

A retailer, on receiving the first delivery of a large order, was annoyed to find the goods not up to sample. "Cancel my order immediately," he wired the manufacturer.

They replied: "Regret cannot cancel immediately. You must take your turn."

295   VARIETY

"What are you raising in your garden this year?"

"Johnson's Plymouth Rocks, Brown's Leghorns and Smith's Wyandottes."

296   ONLY WHEN NECESSARY

Preacher: "Do you say your prayers at night, little boy?"

Jimmy: "Yes, sir."

Preacher: "And do you always say them in the morning, too?"

Jimmy: "No, sir. I ain't scared in the daytime."

297   ONE THAT WAS TOO FAST FOR HIM

A Frenchman was relating his experience in studying the English language. He said: "When I first discovered that if I was quick, I was fast; that if I was tied, I was fast; if I spent too freely, I was fast; and that not to eat was to fast, I was discouraged. But when I came across the sentence, 'The first one won one-dollar prize,' I gave up trying."

298   ACCOUNTING

A colored man doing a hauling job was told that he couldn't get his money until he submitted a statement. After much meditation he evolved the following bill:

"Three comes and three goes, at four bits a went, $3."

299   NO PLACE FOR HER

A new maid had just arrived and her mistress was giving her a list of kitchen utensils to be purchased.

"And don't forget, Emma," she said, "we want a new griller for the kitchen."

Emma stared vacantly.

"You know what a griller is, I suppose?" ventured the lady of the house.

" 'Course I do," returned the girl. "It's a big hairy monkey, and if you want one of those in the kitchen—I'm leaving."

300   She Knew What Happened

Brother and sister were eating ice cream that daddy had brought home. Brother started counting all the goodies they had had that day: "Sis," he said, "do you know we had candy, gum, popsickle, pie, watermelon, and ice cream? Whew!"

"Yeh," said Sis, stuffing her mouth full of ice cream, "I guess we hit the jackpot."

301   Welcome Relief

Little Mary: "Mother, they are going to teach us domestic silence at school now."

Mother: "Don't you mean domestic science?"

Father: "There is a bare hope our little girl means what she is saying."

302   Strange

Little Bobby was sitting with his mother in church during the wedding of her eldest daughter. Halfway through the service, he observed his mother crying.

"Why are you crying, mama?" he asked. "It's not your wedding."

303   Nature Story

A tourist traveling through the Texas Panhandle got into conversation with an old settler and his son at a filling-station.

"Looks as though we might have rain," said the tourist.

"Well, I hope so," replied the native, "not so much for myself as for my boy here. I've seen it rain."

304   Legitimate Objection

The teacher was trying to impress upon her class the advantages of peace and disarmament. "How many of you boys object to war?" she asked. Up went several hands.

"Jimmy, will you tell the class why you object to war?"

" 'Cause wars make history," replied Jimmy soberly.

305   Willing to Reciprocate

Professor: "Er—My dear, what's the meaning of this vase of flowers on the table today?"

Wife: "Meaning? Why, today is your wedding anniversary."

Professor: "Indeed! Well, well, do let me know when yours is so I may do the same for you."

306   Why He Hesitated

The hired man asked little Johnny to pass the salt.

Looking at his mother, the boy hesitated. "Shall I give him the salt?" he whispered. "Daddy said he wasn't worth it."

307   It Stopped Him

Mandy: "Yo' jus' keep on pesterin' foh two bits and yo' gwine to be able to settle a pow'ful big question foh de sciumtific folks."

Sambo: "Yah. Whut am dat question?"

Mandy: "Kin de dead speak?"

308   THE EGOTIST

Him: "I dreamed I was married to the most beautiful girl in the world."
Her: "Were we happy?"

309   O. K. HERE

Target Instructor: "Where the dickens are your shots going?"
Seaman: "I don't know, but they're leaving this end all right."

310   CORRECT

Teacher: "Johnny, can you tell me the name of an animal that travels great distances?"
Johnny: "Yes, a goldfish. It travels around the globe."

311   IN REVERSE

Little Dickie, aged 6, seized with hiccoughs, ran to his mother and said, "Oh Mother, I believe I'm coughing backwards."

312   FLAVOR FOR BATH

The little grandson, who had been using toilet water in his bath called to his mother, saying, "Mother, where is the bath flavoring?"

313   A VOTE OF THANKS

An elderly maiden aunt received this note from her 10-year-old niece: "Dear Aunt: Thank you for your nice present. I have always wanted a pin cushion, but not very much."

314   HARDER THAN A DIAMOND

Dorothy (admiring her engagement ring): "There's nothing in the world harder than a diamond, is there?"
Howard: "Yes, sweetheart—keeping up the installment payments on it."

315   WHY HE COULDN'T DO IT

My 5-year-old son and I made an agreement. He was to make his little bed while I made the large bed. After I had finished straightening my bedroom, I went into his room to see how he was getting along. He was struggling violently to get a clean pillow-slip over a large feather pillow.
"Here, son, this is the way to do that," I said, and taking one end of the pillow firmly in my teeth, slipped the cover on.
"Oh! Mudder," he cried, "I know! I was biting on the wrong end!"

316   CHOICE

Casey and Murphy stood looking into a jeweler's window. "Casey," asked Murphy, "how'd you like to have your pick here?"
"Sure," responded Casey, "I'd rather have my shovel."

317   SUCCESS

Customer: "To what do you owe your extraordinary success as a house-to-house salesman?"
Salesman: "To the first five words I utter when a woman opens the door—'Miss, is your mother in?'"

318   PASSING FANCY

The Boss: "On your way to Smith and Sons you will pass a football ground."
Office Boy (hopefully): "Yes, sir!"
The Boss: "Well, pass it!"

319   NO LACK OF OPPORTUNITY

"Your references are good. I'll try you," said the farmer to a lad who applied
for a job in the poultry yard.
"Is there any chance to rise, sir?" the boy asked.
"I'll say there is," replied the farmer. "You'll rise at four o'clock every
morning."

320   EMBARRASSING FOR TRAIN

Junior was visiting his grandmother who lived near the railroad yards in a
small town. Noticing a train switching back and forth, he exclaimed, "Mother,
the train can't find anywhere to park."

321   A WARNING

Teacher: "Yes, Johnny, what is it?"
Johnny: "I don't want to scare you, but Papa said if I didn't get better
grades someone is due for a licking."

322   CO-ORDINATION

"Is your wife having any success in learning to drive the car?"
"Well, the road is beginning to turn when she does."

323   A MARTYR TO HER FAITH

"Marie," observed Muriel, "has suffered much for her belief."
"Indeed?" asked Millicent, lifting her eyebrows in polite curiosity. "What
is her belief?"
"That she can wear a number four shoe on a number six foot."

324   MODERN MARRIAGE

Mr. Newlywed: "Darling, did you sew the button on my coat?"
Mrs. Newlywed: "No, sweetheart, I couldn't find a button, but it's all right
now. I sewed up the buttonhole."

325   ONE YEAR LATER

"Oh, George, do you realize it's almost a year since our honeymoon, and
that glorious day we spent on the sands? I wonder how we'll spend this one?"
"On the rocks."

326   NOT YET OUT OF DANGER

"How's your wife coming along with her driving?"
"She took a turn for the worse last week."

327   A SHINING FACE

"The new patient in Ward B is very good looking," said the nurse.
"Yes," agreed the matron, "but don't wash his face. He's had that done by
four nurses this morning."

328   REASON FOR BEING PRESENT

Teacher: "How is it you cannot answer any of my questions?"
Pupil: "Well, if I could, what would be the use of my coming here?"

329   A LONG WAY TO GO

Weary Willie's financial position was very shaky, and when he met a kind old lady in the park he decided to tell her his story.

"Yes, ma'am," he said, "I've asked for money, and begged for money, and cried for money."

"Have you ever thought of working for it, my man?" she asked.

"No, not yet, ma'am," said Willie. "You see, it's like this, I'm going through the alphabet, and I ain't got to 'W' yet."

330   HE SHOULD KNOW

Prospective Bridegroom (gaily): "Will it take much to feather a nest?"
Furniture Dealer: "Oh, no: only a little down."

331   SAFETY FIRST

A woman motorist was driving along a country road when she noticed a couple of repair men climbing telephone poles.

"Fools!" she exclaimed to her companion, "they must think I never drove a car before."

332   A SAFE BET

The old martinet was lecturing his nephew.

"Never known such a generation," said the old fellow. "You modern boys want too much."

The boy was tactfully silent.

"Do you know what I was getting when I married your aunt?" asked the uncle.

"No," replied the nephew, realizing the time had come to terminate the argument, "and I bet you didn't, either."

333   NIGHT LIFE

"My, isn't a night club a great place on a rainy night?"
"You said it! Stay outside and get wet and come in and get soaked."

334   DRY COUNTRY

The mayor of a tough border town was about to engage a preacher for the new church.

"Parson, you aren't by any chance a Baptist, are you?"

"No. Why?"

"Well, I was just going to say that we have to haul our water twelve miles."

335   COLD TURKEY

Arctic Explorer: "It was so cold where we were that the candle froze and we couldn't blow it out."

Second Explorer: "That's nothing. Where we were the words came out of our mouths in pieces of ice, and we had to fry them to see what we were talking about."

336   WASTED EFFORT

Professor (finishing long algebra problem): "And so we find X equals zero."
Sophomore: "All that work for nothing."

337   LATE DATE

Mrs. Doe (as John enters house): "What time is it?"
John: "Just one o'clock."
Mrs. Doe (as clock strikes three): "Dear me, how that clock stutters."

338   TAIN'T FAIR

Life isn't fair to us men. When we are born, our mothers get the compliments and the flowers. When we are married, our brides get the presents and the publicity. When we die, our widows get the life insurance and the winters in Florida.

339   FLIVVER SIGNS

Hesit 8
Viber 8
Exasper 8
Spoon Holder
Chicken, Here's Your Coop
Baby, Here's Your Rattle
Shake, Rattle and Roll
Sister, You'd Look Tough Without Paint, Too
Laugh, But I Paid Cash for Mine
Four Wheels, Four Brakes, Four More Installments
Darling, I Am Growing Old
I Rattle in My Rear End But I Don't Strike
Capacity 5,000 Gals (One at a Time)
Tack Finder
It Ain't Gonna Run Much More
True Love Never Runs Smoothly
Dangerous But Passable
Sound Value—Can't You Hear It?
There's Beauty in Every Jar
For Sale, $1.98; While It Lasts
Willie's Nightie
Dodge—No Metal Can Touch You

Northwestern Banker

340   COLD

"The cold in the Arctic was so intense that we couldn't pat our dogs."
"Why not?"
"Their tails were frozen so still that they broke off if they wagged them."

341   NOT ENOUGH

Man (to wife): "What do you mean by saying I have been deceiving you for years?"
Wife: "I just found out the Government allows you $1,500 a year on your income tax for being married and you only allow me a measly $10 a month."

342 JUJITSU
"Did I ever tell you how I tried my jujitsu on a burglar?"
"No."
"Well, I got hold of his leg and twisted it over his shoulder. Then I got hold of his arm and twisted it round his neck, and before he knew where he was I was flat on my back."

343 WRONG NUMBER
Irate subscriber to operator: "Am I crazy or are you?"
Operator: "I am sorry, but we do not have that information."

344 INDEPENDENCE
Wifey: "Oh, Bill, baby can walk."
Hubby: "That's fine. Now he can walk up and down at night by himself."

345 GREAT OAKS
A colored lad killed a man . . . "Don't tell me," the irate judge scowled, "that you killed a man for the paltry sum of three dollars." . . . The lad merely shrugged his shoulders and replied, "You-all don't see, jedge . . . but three bucks here and three bucks there, they all add up!"

346 COMATOSE COURTSHIP
Bier: "The Weavers are so quiet tonight. Is there anything wrong?"
Gardiner: "No; they're always that way. When he proposed, he just held up a diamond ring and said, 'Eh?' and she looked at it and said, 'Uh-huh.'"

347 SQUALL OR SQUEAL
Young Father: "In your sermon this morning you spoke about a baby being a new wave on the ocean of life."
Minister: "That's right. Do you think a fresh squall would have been nearer the truth?"

348 ETIQUETTE
The district engineer and his wife were entertaining at dinner. Suddenly a child's voice was heard from the floor above. "Mother." "What is it, Archie?" she asked. "There's only clean towels in the bathroom. Shall I start one?"

349 SPENDTHRIFT
Tramp: "Lady, I'm almost famished."
Housewife: "Here's a cent. But how did you fall so low?"
Tramp: "I had your fault. I was too extravagant."

350 COMMENCE
A Yale player was teaching some cowboys how to play football. He explained the rules and ended as follows:
"Remember, fellows, if you can't kick the ball, kick a man on the other side. Now let's get busy. Where's the ball?"
One of the cowboys shouted: "T'heck with the ball! Let's start the game!"

351 PRETTY FIX
Woman driver: "Can you fix this fender so my husband will never know I bent it?"

D

Garage mechanic: "No, but I can fix it so that you can ask him in a few days how he bent it."

352 MATRIMONIALLY INCLINED

Doris: "When is your sister thinking of getting married?"
Tom: "Constantly."

353 ECONOMICAL SCOT

"Stand behind your lover, false woman," thundered the Scotsman, "I'm going to shoot you both."

354 EPITAPH

"Here Lies an Atheist; All Dressed Up and No Place to Go."

355 CRAMPED

"That fellow must live in a very small flat."
"How can you tell?"
"Why, haven't you noticed that his dog wags his tail up and down, instead of sideways?"

356 COINCIDENCE

"So he is a reckless driver?"
"Say, when the road turns the same way as he does, it's just a coincidence."

357 THOUGHTFUL

Freshman: "Say, what's the idea of wearing my raincoat?"
Roommate: "Well you wouldn't want your new suit to get wet, would you?"

358 SUBSTITUTE

"Tommy, what is a synonym?" the teacher asked.
"A synonym," said Tommy, wisely, "is a word you use when you can't spell the other one."

359 LIVING ON THEIR INCOME

Householder (to prospective maid): "Why did you leave your last place?"
Maid: "Oh, it was so dull. They were trying to live on their income."

360 WASTED EFFORT

"Ah," sighed the serious-faced passenger, "how little we know of the future and what it has in store for us."
"That's true," responded the other.
"Little did I think when some 30 years ago I carved my initials on the desk in the old country school that I would some day grow up and fail to become famous."

361 HIS SAVING GRACE

Doctor (after examining patient): "I don't like the looks of your husband, Mrs. Brown."
Mrs. Brown: "Neither do I, doctor, but he's good to our children."

362 TEMPUS FUGIT

Sam Watson, a tall, solemn-looking Negro, making his annual trip for his holiday purchases, was a little belated, reaching the city on Christmas eve.

Having finished his shopping, he was hurrying to the station to catch his waiting train, when he stumbled; a jug fell to the sidewalk with a crash and the precious contents at once became a mere wet place on the concrete. Sam stood for a moment, dazed by his misfortune. Then, as he turned away from the heart-breaking sight, he said in a lugubrious tone: "Dah now! Chris'mus done come—an' gone!"

363   OBLIGING

House Mother: "Young man, we turn the lights off at 10:30!"
Freshman: "Oh, boy! that'll be keen."

364   TSCH! TSCH!

Mrs. Knicker: "We are told one-third of the nation is ill-housed, ill-nourished and ill-clad."
Mr. Knicker: "I didn't realize so many go away for the summer."

365   SLIGHTLY SCRAMBLED

Another audition in the family of Mr. and Mrs. Jed Draper occurred Friday night, this time a bouncing boy. *Martinez (Cal.) Citizen*
The bride is a member of Coulton's social set, a member of the Junior League, and a skillet musician. *Coulton (Ore.) Advocate*

366   YOUR CHOICE

The tramp called at a home and asked for food:
Housewife: "And how would you like a nice chop?"
Tramp: "That all depends, lady—is it lamb, pork or wood?"

367   REQUEST NUMBER

Douglas Jerrold was accounted the greatest wit of his generation. They were talking in a certain company about a popular song. One rather silly young enthusiast exclaimed: "That air always carries me away when I hear it."
Jerrold wistfully looked around him. "Can anybody whistle it?" he inquired.

368   IN HUNTING SEASON

"Sorry, sir, but I'm all out of wild ducks. I could let you have a fine end of ham."
"Don't kid me. How could I go home and say I shot an end of ham?"

369   HEAVY FINANCE

Englishman (in poker game): "Well, I'll wager a bally pound on this."
American (holding four aces): "I dunno much about your darn English money, but I'll raise you a couple of tons!"

370   SEZ YOU

"The piano is hard-hit by the radio," says a dealer. And by the little girl next door.

371   TWO OF A KIND

Mr. Nagg: "Those newlyweds are pretty well matched, aren't they?"
Mrs. Nagg: "Yeah, she's a grass widow and he's a vegetarian."

372 A HOWLING SUCCESS

Oletimer: "Is your married life one grand sweet song?"

Newlywed: "Well, since our baby's been born it's more like an opera, full of grand marches, with loud calls for the author every night."

373 TRANSPORT HAS CHANGED

"If witches came back they'd flourish in some parts of the country as much as they ever did," says a writer. "But they'd find it a little awkward getting about on a vacuum cleaner, wouldn't they?"

374 TREES

I think that I shall never see along the road an unscraped tree, with bark intact, and painted white, that no car ever hit at night. For every tree that's near the road has caused some auto to be towed.

Sideswiping trees is done a lot by drivers who are plumb half shot. God gave them eyes so they might see, yet any fool can hit a tree.

375 CONSIDERATE

Soph: "But I don't think I deserve a zero."

Prof: "Neither do I, but it's the lowest mark I'm allowed to give."

376 CAN'T FIRE THE COOK

Woman: "Does your husband kick about the meals?"

Other Bridge Player (smiling): "No, what he kicks about is having to get them."

377 STEPPING ON IT

Employer: "Do you believe in love at first sight, Miss Vamper?"

Stenographer: "Well, I think it saves a lot of time."

378 TRY A SEXTANT

Golfer (far off in the rough): "Say, caddy, why do you keep looking at your watch?"

Caddy: "It isn't a watch, sir; it's a compass."

379 PERMANENT GUEST

A little Logan Heights girl said there was a new baby at her house.

"Has the baby come to stay?" she was asked.

"I think so," she said; "he's taken all his things off."

380 BOTH ENDS AGAINST THE MIDDLE

Two men who had been bachelor cronies met for the first time in five years.

"Tell me, Tom," said one, "did you marry that girl, or do you still darn your own socks and do your cooking?"

"Yes," was Tom's reply.

381 SHE KNEW HER MEN FOLK

A recent speaker before a woman's organization, talking on Persia, was telling about how careless the men over there are with their wives, and said it was no uncommon sight to see a woman and a donkey hitched up together.

Then he laughed, and said when he made that statement in a speech at Detroit one of the ladies in the audience piped up:
"That's not so unusual—you often see it over here too."

382 ONE ON THE BUTTON

Mr. Grouch: "Woman is nothing but a rag, a bone and a hank of hair."
Mrs. Grouch: "Man is nothing but a brag, a groan and a tank of air."

383 A DIPLOMAT

Judge O'Flaherty: "Haven't you been before me before?"
Prisoner: "No, yer honor. Oi never saw but one face that looked loike yours and that was a photygraf of an Irish king."
Judge O'Flaherty: "Discharged! Call the next case!"

384 THIS MODERN AGE

"Why, what are you crying so for, sonny?" asked Dad of his four-year-old heir.
"I heard you say you were going to get a new baby and I suppose that means you'll trade me in on it," he sobbed.

385 LIKE A CRICKET IN A CABBAGE

"When a man is asleep he's a mere vegetable," says a scientific writer. "He is, however, not edible—only audible."

386 CASHING IN ON A CORRESPONDENCE COURSE

My friend laughed when I spoke to the waiter in French, but the laugh was on him. I told the waiter to give him the check.

387 THAT SILVER LINING

Lily: "So yo' done mortgaged our li'l home."
Mose: "Jes' temp'rarily, honey, till de mortgage am foreclosed."

388 COSTLY DELUSION

"My wife had a dream last night and thought she was married to a millionaire."
"You're lucky! My wife thinks that in the daytime."

389 SAFETY FIRST

Diner: "Waiter, this soup is cold. Bring me some that's hot."
Waiter: "What do you want me to do? Burn my thumb?"

390 ALGER HEROES ARE EXTINCT

Gruff father to son: "Why don't you get out and find a job? When I was your age I was working for $3 a week in a store, and at the end of five years I owned the store."
Son: "You can't do that nowadays. They have cash registers."

391 MINUS A MIND

Wife: "I can't decide whether to go to a palmist or to a mind-reader."
Husband: "Go to a palmist. It's obvious that you have a palm."

392   COULDN'T MISS HIM

"Waiter, have you forgotten me?"

"Oh, no, sir, you are the stuffed calf's head."

393   CALL A PLUMBER

City Boy: "Say, dad, how many kinds of milk are there?"

Father: "Well, there's evaporated milk, buttermilk, malted milk and—but why do you wish to know?"

"Oh, I'm drawing a picture of a cow and I want to know how many spigots to put on her."

394   OR TRY HEAD CHEESE

"Yes, I know fish is brain food, but I don't care so much for fish. Hain't there some other brain food?"

"Well, there's noodle soup."

395   HOME TOWN CUSTOM

Boy: "Do you know, dad, that in some parts of Africa a man doesn't know his wife until he marries her?"

Dad: "Why single out Africa?"

396   BOOM IN AGRICULTURE

"How's your farm work coming?"

"Oh, fine! Got the billboard and hotdog stand painted, and the filling station stocked full of gas."

397   READY FOR THE WORST

Dorothy: "How long is it to my birthday?"

Mother: "Not very long, dear."

Dorothy: "Well, is it time for me to begin to be a good girl?"

398   GAME TO THE LAST

"So you are undertaking to keep bees?"

"Yes," answered Farmer Corntossel. "I don't want to miss anything, and I've been stung every other way there is."

399   IMMOBILIZING BOSSY

The little city boy stood and watched the farmer milk the only cow he had. The next morning the farmer was much excited, as the cow had been stolen during the night.

Farmer: "Drat the thief that stole that cow. He's miles away from here by now."

Little Boy: "I wouldn't worry 'bout it, mister; they can't get so far away with it, 'cause you drained her crank-case last night."

400   CUTTING IN

Margery had been watching a fashionable wedding from outside the church. Returning home she reported: "Well, I can't make out who she married. She went in with quite an old man and when she came out she was with a different one altogether."

401 SOLD!

"Do you guarantee this hair-restorer?"

"Better than that, sir. We give a comb with every bottle."

402 WELL, IT HELPS

"Murphy got rich quick, didn't he?"

"He got rich so quick that he can't swing a golf club without spitting on his hands."

403 SOMETHING NICE

Hubby: "The bank has returned that check."

Wife: "Isn't that splendid! What can we buy with it this time?"

404 HE'LL CATCH UP

Neighbor: "Where is your brother, Freddie?"

Freddie: "He's in the house playing a duet. I finished first."

405 THAT'S ONE WAY OF PUTTING IT

Vicar: "I was grieved to hear your husband has gone at last."

Mrs. Black: "Yas, 'e 'as, sir, and I only hope 'e's gone where I know 'e ain't."

406 IN PLAIN ENGLISH

Pastor Jones: "Brethren, we mus' do somethin' to remedy de status quo."

Deacon: "Brother Jones, what am de status quo?"

Pastor: "Dat, brother, am Latin for de mess we's in."

407 A LITTLE LESS OF SOMETHING

He: "You are always wishing for what you haven't got."

She: "Well, what else can one wish for?"

408 HE'LL GET ALONG

Small Bobby had been to a birthday party, and, knowing his weakness, his mother looked him straight in the eye and said, "I hope you didn't ask for a second piece of cake?"

"No," replied Bobby. "I only asked Mrs. Smith for the recipe so you could make some like it and she gave me two more pieces just of her own accord."

409 AND LIKE IT

"I never clash with my boss."

"No?"

"No; he goes his way and I go his."

410 INDEPENDENT

Arthur: "So your new job makes you independent?"

Albert: "Absolutely. I get here any time I want before eight, and leave just when I please after five."

411 JUST A LITTLE SQUIRT

"Are you a doctor?" asked a young lady, stepping into a drug store.

"Naw," replied the youth behind the white counter, "I'm just the fizzician."

412   Two Seasons

It happened in New York's lower East Side.
"How many seasons are there?" asked the teacher.
"Just two," answered Rachel.
"What are they?" inquired the puzzled instructor.
"Slack and busy," replied Rachel.

413   Ask Dad

Young Husband (in early morning): "It must be time to get up."
Wife: "Why?"
Young Husband: "Baby's fallen asleep."

414   Better Ask the Driver

"Are you quite sure this bus is going to Shepherd's Bush?"
"If it isn't, lady," said the conductor, "I'm in a worse mess than you are!"

415   That's Prevarication

Employer (to newly-hired typist): "Now I hope you thoroughly understand
the importance of punctuation?"
Stenographer: "Oh, yes, indeed. I always get to work on time."

416   A Century of Progress

A newly created papa received the glad tidings in a telegram:
"Hazel gave birth to a little girl this morning; both doing well."
On the message was a sticker reading: "When you want a boy, call Western
Union."

417   It's an Expensive Way

"Has your son's college education been of any value?"
"Oh, yes; it cured his mother of bragging about him."

418   Take That

"It's going to be a real battle of wits, I tell you," said the sophomore member
of the debating team.
"How brave of you," said his roommate, "to go unarmed."

419   Nosey People

The teacher was explaining to the class the meaning of the word "recuperate." "Now, Tommy," she said to a small boy, "when your father has worked
hard all day, he is tired and worn out, isn't he?"
"Yes, ma'am."
"Then, when night comes, and his work is over for the day, what does
he do?"
"That's what mother wants to know," Tommy explained.

420   Not at All Exclusive

Diner: "Do you serve crabs here?"
Waiter: "We serve anyone; sit down."

421   Forgive and Forget

A Negro was arrested and brought before a commissioner for having a still

on his premises. He was asked by the commissioner, "How do you plead?"
The Negro said:

"I pleads guilty and waives de hearing."

"What do you mean, 'Waive the hearing'?" asked the commissioner.

"I means I don't wanta heah no mo' abou' it."

422   No Wings Over Rastus

Two Negroes who had not seen each other in five years discovered each
had been married during this time.

"What kinda woman did you-all get, Mose?" asked Rastus.

"She's an angel, Rastus, dat's what she is."

"Boy, you sho' is lucky. Mine's still livin'," Rastus muttered sorrowfully.

423   Milquetoast in Africa

Angry Guide: "Why didn't you shoot that tiger?"

The Timid Hunter: "He didn't have the right kind of expression on his face
for a rug."

424   Pity the Moth

"A moth leads an awful life."

"How come?"

"He spends the summer in a fur coat and the winter in a bathing suit."

425   There's Money in It

"Did you know that I had taken up story-writing as a career?"

"No. Sold anything yet?"

"Yes; my watch, my saxophone and my overcoat."

426   Surprise

He was at the fountain-pen counter making a purchase. "You see," he said,
"I'm buying this for my wife."

"A surprise, eh?"

"I'll say so. You see, she's expecting a car."

427   Happy Combination

The boys of the Fairmont (W. Va.) American Legion Post were discussing
the impending marriage of a buddy.

"That's an accomplished girl Ben is going to marry," observed one of the
men. "She can swim, ride, dance, drive a car and pilot a plane; a real all-around
girl."

"They should get along fine," replied another. "You know Ben is a good
cook."

428   Unbeliever

Doctor Abrams was called to a barber shop where Sam, the Negro porter,
was lying unconscious. Doctor Abrams worked on him for a long time, and
finally revived the man.

"How did you happen to drink that stuff?" he asked the patient. "Didn't
you see the label on the bottle? It said 'poison.'"

Sam: "Yes, doctor, but I didn't believe it."

D*

Doctor Abrams: "Why not?"

Sam: "Because right under that it said 'Lye.'"

429   CHIVALRY

A certain middle-aged spinster has a vivid memory of Texas courtesy.

She was struggling with a hot cup of coffee in a small-town railway station, trying to gulp it before the train pulled out. A cowboy, seated a couple of stools away, noted her plight, and seeing the guard waving to the woman, came to the fore.

"Here, ma'am, you can take my coffee. It's already saucered and blown."

430   NERVE

"I envy the man who sang the tenor solo."

"Really? I thought he had a very poor voice."

"So did I, but just think of his nerve."

431   BANKRUPTCY

First Businessman: "Old Sharklee is going to retire from business."

Second Businessman: "I heard him say that before."

First Businessman: "I know, but the judge said it this time."

432   CONCEIT

"I hope you don't think I'm conceited," he said, after he had finished telling her all about himself.

"Oh, no," she replied, "but I'm just wondering how you can keep from giving three hearty cheers whenever you look at yourself in the glass."

433   ON THE SQUARE

The scene was the interior of a saloon in the Far West, and round the table were gathered as tough a gang as could be found in the whole of California. The game was fast and furious, the stakes were high.

Suddenly the dealer flung his cards on the table, and threateningly pulled out his six-gun.

"Boys," he shouted, "the game ain't a straight one! Slippery Sam ain't playing the hand I dealt him."

434   ARE THEY STRICT?

Frosh: "Are they very strict at Cornell?"

Soph: "Are they? Why, when a man dies during a lecture, they prop him up in the seat until the end of the hour."

435   HOW TO SUCCEED

"My boy," said the businessman to his son, "there are two things that are vitally necessary if you are to succeed in business."

"What are they, dad?"

"Honesty and sagacity."

"What is honesty?"

"Always—no matter what happens, no matter how adversely it may affect you—always keep your word once you have given it."

"And sagacity?"

"Never give your word."

436   UNEXPECTEDLY

Two freshmen were trying to define the word "collision." "Collision," said one freshman, "is when two things come together unexpectedly."

"I know," brightly replied the other freshie. "Twins."

437   NO DESERTER

Judge: "Rastus, do you realize that by leaving your wife you are a deserter?"

Rastus: "Jedge, ef yo' knowed dat woman like Ah does, yo' wouldn't call me no deserter. Ah's a refugee."

438   BOASTING

The young wife was boasting to a friend what a big man her hubby was. "Why, he's bigger than Ford," bragged the wifey. "He's even bigger than Roosevelt." The friend asked, "Is he bigger than God?" "Well, I wouldn't say that," replied the wife, "but he's young yet."

439   A TOUGH ORDER

The meek little gent in the restaurant finally sighed and decided to give up his steak. It was tougher than sole leather. He called the waiter and pleaded that it be taken back to the kitchen. The waiter dolefully shook his head and said: "Sorry, pal, I can't take it back now. You've bent it!"

440   SEEIN' STARS

A high school girl, seated next to a famous astronomer at a dinner party, struck up a conversation with him by asking, "What do you do in life?"

He replied, "I study astronomy."

"Dear me," said the girl. "I finished astronomy last year."

441   HONESTLY?

A candidate came home in the small hours and gave his wife the glorious news:

"Darling, I have been elected."

She was delighted. "Honestly?" she said.

He laughed in an embarrassed way.

"Oh, why bring that up?"

442   NOTHIN' BUT

Mandy Walker, the old negress who washed for Mrs. Frisk, came one day with a tale of woe calculated to awaken pity in the hardest heart.

"Cheer up, Mandy," said Mrs. Frisk consolingly. "There's no use in worrying."

But Mandy held other views. "How come dere's no use in worryin'?" she demanded. "When de good Lawd send me tribulation He 'spect me to tribulate, ain't He?"

443   HOW MANY LEARN IT?

Young Mother: "Nurse, what is the most difficult thing for a young mother to learn?"

Nurse: "That other people have perfect children, too."

444   SUITABILITY

"Aren't some of the hats women wear absurd?"

"Yes," replied Miss Cayenne; "and yet when some people put them on they *do* look *so* appropriate."

445   OPPORTUNITY KNOCKS

A new pulpit having been erected, the minister and the verger tested the acoustics.

"Stand you well to the back and see how this sounds," said the minister, repeating a text.

"Fine, meenister, fine!"

"Now you go up into the pulpit and say anything you like."

The verger went up. "I havena' had a rise o' pay for three years. Hoo does that soond, meenister?"

446   CRAZY

First businessman: "You don't have to be crazy to do business now."

Second businessman: "No, but it helps."

447   ANGLER LOGIC

"What for did ye tell him there was plenty of fishin' when there aren't two trouts in the stream?"

"Well, an' the less fishes there is, the more fishin' to get 'em, ain't there?"

448   TAKE THE BAD WITH THE GOOD

Wife (heatedly): "You're lazy, you're worthless, you're bad-tempered, you're shiftless, you're a thorough liar."

Husband (reasonably): "Well, my dear, no man is perfect."

449   LAST STAND

The father was reading the school-report which had just been handed to him by his hopeful son. His brow was wrathful as he read: "English, poor; French, weak; mathematics, fair"; and he gave a glance of disgust at the quaking lad. "Well, dad," said the son, "it is not as good as it might be, but have you seen that?" And he pointed to the next line, which read: "Health, excellent."

450   SIGN READING

A denizen of the hills of East Tennessee, who was appearing as a witness in a lawsuit, was being questioned as to his educational qualifications by the plaintiff's lawyer.

"Can you write?" asked the lawyer.

"Nope."

"Can you read?"

"Wa'al, I kin read figgers pretty well, but I don't do so good with writin'."

"How is that?"

"Wa'al, take these here signs along the road when I want to go sommers; I kin read how fur, but not whurto."

451 · SALESMANSHIP

Customer: "Are those eggs strictly fresh?"

Grocer (to his clerk): "Feel of those eggs, George, and see if they're cool enough to sell yet."

452 · OVERWORKED

"Boss, has you got a man on your book named Simpson?"

"Yes. What about it?"

"Wall, Ah's dat man, boss. Ah just thought you done had put down Samson."

453 · BUT NO PEDESTRIANS

Tourist: "Did you see a pedestrian pass here?"

Native: "No, I've been sittin' here all afternoon, and nobody's come by 'ceptin' one solitary man; he was afoot."

454 · MORE ECONOMICAL

Grocer: "But why do you want a carrier pigeon instead of a turkey?"

Thrifty young bride: "Because I hear that they go further than any other bird."

455 · PAID UP

Sam: "Listen heah, boy, jes' what kind of life you been livin'?"

Rastus: "Oh, ordinary, jes' ordinary."

Sam: "Well, if yo' pulls any mo' aces out o' yo' shoe, yo' ordinary life is goin' to mature."

456 · ETERNITY CASE

The doctor's five-year-old answered the call at the door. "Is the doctor in?" inquired the caller.

"No, sir."

"Have you any idea when he will be back?"

"I don't know, sir--he went out on an eternity case."

457 · THERE'S A REASON

"These eggs are very small," complained the young housewife to her grocer.

"Straight from the farm this morning, madam," declared the grocer.

"That's the trouble with these farmers," she persisted. "They're so anxious to get their eggs sold they take them off the nest too soon."

458 · ROMEO MIZ'N

Sam held her hand and she held hiz'n,
And then they hugged and went to kiz'n.
They did not know her dad had riz'n,
Madder than hops and simply siz'n;
And really 'tiz'n right to liz'n,
But Sam got hiz'n and went out whiz'n.

459 · YOUNG WEBSTER

School Teacher: "Johnny, can you tell me the difference between perseverance and obstinacy?"

Johnny: "One is a strong will, and the other is a strong won't."

460   He Almost Got Angry

A bricklayer working on top of a high building carelessly dropped a brick, which landed on the head of his negro helper below.

"Yah-all bettah be careful up dere, boss," said the helper, dusting his hat off. "Yah done made me bite mah tongue!"

461   Story-Telling Dad

Six-year-old Mary woke up about two in the morning. "Tell me a story, mamma," she pleaded.

"Hush, darling," said mother. "Daddy will be in soon and tell us both one."

462   A Burned Offering

She (on the 'phone): "I'm afraid your dinner will be burned a little tonight, darling."

He: "What's the matter? Did they have a fire at the delicatessen?"

463   What Mother Calls Father

Teacher (pointing to a deer at the zoo): "Johnny, what is that?"
Johnny: "I don't know."
Teacher: "What does your mother call your father?"
Johnny: "Don't tell me that's a louse!"

464   Cure for Nervousness

Phyllis: "Were you nervous when George proposed?"
Mabel: "No, dear, that's when I stopped being nervous."

465   Another Necktie

Lady Customer: "I want a birthday present for my husband."
Floorwalker: "How long have you been married, madam?"
Lady Customer: "Twelve years."
Floorwalker: "Bargain basement is on the left."

466   Efficient Nagging

"My husband is an efficiency expert in a large office."
"What does an efficiency expert do?"
"Well, if we women did it, they'd call it nagging."

467   We've Tasted Medicine Like That

An invitation to dinner had been sent to the newly settled physician. In reply the hostess received an absolutely illegible letter.

"I must know if he accepts or refuses," she declared.

"If I were you," suggested her husband, "I should take it to the druggist. Druggists can always read doctors' letters, however badly they are written."

His wife followed his advice. The druggist looked at the slip of notepaper, went into his dispensary and returned a few minutes later with a bottle, which he handed over the counter.

"There you are, madam," he said. "That will be seventy-five cents."

468   Practically Bald

Customer: "Does a man with as little hair as I've got have to pay full price to have it cut?"

Barber: "Yes, and sometimes more. We usually charge double when we have to hunt for the hair."

469   OF COURSE

Professor: "I forgot my umbrella this morning."

King Arthur: "How did you remember you forgot it?"

Professor: "Well, I missed it when I raised my hand to close it, after it had stopped raining."

470   RECALCITRANT

Bill (viciously attacking a piece of chicken): "This must be an incubator chicken."

Joe: "Why?"

Bill: "No chicken with a mother could be so tough."

471   BOVINE

Artist: "That, sir, is a cow grazing."

Visitor: "Where is the grass?"

Artist: "The cow has eaten it."

Visitor: "But where is the cow?"

Artist: "You don't suppose she'd be fool enough to stay there after she'd eaten all the grass, do you?"

472   EDITED

An English cub reporter, frequently reprimanded for relating too many details and warned to be brief, turned in the following:

"A shooting affair occurred last night. Sir Dwight Hopeless, a guest at Lady Panmore's ball, complained of feeling ill, took a highball, his hat, his coat, his departure, no notice to his friends, a taxi, a pistol from his pocket and finally his life. Nice chap. Regrets and all that sort of thing."

473   CAUTIOUS

Father was standing at the edge of a cliff admiring the sea below, the sandwiches clutched in his hand. His son approached him and tugged at his coat.

"Mother says it isn't safe here," said the boy, "and you're either to come away or else give me the sandwiches."

474   STRANGLE-HOLD

On a crowded car: "Madam, would you like me to get you a strap?"

"No, thank you, I have one."

"Then, would you mind letting go of my necktie?"

475   CHALLENGE

A hard-driving taxi driver ignored a red signal, threatened a policeman's knees, missed the street island by a hair and grazed a bus, all in one dash.

The policeman hailed him, then strolled over to the taxi, pulling a big handkerchief from his pocket *en route*.

"Listen, cowboy," he growled. "On the way back I'll drop this and see if you can pick it up with yer teeth."

476 ARS LONGA

Auctioneer: "What am I offered for this beautiful bust of Robert Burns?"

Man in Crowd: "That ain't Burns ... that's Shakespeare."

Auctioneer: "Well, folks, the joke's on me. That shows what I know about the Bible."

477 OPEN-HANDED

First Caddie: "What's your man like, Skeeter?"

Second Caddie: "Left-handed, and keeps his change in his right-hand pocket."

478 GRAMMAR

"Are your father and mother in?" asked the visitor of the small boy who opened the door.

"They was in," said the child, "but they is out."

"They was in. They is out. Where's your grammar?"

"She's gone upstairs," said the boy, "for a lay-down."

479 ADDITION

Rich Man: "There's no sense in teaching the boy to count over 100. He can hire accountants to do his bookkeeping."

Tutor: "Yes, sir, but he'll want to play his own game of golf, won't he?"

480 MONEY IN IT

Uncle: "And what are you going to be when you grow up, Freddy?"

Freddy: "I'm going to be a philanthropist; those people always seem to have such a lot of money."

481 WASHING UP

Smith: "I wear the trousers in my home."

Friend: "Yeah, but right after supper I notice you wear an apron over them."

482 NEW

Teacher: "If you have ten potatoes and must divide them equally among three persons, how would you do it?"

Johnny: "I'd mash them."

483 COLLECTIVE

Teacher: "Name three collective nouns."

Tommy: "Fly-paper, waste-basket and vacuum-cleaner."

484 SECOND ATTACK

Diner: "Waiter, I was here yesterday and had a steak."

Waiter: "Yes, sir; will you have the same today?"

Diner: "Well, I might as well, if no one else is using it."

485 RECOGNITION

A recruit failed to salute a Captain. The Captain followed him inside and demanded: "Don't you recognize the uniform?"

"Yes, sir," replied the recruit, feeling of the Captain's coat. "Pretty nice uniform; look at this thing they issued me."

486   SIMPLER

"Give me a glass of milk and a muttered buffin."
"You mean a buffered muttin."
"No, I mean a muffered buttin."
"Why not take doughnuts and milk?"

487   VIEW-POINT

She: "Doesn't the bride look stunning?"
He: "Yeah, and doesn't the groom look stunned?"

488   HAPPY ENDING

Three Britons, each hard of hearing:
First Limey: "Is this Wembley?"
Second Pelter: "No, it's Thursday."
Third Limey: "So am I. Let's have a Scotch and soda."

489   CURRENT CASE

A chap was arraigned for assault and brought before the judge.
Judge: "What is your name, occupation, and what are you charged with?"
Prisoner: "My name is Sparks; I am an electrician, and I'm charged with battery."
Judge (after recovering his equilibrium): "Officer, put this guy in a dry cell."

490   IN A BIG WAY

A tourist was enjoying the wonders of California as pointed out by a native.
"What beautiful grapefruit," he said, as they passed through a grove of citrus trees.
"Oh, those lemons are a bit small owing to a comparatively bad season," explained the Californian.
"What are those enormous blossoms?" questioned the tourist a little bit farther on.
"Just a patch of dandelions," answered the guide.
Presently they reached the Sacramento River.
"Ah," said the tourist, "some one's radiator is leaking."

491   DOUBTING THOMAS

The one-ring circus was visiting a town in the hills. The folks there recognized all the instruments of the band except the slide trombone.
One old settler watched the player for quite some time, then said:
"There's a trick to it; he ain't really swallerin' it."

492   GHOSTS

Two colored boys were having an argument about ghosts. One of them claimed to have seen a ghost the night before.
"What was dis here ghos' doin' when you las' seen him?" asked the doubting one.
"Jes' fallin' behin', mistah; fallin' behin' rapid."

493   Yes!

"Mr. Brown, these are very small oysters you are selling me."

"Yes, ma'am."

"They don't appear to be very fresh, either."

"Then it's lucky they're small, ain't it?"

494   Ho, Hum

An English tourist was on his first visit to Niagara Falls, and the guide was trying to impress him with its magnificence.

"Grand," suggested the guide.

The visitor did not seem much impressed.

"Millions of gallons a minute," explained the guide.

"How many in a day?" asked the tourist.

"Oh, billions and billions," answered the guide.

The visitor looked across, and down and up, as if gaging the flow. Then he turned away with a shrug, apparently unaffected.

"Runs all night, too, I suppose," he remarked.

495   A Riddle to End All Riddles

A train operated by a Norwegian engineer starts to New York from Albany just as a train with a drunken engineer leaves New York for Albany. There's only one track, no switches or sidings, yet the trains do not collide. Why? Because Norse is Norse and Souse is Souse and never the twain shall meet.

496   Economics

"It's tough to pay forty cents a pound for meat."

"Mmm. But it's tougher when you pay only twenty."

497   Service

The motorist had just bought a tankful of gasoline, and the station attendant was going through his little ritual.

Attendant: "Check your oil, sir?"

Motorist: "No, it's O.K."

Attendant: "Got enough water in your radiator?"

Motorist: "Yes, filled up."

Attendant: "Anything else, sir?"

Motorist: "Yes, would you please stick out your tongue so I can seal this letter?"

498   It's Perfect

"Is that hair tonic any good?"

"Say, I spilled some of it on my comb last week and now it's a brush."

499   And Still Hungry

"What is a cannibal, Tommy?"

"I don't know."

"Well, if you ate your mother and father, what would you be?"

"An orphan."

500   6500 Jingling Noises

Along a country road came a $7,000 limousine. As it caught up with the small car, the owner of the big car could not resist the temptation to slow down and jolly the other driver a bit.

"Heavens, man," he said, "what is it about your car that makes such a dreadful rattling sound?"

"That? Oh, that's the $6,500 jingling around in my pocket," said the small car driver.

501 DARN!

"Does your husband talk in his sleep?"

"No, and it's terribly exasperating. He just grins."

502 INJUSTICE

Tenant: "This roof is so bad that it rains on our heads. How long is this going to continue?"

Owner: "What do you think I am, a weather prophet?"

503 DEFINITION

Sometimes you run across a farmer who wants to know just what the Russians mean by a "kulak." Well, there may be exact definitions, but an example can be given of the "gentleman farmer," whose daughter was asked if their hens laid eggs.

"They can, of course," she replied haughtily, "but in our position, you understand, they don't have to."

504 CURE

Voice over 'Phone: "I can't sleep, Doctor. Can you do anything for me?"

Doctor: "Hold the 'phone and I'll sing you a lullaby."

505 WITNESS

The men were swapping stories.

"When I was logging up in Oregon," said one of them, "I saw a wildcat come right up to the skidder one day. It was a fierce beast, but with great presence of mind, I threw a bucket of water in its face and it slunk away."

"Boys," said a man sitting in the corner, "I can vouch for the truth of that story. A few minutes after that happened, I was coming down the side of the hill. I met this wildcat and, as is my habit, stopped to stroke its whiskers. Boys, those whiskers were wet!"

506 TRUTH

Teacher (brightly): "As we walk out-of-doors on a cold winter's morning and look about us, what do we see on every hand?"

Class (as a man): "Gloves!"

507 WORRIED

A visitor at the Capitol was accompanied by his small son. The little boy watched from the gallery when the House came to order.

"Why did the minister pray for all those men, Pop?"

"He didn't. He looked them over and prayed for the country."

508 WE WONDER TOO

Husband: "Have you ever wondered what you would do if you had Rockefeller's income?"

Wife: "No, but I have often wondered what he would do if he had mine!"

509   He Must Be an Economist

"I'm glad you're so impressed, dear, by all these explanations I have been giving you about banking and economics," remarked the young husband.

"Yes, darling. It seems wonderful that anybody could know as much as you do about money without having any."

510   Or Minnie the Moocher

"Now boys," said the teacher, "tell me the signs of the zodiac. You first, Thomas."

"Taurus, the Bull."

"Right! Now, you, Harold, another one."

"Cancer, the Crab."

"Right again. And now it's your turn, Albert."

The boy looked puzzled, hesitated a moment, and then blurted out, "Mickey, the Mouse."

511   Commercial

British Guide (showing places of historical interest): "And it was in this room that Lord Wellington received his first commission."

Insurance man: "How many renewals?"

512   Go Easy

The girl had just said "yes."

"Do your people know that I write poetry?" he asked.

"Not yet, dear," she said. "I've told them about your drinking and gambling, but I couldn't tell them everything at once."

513   Or Buckshot

"Engaged to five girls at once!" exclaimed a horrified father. "How do you explain such a situation?"

"I don't know," replied the son, "unless Cupid shot me with a machine gun."

514   Or Jump Up

The excited sportsman heaved a mighty heave, then reeled madly till the poor troutling was nine feet aloft, with its head against the tip of the rod, flapping feebly there.

"Now what'll I do?" he demanded.

"So fur ez I can see," said the puzzled lumberjack, "there ain't nuthin' fur you to do except climb the pole."

515   A Searching Examination

A minister was loud in his praise of the fat and juicy bird his colored host served for dinner, and finally he asked: "Where did you get such a fine goose as that?"

"Pahson," replied his host, "when you preaches a good sermon Ah doan ax you whar you got it. Ah hopes you'll hab de same consideration fo' me."

516   Knew It All the Time

Jim: "When you proposed to her, I suppose she said 'This is so sudden'?"

George: "No, she was honest about it and said: 'The suspense has been terrible.'"

517 IN TRAINING

The vicar was paying a visit to the houses of his poorer parishioners, and in one of the houses he asked a good many questions about the family. A very grubby but very cheerful little boy attracted the kindly cleric's attention, and he asked him his name.

"Reginald d'Arcy Smif, sir," replied the boy with a grin.

The vicar turned to the boy's father.

"What made you give the boy a name like that?" he asked.

" 'Cause I want 'im to be a professional boxer," returned the parent, "an' wiv a name like that he'll get plenty o' practice at school."

518 DOUBTFUL CHARACTER

Customer: "Remember that cheese you sold me yesterday?"

Grocer: "Yes, madam."

Customer: "Did you say it was imported or deported from Switzerland?"

519 TWO OF A KIND

Mrs. John: "Wake up, John, there's a burglar going through your pants pockets."

John (turning over): "Oh, you two just fight it out between yourselves."

520 TOO COARSE

Mr. Newlywed: "What's wrong with this cake, dear? It tastes kind of gritty."

Mrs. Newlywed: "Don't be silly, darling. The recipe calls for three whole eggs and I guess I didn't get the shells beaten up fine enough."

521 SPONGED CAKE

Hubby: "What are we having for dessert tonight, dear?"

Wife: "Sponge cake. I sponged the eggs from Mrs. Brown, the flour from Mrs. Smith and the milk from Mrs. Jones."

522 TOO LONG TO WAIT

"What inspired the old-time pioneers to set forth in their covered wagons?"

"Well, maybe they didn't want to wait about 30 years for a train."

523 THE LET-DOWN

For months he had been her devoted admirer. Now, at long last, he had collected up sufficient courage to ask her the most momentous of all questions.

"There are quite a lot of advantages in being a bachelor," he began, "but there comes a time when one longs for the companionship of another being— a being who will regard one as perfect, as an idol; whom one can treat as one's absolute property; who will be kind and faithful when times are hard; who will share one's joys and sorrows ——"

To his delight he saw a sympathetic gleam in her eyes. Then she nodded in agreement.

"So you're thinking of buying a dog?" she said. "I think it's a fine idea. Do let me help you choose one!"

524 MODERN YOUTH

"Is your daughter home from school for the holidays?"

"I think so. One of the servants said she saw her dav before yesterday."

525   UNPREDICTABLE

"I turned the way I signaled," said the lady, indignantly, after the crash.
"I know it," retorted the man. "That's what fooled me."

526   LIVE ON HIS INCOME

"Do you love me?"
"Yes, handsome."
"Can you live on my income?"
"Yes, but what will you live on?"

527   SPEAKING FROM EXPERIENCE

Wally: "Gee, pop, there's a man in the circus who jumps on a horse's back, slips underneath, catches hold of its tail, and finishes up on the horse's neck."
Father: "That's nothing. I did all that, and more, the first time I ever rode a horse."

528   WHY WORRY ABOUT IT?

Teacher: "Take 13½ from 29¼ and what's the difference?"
Class Dunce: "Yeah, that's what I say, who cares anyhow?"

529   DIFFICULT DAYS

A person has to be a contortionist to get along these days. First of all he's got to keep his back to the wall, and his ear to the ground. He's expected to put his shoulder to the wheel, his nose to the grindstone, keep a level head and both feet on the ground. And, at the same time have his head in the clouds, so he can look for the silver lining.

530   MODEST

Goolsby: "Did anyone in your family ever make a brilliant marriage?"
Harefoot: "Only my wife."

531   THE INEVITABLE END

Man wants but little here below,
   He's ready to admit it,
And if Uncle Sam keeps taxing him
   He's pretty sure to git it.

532   REMISS

Vicar (benevolently): "And what is your name, my little man?"
Small boy: "Well, if that ain't the limit. Why, it was you that christened me."

533   TIME TO REPEAT

Mose: "Don't you start no fight with me, big boy. Remember Ah was decorated foh bravery in the Spanish war."
Sambo: "Maybe yo' was, but it done give you such a swell head you'se about ripe to be redecorated."

534   HAVING WONDERFUL TIME

Says a postcard from a truth-telling vacationist at an expensive mountain resort: "Having a wonderful time; wish I could afford it."

535   SPOILED HIS WISH

Sonny: "Kin I have the wishbone, mother?"
Mother: "Not until you've eaten your spinach."
Sonny: "Yes, but I wanted to wish I didn't have to eat it."

536   HIS OVERSIGHT

Waiter: "How did you order your steak, sir?"
Diner (impatiently): "Orally, but I realize now I should have ordered it by mail in advance."

537   CANDID ANSWER

Boy Friend: "You're dancing with me tonight, and I suppose tomorrow you'll be making a date with some other man."
Girl Friend: "Yes, with my chiropodist."

538   SPELLING

Teacher: "Why did you spell pneumatic 'neumatic'?"
Pupil: "The 'k' on my typewriter isn't working."

539   STAYING HOME

"Boy, if I had a wife like yours, I'd stay home every night in the week."
"I'll say you would, or get your neck broken."

540   QUITE IMPORTANT

A Chinaman was worried by a vicious looking dog.
"Don't be afraid of him," the owner reassured. "You know the old proverb, 'A barking dog never bites.' "
"Yes," replied the Chinaman, "you know ploverb, me know ploverb, but do dog know ploverb?"

541   TAKING NO CHANCES

Passerby: "Kinda cold sitting on your front porch this weather, isn't it, Mr. Davis?"
Mr. Davis: "Well, yes, a little, but you see my wife is taking her singing lesson, and I don't want the neighbors to think I'm beating her up."

542   THE WORLD MOVES TOO FAST

"Nothing to read around this place," stormed the man of the house who had settled down for an evening, "but some old next month's magazines!"

543   'TWAS EVER THUS

"Has your wife changed very much since you married her?"
"Yes, she's changed my friends, my habits and my hours."

544   TRUTHFUL ANSWER

Caller: "Won't you walk as far as the street car with me, Tommy?"
Tommy: "Nome, I can't."
Caller: "Why not?"
Tommy: " 'Cause we're gonna eat dinner soon's you're gone."

545   REASON ENOUGH

"Just tell me one good reason why you can't buy a new car now," said the persistent automobile salesman.

"Well, I'll tell you, man," replied the farmer, "I'm still paying installments on the car I swapped for the car I traded in as part payment on the car I own now."

546   O WONDERFUL HORSE!

O horse, you are a wonderful thing;
No buttons to push, no horn to honk;
You start yourself, no clutch to slip;
No spark to miss, no gears to strip;
No license buying every year,
With plates to screw on front and rear;
No gas bills climbing up each day,
Stealing the joy of life away;
No speed cops chugging in your rear,
Yelling summons in your ear.
Your inner tubes are all O.K.
And thank the Lord, they stay that way;
Your spark plugs never miss and fuss;
Your motor never makes us cuss.
Your frame is good for many a mile;
Your body never changes style.
Your wants are few and easy met;
You've something on the auto yet.
                              Northwestern Banker

547   SLIGHT TRANSPOSITION

The visitor paid his bill at the fashionable hotel, and as he went out, he noticed a sign near the door, "Have you left anything?"

So he went back and spoke to the manager. "That sign's wrong," he said. "It should read 'Have you anything left?'"

548   WHAT MODEL?

"Mah bredern," said a Negro preacher, "when yo' hears Gabriel sound his horn yo' wants to be ready to jump."

"Mah goodness," exclaimed one of the congregation, "am he comin' in an auto?"

549   FOLLOWING ORDERS

Bill: "You look all out of sorts. What's the matter?"
Jack: "Plenty. On account of my rheumatism the doctor told me to avoid all dampness—and you've no idea how silly I feel sitting in an empty bathtub and going over myself with a vacuum cleaner."

550   SCHEMER

Billy (who has eaten his apple): "Let's play Adam and Eve."
Small Sister: "How do you play that, Billy?"
Billy: "Well, you tempt me to eat your apple and I'll give in."

551   SHORT ON COLLATERAL

Two Georgia darkeys were discussing the financial condition of the country. They didn't agree.

"You's all wrong," one vociferated. "Dey ain't no money sho'tage. Ah asked mah bankuh is he out o' money and he tuk me in de vault and showed me piles an' piles o' money. And Ah says could he let me have a little. And he says he sho' could. Has Ah any collat'rul? Ah hasn't. Now, dat's what's de mattuh wid dis country. Dey's plenty o' money, but we's jest runnin' sho't on collat'rul."

552   POWER

"What is the greatest water power known to man?"
"Woman's tears."

553   WRONG NUMBER

"I called on Mabel last night, and I was hardly inside the door before her mother asked me about my intentions."
"That must have been embarrassing."
"Yes. But the worst of it was Mabel called from upstairs and said: 'That isn't the one, mother!' "

554   SLIGHTLY SCRAMBLED

A newspaper account of a disastrous shipwreck stated: "The vessel sank with all aboard except one lady passenger. She was insured for a large sum and loaded with pig iron."

555   SLOW MOTION

Patient: "What do you charge for extracting a tooth?"
Dentist: "$5."
Patient: "$5 for only two seconds' work?"
Dentist: "Well, if you wish, I can extract it very slowly."

556   WORKING LATE AT THE OFFICE

"I don't see Charlie half as much as I used to."
"You should have married him when you had the chance."
"I did."

557   SAD MISTAKE

Mr. Brown: "So your son had to leave college on account of poor eyesight?"
Mr. White: "Yes, he mistook the dean of women for a coed."

558   IMPORTS

Gibbs: "Did you see much poverty in Europe?"
Biggs: "A great deal. In fact, I brought some home with me."

559   NOT THAT BOLD

Ma: "That new couple next door seem to be very devoted. He kisses her every time they meet. Why don't you do that?"
Pa: "I don't know her well enough."

560   CREDIT

A man mortgaged his home to buy an automobile. Then he went around and tried to mortgage the car to get money to build a garage.

"How are you going to buy gas?" curiously inquired the man of whom the loan was asked.

"Well," replied the other slowly, "if I own a house, a car and a garage, I should think any dealer would be willing to trust me for gas."

561   CORRECT

New Teacher: "Where is the elephant found?"

Jane: "It's so big, it's hardly ever lost."

562   TIT FOR TAT

Boarder: "This steak is like a cold day in June—very rare."

Landlady: "Yeah, and your bill is like a day in March, very unsettled."

563   STILL CIRCULATING

An old gentleman approached a nattily attired Negro at an elaborate dark-town wedding.

"Pardon me, suh," said the old pappy, "is you de bridegroom?"

The young Negro shook his head dolefully. "No, suh," he replied, "Ah wuz eliminated in de semi-finals!"

564   TWO YEARS SHOULD DO IT

Her Suitor: "Sir, I came to—er—ask you whether you would object—er—to my marrying your daughter."

Her Father: "My boy, you're only twenty-one and my daughter is twenty-seven. Why not wait a few years till you're both about the same age?"

565   HIGHLY COMPETENT

A man of six feet eight inches applied for a job as a life guard.

"Can you swim?" asked the official.

"No, but I can wade to beat the devil."

566   DIPLOMACY

Telegraph messengers are often called upon to exercise wily diplomacy with drunks or enraged addressees, who think a bicycle can go thirty miles an hour.

One once proved himself a past master at the diplomatic game of flattery, when he entered an elevator and forgot to take off his hat. There was only one other passenger in the elevator, but she was a rather fussy, middle-aged woman, and she asked: "Don't you take off your hat to ladies?"

"Only to old ones, madam," he replied, with a little bow.

567   EPITHET

"Yes, the smallest things seem to upset my wife. The other day she was doing a crossword puzzle and she asked me, 'What is a female sheep?' I said, 'Ewe,' and she burst into tears."

568   NEW TROUBLE

Man (to small son of workman who has met with an accident): "When will dad be fit to work again?"

Boy: "Can't say for certain, but it will be a long time."
Man: "What makes you think that?"
Boy: " 'Cause compensation's set in."

GENEROUS

69

The young bride was extolling the virtues of her husband to a friend.
"George is just the most generous man in the world," she declared. "He gives me everything credit can buy."

EYE FOR EYE

70

A small boy leading a donkey passed by an army camp. A couple of soldiers wanted to have some fun with the lad.
"What are you holding on to your brother so tight for, sonny?" said one of them.
"So he won't join the army," the youngster replied without blinking an eye.

AMELIORATING CIRCUMSTANCES

71

An old farmer was moodily regarding the ravages of the flood.
"Hiram," yelled a neighbor, "your pigs were all washed down the creek."
"How about Flaherty's pigs?" asked the farmer.
"They're gone, too."
"And Larsen's?"
"Yes."
"Humph!" ejaculated the farmer, cheering up. " 'Tain't as bad as I thought."

INTRICACIES OF FINANCE

72

Rastus borrowed $35 from his friend Amos and gave a note for the amount. The note became long past due. One day Amos called on Rastus and demanded: "When you-all gwine pay dat note?"
"Ah ain't got no money now, but Ah gwine pay just as soon as Ah kin."
"Dat don't git me nothin'," retorted Amos. "If you-all don't pay me here an' now, Ah gwine burn up your old note; den where you-all gwine be at?"
"You better not! You better not!" shouted Rastus. "You just burn dat note of mine, and Ah'll burn you up wid a lawsuit."

DEFINITION

573

The identity of the young lady is withheld, but the memory of her answer lingers with the instructor conducting a science course at a local high school. One of the requirements in the written quiz was: "Define a bolt and nut and explain the difference, if any." The girl wrote:
"A bolt is a thing like a stick of hard metal such as iron with a square punch on one end and a lot of scratching wound around the other end. A nut is similar to the bolt only just the opposite being a hole in a little chunk of iron sawed off short with wrinkles around the inside of the hole."
The startled professor marked that one with a large "A."

OBLIGING

574

Fat Man (in a movie to little boy sitting behind him): "Can't you see, little fellow?"
Little Fellow: "Not a thing."
Fat Man: "Then keep your eye on me and laugh when I do."

575   GETTING RIGHT ALONG

"A telegram from George, dear."

"Well, did he pass the examination this time?"

"No, but he is almost at the top of the list of those who failed."

576   DIFFERENCE

"That means fight where I come from!"

"Well, why don't you fight then?"

" 'Cause I ain't where I come from."

577   HINT

The Vicar: "I want to speak to you, Fishner, about the milk you've been delivering lately. We don't require it for christenings."

578   THE WAY OF FAME

Author: "Well, sir, the upshot of it was that it took me ten years to discover that I had absolutely no talent for writing literature."

Friend: "You gave up?"

Author: "Oh, no; by that time I was too famous."

579   MAKES A DIFFERENCE

Passenger: "Have I time to say good-by to my wife?"

Porter: "I don't know, sir; how long have you been married?"

580   QUITE DIFFERENT

The banker was questioning the Negro applicant for a chauffeur's job.

"Are you married?" the banker asked.

"Nawsah, boss," replied the applicant, "nawsah; Ah makes mah own livin'."

581   GRADUAL PROGRESS

Victim: "Hey, that wasn't the tooth I wanted pulled."

Dentist: "Calm yourself, I'm coming to it!"

582   VOYAGEUR

Visitor: "How far is it to Washington?"

Native: "Wa'al, I don't rightly know, but I'll call Eph. Eph'll know. He's traveled all over. He's got shoes."

583   CLOSE SHAVE

A couple of boys out in Nebraska were discussing the recent drought. One fellow had some wheat which he managed to harvest.

"The drought sure has made the wheat short this year."

"Short? Say, I had to lather mine to mow it!"

584   BOOK LARNIN'

The Southern father was introducing his family of boys to a visiting Governor.

"Seventeen boys," exclaimed the Governor. "And all Democrats, I suppose."

"All but one," said the father proudly. "They're all Democrats but John, the little rascal. He got to readin'."

585   AGREED

Telephone Operator: "Is this 1749?"
Colored Maid: "Yassum."
T. O.: "Is this Mrs. Blots' residence?"
C. M.: "Yassum."
T. O.: "Long distance from Washington."
C. M.: "Yassum, sho' is."

586   STEADY CUSTOMER

Housewife: "Look here, my man, why do you always come to my house
to beg?"
Tramp: "Doctor's orders, madam."
Housewife: "Doctor's orders?"
Tramp: "He told me that when I found food that agreed with me I should
stick to it."

587   SECONDHAND

Daughter of first film star: "How do you like your new father?"
Daughter of second film star: "Oh, he's very nice."
Daughter of first film star: "Yes, isn't he? We had him last year."

588   TACTFUL

First Clerk: "Have you and your boss ever had any differences of opinion?"
Second Ditto: "Yes, but he doesn't know it!"

589   GENESIS

A surgeon, an architect, and a politician were arguing as to whose profession was the oldest.
Said the surgeon: "Eve was made from Adam's rib, and that surely was a
surgical operation."
"Maybe," said the architect, "but prior to that, order was created out of
chaos, and that was an architectural job."
"But," interrupted the politician, "somebody created the chaos first!"

590   SAME RESULT

"Are you a college man?"
"No; a horse stepped on my hat."

591   NO PLACE FOR HIM

A young lawyer from the North sought to locate in the South. He wrote to
a friend in Alabama, asking him what the prospects seemed to be in the city
for "an honest young lawyer and Republican."
In reply the friend wrote: "If you are an honest lawyer, you will have absolutely no competition. If you are a Republican, the game laws will protect
you."

592   A LITTLE SLOW

New typist (following rapid-fire dictation): "Now, Mr. Jones—what did
you say between—'Dear Sir' and 'Sincerely yours'?"

593   EVOLUTION

Evolution of a man's ambition:
    To be a circus clown.
    To be like dad.
    To be a fireman.
    To make All-State.
    To do something noble.
    To get wealthy.
    To make ends meet.
    To get the old-age pension.

594   So UNSELFISH

Teacher: "Unselfishness means going without something you need, voluntarily. Can you give me an example of that, Bobby?"
Bobby: "Yessum. Sometimes I go without a bath when I need one."

595   A REMINDER

I rose and gave her my seat—
I could not let her stand.
She made me think of Mother,
With that strap held in her hand.

596   CLOSE RESEMBLANCE

Joe: "The boss told us when he was a boy on a farm they had a mule that was just like one of the family."
Jim: "Yeah, and I know which one."

597   A NEW ANGLE

As he was drilling a batch of recruits the sergeant saw that one of them was marching out of step. Going to the man as they marched, he said sarcastically:
"Do you know they are all out of step except you?"
"What?" asked the recruit innocently.
"I said they are all out of step except you," repeated the sergeant.
"Well," was the retort, "you tell 'em. You're in charge."

598   WHAT A LIFE!

Husband (reading): "The tusks of 4,700 elephants were used last year to make billiard balls."
Wife: "Isn't it wonderful that such big beasts can be taught to do such delicate work!"

599   FOLLOWING ORDERS

Mr. Wimpus: "You sure made a poor job of painting this door."
Mrs. Wimpus: "Well, you declared this morning that it needed painting badly."

600   No RESPONSIBILITY

Worker: "Would you increase my wages; I was married yesterday?"
Foreman: "Sorry, but we are not responsible for accidents that occur outside the factory."

01 CONSCIENCE ON THE INSTALLMENT

A man who had his purse stolen some years previously, received the following letter:

"Sur, sum years ago I stole your muny. Remorse is gnawin' me, so I send um back. Wen it gnaws me again I will send sum more."

02 GRAMMAR

The head of the firm was frowning over a letter. Calling his chief clerk he said, "That new stenographer—you surely did not hire her on account of her grammar!"

"Grammar!" echoed the clerk. "Gosh, Boss, I thought you told me to pick ne out for Glamor."

03 IT'S A CLEAN LIFE!

Mother: "Junior, go wash your hands and face."
Junior: "Aw, I just took a bath this morning."
Mother: "Then go wash the bathtub."

04 SHORT STORY

"How is your father getting along?"
"Well, the doctor told him not to start any continued stories."

05 SUCCESS STORY

The corpulent self-complacent Irishman sank into his most comfortable chair and remarked to his wife, "Well, Kate, me dear, life to me seems to have been one long run of prosperity. First I was plain Hooley; then I married you and became Mr. Hooley; then I was made Councillor Hooley, and later Alderman Hooley. To cap the lot, as I wint into church yisterday all the congregation with one accord rose and sang, 'Hooley, Hooley, Hooley'!"

06 FOOD JARGON

She balanced herself daintily on a stool at the hamburger counter, looked over the pastries and, after a few minutes of indecision, addressed the counter man: "I would like to have two hamburgers well done; no pickle, but you may put a little mustard on them, if you don't mind."

Without turning his head the counter man shouted to the short order cook: Elmers, on two; hobnailed; hold the pucker and make 'em dirty."

07 WRONG IMPRESSION

Junior: "That man wasn't a painless dentist like he advertised."
Senior: "Why? Did he hurt you?"
Junior: "No, but he yelled when I bit his thumb, just like any other dentist."

08 CORRECT

Teacher: "Now, which boy can name five things that contain milk?"
Jimmie: "Butter, cheese, ice cream, and two cows."

09 MORE THAN SATISFIED

Son: "Dad, what was your greatest ambition when you were a kid?"
Dad: "To wear long pants. And I've had my wish. If there is anybody else n this country who wears his pants longer than I do, I'd like to see him."

610 GENEROUS

"When I was a little boy, I always ate my crusts," said Willie's father.
"Did you like them?" asked Willie.
"Of course I did," quickly responded his father.
"Then you may have mine," replied his son, graciously.

611 WRONG RECIPE

Groom: "How did you make this cake, dear?"
Bride: "Here's the recipe. I clipped it from a magazine."
Groom: "Are you sure you read the right side? The other side tells how
to make a rock garden."

612 HIS ERROR

The owner of a cheap watch brought the timepiece into the jeweler's shop
to see what could be done for it. "The mistake I made, of course," he admitted, "was in dropping this watch."
"Well, I don't suppose you could help that," the jeweler remarked. "The
mistake you made was picking it up."

613 HIS GOOD DEED!

A naval officer fell overboard. He was rescued by a deck hand. The officer
asked how he could reward him.
"The best way, sir," said the gob, "is to say nothing about it. If the other
fellows knew I'd pulled you out, they'd chuck me in."

614 HOPES REALIZED

Bill: "Have you ever realized any of your childhood hopes?"
Pete: "Yes; when mother used to comb my hair, I often wished I didn't
have any."

615 A "TENSE" SITUATION

A school teacher was correcting a boy who said, "I ain't gwine."
Teacher: "You have not studied your lesson. Listen: 'We are not going.
You are not going. They are not going'. Now do you understand?"
Boy: "Yes, teacher. Nobody ain't gwine."

616 IDEAL JOB

He had managed to get a job as collector for a gas company.
"Take this master key and go round and empty all the coin boxes; get all
the pennies and quarters," said the manager.
He was gone for three weeks. Then he walked into the office and an-
nounced: "Can I have another key? I've lost t'other one."
"Certainly," replied the manager. "But where have you been all this time?
The cashier has stayed late every Friday night expecting you to come for
your wages."
"What!" exclaimed the man, beaming; "do I get wages as well?"

617 IN FULL ACCORD

Housewife: "I don't suppose you know what good honest work is?"
Hobo: "No, I don't. What good is it?"

618 IDENTIFIED

Sentry: "Halt; who's there?"

Voice: "American."

Sentry: "Advance and recite the second verse of 'The Star Spangled Banner.'"

Voice: "I don't know it."

Sentry: "Proceed, American."

619 FOLLOWING THE RULES

Sam had applied to the teller at the bank window to withdraw a dollar. The teller told him it was a rule of the bank not to permit any withdrawal less than five dollars.

Sam: "All right. Ah'll take five dollars, and then ah would like to make a deposit of four dollars to my account."

620 SUPERFLUOUS

"George, dear, do you remember what Wordsworth said about daffodils?"

"No. And what's the use of bothering when we pay a gardener?"

621 UPSET

The president of the local gas company was making a stirring address.

"Think of the good the gas company has done," he cried. "If I were permitted a pun I should say, 'Honor the Light Brigade.'"

And a customer immediately shouted, "Oh, what a charge they made!"

622 POSSIBLY

"What a boy you are for asking questions," said the father. "I'd like to know what would have happened if I'd asked as many questions when I was a boy."

"Perhaps," suggested the young hopeful, "you'd have been able to answer some of mine."

623 HEAD OF THE FIRM

"Is this Peabody, Finchley, Longworth, and Fitzgerald?"

"Yes, this is Peabody, Finchley, Longworth, and Fitzgerald."

"I want to speak to Mr. Smith."

624 PEOPLE ARE TOO SUSPICIOUS

Judge: "How could you swindle people who trusted in you?"

Prisoner: "But, judge, people who don't trust you cannot be swindled."

625 STRIKE UP THE BAND

Madge: "Why do you prefer Wagner?"

Marjorie: "Because he composes about the only kind of music one can hear above the conversation."

626 SUNK

Two old settlers, confirmed bachelors, sat in the backwoods. The conversation drifted from politics and finally got around to cooking.

"I got one o' them cookery books once, but couldn't do nothing with it."

"Too much fancy work in it, eh?"

E

"You've said it! Every one o' them recipes began the same way: 'Take a clean dish'—and that settled me."

627   STRATEGY

"Father," said the small boy, "what is psychology?"

"Psychology, my son, is a word of four syllables that you ring in to distract attention when the explaining gets difficult."

628   DOMESTIC CORPORATION

"So your wife takes in washing?" the Montgomery County judge asked a man who was up for vagrancy. "What do you do?"

"Well, Judge," explained the accused, "I takes in the washin', the old woman does the washin', I takes the washin' back, the old woman collects the money and I talks her out of most of it."

629   RAPID

A golf professional, hired by a big department store to give golf-lessons, was approached by two women.

"Do you wish to learn to play golf, madam?" he asked one.

"Oh, no," she said, "it's my friend who wants to learn. I learned yesterday."

630   HOW'RE YOU BETTING?

"The people in our part of town are watching the result of a very interesting conflict."

"What is it?"

"An irresistible blonde has just met an immovable bachelor."

631   POSER

"Why does a woman say she's been shopping when she hasn't bought a thing?"

"Why does a man say he's been fishing when he hasn't caught anything?"

632   OBVIOUSLY

"My poor husband was a wonderful artist," sighed the landlady as she hacked at the pie crust, "and always said he found inspiration in my cooking."

"A sculptor, I presume," said the gloomy boarder, surveying his bent fork.

633   DON'T LIKE THE TYPE

Mrs. Brown: "Do you know, dear, I was reading the other day that an ostrich can see very little, and can digest anything."

Mrs. Smith: "What an ideal husband!"

634   HANG HIM OUT

An Irish Guards officer called up a sergeant and spoke of the unsoldierly appearance of a recruit.

"He looks very slovenly, sergeant."

"Yes, sor."

"Are you sure he washes?"

"Yes, sor."

"Absolutely certain he washes?"

"Yes, sor, but he dries a bad color, sor."

635 ### ALL IS WELL

"Mose, you lazy rascal, do you think it right to leave your wife at the wash-tub while you spend your time fishing?"

"Oh, yassuh, mah wife doan need no watchin'. She wuk jest as hard as if'n I wuz dere."

636 ### MORE NEXT WEEK

Dora had returned from Sunday-school where she had been for the first time.

"What did my little daughter learn this morning?" asked her father.

"That I am a child of Satan," was the beaming reply.

637 ### NOTHING TO WORRY ABOUT

Overheard on the Beach: "Mummy, may I go in for a swim?"

"Certainly not, my dear, it's far too deep."

"But daddy is swimming."

"Yes, dear, but he's insured."

638 ### ON THE FAIRWAYS

Golfer: "Listen, kid, I'll swat you with a club if you don't stop wisecracking me about my game!"

Caddie: "Yeah, but you wouldn't know which club to use!"

639 ### THAT'S IT

Woman Learning to Drive: "But I don't know what to do!"

Husband: "Just imagine that I'm driving."

640 ### THAT'S DIFFERENT

A Negro was telling his minister that he had "got religion."

"Dat's fine, brothah; but is you sure that you is going to lay aside sin?" asked the minister.

"Yessuh, Ah's done it already."

"An' is you gwine to pay up all your debts?"

"Wait a minute, pahson. You ain't talking religion now—you is talking business."

641 ### HERE WE GO

Lady: "So you are on a submarine. What do you do?"

Sailor: "Oh, I run forward, ma'am, and hold her nose when we want to take a dive."

642 ### 'S TRUTH

A Negro was endeavoring to make clear to a friend just what constitutes oratory. "I will elucidate," he said. "If you say black am white, dat am foolish. But if you says black am white an' bellers like a bull, an' pounds de table with both fists, dat am oratory!"

643 ### BAD COMPANY

An elderly man of convivial habits, but also bookish, was hailed before the bar of justice in a small country town.

"Ye're charged with bein' drunk and disorderly," snapped the magistrate. "Have ye anything to say why sentence should not be pronounced?"

"Man's inhumanity to man makes countless thousands mourn," began the prisoner, in a flight of oratory. "I am not so debased as Poe, so profligate as Byron, so ungrateful as Keats, so intemperate as Burns, so timid as Tennyson, so vulgar as Shakespeare, so——"

"That'll do, that'll do," interrupted the magistrate. "Seven days. And, officer, take down that list of names he mentioned and round 'em up. I think they're as bad as he is."

644   DEPENDS UPON THE VIEW-POINT

A London doctor touring in the provinces had difficulty in obtaining suitable lodgings in a small town.

One landlady, showing him a dingy bedroom, remarked persuasively, "As a whole, this is quite a nice room, isn't it?"

"Yes, madam," he agreed, "but as a bedroom it's no good."

645   PLAYING SAFE

The hotel clerk was growing impatient as the prospect took so long to read the names on the register. "Just sign on that line, please," said the clerk.

The prospect was indignant and retorted: "Young man, I'm too old a hand to sign anything without reading it."

646   JUSTIFIED

Johnnie was gazing at his one-day-old brother, who lay squealing and wailing in his cot.

"Has he come from heaven?" inquired Johnnie.

"Yes, dear."

"No wonder they put him out."

647   GIVE US A COUPLE

Joking Customer: "How much are your four-dollar shoes?"
Smart Salesman: "Two dollars a foot."

648   STORM COMING

Magistrate (to man accused of begging): "What have you to say?"
Prisoner: "It wasn't my fault, sir. I just held out my hand to see if it was raining and the gent dropped a penny in it."

649   CALL THE MANAGER

"Look here, waiter, is this peach or apple pie?"
"Can't you tell from the taste?"
"No, I can't."
"Well, then, what difference does it make?"

650   AND COLLECT YOUR COMMISSION

"Doctor, I want you to look after my office, while I'm on my vacation."
"But I've just graduated, doctor. I've had no experience."
"That's all right, my boy. My practice is strictly fashionable. Tell the men to play golf and send the lady patients abroad."

651   LET'S GO!

Sonny: "Mother, we're going to play elephants at the zoo and we want you to help us."

Mother: "What on earth can I do?"

Sonny: "You can be the lady who gives them peanuts and candy."

652   TRAGIC

"I understand," said a young woman to another, "that at your church you are having very small congregations. Is that so?"

"Yes," answered the other girl, "so small that every time the rector says, 'Dearly Beloved,' you feel as if you had received a proposal."

653   BUDGET

"What is a budget?"

"Well, it is a method of worrying before you spend instead of afterward."

654   GENTLEMEN OF THE JURY

The prosecuting counsel was having a little trouble with a rather difficult witness. Exasperated by the man's evasive answers, he asked him if he was acquainted with any of the jury.

"Yes, sir, more than half of them," replied the man in the box.

"Are you willing to swear that you know more than half of them?" asked the counsel.

"If it comes to that, I'm willing to swear that I know more than all of 'em put together," came defiantly from the witness.

655   WHO'S DRIVING THIS CAR?

Timid Wife (to husband who has fallen asleep at the wheel): "I don't mean to dictate to you, George, but isn't that billboard coming at us awfully fast?"

656   PLAYING SAFE

Teacher: "Johnny, why does Missouri stand at the head in mule-raising in the United States?"

Johnny: "Because the other end is dangerous."

657   THAT SETTLES IT

Man Motorist (after barely avoiding a collision): "Why, in the name of common sense, didn't you signal?"

Woman Driver (who had just turned into her home driveway): "Why I always turn here, stupid!"

658   AND A DOLLAR

Teacher: "Tommy, if your father could save a dollar a week for four weeks what would he have?"

Tommy: "A radio, a new suit, and a set of furniture."

659   WHERE IT BELONGED

Judge (to amateur yegg): "So they caught you with this bundle of silverware. Whom did you plunder?"

Yegg: "Two fraternity houses, Your Honor."

Judge (to Sergeant): "Call up the downtown hotels and distribute this stuff."

660   REVERSE ENGLISH

Teacher: "Correct the sentence, 'Before any damage could be done the fire was put out by the volunteer fire brigade.' "

Boy: "The fire was put out before any damage could be done by the volunteer fire brigade."

661   DEFINITION

"What is an 'optimist,' Daddy?"

"Well, child, he is a fellow who goes into a hotel without baggage and asks to have a check cashed."

662   SENSITIVE

Two men were seated together in a crowded street car. One of them noticed that the other had his eyes closed.

"What's the matter, Bill," he asked, "feeling ill?"

"I'm all right," answered Bill, "but I hate to see ladies standing."

663   ECONOMY

"Jack," said Capt. Angus to his cook, "here's a wee ticket for tonight's conjuring show at the Beacon. Noo, when he comes to that part where he takes a spoonful o' flour and one egg, and makes 20 omelettes, watch very closely, laddie."

664   DON'T WAIT

A mistress engaging a new maid said: "Mary, we have breakfast promptly at 8 A.M."

New Maid: "All right, mum. If I ain't down, don't you wait!"

665   ACQUAINTED

Judge: "Have you ever seen the prisoner at the Bar?"

Witness: "Yes, that's where I met him."

666   CITY AND COUNTRY

Amos: "Did you find much difference between the city and the country, Hiram?"

Hiram: "They hain't much difference. In the country you go to bed feeling all in, and you get up feeling fine. In the city you go to bed feeling fine, and you get up feeling all in."

667   NO OBJECTION

Suitor: "I am seeking your daughter's hand, sir. Have you any objection?"

Father: "None at all. Take the one that's always in my pocket."

668   NO AMBITION

Servant: "I want to give notice to leave on the first of next month, ma'am."

Mistress: "Why is that? Do you want to better yourself?"

Servant: "Oh, no, ma'am. I want to get married."

669 GOOD TASTE

"Rastus, don't you know that it is bad form to sop up your gravy with your bread?"

"Liza, it might be bad form, but it sho' am good taste."

670 NOT SO DUMB

Jack: "Why is your car painted blue on one side and red on the other?"

Mac: "It's a great scheme. You should hear the witnesses contradicting each other."

671 FOOLIN' HIMSELF

A colored boy was taking a stroll through a cemetery and reading the inscriptions on tombstones. He came to one which declared: "Not dead, but sleeping."

After contemplating the phrase for a moment, and scratching his head, the Negro exclaimed: "He sure ain't foolin' nobody but hisself."

672 REPARTEE

The audience in the college auditorium was impatiently awaiting the appearance of the out-of-town entertainer, who was already an hour late. The chairman of the evening, fearing the people would leave, scribbled a frantic appeal for help and had it passed down the aisle to Professor B., who was a ready and witty speaker. Thinking to break up the stony atmosphere, Professor B. began: "I've just received a message asking me to come up here and say something funny."

A young student at the back of the room called loudly: "You'll tell us when you say it, won't you?"

To which the grave professor made instant reply: "I'll tell *you*; the rest will know!"

673 SIDE-SEAT DRIVER

A husband drew his chair beside his wife's sewing machine.

"Don't you think you're running too fast?" he said. "Look out! You'll sew the wrong seam! Mind that corner, now! Slow down, watch your fingers! Steady!"

"What's the matter with you, John?" said his wife, alarmed, "I've been running this machine for years!"

"Well, dear," replied her husband, "I thought you might like me to help you, since you help me drive the car."

674 WRONG DIAGNOSIS

Doctor: "Did you tell that young man I think he is no good?"

Daughter: "Yes, I did, Dad, but he did not seem at all upset. He said it wasn't the first wrong diagnosis you have made."

675 TRANSLATED

"I advise you, Madam," instructed the doctor, "to take frequent baths, get plenty of fresh air, and dress in cool clothes."

"What did the doctor say?" inquired her husband an hour later.

"He said I ought to go to Atlantic City, and then to the mountains," replied his wife. "Also that I must get some new light gowns at once."

676 LOST CAUSE

"They say your daughter has made up her mind to marry a struggling young doctor."

"Well, if she's made up her mind, he might as well stop struggling."

677 THAT'S DIFFERENT

"What is the matter, my little man?" asked a sympathetic stranger to a small boy whom he saw crying.

"Please, sir, my dog's dead," sobbed the boy.

"Well," said the man, "you mustn't make such a trouble of it. My grandmother died last week, and I'm not crying."

"No," said the boy, "but you didn't bring her up from a pup."

678 X MARKS THE SPOT

Gus and Ole, at a Northern fishing resort, rented a hotel boat and found great fishing at a certain spot in a nearby lake, so great that they decided to mark the place and come back for more sport the next day. At the dock Gus said, "Ole did you mark the spot?"

"Yah," replied Ole. "Ay put a chalk mark on this side of the boat."

"Boy, are you dumb!" exclaimed Gus. "Maybe ve von't get the same boat."

679 HER RESPONSIBILITY

There was a terrible crash as the train struck the car. A few seconds later, Mr. and Mrs. crawled out of the wreckage. Mrs. opened her mouth to speak, but her husband stopped her. "Don't say a word," he snapped. "I got my end of the car across. You were driving in the back seat, and if you let it get hit it's no fault of mine."

680 MIGHT HAVE BEEN A HICCUP

The tenderfoot thought he could ride, and mounted a pony in front of a lot of cowboys. The pony soon threw him. A cowboy, helping him up, said: "Well! What threw you?"

"What threw me? Why she bucked something fearful! Didn't you see her buck?" cried the tenderfoot.

"Buck!" said the cowboy. "Heck! She only coughed."

681 THE CAD AT EVE

Husband: "If a man steals, no matter what, he will live to regret it."

Wife (coyly): "You used to steal kisses from me before we were married."

Husband: "Well, you heard what I said."

682 WHY WORRY?

Father: "Ned, why are you always at the bottom of your class?"

Ned: "It doesn't really matter, dad. We get the same instruction at both ends of the class."

683 FRANK

He: "You know you are not a bad looking sort of girl."

She: "Oh, you'd say so even if you didn't think so."
He: "Well, we're squared, then. You'd think so even if I didn't say so."

684 RIGHT PLACE

Customer: "Waiter, I'm so hungry I could eat a horse."
Waiter: "You came to the right place, sir."

685 A BEGINNER

Farmer: "Come on, I'll show you how to milk a cow."
Novice: "Perhaps I'd better start on a calf."

686 WELL ON THEIR WAY

"One more payment and the furniture's ours."
Wife: "Good! Then we can throw it out and get some new stuff."

687 TAKING NO CHANCES

Old Lady to Old Tar: "Excuse me Do those tattoo marks wash off?"
Old Tar: "I can't say, lady."

688 LOOKING BACKWARD

"George comes from a very poor family."
"Why, they sent him to the university, didn't they?"
"Yes, that's how they got so poor."

689 THE WHOLE STORY

Johnny had been the guest of honor at a party the day before, and his friend was regarding him enviously.
"How was it? Have a good time?" he asked.
"Did I?" was the emphatic answer. "I ain't hungry yet!"

690 TACT

That a certain young man is wise beyond his years was proved when he paused before answering a widow who had asked him to guess her age.
"You must have some idea," she said.
"I have several ideas," said the young man, with a smile. "The only trouble is that I hesitate whether to make you ten years younger on account of your looks, or ten years older on account of your intelligence."

691 POLISHED

He: "She certainly is polished, doncha think so?"
She: "Yeah. Everything she says casts a reflection on someone."

692 DID HE GET THE JOB?

Employer: "Personal appearance is a helpful factor in business success."
Employee: "Yes, and business success is a helpful factor in personal appearance."

693 ADD GOLF WOE

"When I put the ball where I can reach it," said the stout golfer, when asked how he liked the game, "I can't see it, and when I put it where I can see it, I can't reach it."

E

694   CAN'T COMPLAIN, SIR

"Are you the waiter who took my order?"

"Yes, sir."

"H'm, still looking well, I see. How are your grandchildren?"

695   PRESTO!

Teacher was giving a lesson on the weather idiosyncrasies of March. 'What is it," she asked, "that comes in like a lion and goes out like a lamb?'

And little Julia, in the back row, replied: "Father."

696   SALT SELLER

A tourist stopped in front of a little country store, dumfounded a, the sight of an enormous display of salt piled high on the premises. Stack after stack. Boxes, barrels, bags. Tons of salt, inside the store and out.

"You must sell a lot of salt," exclaimed the tourist.

"No, I don't sell much," replied the storekeeper. "But you shoulda seen the guy that came here last week. He could really sell salt."

697   WE'RE STILL FRIENDS

Mrs. Jones: "I understand you've got your divorce, Sally. Did you get any alimony from your husband?"

Laundress: "No, Mrs. Jones, but he done give me a first-class reference."

698   THAT'S HIGH GEAR

Traffic Cop: "Now, Miss, what gear were you in at the time of the accident?"

Demure Miss: "Oh, I had on a black beret, tan shoes, and a tweed sports dress."

699   DAY OF DOOM

Flo: "I don't intend to be married until I'm thirty."

Rea: "I don't intend to be thirty until I'm married!"

700   SHE'D NO MECHANICAL TASTE

Betty (who has been served with a wing of chicken): "Mother, can't I have another bit? This is nothing but hinges."

701   MODERN MODEL

Wife (reading): "It says here they have found sheep in the Himalaya mountains that can run forty miles an hour."

Her Hubby: "Well, it would take a lamb like that to follow Mary nowadays."

702   SHH!

A Union Pacific shopman had been drawn on a Federal grand jury and didn't want to serve. When his name was called he asked Judge Pollock to excuse him. "We are very busy at the shops," said he, "and I ought to be there."

"So you are one of those men who think the Union Pacific couldn't get along without you," remarked the judge.

"No, your honor," said the shopman. "I know it could get along without me, but I don't want it to find out."

"Excused," said the judge.

703 SIT DOWN

Teacher: "Johnny, can you define nonsense?"

Johnny: "Yes, teacher—an elephant hanging over a cliff with his tail tied to a daisy."

704 THE RESTLESS AGE

Teacher: "Willie, give the definition of home."

Willie: "Home is where part of the family waits until the others are through with the car."

705 THE NEW ORDER

A school teacher from the city was questioning her small farm nephew to see how his country school education was progressing. "If a farmer had 5,000 bushels of corn," she asked, "and corn is worth 40 cents a bushel, what will he get?"

"A government loan!" promptly replied the nephew.

706 ONE KIND

Teacher: "What is capital punishment?"

Pupil (whose father was a big business man): "It's when the government sets up business in competition with you, and then takes all your profits with taxes in order to make up its loss."

707 BOSSY'S EPITAPH

A farmer was trying hard to fill out a railway company claim sheet for a cow that had been killed on the track. He came down to the last item: "Disposition of the carcass." After puzzling over the question for some time, he wrote: "Kind and gentle."

708 STAND IT ON ITS HEAD

"Have you any alarm-clocks?" inquired the customer. "What I want is one that will rouse father without waking the whole family."

"I don't know of any such alarm-clock as that, madam," said the shopkeeper. "We keep just the ordinary kind that will wake the whole family without disturbing father."

709 TIT FOR TAT

She: "You certainly do keep your car nice and clean."

He: "It's an even deal—my car keeps me clean, too."

710 SOLOMON SAID IT FIRST

"Anything new in the paper today, George?"

"No, my dear—just the same old things, only happening to different people."

711   GIVE HIM SOME OXYGEN, NURSIE

Homely Wife (in hospital): "My husband seems a lot brighter this morning. He said he's just longing to get home again."

Nurse: "Yes; I'm afraid the anesthetic hasn't worn off yet."

712   SAUCE FOR GOOSE AND GANDER

The elderly gentleman's wife was entering a railway carriage, and he neglected to assist her. "You are not so gallant, John, as when I was a gal," she exclaimed in gentle rebuke.

"No" was his ready response, "and you are not so buoyant as when I was a boy."

713   GROWLS OF RECOGNITION

While on the bench one day Judge Daniel called a case for trial, and two lawyers appeared as attorneys for the litigants.

"You're a dirty shyster," snarled one of the lawyers to the other, "and before this case is through I'll show you up for the crooked ape that you are."

"Sez you," snapped the other. "You are a cheat and a liar."

"Come, come," broke in the judge. "Let the case proceed now that the learned counsel have identified each other."

714   ONE-ARM DRIVING BARRED

"I wonder why there are so many more auto wrecks than railway accidents?"

"That's easy. Did you ever hear of the fireman hugging the engineer?"

715   CALL AN AMBULANCE

"Cup o'tea, weak," said a customer at a London coffee stall. When the decoction was brought to him, he eyed it critically.

"Well, what's wrong with it? You said weak, didn't you?"

"Weak, yes," was the reply, "but not helpless."

716   FINALLY

Diogenes met a World War veteran.

"What were you in the war?" he asked.

"A private," the soldier answered.

And Diogenes blew out his lamp and went home.

717   FASHIONS

A man who had been waiting patiently in the post office could not attract the attention of either of the girls behind the counter.

"The evening cloak," explained one of the girls to her companion, "was a redingote design in gorgeous lamé brocade with fox fur and wide pagoda sleeves."

At this point the long suffering customer broke in with, "I wonder if you could provide me with a neat purple stamp with a dinky perforated hem. The tout ensemble deliberately treated on the reverse side with mucilage. Something about 3 cents."

718   SCHOOL
"Were you copying his paper?"
"No, sir, I was only looking to see if he had mine right."

719   SKATING
1st Frosh: "My, what a skating rink!"
2nd Frosh: "Yes. It has a seating capacity of 5,000."

720   AMAZING
Professor: "What happens when the human body is immersed in water?"
Student: "The telephone rings."

721   LESSER OF TWO EVILS
During the recent flood in the Kentucky lowlands, one family sent its
little boy to stay with an uncle in another part of the state, accompanied by
a letter explaining the reason for the nephew's sudden and unexpected visit.
Two days later the parents received the telegram: "Am returning your boy.
Send the flood."

722   ANOTHER VERSION
Prof: "Mr. Smith, will you tell me why you look at your time-piece so
often?"
Smith (suavely): "Yes, sir! I was afraid, sir, that you wouldn't have time
to finish your interesting lecture, sir."

723   QUICKLY EXPLAINED
In speaking of the song, "The Bonnie Banks o' Loch Lomond," a country
teacher asked his pupils for an explanation of the line, "Yu'll tak' the high
road and I'll tak' the low road."
"One was going by air and the other by bus," answered a boy.

724   NEW RECRUIT
"Does the Sergeant know about this?" inquired the Colonel as he surveyed
a barricade of sandbags which had just collapsed.
"He ought to," replied a private, "he's underneath!"

725   DISAPPOINTMENT!
"John, dear," said Mrs. Brown, "such an odd thing happened today. The
clock fell off the wall, and if it had fallen a moment sooner, it would have
hit mother."
"I always said that clock was slow."

726   BREAKING IT GENTLY
"Mrs. Upton's pet dog has been run over; she'll be heartbroken."
"Don't tell her abruptly."
"No, I'll begin by saying it's her husband."

727   DEBTOR OR CREDITOR
"What is a debtor, pa?"
"A man who owes money."

"And what is a creditor?"

"The man who thinks he's going to get it."

728   TRY A MERRY-GO-ROUND

Salesman: "What kind of car would you like, madam, four, six or eight cylinders?"

Timid Customer: "Couldn't I begin with one?"

729   ALL SET FOR THRIFT WEEK

An insurance man walked into a lunch-room and taking his place on one of the vacant stools, ordered bread and milk. The fellow sitting on the next stool asked:

"On a diet?"

"No. Commission."

730   ANCESTRY

A modest gentleman, in speaking of his family, said: "The Hardson family is a very, very old family. The line runs away back into antiquity. We do not know how far back it runs, but it's a long, long way back, and the history of the Hardson family is recorded in five volumes. In about the middle of the third volume, in a marginal note, we read, 'About this time the world was created.' "

731   USUAL

A lady was entertaining her friend's small son.

"Are you sure you can cut your meat?" she asked, after watching his struggles.

"Oh, yes," he replied, without looking up from his plate. "We often have it as tough as this at home."

732   MODERN

Grandma: "Would you like to go to the fair and ride in the merry-go-round, dear?"

Modern Child: "I don't really mind, if it will amuse you."

733   SUSPENSE

Old Lady (to parachutist): "I really don't know how you can hang from that silk thing. The suspense must be terrible."

Parachutist: "No, mum; it's when the suspense ain't there that it's terrible."

734   TOUCHY

Barry Winton remarks that a college boy's definition of a male parent is, "The KIN you love to touch."

735   INDIFFERENT

Gus: "The horn on your car must be broken."

Mr. ——: "No, it's just indifferent."

Gus: "Indifferent! What do you mean?"

Mr. ——: "It just doesn't give a hoot."

736   SERVICE

Barber: "Hair-cut?"
Sap: "No, just change the oil."

737   YOUR MORNING SMILE

A divinity student named Tweedle
Refused to accept his degree;
He didn't object to the "Tweedle,"
But hated the "Tweedle, D.D."

738   STRATEGY

"Talk about Napoleon! That fellow Johnson is something of a strategist
himself."
"As to how?"
"Got his salary raised six months ago, and his wife hasn't found it out yet."

739   DUAL PURPOSES

A husband and wife came to a bank to open a joint account. Being in a
hurry, the man made out his signature card and left.
"Let me see," an official of the bank said to the wife. "This is to be a joint
account, is it not?"
"That's right," smiled the wife. "Deposit for him—checking for me."

740   SUCH GALLANTRY

"Dearest Annabelle," wrote a lovesick swain, "I could swim the mighty
ocean for one glance from your lovely eyes. I could walk through a wall of
flame for one touch of your little hand. I would leap the widest stream for a
word from your warm lips.—As always, Your Own Oscar.
"P.S.—I'll be over to see you Sunday night, if it doesn't rain."

741   HIS POLITICAL OPPONENT

English political speeches, at their best, have long been noted for their
pungent humor. A rejoinder of John Morley, given in the heat of battle, is a
typical example.
Morley had just finished a campaign address by requesting his listeners to
vote for him, when a man jumped angrily to his feet and shouted, "I'd rather
vote for the devil!"
"Quite so," rejoined Morley with a smile, "but in case your friend declines
to run, may I count on your support?"

742   MEMORIES

"Dear Clara," wrote the young man, "pardon me, but I'm getting so forgetful. I proposed to you last night, but really forgot whether you said yes or
no."
"Dear Will," she replied by note, "so glad to hear from you. I knew that I
had said no to somebody last night, but had forgotten who it was."

743   JUST A DIFFERENCE

"Oh, what a strange looking cow," exclaimed the sweet young thing from
Chicago. "But why hasn't she any horns?"

"Well, you see," explained the farmer, "some cows is born without horns and never had any, and others shed theirs, and some we dehorn, and some breeds ain't supposed to have horns at all. There's a lot of reasons why some cows ain't got horns, but the reason why that cow ain't got horns is because she ain't a cow—she's a horse."

744 LIKEWISE

Conductor: "Next station is Long Wait Junction. Change cars for Mauch Chunk, Squeedunk, Quakake and Podunk, Hokendaqua, Catasaqua, Mecanaqua, and Tamaqua."

Green Brakeman (at other end of car): "Same at this end."

745 RAW RECRUIT

Rifle Instructor: "Do you know where you are aiming?"

New Recruit: "No, sir. I'm a stranger in this district."

746 CORPSE

Mathematics Teacher: "Robert, can you tell me what is meant by a polygon?"

Robert (a freshman): "I guess it means a parrot that's died, doesn't it?"

747 SPEED

Man: "Say, conductor, can't you run any faster than this?"

Conductor: "Yes, I can, but I have to stay in the car."

748 EASILY PLEASED

Father: "Remember, son, beauty is only skin deep."

Son: "'Sdeep enough for me. I ain't no cannibal."

749 DO AS I SAY, ETC.

Student (to Prof.): "What's that you wrote on my paper?"

Prof: "I told you to write plainer."

750 ONE ADVANTAGE OF IRRIGATION

Customer: "Say, this hair restorer you sold me didn't grow one hair on my head."

Barber: "Mebbe not, but it has a nice cooling effect when it runs down around your ears, hasn't it?"

751 STATISTICS

Office Boy: "I et six eggs for breakfast this morning."

Bookkeeper: "You mean ate, don't you?"

Office Boy: "Well maybe it was eight I et."

752 BITING

Game Warden: "Are the fish biting today?"

Weary Angler: "I don't know. If they are, they're biting each other."

753 IGNORANT

Lecturer: "Of course you all know what the inside of a corpuscle is like."

Chairman (interrupting): "Most of us do, but you had better explain for the benefit of them as has never been inside one."

754   INFORMATION, PLEASE

An example of youthful pessimism was provided by a little colored boy
who was about to start on a railway journey. It was the first time he had ever
traveled alone, and his mother told him to write his name and address on a
card and keep it in his pocket. He wrote: "In case of accident, dis was Johnny
Jones."

755   TWO TO ONE

Some few years ago, just after Jimmy Foxx had broken into the regular
lineup with the Philadelphia Athletics, the Boston Red Sox came to Philly
to play a series. George Moriarty was umpiring behind the plate.

Foxx took two terrific cuts at the first two pitches, and let the third one
float by.

"Strike three, you're out," said Moriarty.

Foxx turned indignantly, "You missed that one, George."

"Well, you missed the other two," Moriarty replied. "You're still one up
on me."

756   EARNING HIS BIT

The plumber was working and his new assistant was looking on. The latter
was learning the trade and this was his first day.

"Say," he inquired, "do you charge for my time?"

"Certainly," was the reply.

"But I haven't done anything."

The plumber had been inspecting the finished job with a lighted candle,
which he handed to his helper. "Here," he said, "if you've got to be so conscientious, blow that out!"

757   DUMB TREES

Sonny sat on the lower steps, his face resting in his two chubby hands.

"What's the matter, Sonny?"

"Nothin'—just thinkin'."

"What about?"

"Thinkin' how dumb trees are to take off their clothes in winter and put
'em on in summer."

758   SINISTER CONNOTATION

"I wish you boys wouldn't call me Big Bill."

"Why not?"

"Those college names stick—and I'm going to be a doctor."

759   TOO BAD

Mary had a little lamb
　'Twas awful dumb and so
It couldn't tell the red from green
　Nor which was stop or go.
It followed her to school one day
　A silly thing to do
Was caught between the red and green
　And now it's mutton stew.

760   TWO-THIRTY PLENTY

Chinese patient (on telephone): "Doctor what time you fixee teeth for me?"
Doc: "Two-thirty—all right?"
Chinese: "Yes, tooth hurty, all right, but what time you fixee?"

761   MINISTERIAL TACT

A minister was known by a few of his parishioners to be fond of Cherry
Brandy and one of them in a mischievous frame of mind offered to present
him with a bottle on condition that it was fully acknowledged in the next
issue of the Church Magazine. The offer was promptly accepted and in due
course the notice appeared in the magazine: "The Vicar thanks Mr. McTavish
for his gift of fruit and the spirit in which it was given."

762   ONE DRAWBACK

Tom: "How do you like your new job selling on the road?"
Harry: "Oh, it's dandy. You meet some fine fellows at the hotels and have
lots of fun in the evenings, but what I don't like is calling on those jobbers
every day."

763   OBSERVANT

"Mother, I'm the best looking boy in Sunday School."
"Why, Tommy! Who told you that?"
"Nobody, mother. Nobody didn't have to tell me. I saw all the rest of 'em."

764   THERE MUST HAVE BEEN SEVERAL

A Civil War veteran had spent a week at a New York hotel. When he
went to pay his bill the clerk asked:
"What was your rank?"
"Oh, just a private," the old soldier replied.
"Well, I won't charge you anything. You are the first private I ever met."

765   LEFT IN DOUBT

Policeman (after the collision): "You saw this lady driving toward you. Why
didn't you give her the road?"
Motorist: "I was going to, as soon as I could discover which half she
wanted."

766   A BREAK FOR THE BIRDS

After a day's shooting in India, a young Englishman who was a poor shot
said to his Indian attendant: "I did not do so well today."
"Oh, the young sahib shot very well, very well indeed," said the diplomatic
Hindu, "but God was very merciful to the birds."

767   WHAT GOES UP

It seems that one of the boys in Army maneuvers in Texas came floating
into camp near the Davis Mountains. When he was brought to the officer's
tent, slightly bruised, he was told, "You've got real nerve to come down in a
parachute with this 100-mile wind blowing. That's dangerous!"
"I didn't come down in a parachute," said the private. "I went up in a
tent."

768 WISE GIRL

Student: "To whom was Minerva married?"
Professor: "My boy, when will you learn that Minerva was the Goddess of Wisdom? She wasn't married."

769 NUT SHELL

Student: "Yes, sir; I always carry my notes in my hat."
Prof: "I see—knowledge in a nut shell."

770 A STRAIGHT FACE

Father: "I never kissed a girl until I met your mother. Will you be able to say the same to your son when you become a married man?"
Son: "Not with such a straight face as you can, father."

771 DIRECT HIT

The squad of recruits had been out to the rifle range for their first try at marksmanship. They knelt at 250 yards and fired. Not a hit. They moved up to 200 yards. Not a hit. They tried at 100 yards. Not a hit.
" 'Tenshun!" the sergeant drawled. "Fix bayonets! Charge! It's your only chance."

772 RECONDITIONED

Draftee: "Was that your new girl I saw you with last night?"
Regular: "No; just the old one painted over."

773 GOLF CLUB LUNCH MENU

Scotch Broth
Club Sandwich   Sliced Tomatoes
Link Sausage
Dandelion Green   Puttatoes
Parsnips
Cup Custard
Rolls   Nuts
Tea

774 HE'S SAFE

"You know the old saying, what you don't know won't hurt you."
"So what?"
"You lucky dog, you're invulnerable."

775 CONSIDERABLE DIFFERENCE

"Give me a chicken salad," said the man in a suburban restaurant.
"Do you want the 40-cent one or the 50-cent one?" asked the waitress.
"What's the difference?"
"The 40-cent ones are made of veal and pork and the 50-cent ones are made of tuna."

776 MOUNTAIN GUIDE

Be careful not to fall here. It's dangerous. But if you do fall, remember to look to the left. You get a wonderful view on that side.

777   IT HELPS

"I drink about fifty cups of coffee a day."

"Doesn't that keep you awake?"

"It helps."

778   NUMBER, PLEASE

A gentleman visiting in Washington wanted to 'phone someone in Baltimore. It proved annoying when the operator said: "Deposit twenty-five cents, please."

"What!" he cried, "twenty-five cents to call Baltimore? Why, at home we can 'phone to hades and back for a nickel."

"Oh, yes," she replied, "but that's a local call."

779   COLLEGE EXAMS

Prof (gazing over the room during an examination): "Will some kind gentleman who isn't using his textbook be so kind as to permit me to have it for a few minutes?"

780   CAPITAL AND LABOR

Willie: "What is the difference between capital and labor, Dad?"

Dad: "Well, son, the money you lend represents capital—and getting it back represents labor."

781   CROSS-EXAMINATION

State's Attorney: "Are you sure this is the man who stole your car last Thursday?"

Much befuddled plaintiff: "Well, I was. Now after the cross-examination, I'm not sure I ever even owned a car."

782   NEVER MIND THE DETAILS

A somewhat inebriated gentleman was walking down State Street and did not know his location. He turned to a passerby and said, "Mister, where am I?" The passerby answered, "You are at the corner of State and Madison Streets." The inebriated gentleman said, "Never mind the details, what city?"

783   CONSPICUOUS

An American advertising man told an Englishman that an electric sign being constructed had 30,000 white lights, 40,000 green lights, 60,000 pink lights, and, in addition, it would have a great sunburst of 100,000 orange lights. The Englishman looked at it a moment and said, "Yes, that's a marvelous sign, but don't you think it is going to be a little bit conspicuous?"

784   TROUBLE

Two little boys were playing in a train. The conductor said the children must behave or he would make trouble. The boys' father said, "You don't know what trouble is. My wife's in the hospital. I am on my way to see my sick mother-in-law; my daughter has had triplets; one of the boys has just smashed his finger and the other has chewed up our tickets. To top it all off, we are on the wrong train."

785   A DIFFICULT GOLF COURSE

A guest on a golf course placed the ball in position, missed three times, hit it the fourth time, and then turned to his host and said, "This is a difficult course, isn't it?"

786   FAST DRIVING

Two fraternity brothers headed toward Philadelphia. They were zipping along the highway at some eighty or ninety miles an hour, when a policeman appeared from nowhere and forced them over to the curb.

"What's the matter, officer?" they asked. "Were we driving too fast?"

"No," he answered sarcastically. "You were flying too low."

787   FARSIGHTED

Doctor: "I'd like to have a quart of blood for a transfusion. Can you give it?"

Stude: "I can only give you a pint. I gotta shave tomorrow."

788   TIN YOU

I bought a wooden whistle,
But it wooden whistle,
So I bought a steel whistle,
But steel it wooden whistle,
So I bought a lead whistle,
Still they wooden lead me whistle,
So I bought a tin whistle,
And now I tin whistle.

789   THE OLD GENT SHOULD KNOW

"Now," said the lad to his father, at the college football game, "you'll see more excitement for two dollars than you ever saw before."

"I don't know," replied the old gent. "That's what my marriage license cost me."

790   THAT'S ALL

"Say, pal, how much money does your wife demand every pay day?"

"Don't ask foolish questions. You know my salary is fifty dollars a week."

791   EXPENSIVE

"Can you tell if the defendant was expensively garbed?"

"'Deed she was, suh. Ah knows expensive garbage when Ah sees it."

792   INVOICE

Hubby: "You never tell me what you buy! Don't I get any voice in the buying?"

Wifey: "Certainly, darling! You get the invoice."

793   CLEVER, THESE CHINESE

A sailor, after placing some flowers on a grave in a cemetery, noticed an old Chinaman placing a bowl of rice on a nearby grave, and asked: "What time do you expect your friend to come up and eat the rice?"

The old Chinaman replied with a smile: "Same time your friend come up to smell flowers."

794   COURT SCENE

Judge to Prisoner: "Say, when were you born?"
(No reply.)
Judge: "I say, when was your birthday?"
Prisoner (sullenly): "Wot do you care? You ain't gonner give me nothin'!"

795   BACK IN THE GOOD OLD DAYS

"Crop failures?" asked the old timer.
"Yep, I've seen a few of 'em in my days. Now in 1884 the corn crop was purt' nigh nothing. We cooked some for dinner one day, and paw ate fourteen acres of corn at one meal!"

796   NEAR BY

He: "Meet me at the Waldorf-Astoria at eight."
She: "The Waldorf? . . . Say, that's a nice place."
He: "Yeah, and it's close to where we're going, too."

797   BEHIND HIS EARS

In a church, at the font, her small brother was being christened.
Little Girl—*"Behind his ears, too, Reverend Smyth!"*

798   PLAY BALL

In a small town in Mississippi on a hot dusty day, two Negro baseball teams, surrounded by their dusky devotees, were engaged in a very important baseball game.

The colored preacher of the community had been approved by both teams for the position of umpire in this contest—because, as the home team pointed out, a parson couldn't do wrong.

The visiting team's clean-up man stood in the batter's box. The bases were loaded.

"Ball one, high!" the voice of authority boomed.
"Ball two, low!"
"Ball three, inside!"
"Ball fo', low and wide—you is out!"
"How does you talk, Mister Ump? Ah gets a base fo' dat!" screamed the mutinous batsman.

"Brother, you is right—but de bases am loaded, an' Ah ain't got no place to put you. You is out!"

799   UNDECIDED

Little Willie is so distressed, he got a pair of pink P-jams and a military hair brush for Christmas and now he doesn't know whether to go to Harvard or West Point.

800   LOW DOWN

Mose recently joined a colored lodge and shortly after met a friend who was not a member. "How yo' all like the lodge?" asked friend Rastus.

"That am a great lodge," said Mose, "an' they done give me an office in de lodge."

"What am de name of the office?" asked his friend.

"I am de Supreme Dictator of the Universe," said Mose.

"My, my, sho enuff. Dat must be some big office."

"No," answered Mose, "dat am de lowest office in de lodge."

801 NOT ASHAMED OF DAD!

"My boy," said the millionaire, "when I was your age, I carried water for a gang of bricklayers."

"I'm mighty proud of you, Father. If it hadn't been for your pluck and perseverance, I might have had to do something like that myself."

802 NOT SO BIG

"He's not as big a fool as he used to be."

"Getting wiser?"

"No, thinner."

803 TO THE POINT

Chairman: "Congratulations, my boy, congratulations on your typical married man's speech!"

Timid Speaker: "But I said only a couple of words."

Chairman: "Precisely!"

804 THAT SUFFOCATING FEELING

Have you ever had that cooped-up feeling as if you were in a very small cell? Have you ever felt that closed-in suffocating feeling? Have you ever found yourself talking when there was actually no one present for you to talk to? Were you ever worried by this condition? Then, why didn't you get out of the telephone booth?

805 ARCHITECTURAL TRIUMPH

Two ladies were attending a concert or something at the Civic Auditorium. Seated in the parquet, they looked about them.

"Nice building," said one lady. "What style of architecture is it?"

"I'm not quite sure," said the other lady, "but I think it's Reminiscence."

806 AND LADY UNCLES ARE O.K.

A school-teacher asked the pupils to write a short essay and to choose their own subjects.

A little girl sent in the following paper:—

"My subjek is 'Ants.' Ants is of two kinds, insects and lady uncles.

"Sometimes they live in holes and sometimes they crawl into the sugar bole, and sometimes they live with their married sisters.

"That is all I know about ants."

807 NEEDLES AND PINS

They had just become engaged.

"I shall love," she cooed, "to share all your troubles."

"But darling," he murmured, "I have none."

"No," she agreed, "but I mean when we are married."

808　　　　　　STOLEN SWEETS

The rector had invited the village boys to the rectory for a strawberry tea. After they had finished he, seeking to point the moral said: "Now, boys, wasn't that nicer than breaking into my garden and helping yourselves?"

"Oh, yes," chorused the boys.

"And why was it nicer?" he asked a chubby-faced boy.

"Because, sir," was the reply, "we shouldn't have had any sugar and cream with them."

809　　　　　　BIRD OF PARADISE

Customer: "That chicken I bought yesterday had no wish-bone."

Butcher (smoothly): "It was a happy and contented chicken, madam, and had nothing to wish for."

810　　　　　A POSITIVE SITUATION

Jack: "My wife talks to me positively awful."

Ed: "That's nothing. Mine talks to me awfully positive."

811　　　　　　EXPERIENCED

Henry: "My dear, I really don't believe you can ever teach that dog to obey you."

Mrs. Peck: "Nonsense, darling. Just remember how obstinate you were when we were first married."

812　　　　　HEARD ON THE LINKS

At the last home talent golf tournament the club secretary caught one of the entrants driving off about a foot in front of the teeing mark.

"Here!" he cried indignantly, "you can't do that. You're disqualified!"

"What for?" demanded the golfer.

"Why, you're driving off in front of the mark."

The player looked at the secretary with pity. "G'wan back to the clubhouse," he said tersely. "I'm playin' my third stroke!"

813　　　　　　A GOOD START

The first morning after the honeymoon, the husband got up early, went down to the kitchen and brought his wife her breakfast in bed. Naturally, she was delighted. Then her husband spoke:

"Have you noticed just what I have done?"

"Of course, dear; every single detail."

"Good. That's how I want my breakfast served every morning after this."

814　　　　　WINS HER DIPLOMA

An inspector, examining a class in religious knowledge, asked the following question of a little girl intending it for a catch:

"What was the difference between Noah's Ark and Joan of Arc?" He was not a little surprised when the child, answering, said: "Noah's Ark was made of wood and Joan of Arc was maid of Orleans."

815　　　　　　THAT'S DIFFERENT

"Ah wins."

"What yuh got?"

"Three aces."
"No yuh don't. Ah wins."
"What yuh got?"
"Two eights and a razor."
"Yuh sho' do. How cum yuh so lucky?"

816   VETERAN SPEAKS

Young Harry: "Father, what's the difference between a gun and a machine gun?"
Dad: "There is a big difference. It is just as if I spoke, and then your mother spoke."

817   DOUBLE-JOINTED

Fifer: "What sort of fellow is Groot?"
Zimpir: "Oh, he's one of those people who will pat you on the back before your face and hit you in the face behind your back."

818   BLACK OUT

A New Orleans mother noticed the other night that her high school son who was getting ready to go to a dance got dressed in record time.
"Boy, did you take a bath?" she asked him accusingly.
"No," came the reply.
"Now listen, son," she remonstrated, "you wouldn't go to a dance without taking a bath, would you?"
"Sure I would, Mom," came the reply. "It's not formal."

819   KNOWS HIS NEPTUNE

A young naval student was being put through the paces by an old sea-captain.
"What would you do if a sudden storm sprang up on the starboard?"
"Throw out an anchor, sir." "What would you do if another storm sprang up aft?" "Throw out another anchor, sir." "And if another terrific storm sprang up forward, what would you do?" "Throw out another anchor." "Hold on," said the Captain, "where are you getting all your anchors from?" "From the same place you're getting your storms, sir."

820   DOMESTIC BUSINESS COLLEGE

Momma (singing): "By low, my baby."
Poppa: "That's right; you tell him to buy low and I'll teach him to sell high."

821   NEW GADGET

Traffic Cop: "Use your noodle, lady! Use your noodle!"
Lady: "My goodness! Where is it? I've pushed and pulled everything in the car."

822   TRIUMPH OF COMFORT

"I'm not sure I quite understand those knee-action wheels."
"Why, it's like this—the wheels give. So if you run over a pedestrian you hardly feel it."

823   SHOULDN'T BE TIGHT

He: "What part of the car causes the most accidents?"
She: "The nut that holds the wheel."

824   STOP THIEF!

Niece (in the picture gallery): "Aunt Sarah, this is the famous 'Angelus,'
by Millet."
Aunt Sarah: "Well, I never! That man had the nerve to copy the calendar
that has hung in our kitchen for a dozen years or more."

825   RATTLING THE SKELETON

Pupil (after lesson on creation): "But, teacher, daddy says we are descended
from monkeys."
Teacher: "We can't discuss your private family affairs in class."

826   TRY BRAN MASH

Neighbor: "How is that incubator doing that you bought?"
Mrs. Newbride: "I suppose it's all right, but I'm a little worried about it.
It hasn't laid a single egg yet."

827   GETS 'EM GOING AND COMING

Schultz: "Your opening sale has closed. What now?"
Schwartz: "Our closing sale opens."

828   IMPROMPTU HOWLER

Teacher: "William, construct a sentence using the word 'archaic.'"
William: "We can't have archaic and eat it too."

829   COVER CHARGE

Waiter: "Would you mind settling your bill, sir? We're closing now."
Irate Patron: "But, hang it all, I haven't been served yet."
Waiter: "Well, in that case, there'll only be the cover charge."

830   TRAVEL NOTE

"What is the difference between valor and discretion?"
"Well, to travel on an ocean liner without tipping would be valor."
"I see."
"And to come back on a different boat would be discretion."

831   SHE KNEW HER NECK

The barber had used his electric clippers in cutting small Betty's hair. "I
guess my neck wasn't clean," she told her mother on coming home, "'cause
that man used his vacuum cleaner on it."

832   PLENTY BACK SEAT DRIVING

Sunday School Teacher: "Why was Solomon the wisest man in the world?"
Sarkis: "Because he had so many wives to advise him."

833   AND WAS HIS FACE RED!

In the congregation of an Oak Park church during Sunday morning service
was a young bride whose husband was an usher. Becoming terribly worried

about having left the roast in the oven, she wrote a note to her husband, sending it to him by another usher.

The latter, thinking it was a note for the pastor, hurried down the aisle and laid it on the pulpit. Stopping abruptly in the middle of his sermon to read the note, the astonished pastor was met with this written injunction:

"Please go home and turn off the gas."

834 BUT DID SHE FALL FOR IT?

Wife: "Mrs. Jones has another new hat."

Hubby: "Well, if she were as attractive as you are, my dear, she wouldn't have to depend so much upon the milliner."

835 BRINGING HOME THE BACON

Judge: "Mose, is your wife dependent upon you?"

Mose: "She sho is, jedge. If I didn't go out and get de washin's, she'd starve plum to death."

836 "ATCHOO!"

"Who invented the hole in the doughnut?"

"Oh, some fresh air fiend, I suppose."

837 NOBLESSE OBLIGE

Professor: "This exam will be conducted on the honor system. Please take seats three seats apart and in alternate rows."

838 CURE FOR EXTRAVAGANCE

"Are you saving any money since you started your budget system?"

"Sure. By the time we have balanced it up every evening it's too late to go anywhere."

839 STAYING POWER

"Your wife seems a garrulous woman."

"Garrulous? Why, if I suddenly went dumb it would take her a week to find it out."

840 CRAMPING HIS STYLE

Golfer: "Hi, caddie! Isn't Major Pepper out of that bunker yet? How many strokes has he had?"

Caddie: "Seventeen ordinary, sir, and one apoplectic!"

841 NEVER ENDING MARATHON

Gibbs: "My wife always has the last word."

Gabbs: "You're lucky. Mine never gets to it."

842 PERFECT ALIBI

Hubby: "What became of that unpaid bill Dunn and Company sent to us?"

Wife: "Oh, that? I sent it back marked insufficient funds."

843 GIVING IT THE WORKS

Maud: "So Jack said that I had a skin one loves to touch."

Marie: "Not exactly, dear; he said you had a skin you love to retouch."

844 ROCK OF AGES

"What is the mortar board I hear mentioned so often?" asked the little girl.

"I'll try to explain," said Miss Cayenne, "although it is a slightly complicated matter. A mortar board carried by a builder often has cement on top and worn by a college professor often has concrete under it."

845 ALL SEWED UP

"John, I found this letter in your coat pocket this morning. I gave it to you a month ago to mail."

"Yes, dear, I remember. I took that coat off for you to sew a button on and I'm still waiting."

846 A LITTLE WIDER, PLEASE

Judge (in dentist chair): "Do you swear that you will pull the tooth, the whole tooth, and nothing but the tooth?"

847 DEAD LETTER BARITONE

"Yessah, Ah's a great singah."

"Wheah did you-all learn to sing?"

"Ah graduated from a correspondence school."

"Boy, you sho' lost lots of yo' mail."

848 SUCCESS

Bride: "I cooked my first meal last night—it was a grand success."

Visitor: "How nice!"

Bride: "Yes, he's going to get me a cook right away."

849 WHEN WORDS FAIL

The golfer stepped up to the tee and drove off. The ball sailed straight down the fairway, leaped onto the green and rolled into the hole. The golfer threw his club in the air with excitement.

"What have you suddenly gone crazy about?" asked his wife, who was trying to learn something about the game.

"Why, I just did a hole in one," yelled the golfer, a wild gleam of delight in his eyes.

"Did you?" asked his wife placidly. "Do it again, dear, I didn't see you."

850 OH YOU CALIFORNIA!

Millionaire Jones was recalling the struggles of his youth. "I was living in California, and my parents in New York," he said, "and I had just managed to save enough money to buy myself a bicycle when my father wrote that my mother was ill.

"I jumped on my bicycle and rode across the continent, only to be told that California air was all that would save my mother.

"So I dragged the bike in beside the bed, let the California air out of the tires, and she lived to the good old age of 95."

851 OUT OF TUNE

Two elderly men at a club were discussing the table manners of a new member.

"Well, what do you think of him?" asked one.

"Very remarkable," replied the other, thoughtfully, "I've heard soup gargled and siphoned, but upon my word, that's the first time I've ever known it to be yodeled."

852   SLIGHT ERROR

Joan: "John, dear, your office is on Broad Street, isn't it?"
John: "Yes, why?"
Joan: "That's funny. I told that to Daddy and he said he'd been looking you up in Bradstreet."

853   CHRONIC KNOCKER

"Anything the matter with the car?"
"Well, there's only one part of it that doesn't make a noise and that's the horn."

854   PRINCIPLES ARE PRINCIPAL

When William died suddenly the neighbors were shocked, and a kindly woman proceeded to comfort William's wife by describing his good points.
"He was such a man of principle," said the neighbor.
"And am I not the one to know it?" said the bereaved woman. "Every Saturday night didn't he come home and place his pay envelope in front of me as regular as clockwork? Not a night did he miss all the time we were married.
"Of course, the envelope was always empty, but look at the principle of the thing!"

855   IRRESISTIBLE

Customer: "I've come back to buy that car you showed me yesterday."
Salesman: "That's fine, I thought you'd be back. Now tell me what was the dominant feature that made you decide to buy this car?"
Customer: "My wife, sir."

856   UNANIMOUS

Warden: "Boys, I've had charge of this prison for ten years and we ought to celebrate the occasion. What kind of party would you suggest?"
Prisoners (in unison): "Open house."

857   WHAT THEY THINK

What they think when little Oswald starts to school for the first time.
His mother: "Just think, my little darling is almost grown up."
His father: "I hope he makes a fullback."
His older sister: "That means I've got to walk to school with him and can't go to school with the kids."
His teacher: "I hope he's smarter than he looks."
His neighbors: "Thank heaven! Now we can have peace for a few hours a day."
His dog: "Yo-o-ow-l-l-l."

858   A MATTER OF CONVENIENCE

Teacher: "Why does the cream rise to the top of the milk?"
Johnny: "So the people can get it."

859 HE KNOWS

Teacher: "Johnny! Can you tell me what a waffle is?"
Johnny: "Yes'm: it's a pancake with a non-skid tread."

860 AN OMISSION

A London welfare club gives an annual bathing outing to newsboys.
Said one: "I say, Bill, ain't you dirty!"
Bill: "Yes, I missed the train last year."

861 "SOCIALIZED" MEDICINE

Janice: "So Lillie threw over that young doctor she was going with!"
Clarice: "Yes, and what do you think? He not only requested her to return his presents but sent her a bill for forty-seven visits."

862 ETERNAL FEMININE

Young Coed: "Oh, Dad, I've just discovered that the girl who sits next to me in Bio. has a hat exactly like mine."
Father: "So I suppose you want me to buy a new one?"
Coed: "Well, darling, that would be cheaper than changing schools."

863 QUIZ

"Are you a good student?"
"Yes and no."
"What do you mean?"
"Yes, I am no good."

864 LADIES NOTE

Quiggle: "Why is it that you women always insist on having the last word?"
Mrs. Quiggle: "We don't. The only reason we get it is that we always have a dozen arguments left when you stupid men are all run out."

865 A NAG, A BONE AND A HUNK OF HAY

He: "How do you feel after your ride on that horse?"
She: "Gosh! I never thought anything filled with hay could be so hard!"

866 DIPLOMACY

Customer: "Have you anything for gray hair?"
Conscientious Druggist: "Nothing, madam, but the greatest respect."

867 BAFFLING

She had spent a full hour instructing her third grade class in some of the wonders of nature, and just by way of a clincher she said: "Isn't it wonderful how little chickens got out of their shells?" One little eight-year old lad, quite practical, quizzed back, "What gets me is how they got in!"

868 CARELESS

Old Lady (meeting a one-legged tramp on the street): "Poor man, you have lost a leg, haven't you?"
Tramp (looking down): "Well, I'll be darned if I haven't!"

69   CAREFUL

The alert Shelby (Ala.) Democrat reports the case of a man who was
efeated ignominiously when he ran for the office of Sheriff.
He got 55 votes out of a total of 3,500, and the next day he walked down
Main Street with two guns hanging from his belt.
"You were not elected, and you have no right to carry guns," fellow-citizens
ld him.
"Listen, folks," he replied, "a man with no more friends than I've got in
iis county needs to carry guns." *The American Mercury*.

70   RESULTS DUBIOUS

"Did Mr. Borer sing a popular song at the concert?"
"Well, it had been popular before he sang it."

71   NO BLUFFING NECESSARY

"Now that you're a success as a character actor and are going to be married,
ill you build your house on a bluff?"
"I should say not—her father's paying for it."

72   WITH ONE EXCEPTION

"Why, he's the loudest-mouthed man I ever heard."
"Shush, dear, you forget yourself."

73   IT'S EASY

Hunter: "How do you detect an elephant?"
Guide: "You smell a faint odor of peanuts on his breath."

74   THE OLD THIEF

"The new washerwoman has stolen two of our towels."
"The thief! Which ones, dear?"
"The ones we got from the hotel in Miami."

75   HOPEFUL

Boss: "Henry, you're a liar. You took a day off to bury your mother-in-law,
nd I met her in the park this morning."
Henry: "Oh, I didn't say she was dead, sir. I just said I would like to go to
er funeral."

76   CLIPPED WINGS

At a fancy dress dance for children a policeman stationed at the door was
istructed not to admit any adults.
An excited woman came running up to the door and demanded admission.
"I'm sorry, ma'am," replied the policeman, "but I can't let anyone in but
iildren."
"But my child is in there as a butterfly," exclaimed the woman, "and has
rgotten her wings!"
"Can't help it," replied the policeman, "orders is orders. You'll have to let
er represent a caterpillar!"

877   SISTER'S VIEWPOINT
Coed: "What position does your brother play on the team?"
Sister: "A sort of crouched, bent position."

878   A GRACIOUS RIVAL
Modern political campaigners might take a lesson in graciousness and kind
ness from Edward Campbell, the great British statesman.
Once when Campbell was opposing Thackeray for a seat in Parliament, the
two contenders, in the course of their campaigning, met and engaged in
friendly conversation.
On taking leave of his rival Thackeray remarked, "May the best man win!"
"Oh, no," replied Campbell. "I hope not, I want to win!"

879   HIGHLAND PLAYBOYS
MacGregor and MacPherson decided to become teetotalers, but MacGregor
thought it would be best if they had one bottle of whisky to put in the cupboard
in case of illness.
After three days MacPherson could bear it no longer and said: "MacGregor
Ah'm not verra weel."
"Too late, MacPherson, Ah was verra sick m'sel' all day yesterday."

880   WANTED A LESSON
Gentleman (at police station): "Could I see the man who was arrested
for robbing our house last night?"
Desk Sergeant: "This is very irregular. Why do you want to see him?"
Gentleman: "I don't mind telling you. I only want to ask how he got in
the house without awakening my wife."

881   SLAM
The landlady brought in a plateful of extremely thin slices of bread and
butter, which rather dismayed her hungry men boarders.
"Did you cut these, Mrs. Brown?" asked one.
"Yes, I cut them," came the stern reply.
"Oh," said the boarder, "all right, I'll deal!"

882   LEAVE IT OUT
Mrs. Newbride: "I took the recipe for this cake out of the cook book."
Hubby: "You did perfectly right, dear. It never should have been put in."

883   FORGETFUL
The mill foreman came upon two darkies walking slowly up the road, single
file.
"Say, you, why ain't you working?"
"We's working, boss, sho' nuff. We's carrying this plank up to the mill."
"What plank? I don't see any plank."
"Well, fo' de land's sake, Abe, ef we ain't gone an' forgot de plank."

884   GOOD SWIMMER
Sally Anne (aged six): "Granddad, were you in the ark?"

Granddad: "Why no, honey."
Sally Anne: "Then why weren't you drowned?"

885 SHORT CUT

"Officer, what's the quickest way to the hospital?"
"Close your eyes, cross this street, and you'll be there in fifteen minutes."

886 INVOLUNTARY CONTRIBUTION

Preacher: "And when I get through with my sermon I'll ask those of the congregation who want to contribute $5 toward the mortgage on the church to stand up. In the meantime you play appropriate music."
Organist: "What do you mean, appropriate music?"
Preacher: "You play The Star Spangled Banner."

887 SAFETY FIRST

Singer: "Now that you've heard my voice, what would you suggest to accompany me?"
Impresario: "A body-guard."

888 THE AVERAGE MOTORIST

Service station man: "How much gasoline does the tank in your car hold?"
Autoist: "I don't know. I've never had enough money to get it filled yet."

889 SOME REST

Sergeant: "Did you sleep well on your cot? I'm afraid it was a little hard and uneven, but ——"
Conscript: "It was all right, sir. I got up now and then during the night and rested a little, you know."

890 FLATTERED

The new traffic cop had been told by his inspector to overtake and stop a speeding car. Ten minutes later he rang up to report: "Car was being driven by an actress. I stops her, pulls out my notebook. She snatches it, writes her autograph and leaves me standing."

891 ARCTIC STYLE HINTS

Teacher: "Now, Freddy, why does a polar bear wear a fur coat?"
Freddy: "Oh—er, well, I suppose he would look funny in a tweed one."

892 SAME BREAD

The orderly officer received a complaint about the issue of bread.
"Soldiers should not make a fuss about trivialities, my man," he said. "If Napoleon had had that bread when he was crossing the Alps, he'd have eaten it with delight."
"Yes, sir," said the lance corporal, "but it was fresh then."

893 SPHERE OF INFLUENCE

Frederick S. Isham, the novelist, has offered this story to refute the belief that the Chinese are not a humorous people.
Two Chinese many years ago were discussing a visit William Howard Taft had just made to Shanghai.

F

"Taft is a big man," one of them exclaimed, making a gesture to outline a large circle.

"Big man," the other repeated. "We have certainly had large sphere of American influence in our midst recently."

894   PERFECT FIT

Salesman: "See there, mister, that hat fits perfectly. How does it feel?"
Buyer: "Okay, unless my ears get tired."

895   STANDING ROOM

Patient: "Doctor, is my mouth opened wide enough?"
Doctor: "Yes. You see, I always stand on the outside while pulling a tooth."

896   SAFETY ZONE

Cop: "Hey, what are you doing there?"
Driver: "Parking my car. It seemed such a good place. The sign said 'Safety Zone.'"

897   OF COURSE NOT

Interviewer: "What have you to say about anonymous letters?"
Professor: "They're stupid; I read them, but I never answer them."

898   JUST A PAWN

"He is the secretary of a chess club."
"But what does he do?"
"He reads the hours of the last meeting."

899   FAR BEHIND

"European military leaders claim they have the people behind them."
"In war, of course, the positions are immediately reversed."

900   ALWAYS FAITHFUL

"Is he the sort of fellow who forgets you when you have no money?"
"No, he's an installment collector."

901   GENEROUS

Sue: "I believe my husband is the most generous man in the world."
Lou: "How's that?"
Sue: "Well, I gave him a dozen of the loveliest neckties for Christmas, and he took them right down and gave them to the Salvation Army."

902   THE POWER OF EDUCATION

The new minister in a Georgia church was delivering his first sermon. The janitor was a critical listener from a back corner of the church. The minister's sermon was eloquent and his prayers seemed to cover the whole category of human wants.

After the service one of the deacons asked the old janitor what he thought of the new minister. "Don't you think he offers up a good prayer, Joe?"

"Ah mos' suhtainly does, boss. Why, dat man axed de good Lord fo' things dat de odder preacher didn't even know He had!"

903   FITTING COMPARISON

She: "You remind me of the ocean."
He: "Wild, restless and romantic?"
She: "No; you just make me sick."

904   THE PROOF WAS THERE

"It says the man was shot by his wife at close range."
"Then there must have been powder marks on the body."
"Yes, that's why she shot him."

905   JUST CURIOUS

Boss: "Now what do you want? I thought I fired you two weeks ago."
Ex-Office Boy: "Oh, I just came back to see if you were still in business."

906   SLIGHTLY SUSPICIOUS

Defense Counsel: "Do you mean to insinuate that my client is a thief?"
Witness: "No sah, Ah don't, Mistah Lawyah, but Ah do say effen Ah wuz
a chicken an' Ah saw him hangin' around, Ah sho'ly would roost way up high."

907   FOREWARNED

Mistress: "Marie, when you wait on the table tonight for my guests, please
don't spill anything."
Maid: "Don't you worry, ma'am, I never talk much."

908   CLASSROOM CANDOR

The president of the school board, being of a conscientious nature, made it
a point to visit all the schoolrooms frequently. In each room he would make a
little talk in an effort to interest the children in the everyday things of life.
On one such occasion, he was telling them of the blacksmith. "And what
kind of arm has the blacksmith?" he asked.
"Big!" shouted the children.
"And why is the blacksmith's arm bigger than mine?"
"He works!" came the chorused reply.

909   BROADMINDED TRAVELER

Mr. Newrich (touring in his new car): "Where are we now?"
Chauffeur: "Halfway between Paris and Marseilles, sir."
Mr. Newrich: "Don't bother me with niggling little details. What country
are we in?"

910   MUG DRILL

Sergeant: "Did you shave this morning, Jones?"
Recruit: "Yes, sergeant."
Sergeant: "Well, next time stand a bit closer to the razor."

911   STREAMLINED

"Say," said the woman customer over the 'phone, "the next time I order
chicken don't send me any more airplane fowls."
"What do you mean—airplane fowls?" asked the butcher.
"You know what I mean; all wings and machinery and no body."

912   FRESH EGGS

A bachelor was breakfasting in a restaurant when he saw an inscription on an egg: "Should this meet the eye of some young man who desires to marry a farmer's daughter, age 20, write. . . ."

The bachelor wrote and in a few days received the following note: "Your letter came too late. I am now married and have four children."

913   "ENNUI"

A very dull play was talked of, and one attempted a defense by saying, "It was not hissed."

"True," said another, "no one can hiss and yawn at the same time."

914   CHEERFUL DEADHEAD

Filling-station Attendant: "Here comes another I.W.W. customer."

Patron: "What's that?"

Attendant: "A motorist who wants only Information, Wind and Water."

915   ANOTHER SCOTCH STORY

"How much are your peaches?"

"Penny each, lady."

"I'll have one, please."

"Givin' a party?"

916   UNSCRAMBLING HES AND SHES

The vicar, awarding prizes at the local dog show, was scandalized at the costumes worn by some members of the younger fair sex.

"Look at that youngster," said he; "the one with cropped hair, the cigarette and breeches, holding two pups. Is it a boy or a girl?"

"A girl," said his companion. "She's my daughter."

"My dear sir!" The vicar was flustered. "Do forgive me. I would never have been so outspoken had I known you were her father."

"I'm not," said the other. "I'm her mother."

917   ALPINE JOURNEY

"Does the giraffe get sore throat if he gets wet feet?"

"Yes, but not until the next week."

918   CANINE ERUDITION

"Lay down, pup; lay down," ordered the man. "Good doggie—lay down, I say."

"You'll have to say, 'Lie down,' mister," declared a small bystander. "That's a Boston terrier."

919   PRIMITIVE CELLOPHANE

Teacher: "Robert, explain what are the functions of the skin."

Bobby: "The chief function of the skin is to keep us from looking raw."

920   HUSH! THE WALLS HAVE EARS

Willie: "Paw, does bigamy mean that a man has one wife too many?"

Paw: "Not necessarily, my son. A man can have one wife too many and still not be a bigamist."

921 TIME TO DUCK

"I see you advertised your saxophone for sale," said the friend.

"Yes," he sighed, "I saw my neighbor in the hardware store yesterday buying a gun."

922 RUSHED

Joe: "Are you doing much in your business now?"

Harry: "I should say so! Why, we are so busy that we employ a man to insult new customers."

923 NOWADAYS ONE SPECIFIES

"Get my broker, Miss Jones."

"Yes, sir, stock or pawn?"

924 UP THE OTHER ALLEY

The Congressman's wife sat up in bed, a startled look on her face. "Jim," she whispered, "there's a robber in the house."

"Impossible," was her husband's sleepy reply. "In the Senate, yes, but in the House, never."

925 MODERN CHILD

Photographer: "Watch and see the dicky bird."

Child: "Just pay attention to your exposure so that you do not ruin the plate."

926 ON THE SAFE SIDE

Rastus was in trouble again, and the judge asked him if he were guilty or not guilty.

"Guilty, suh, Ah thinks, but Ah'd rather be tried'n make sure of it."

927 CONTRAST

"I'll bet if I was married I'd be boss and tell my wife where to head in," declared the bachelor.

"Yes," retorted the old married man, "and I suppose when you get to a railroad crossing you honk your horn to warn the oncoming express to get out of your way, don't you?"

928 FRANK PROSPECT

Life Insurance Agent: "Do you want a straight life?"

Prospect: "Well, I like to step out once in a while."

929 LOST OPPORTUNITY

Wife (to husband inquiring what she thought of his speech): "You didn't make the most of your opportunities."

Husband: "What opportunities?"

Wife: "Why, the opportunities you had of sitting down."

930 WHILE THERE'S LIFE THERE'S HOPE

Husband: "I've got to get rid of my chauffeur. He's nearly killed me four times."

Wife: "Oh, give him another chance."

931   LANDLUBBER

Rastus, on his first ocean trip, was desirous of getting off the boat.

"Say, Rastus," said a friend, "it's easy to see you're a landlubber, all right."

"You're right, boy," murmured Rastus. "And I'se just finding out how much I really lubs it."

932   NOT A BAD WISH

Mother was telling stories of the time she was a little girl. Little Harold listened thoughtfully as she told of riding a pony, sliding down the haystack, and wading in the brook on the farm.

Finally he said with a sigh, "I wish I had met you earlier, Mother."

933   PERFECT SPECIMEN

"And at her request you gave up drinking?"

"Yes."

"And you stopped smoking, for the same reason?"

"I did."

"And it was for her that you gave up dancing, card parties, and billiards?"

"Absolutely."

"Then why didn't you marry her?"

"Well, after all this reforming I realized I could do better."

934   ONE AT A TIME

A very stout man was walking on the promenade of a seaside town when he noticed a weighing machine with the notice: "I speak your weight."

He put a penny in the slot and stood on the platform. A voice answered: "One at a time, please!"

935   GR-R-R!

Noticing that little Joan was struggling with an ear of corn, her mother offered to cut off the kernels. However, she was quickly rebuffed when Joan replied:

"No, I like it on the bone!"

936   COMPARISONS

She: "The Brownes must be awfully rich, judging from the clothes they wear."

He: "Oh, one can never tell. Some of the most gorgeous flowers haven't got a scent."

937   WISE BOY

Teacher: "Jimmy, name a great time saver."

Jimmy: "Love at first sight."

938   BACK ON THE PAY ROLL

"Did that star football player graduate last year?"

"No, he renewed his contract for another year."

939   SPEED

A tourist grouch was traveling in a desolate part of a southern state. He stopped at a filling station and waited impatiently while the attendant slowly serviced his car. Lolling lazily in the shade next to the station were two natives. The tourist mumbled under his breath, but loud enough for all to hear, "These people around here are the laziest I ever saw."

One of the lollers turned to the other and drawled, "Say, Bill, I seed a dog chasin' a rabbit yes'erday, but they weren't in no hurry—both were walkin'."

940 OLD-TIMER

"What model is your car?"

"This car ain't no model—it's a horrible example."

941 HIS ERROR

Him: "Well, I suppose you're plenty angry because I came home with this black eye last night."

Her (sweetly): "Not at all, dear. You may not remember it, but when you came home you didn't have that black eye."

942 BRAGGING

"I started in life without a penny in my pocket," said Smith.

"And I," put in Jones, "started in life without a pocket."

943 SURELY FEMININE

Visitor: "And what will you do, little girl, when you get as big as your mother?"

Little Girl: "Diet!"

944 EFFICIENCY MEASURE

Customer: "Why do you have magazines on the table here, with stories of horrible murders, mysteries and ghosts?"

Barber: "Well, it makes the customer's hair stand on end, and then it's easier to cut."

945 PLAYING SAFE

"You remembers when you cured mah rheumatism a year ago, don't you, Doctah?" asked the colored patient, "and told me not to get mahself wet."

"Yes, Ephraim," replied the doctor.

"Well, I jes wants to ask you if you thinks it's safe for me to take a bath now?"

946 PERFECTLY GENTLE

Insurance Agent: "Now that you're married and have the responsibility of a wife, you will want to take out some insurance."

Mr. Newlywed: "Insurance? Shucks, no. Why she's not the least bit dangerous."

947 WELL CHARGED

Two women were discussing a mutual acquaintance.

"She has a very magnetic personality," said one woman.

"She ought to have," replied the other woman, "every stitch she has on is charged."

948 HI-HAT POOCH

Customer: "Has this dog a good pedigree?"

Salesman: "Has he? Say, if that dog could talk, he wouldn't speak to either of us."

949 ON THE WAY

Actor (to Manager): "Poor house, tonight!"

Manager: "You're wrong. It's the poorhouse tomorrow."

950 BELOW PAR

Ned: "What did Miss Petite say after you kissed her?"

Ted: "She told me to call on Friday hereafter, because that was Amateur Night."

951 TRIED THEM ALL

"Do we have to wait very much longer for mummy, Daddy?"

"No, not now. They've just taken the last pair of shoes out of the window."

952 COURTEOUS RETORT

Operator: "Pardon me, madam, but your girl seems more than twelve."

Her Mother: "Operator, would you take me to be the mother of a girl that age?"

Operator: "Lady, don't tell me you're her grandmother!"

953 COMMON FAILING

Mother: "Do you know what happens to little girls who tell lies?"

Small Betty: "Yes, they grow up and tell their little girls they'll get curly hair if they eat their spinach."

954 THE BIGGEST HEAD

A Sunday-school teacher had been telling her class of boys about the crowns of glory they might wear in the hereafter.

"Now, boys," she said, "can you tell me who will get the biggest crown?"

"Yes, mum," said one of the pupils. "Him wot's got the biggest head!"

955 COMPLIMENT

Stout lady (at a street crossing): "Officer, could you see me across the street?"

Officer (inclined to flattery): "Why Ma'm, I could see you a mile off."

956 NEW JOB

"I'se got a new job, so I cain't do yo' washin' no mo'."

"What is it, Mandy?"

"My new job is dat I cain't work. I'se on relief."

957 STRENGTH

On a certain Sunday morning the pastor of a Negro congregation noticed that an old face had reappeared among his flock, and after the sermon made it a point to welcome the supposedly repentant backslider.

"This is the first time I have seen you at church for a long time," he said. "I'm sh'ly glad to see you here."

"Ah done had to come," explained Rastus. "Ah needs strengthenin'. I'se got a job whitewashin' a chicken coop and buildin' a fence aroun' a watermelon patch."

958   HM-M

It was during the impaneling of a jury that the following colloquy occurred:
"You are a property holder?"
"Yes, your Honor."
"Married or single?"
"I have been married five years, your Honor."
"Have you formed or expressed an opinion?"
"Not in five years, your Honor."

959   RIGHT

"So you want to try that proofreader job, eh?"
"Yes, sir."
"And do you understand all the responsibility attached to it?"
"Yes, sir, when you make a mistake, I take all the blame."

960   UNNATURAL HISTORY

Teacher: "Can anyone tell me what causes trees to become petrified?"
Bright Student: "The wind makes them rock."

961   NO END

"Mamie," said Maud, "what is an ultimatum?"
"I don't know exactly," was the reply. "But judging from the way it is used in diplomatic correspondence I should say it was modern Latin for 'to be continued in our next.'"

962   PARTNERSHIP

Mose: "Does yo' wife take in washin'?"
Rastus: "Ah shud say not. Ah takes it in an' Ah takes it out. All she does is stay home an' wash it."

963   HOUSE DETECTIVE

"Mummy, I want to whisper something."
"Darling, big girls that are nearly five never whisper before company."
"All right then, but that gentleman over there took another cake when you weren't looking."

964   ECONOMIZING ON THE PIANO

A tramp paused outside a large house, and as he did so another of his kind came shuffling out of the gate.
"Any luck, mate?" asked the first tramp.
"It ain't no use tryin' there," was the reply. "It's a poverty-stricken 'ole. There was a couple o' women tryin' to play on one blinkin' pianner!"

965   NEW CROP

"What do you think is the trouble with farming?"
"Well," replied Farmer Bentover, "in my day when we talked about what we could raise on 60 acres, we meant corn—not loans."

F*

966   No Hurry

A doctor had an urgent 'phone call from a gentleman saying his small son had swallowed his fountain pen.

"All right! I'll come at once," replied the doctor, "but what are you doing in the meantime?"

Whereto came the unexpected answer, "Using a pencil."

967   Nothing to It

"We don't need any of them new-fangled scales in Ireland," said O'Hara. "There's an aisy way to weigh a pig without scales. You get a plank and put it across a stool. Then you get a big stone. Put the pig on one end of the plank and the stone on the other end of the plank, and shift the plank until they balance. Then you guess the weight of the stone and you have the weight of the pig."

968   Evolution

Teacher: "Yes, go on, Tommy. After the horse comes the motor car, and (prompting) after the motor car comes the ——"

Tommy (whose father has a car): "Installment man, miss."

969   More Than Was Expected

Johnny, 10 years old, applied for a job as grocery boy for the summer. The grocer wanted a serious-minded youth, so he put Johnny to a little test. "Well, my boy, what would you do with a million dollars?" he asked.

"Oh, I don't know—I wasn't expecting so much at the start," said Johnny.

970   Hey, That Man's in Again!

"I must pay my tailor's bill first."

"Why so?"

"Well, it's the most pressing one."

971   House-Broken

"Does your husband expect you to obey him?"

"Oh, dear, no. You see he's been married before."

972   All Explained

Johnnie: "Why does the whistle blow for a fire?"

Billy: "It doesn't blow for the fire, it blows for water. They've got the fire."

973   Wasted Alarm

"Pat," said the manager of the factory, "I want you to report to me at 6 o'clock tomorrow morning. Here's an alarm clock."

The next morning arrived. Pat was met by a frowning manager.

"Well, what was the matter? Didn't the alarm clock go off?"

"Oh, yes, sorr, it went off all right, but the trouble was that it went off while I was asleep."

974   Theological Mainspring

Two ministers were driving in a cab to the station, and were in some anxiety lest they should miss their train. One of them pulled out his watch and discovered it had stopped.

"How annoying!" he exclaimed. "And I always put such faith in that watch!"

"In a case like this," answered the other, "good works would evidently have answered the purpose better."

975   STILL CACKLING

Customer: "Are these eggs fresh?"

Grocer: "Fresh! Why, the hens haven't missed them yet."

976   LUCID INTERVALS

An American film actress was applying for a passport.

"Unmarried?" asked the clerk.

"Occasionally," answered the actress.

977   ALIBI IKE

Bobby: "Mamma, what is a 'Second-Story Man'?"

Mrs. Joe Bungstarter: "Your father's one. If I don't believe his first story, he always has another one ready."

978   LONG, LONG TRAIL

The chief objection to the school of experience is that you never finish the post-graduate courses, says an exchange.

When you graduate from that school, brother, your diploma is a tombstone.

979   FLEAS AND ELEPHANTS

Teacher (to bring out the idea of size): "Mention a difference between an elephant and a flea."

Tommy: "Well, an elephant can have fleas, but a flea can't have elephants."

980   STRICTLY ORIGINAL BLUNDERING

Teacher: "Did your father help you with the problem?"

Willie: "No, I got it wrong myself."

981   PENALTY OF BEING ADORED

First Guy: "She treats her husband like a Grecian god."

Second Guy: "How's that?"

First Guy: "She places a burnt offering before him at every meal."

982   DOWN AND OUT

The aviation instructor, having delivered a lecture on parachute work, concluded:

"And if it doesn't open—well, gentlemen, that's what is known as 'jumping to a conclusion.'"

983   BOSSIE'S LITTLE WEAKNESS

A city girl visiting her uncle on the farm was watching a cow chewing her cud.

"Pretty fine cow, that," said her uncle as he came by.

"Yes," said the girl, "but doesn't it cost a lot to keep her in chewing gum?"

984   WHEN MAUDE GETS LEFT

"Doesn't that mule ever kick you?"

"No, sah, he ain't yet, but he frequently kicks de place where Ah recently was."

985   ALL QUIET AMIDSHIPS

"I'm planning to travel on one of those stabilized steamships."

"It will cost you more."

"Maybe, but expenses aren't what I have to keep down on my sea trips."

986   CHAPTER AND VERSE

"My wife has the worst memory I ever heard of."

"Forgets everything, eh?"

"No; remembers everything."

987   OUT FOR THE LONG SHOTS

"Where's the cashier?"

"Gone to the races."

"Gone to the races in business hours?"

"Yes, sir, it's his last chance of making the books balance."

988   NO LAGGING VETERAN

Betty on a visit to her aunt, being offered some left-over fragments, politely declined them.

"Why, dear, don't you like turkey?" inquired her aunt.

"Only when it's new," said Betty.

989   OUT OF THE FRYING-PAN

Teacher: "Really, Johnny, your handwriting is terrible. You must learn to write better."

Johnny: "Well, if I did, you'd be finding fault with my spelling."

990   PATIENT RESEARCH

A party of tourists were enjoying the wonders of the Grand Canyon. A native passing by was asked by the driver of the car:

"I say, neighbor, can you tell us what caused this terrible gorge?"

"Well, they say a Scotchman once owned a ranch near here, and one day he lost a golf-ball down a gopher hole."

991   EMULATING A MASTER

"You say your son plays the piano like Paderewski?"

"Yes. He uses both hands."

992   ONE-WAY ARGUMENT

Telephone Operator: "It costs seventy-five cents to talk to Bloomfield."

Caller: "Can't you make a special rate for just listening? I want to call my wife."

993   EDUCATIONAL LIMITATIONS

"How soon shall I know anything after I come out of the anesthetic?"

"Well, that's expecting a lot from an anesthetic."

994   BLESSED ARE THE HUMBLE

Editor: "Do you know how to run a newspaper?"
Applicant: "No, sir."
Editor: "Well, I'll try you. You talk like you've had experience."

995   SHOCKING POLITENESS

Policeman: "How did you knock him down?"
Motorist: "I didn't! I pulled up to let him go across—and he fainted."

996   TOO MUCH COMPETITION

Not long ago a jury went out early in the day on a simple case, and when it came near the time for court to adjourn, his honor sent for the jury, and asked the foreman if they required any further instruction. "We need no instruction, your Honor," replied the foreman, "but here are eleven prejudiced and unreasonable men who won't agree to anything."

997   IN A CONFERENCE

A little boy was saying his go-to-bed prayers in a very low voice.
"I can't hear you, dear," his mother whispered.
"Wasn't talking to you," said the small one firmly.

998   PEDAGOGY

At a recent "panel discussion" in one of our great universities several speakers aired their views on "creative education," solemnly or otherwise. One speaker got up to remark: "I have discovered that if you have pupils of greater ability, you will get better results"; and the walls of that university (it is averred) rocked with this momentous announcement. Someone suggested that the speaker would have been much better advised had he said something like this: "If the correlation of intrinsic competency to actual numerical representation is definitely high, then the thoroughly objective conclusion may inexpugnably be reached that the scholastic derivations and outgrowths will attain a pattern of unified superiority." No one would have known what he was talking about, and he would thereafter have been regarded with awe as a pedagogical pundit.—*Henry Grattan Doyle*

999   CHEERS FOR WILLIE!

"Who gave the bride away?"
"Her little brother, Willie. He stood right up in the middle of the ceremony and yelled, 'Hurray, Louise, you've got him at last!'"

1000   NO REFERENCE

Would-be employer: "Young man, do you have references from your last place of employment?"
Applicant: "Yes, sir. Here's their letter. It reads:
'To whom it may concern. We had Sam Jones working for us for three weeks and we can truthfully say we are satisfied!'"

1001   FRIGID AIR

An electrician was examining an electric refrigerator that was using too much electricity and could not find the reason.

He idly asked the cook, "How do you like the refrigerator?"

"I like it fine," she said. "I open the door and it cools off the whole kitchen."

1002 FASHION NOTES

"Anna Mae," said the mistress of the house, finally giving way to curiosity, "I notice you have been taking our empty grapefruit hulls home with you. Do you mind telling me what you do with them?"

"Yes'm," the maid admitted, "I been takin' 'em 'cause I think they make my garbage look so stylish."

1003 CALL AN AMBULANCE

"Waiter, are you sure this ham was cured?"

"Yes, sir."

"Well, it's had a relapse."

1004 INN LUCK OR INN DUTCH

"Why don't you give your new bungalow a name? Something appropriate. Other people do. There's 'Seldom Inn,' 'Walk Inn,' 'Cosy Inn,' and a lot of others."

"That's an idea. As I've just finished paying for it, I'll name it 'All Inn.'"

1005 WHAT PRICE "K"?

Mother (teaching alphabet): "Now, dear, what comes after O?"

Child: "Yeah!"

1006 MOM WAS NO PROPHET

When supper was served Helen refused a second helping of ice cream with a polite but wistful, "No, thank you!"

"Do have some more, dear!" her hostess urged.

"Mother told me to say, 'No, thank you,'" Helen explained naïvely, "but I don't think she could have known how small that first helping was going to be!"

1007 SUPER SERVICE

Speaking of banks, there was an Irishman who opened an account, his first. At the end of the month he got a statement, which meant absolutely nothing to him, but he was delighted to receive his checks.

"Sure, an' it's a smart bank I'm after dealin' with," he told a pal.

"Is it that now?" was the rejoinder.

"Faith, an it is. Them fellers was smart enough to get every one av me checks back for me."

1008 SOUTHPAW

"Does it make any difference on which side of you I sit?" she asked.

"Not a bit," he replied. "I'm ambidextrous."

1009 ALIVE AND FRESH

Fish Dealer: "Lobsters, madam; nice lobsters? Look, they're all alive."

Lady: "Yes, but are they fresh?"

1010   MRS. BEAVER: MR. MUD-TURTLE

Mistress: "So your married life was very unhappy? What was the trouble? December wedded to May?"

Chloe Johnson: "Lan' sake, no, mum! It was Labor Day wedded to de Day of Rest!"

1011   SHORT CIRCUIT

An electrician returned home from work one night to find his small son waiting for him with his right hand swathed in a bandage.

"Hello, sonny!" he exclaimed. "Cut your hand?"

"No, Dad," was the reply. "I picked up a pretty little fly and one end wasn't insulated."

1012   THUMBS DOWN SLIGHTLY

Children have their own peculiar way of expressing themselves.

"Well, Peggy," said the neighbor, "and how do you like your new governess?"

Peggy thought a moment and then said: "I half like her and I half don't like her, but I think I half don't like her the most."

1013   ANNUAL STEW

"Do you summer in the country?"

"No, I simmer in the city."

1014   JOB FOR THE ICEMAN

Bride: "I made this pudding all by myself."

Hubby: "Splendid! But who helped you lift it out of the oven?"

1015   EARLY BIRD VARIETY

"Is your husband a bookworm?"

"No, just an ordinary one."

1016   ALWAYS A NIGHT OWL

The young bride was asked what she thought of married life.

"Oh, there's not much difference," she replied. "I used to wait up half the night for George to go, and now I wait up half the night for him to come home."

1017   THE WORST BOOM

When the president of the Los Angeles Chamber of Commerce was asked recently how the depression had hit Los Angeles, he replied, "Depression? We have no depression in Los Angeles, but I will admit that we are having the worst boom in many, many years."

1018   CHEERING INNOVATION

Real Estate Agent: "Well, what do you think of our little city?"

Prospect: "I'll tell you, brother. This is the first cemetery I ever saw with lights."

1019   When Dads Disappoint

Tommy: "That problem you helped me with last night was all wrong, Daddy."

Father: "All wrong, was it? Well, I'm sorry."

Tommy: "Well, you needn't exactly worry about it, because none of the other daddies got it right, either."

1020   Call for Progress

Little Joan: "What do the angels do in heaven, mummy?"

Mother: "They sing and play harps."

Little Joan: "Haven't they any radios?"

1021   Where Whoppers Breed

"Can any of you," the teacher asked, "tell me what 'amphibious' means, and give a sentence to illustrate?"

A bright little Negro held up his hand. "I know, sah! It's fibbing. Rastus' fish stories am fibious!"

1022   Domestic Treasure

Wife: "How do you like the potato salad, dear?"

Hub: "Delicious! Did you buy it yourself?"

1023   Ducking Destiny

"Pop, will I look like you when I grow up?"

"Everybody seems to think so, son."

"Well, I won't have to grow up for a long time, will I, Pop?"

1024   Accredited Delegate

"Who will help a man to correct personality defects if not his wife?" asks a heart-throb editor.

Well, sister, there is his wife's mother.

1025   Lets Him Do His Stuff

"What! Another new dress? How ever do you think I can find the money to pay for it?"

"Darling, you know I'm not inquisitive."

1026   Financial Genius

"Father," said Junior, "what is a financial genius?"

"A financial genius, my son," answered his harassed pater, "is a man who can earn money faster than his family can spend it."

1027   When Nerves Are Raw

His wife: "It's about time to think about where we shall spend the summer."

Closeman: "I wish you'd say 'pass' the summer, Helen; 'spend' is so confoundedly suggestive."

1028   Human Nature

"My gosh, Bill," groaned the managing editor of the tabloid, "nothing scandalous has happened in twenty-four hours. What'll we do for the front page?"

"Aw, don't get discouraged, Steve," the city editor comforted. "Something'll happen. I've still got faith in human nature."

1029 HOUSE-BROKEN

We congratulated a lady on her silver wedding anniversary for living twenty-five years with the same man.

"But he is not the same man he was when I first got hold of him," she replied.

1030 FIGS OF THISTLES

"Your methods of cultivation are hopelessly out of date," said the youthful agricultural college graduate to the old farmer. "Why, I'd be astonished if you got even ten pounds of apples from that tree."

"So would I," replied the farmer. "It's a pear tree."

1031 BALANCING THE BUDGET

Teacher: "We borrowed our numerals from the Arabs, our calendar from the Romans, and our banking from the Italians. Can any one think of other examples?"

Charlie: "Our lawn-mower from the Smiths, our phonograph from the Browns, and a pair of steps from Miss Evans."

1032 ON THE FRONTIER

A backwoodswoman, the soles of whose feet had been toughened by a lifetime of shoelessness, was standing in front of her cabin fireplace one day when her husband addressed her:

"You'd better move your foot a mite, maw, you're standin' on a live coal."

Said she, nonchalantly: "Which foot, paw?"

1033 PAWNSHOP

"What do the three balls in front of a pawnshop mean?"

"Two to one you don't get it back."

1034 MUST HAVE BEEN A CLOSE SHAVE

Barber: "What's the matter? Ain't the razor takin' holt?"

Victim: "Yeah, it's taking holt all right, but it ain't lettin' go again."

1035 WANTED TO HELP ON THE TREASURE HUNT

A burglar, who had entered a poor minister's house at midnight, was disturbed by the awakening of the occupant of the room he was in. Drawing his weapon, he said:

"If you stir, you are a dead man. I'm hunting for your money."

"Let me get up and strike a light," said the minister, "and I'll hunt with you."

1036 MAYBE SHE WAS TIRED

"When you asked her to dance did she accept quickly?"

"Did she? Why, she was on my feet in an instant."

1037 CONCLUSIONS

The young bachelor was asked which he thought were happier, people who were married or people who were not.

"Well, I don't know," he replied, "sometimes I think there is as many as is that ain't, as ain't that is."

1038   A Perfect Example

The lecturer waxed eloquent as he warmed up to his subject. He wound up in this manner:

"Man, as we have seen, is a progressive being, but many other creatures are stationary. Take the ass, for example. Always and everywhere the ass is the same creature. You never have seen, and never will see, a more perfect ass than you see at the present moment!" A fellow in the back row: "Brother, you said it."

1039   Read the Directions That Come with Each One

The city girl watching the farmer milk a cow: "That looks easy, but how do you turn it off?"

1040   When Greek Meets Greek

Greek Tailor (looking at men's trousers just brought in): "Euripides?" Greek Customer: "Yah; Eumenides."

1041   Boys Who Tell Lies

Mother: "Do you know what happens to little boys who tell lies?" Johnny: "Yes, mother; they travel for half-fare."

1042   Center Aisle

A woman who had approached the office of a Broadway theater, was making a great fuss over the seat they gave her.

"Are you quite positive," she asked for the third time, "that this seat is near enough to the stage?"

"Madam," said the box office man, "if it was much nearer, you'd have to act in the play."

1043   Calling All Cost Accountants

"Why does cream cost more than milk?"
"Because it's harder for the cows to sit on the small bottles."

1044   In Reverse

Motorist (to man he just ran over): "Hey, look out back there!"
Defeated Soul: "What's the matter, y' ain't comin' back, are ya?"

1045   English

A Frenchman learning English said to his tutor: "English is a queer language. What does this sentence mean: 'Should Mr. Noble, who sits for this constituency, consent to stand again, he will in all probability have a walk-over'?"

1046   Page the Government Weather Bureau

A Swedish farmer who wanted to make his permanent home in this country appeared for his naturalization papers.

"Are you satisfied with the general conditions of this country?" he was asked.

"Yah, sure," answered the hopeful one.
"And does this government of ours suit you?"
"Well, yah, mostly," stammered the man, "only I lak see more rain."

1047 ALMOST MISSED

A big buck Indian had just ordered a ham sandwich at a drug-store and was peering between the slices of bread when he turned and said to the waiter: "Ugh, you slice 'em ham?"
The waiter replied: "Yes, I sliced the ham."
"Ugh," grunted the Indian. "You darn near miss 'em."

1048 NO LUMPS

"She asks how many lumps I'll have in my tea ——"
"Yeah?"
"So I tells her, 'I'll take mine smooth, please.'"

1049 NO CAUSE FOR COMPLAINT

"What's wrong, Henry?" asked his wife.
"My razor," boomed the voice within the bathroom. "It doesn't cut at all."
"Don't be silly. Your beard can't be tougher than linoleum."

1050 HE NEEDS A LITTLE MORE PRACTICE

"Melvin! MELVIN!"
"What, ma?"
"Are you spitting in the fish bowl?"
"No, ma, but I'm comin' pretty close."

1051 THE REWARDS OF AUTHORSHIP

The critic started to leave in the middle of the second act of the play.
"Don't go now," said the manager. "I promise there's a terrific kick in the next act."
"Fine," was the retort; "give it to the author."

1052 GOOD REASON

"But this officer says that while you were in a drunken state you tried to climb a lamp-post."
"Yes, I did, your worship, but three crocodiles had been following me about all night, and they were getting on my nerves."

1053 IT'S ALL CLEAR NOW

A cockney telephoned to inquire the rate to Ealing, a suburb of London. The man at the other end of the line couldn't catch the name of the station, so in desperation he asked the cockney to spell it. Quickly came the reply: "E—for 'Erbert, A—wot the 'orses heat, L—w'ere yer goes w'en yer dies, I—wot yer sees wiv, N—wot lays a hegg, G—Gowd bless me. Get me?" *Wall St. Journal.*

1054 NOT SURE

"You've been out with worse-looking fellows than I am, haven't you?"
She did not reply.

"I said, you've been out with worse-looking fellows than I am, haven't you?"
"I heard you the first time. I was trying to think."

1055 How to Paraphrase

The pupil was asked to paraphrase the sentence: "He was bent on seeing her."

He wrote: "The sight of her doubled him up."

1056 Never Over Thirty

Friend: "You can't cheat old father time."
Man: "No, but some of the women drive a mighty close bargain with him."

1057 Not Brave But Generous

"Did he take his misfortunes like a man?"
"Precisely. He laid the blame on his wife."

1058 Stew Bad

Diner: "Waiter! This stew is terrible. What kind is it?"
Waiter: "The chef calls this his enthusiastic stew."
Diner: "Why?"
Waiter: "He puts everything he has into it."

1059 One Time They Don't Change Their Minds

A little girl, sitting in church watching a wedding, suddenly exclaimed:
"Mummy, has the lady changed her mind?"
"What do you mean?" the mother asked.
"Why," replied the child, "she went up the aisle with one man and came back with another."

1060 Slightly Sarcastic

"How is it that you are late this morning?" the clerk was asked by his manager.
"I overslept," was the reply.
"What? Do you sleep at home as well?" inquired the manager.

1061 So That's Where They Go After Graduation

Tourist (in Yellowstone Park): "Those Indians have a blood-curdling yell."
Guide: "Yes, ma'am; every one of 'em was a college cheer leader."

1062 The Enemy

"Sir, the enemy are before us as thick as peas!"
"All right, shell them!"

1063 Why Stay Longer

Mother (to small son who is going to a party): "Now, dear, what are you going to do when you've had enough to eat?"
Little Tommy: "Come home."

1064 Three Beans

A teacher called for sentences using the word "beans."
"My father grows beans," said the bright boy of the class

"My mother cooks beans," said another pupil.
Then a third popped up: "We are all human beans."

1065   No, Thanks

Mother: "Marilyn, were you a good little girl at church today?"
Marilyn: "Yes, mother. A man offered me a big plate of money, and I said, 'No, thank you.'"

1066   Using His Head

Sergeant: "Why is it important not to lose your head in an attack?"
Recruit: "Because that would leave no place to put the helmet."

1067   Higher Mathematics

Judge: "What's the charge against this man, officer?"
Officer: "Bigotry, yer honor. He's got three wives."
Judge: "I'm surprised at your ignorance, officer. That's trigonometry, not bigotry."

1068   The Frog Are a Wonderful Bird

This short essay on frogs, by a young immigrant from Norway, was reported by the Chicago Board of Education: "What a wonderful bird the frog are. When he stand, he sit almost. When he hop, he fly almost. He ain't got no sense hardly. He ain't got no tail hardly, either, when he sit on what he ain't got almost." *Houston Chronicle.*

1069   Hash

"Bring me a plate of hash," said the diner.
The waiter walked over to the kitchen elevator. "Gent wants to take a chance," he called down the speaking tube.
"I'll have some hash too," said a second customer.
The waiter picked up the tube again. "Another sport," he yelled.

1070   Of One Mind

"You say you never have a quarrel with your wife?"
"Never. She goes her way and I go hers."

1071   Smart Worms

Earth flew in all directions as the crimson-faced would-be golfer attempted to strike the ball. "My word," he blurted out to his caddie, "the worms will think there's been an earthquake."
"I don't know," replied the caddie, "the worms 'round here are smart. I'll bet most of them are hiding underneath the ball for safety."

1072   That Makes Them Even

Matron (at the counter): "I suspect that you're giving me awfully short weight for my money!"
Grocer: "Well I'm positive you're giving me an awfully long wait for mine."

1073   The Last Word

Wife: "Must I persuade you to have some more alphabet soup?"
Hubby: "No, thanks, not another word."

1074 DEFINITELY

"My wife doesn't know what she wants."
"Hah, you're lucky. Mine does!"

1075 IT SOUTHERNLY WAS

He: "Honey, will yo' all marry me?"
She: "Oh, this is so southern!"

1076 AQUATIC ENGINEER

"My brother's an aquatic engineer."
"What's that?"
"He's in charge of the dish-washing!"

1077 MAKE MINE WELL

An old cowpuncher entered a restaurant and ordered a steak. The waiter brought it to him, and it was rare, very rare. The cowpuncher demanded that it be taken back and cooked.
"It's already cooked," the waiter snapped.
"Cooked," roared the cowpuncher. "I've seen cows hurt worse than that and they got well."

1078 WEIGHTY EVIDENCE

The portly man was trying to get to his seat at the circus. "Pardon me," he said to a woman, "did I step on your foot?"
"Possibly so," she said, after glancing at the ring. "All the elephants are still out there. You must have."

1079 HOW MANY RABBITS MAKE A MINK COAT?

Glad: "Wonder why the magician wanted to borrow my mink coat."
Puss: "He probably wanted to pull rabbits out of it."

1080 A SOUND SLEEPER

"I slept like a log."
"Yes, I heard the sawmill."

1081 ONE IS ENOUGH

"There are ten reasons why I won't marry Joe."
"What are they?"
"Well, the first is he hasn't any money and the other nine are things I want."

1082 A SHIN-BRUISING GAME

"Is your wife a bridge fiend?"
"Yes, only a fiend could kick as hard as she does."

1083 SWEET YOUNG THING

Virginia Military Institute, the pride of the South, is sometimes referred to as "The West Point of the South." A sweet young thing from Lexington, Va., had been invited to one of the dances at West Point, and after a busy day of sightseeing over the grounds, she was asked by her escort how it had impressed her.

"Oh, it's wonderful," she answered admiringly. "Why, this must be the V.M.I. of the North."

1084 Too Thin

"Bring me another sandwich, please."
"Will there be anything else?"
"Yes, a paper weight. The last sandwich blew away."

1085 Caught in the Rain

"Waiter! Why is this milk so weak?"
"Why, the cows got caught in the rain."

1086 Poor Memory

Scientist (to Pharmacist): "Give me some prepared monaceticacidester of salicylic acid."
Pharmacist: "Do you mean aspirin?"
Scientist: "That's right! I can never think of that name."

1087 A Sizzler

A man in Chicago was grumbling about the heat. Said another, who had just returned from a trip through the South:
"Hot! Boy, you don't know what hot is. One day this week in Mississippi I saw a dog chasing a cat and they were both walking."

1088 Disillusioned

Every year college deans pop the routine question to their undergraduates: "Why did you come to college?" Traditionally the answers match the question in triteness. But last year one University of Arizona co-ed unexpectedly confided: "I came to be went with—but I ain't yet!"

1089 Fowl Talk

"Gosh, this is a tough chicken."
"Yeah, must have been a bad egg in its youth."

1090 How to Reduce in One Lesson

"What's the best exercise for reducing?"
"Just move the head slowly from right to left when asked to have a second helping."

1091 A Vacuum Tank

"His ears remind me of a pair of front fenders."
"They are big, aren't they?"
"And they're on the two sides of a vacuum tank."

1092 Too Personal

Judge: "Are you guilty or not guilty?"
Prisoner: "It seems to me that is a mighty personal question."

1093 Well Laid Out

"Isn't this town laid out prettily?"
"It's laid out all right. How long has it been dead?"

1094   Two Sides to Every Question

"There are two sides to every question," proclaimed the wise man.

"Yes," said the fool, "and there are two sides to a sheet of flypaper, but it makes a difference to the fly which side he chooses."

1095   One Stranger Present

The preacher was at ease after service Sunday night.

"Many folks in church?" asked his wife.

"Yes, good attendance—and a stranger was present, but I did not see him."

"But how do you know?"

"There was a dollar bill in the contribution box."

1096   Coward

"How'd you get along with that fight with your wife, the other night?"

"Aw, she came crawling to me on her knees."

"Yeah, what did she say?"

"Come out from under that bed, you coward."

1097   Honest

"Are your neighbors honest?" the old negro was asked.

"Yassir, dey is."

"But you keep that loaded shotgun near your hen coop."

"Yes, dat's to keep 'em honest."

1098   The American Tourist

"Yes, there is something smaller still than an atom," said a patriotic citizen to his friend.

"What is it?"

"The American tourist in Europe who curries favor by knocking his own country."

1099   Holding Out

Mr. Meek: "Darling, haven't I always given you my salary check the first of every month?"

Mrs. Meek: "Yes, but you never told me you got paid twice a month—you low-down, unprincipled embezzler."

1100   Too Fresh

Mrs. Newlywed: "Aren't these eggs rather small today?"

Grocer: "Yes'm, but the farmer who sells me my eggs had to start to town early this morning and took them out of the nest too soon."

1101   Ghost Stories

"I'm a great lover of ghost stories."

"So'm I, pal. Let's shake."

1102   There Is a Difference

Teacher: "What is the difference between results and consequences?"

Bright Pupil: "Results are what you expect; consequences are what you get."

1103   COLLEGE

"Do you think your son will forget everything he learned in college?"
"I hope so. He can't make a living just making love to the girls."

1104   POOR MANAGEMENT

Ole, the night porter, was testifying before the jury after the big bank robbery.

"You say," thundered the attorney, "that at midnight you were cleaning the office, and eight masked men brushed past you and went on into the vault room with revolvers drawn?"

"Yah," said Ole.

"And a moment later a terrific explosion blew the vault door off, and the same men went out past you carrying currency and bonds?"

"Yah," said Ole.

"Well, what did you do then?"

"Aye put down my mop."

"Yes, but what did you do after that?"

"Vel, Aye say to myself, 'dis bane hell of a way to run a bank.'"

1105   COURTESY

"What would be the proper thing to say if, in carving the duck, it should skid off the platter and into your neighbor's lap?"

"Be very courteous. Say, 'May I trouble you for that duck?'"

1106   IN THE DUMPS

"Whenever I'm in the dumps I just get myself another hat."
"I wondered where you get them."

1107   THE EFFECT OF RADIO

The Man: "I want a loaf of Mumsie's Bread, a package of Krunchies, some Goody Sanny Spread, Ole Mammy's Lasses, Orange Pully, a pound of Aunt Annie's sugar candy, Bitsey-Bite size."

The Clerk: "Sorry. No Krunchies. How about Krinkly Krisps, Oatsie-Toasties, Malty-Wheaties, Riceltes, or Eatum-Wheatums?"

The Man: "The Wheatums, then."

The Clerk: "Anything else? Tootsies, Tatery Chips, Cheesie Weesies, Gingile Bits, Itsey Cakes, Sweetzie Toofums, or Dramma's Doughnies?"

The Man (toddling toward the meat department): "Dot to det some meat."

1108   WEIGHED AND FOUND WANTING

"So you met Marian today?"
"Yes. I hadn't seen her for ten years."
"Has she kept her girlish figure?"
"Kept it? She's doubled it."

1109   DEFINITE PROOF

Counsel (to police witness): "But if a man is on his hands and knees in the middle of the road, that does not prove he is drunk."

Policeman: "No, sir, it does not. But this one was trying to roll up the white line!"

1110 SPECIAL SERVICE

Owner of Midget Car: "I want a half a pint of gasoline and a teaspoonful of oil, please."

Garage Hand: "And shall I cough into the tires, sir?"

1111 VEGETARIANS

"Ever bothered with tramps out your way?"

"No, I have a sign on the gate reading: 'We are vegetarians, but our dog isn't.'"

1112 A RAISE WAS NECESSARY

Bookkeeper: "I'll have to have a raise, sir; there are three other companies after me."

Employer: "Is that so? What companies?"

Bookkeeper: "Light, 'phone and gas."

1113 COLORFUL WRITING

The native student, writing a letter to the superintendent of the mission, desired to end with the words: "May Heaven preserve you."

Not being quite confident of the meaning of "preserve," he looked it up in a dictionary. When the letter reached the superintendent, it ended with the words: "And may Heaven pickle you."

1114 THE WRONG TIME

One night, as a messenger from the office of an evening paper was passing along the ways on the banks of the river, he heard the sound of someone struggling in the water.

"Are you drowning?" he shouted.

"I am," replied a feeble voice from the water.

"What a pity!" said the lad consolingly. "You are just too late for the last edition tonight. But cheer up; you'll have a nice little paragraph all to yourself in the morning."

1115 OBSTINATE

The clergyman was walking through the village when he met one of his parishioners.

"How's your cold, Donald?" he asked.

"Verra obstinate," replied the parishioner.

"And how is your wife?"

"About the same."

1116 WILD OATS AND RYE

Mother: "After all, he's only a boy, and boys will sow their wild oats."

Father: "Yes, but I wouldn't mind if he didn't mix so much rye with it."

1117 HE MAY BE RIGHT

"How many students are there in the university?"

"About one in every five."

1118   HYPNOTISM AND MARRIAGE

"I was hypnotized last week."

"What's hypnotized mean?"

"Why, to hypnotize is to get a man in your power, and make him do whatever you want."

"That's not hypnotism, that's marriage."

1119   NO MIND READER

First New Year's Eve celebrator: "What are you doing?"

Second celebrator: "Writing a letter to myself."

First: "What does it say?"

Second: "I don't know. I won't get it until tomorrow."

1120   SPELLING

School Visitor: "What's the matter, my boy?"

Pupil: "Palpitation and insomnia."

School Visitor: "But you can't be suffering from these things."

Pupil: "It isn't suffering, sir. It's spelling."

1121   HE LOOKED FAMILIAR

An enthusiastic golfer came home to dinner. During the meal his wife said: "Willie tells me he caddied for you this afternoon."

"Well, do you know," said Willie's father, "I thought I'd seen that boy before."

1122   TEACHING BY ILLUSTRATION

Prof: "How much does a twelve-pound shot weigh?"

Frosh: "Don't know, sir."

Prof: "Well, then, what time does the ten o'clock train leave?"

Frosh: "Ten o'clock."

Prof: "Then what is the weight of the twelve-pound shot?"

Frosh: "Ten pounds, sir."

1123   GIVING THE PASSWORD

The young negro recruit was the victim of so many practical jokes that he doubted all men and their motives. One night while he was on guard, the figure of one of the officers loomed up in the darkness.

"Who goes dere?" he challenged.

"Major Moses," replied the officer.

The young negro scented a joke.

"Glad to meet yuh, Moses," he said cheerfully. "Advance and give de ten commandments."

1124   IMPOSSIBLE

Visiting Delegate (to hotel clerk): "Why didn't you call me at 7:30 this morning?"

Clerk (politely): "Because you didn't go to bed till eight."

1125   PUNCTUAL

"Well, son," wrote the fond mother to her soldier son, "I hope you have been punctual in rising every morning so that you haven't kept the regiment waiting breakfast for you."

1126   THE TIDE AND THE UNTIED

Inquiring Schoolboy: "Dad, what effect does the moon have on the tide?" Dad (from the depths of his newspaper): "Not any, son. Only on the untied."

1127   FIVE MEN ON A HORSE

Beta (at riding academy): "I wish to rent a horse."
Groom: "How long?"
Beta: "The longest you've got, there will be five of us going."

1128   WITHOUT ASKING QUESTIONS

A doctor was called in to see a very testy aristocrat. "Well, sir, what's the matter?" he asked cheerfully.

"That, sir," snapped the patient, "is for you to find out."

"I see," said the doctor thoughtfully. "Well, if you'll excuse me for an hour or so, I'll go along and fetch a friend of mine—a veterinarian. He's the only chap I know who can make a diagnosis without asking questions."

1129   TREES TO A GOLFER POET

"I think that I shall never see a hazard rougher than a tree—a tree o'er which my ball must fly if on the green it is to lie; a tree which stands that green to guard, and makes the shots extremely hard; a tree whose leafy arms extend, to kill the mashie shot I send; a tree that stands in silence there, while angry golfers rave and swear. Niblicks were made for fools like me, who cannot ever miss a tree."

1130   HE KNEW THE ANSWERS

A member of a psych class on tour asked an inmate his name.

"George Washington," was the reply.

"But," said the perplexed lad, "last time we were here you were Abraham Lincoln."

"That," said the inmate sadly, "was by my first wife."

1131   DID SHE ASK FOR THIS?

Woman Political Speaker: "What is home without a mother?"
Man in the Back Row: "Your baby!"

1132   THE SERGEANT AND THE ROOKIE

"Com-pa-nee atten-shun," bawled the drill sergeant to the awkward squad. "Com-pa-nee, lift your left leg and hold it straight in front of you."

By mistake one member held up his right leg, which brought it out side by side with his neighbor's left leg.

"And who is the galoot over there holding up both legs?" shouted the hard-boiled sergeant.

1133   COUNSEL FOR THE DEFENSE RESTS

A case was being heard in court in which a farmer was claiming indemnity for a cow killed by a railway train. Counsel for the defense put many tedious and superfluous questions.

"Was the cow on the track?" he asked the engineer.

The engineer had had about enough. He replied: "No, of course not. She was in a field half a mile away. But when it saw her, the engine left the rails, jumped the fence, and chased her across the field and up a tree. There it strangled her to death."

1134   STRAIGHT TO THE POINT

During the progress of a law suit a witness was on the stand for cross-examination regarding the character and habits of the defendant. "I believe you testified a little while ago," began the counsel for the plaintiff, "that Mr. Smith, defendant in this case, has a reputation for being very lazy and personally incompetent."

"No, sir; no, sir," protested the witness. "I didn't say that. What I said was he changed jobs pretty often; that he seemed to get tired of work very quickly."

"Has he or has he not a reputation in the community for being lazy?" persisted the lawyer.

"Well, sir, I don't want to do the gentleman any injustice, and I don't go so far as to say he is lazy; but it's the general impression around the community that if it required any voluntary and sustained exertion on his part to digest his food, he would have died years ago from lack of nourishment."

1135   STREAMLINED

A young woman walked into a railroad ticket office in Chicago and asked for a ticket to New York. "Do you wish to go by Buffalo?" asked the ticket agent. "Certainly not!" she replied, "I want to go by train."

1136   WORRIED ABOUT HIS FUTURE

Joe: "You look down-hearted, old man. What are you worried about?"

Bill: "My future."

Joe: "What makes your future seem so hopeless?"

Bill: "My past."

1137   THE POOR ANIMAL

When Mrs. Berg's expensive new fur coat was delivered to her home, she fondled it ecstatically for a time, and then looked sad for a moment.

"What's the matter, aren't you satisfied with it?" inquired her husband.

"Yes," she answered, "but I feel so sorry for the poor thing that was skinned."

"Thanks," said Mr. Berg.

1138   INFORMATION PLEASE

Mother: "Stop asking so many questions. Don't you know that curiosity killed the cat?"

Small daughter: "Is that so? What did the cat want to know?"

1139   THE STRATEGY OF HANDLING PEOPLE

A girl was driving in her new car when something went wrong with the engine. The traffic light changed from green to red and back to green and still she could not get the car to budge. The traffic cop came up.

"What's the matter, Miss?" he inquired. "Ain't we got colors you like?"

1140   CURIOUS

"These rock formations," explained the guide, "were piled up here by the glaciers."

"But where are the glaciers?" asked a curious old lady.

"They've gone back, Madam, to get more rocks," said the guide.

1141   POLITENESS

Father: "Well, Willie, what did you learn at school today?"

Willie (proudly): "I learned to say 'Yes, sir' and 'No, sir' and 'Yes, ma'am' and 'No, ma'am'."

Father: "You did?"

Willie: "Yeah."

1142   SHOWERS FOR THE GROOM

"Daddy," said Bobby, "don't they ever give any showers for the groom?"

"No, son," replied his dad, "there will be plenty of storms for him after the bride begins to reign."

1143   ALL PREPARED

"I want to grow some trees in my garden. Can you sell me a few seeds?" inquired Mrs. Newlywed.

"Certainly, madam," replied the clerk. He fetched her a packet.

"Can you guarantee these?" she asked.

"Yes, madam, we can."

"Will the trees be tall and thick in the trunk?"

"They should be, madam."

"And quite strong at the roots, I suppose?"

"Oh yes, madam."

"Very well, I'll take a hammock at the same time."

1144   A POOR SUBSTITUTE

There is a colored church in the South that holds annual strawberry festivals. Each year they put out the same large sign in front of the church. A Northerner was driving through the town. He saw the big sign in front of the church reading, "Everybody come to the annual strawberry festival. All the delicious strawberry shortcake you can eat for 25¢. Everybody welcome at the strawberry festival." Then at the bottom, they had tacked on this small notice: "P.S. This year, because of the drought, we is serving prunes." (This story can be used when one is called upon to substitute for another speaker. To illustrate, the substitute speaker might say after telling the story, "I rather fear that tonight what you will get will be prunes compared to the strawberry shortcake you would have received if the distinguished speaker who is absent could have addressed you.")

145   THE REASON THEY HURRY

Recently I told a fireman that I could understand why they hurried to the
fires, but I never could understand why they hurried back from them so
rapidly. He said they had to hurry back, because if they didn't they would
forget what was trump.

146   ALL OF ONE MIND

It is sometimes dangerous to have only one idea. In this case, there were
three men who had taken a few too many drinks. They had one idea in mind,
which was to catch the 11:05 P.M. train. A moment before train time they
rushed into the depot and got to the train just as it was pulling out. One of
them managed to get aboard; the second one caught hold of the hand-rail on
the coach and finally pulled himself up; the third fellow missed the train
altogether. As he sat on the platform, he began laughing, and one of the
spectators said, "I don't see what you have to laugh about, when you missed
the train." He said, "Well, the joke is on the other fellows who caught the
train, because they just came down to see me off."

147   CREDIT ONLY

Mr. Smith, a southern merchant, had sold Rastus, a cotton planter, on
credit during the period before the cotton was ready to be picked and sold.
When Rastus sold his cotton, he went to Smith's competitor across the street
and bought for cash. The next time Smith met Rastus he said, "Rastus, I sold
you on credit for months and now the first time you get cash you go across
the street and buy, instead of coming to me. What's the idea?" Rastus said,
"Boss, I'se sorry, but I didn't even know yo'all sold for cash."

148   PROFESSOR

I once had a classmate named Guesser
Whose knowledge got lesser and lesser.
  It at last grew so small
  He knew nothing at all—
And now he's a college professor.

Arizona Kitty Kat

149   THE GOLFER

"Who's that stranger, mother dear—
Look, he knows us, ain't he queer?"
"Hush, my own, don't talk so wild;
That's your father, dearest child."
"That's my father? No such thing!
Father died away last spring."
"Father didn't die, you dub;
Father joined a golfing club.
Now the club is closed, so he
Has no place to go, you see.
No place left for him to roam,
That is why he's coming home.

Kiss him, he won't bite you, child;
All them golfing guys look wild."

Boardwalk Illustrated News

1150   SAME FELLOW

The guide was showing the tourist the sights of Italy. He said, "Now here is the Leaning Tower of Pisa." The tourist said, "I didn't get the name." The guide repeated, "This is the Leaning Tower of Pisa." The tourist answered, "I still don't recognize the name, but it looks like the work of the contractor who built my garage."

1151   IT HAS TO BE HEARD

A musical critic wrote: "Here is Tchaikovsky at his best. Music so beautiful it has to be heard to be appreciated."

A lot of music is like that.

1152   A FRESH START

The famous Colonel Page of Civil War days, having been given the command of a company of raw recruits, put them through a preparatory drill, and then led them down a street in Philadelphia.

Suddenly from out of the ranks, came the command, "Halt!"

Involuntarily the men came to a stop.

"Who gave that command?" yelled the enraged colonel.

"Potts, sir, Potts," answered a dozen voices.

"What do you mean, sir, by giving that command?" the colonel profanely inquired.

"Well, sir," replied Private Potts, "I've been trying for two blocks to get the company to keep step with me, and they wouldn't do it. So I had to stop them so they could get started all over again."

1153   UP ON HIS HYBRIDS

Little Jimmy, age four, was looking at a picture book. When he came to a picture of a zebra, mother asked him what animal that was.

Jimmy thought a moment, then replied, "That's a cow that ate hybrid corn."

1154   NO OBJECTION

It was the young man's first visit to the home of his adored one, and he seemed to be making a very good impression.

"Have you any objection to a whisky-and-soda?" asked his prospective father-in-law.

"Well," replied the young man, "I've never had one before."

The father stared. "What, never had a whisky-and-soda?"

"No, sir; never had an objection."

1155   TROUBLED HIM JUST ONCE

Doctor: Have you ever had trouble with dyspepsia?

Patient: Only once.

Doctor: And when was that?

Patient: When I tried to spell it.

1156   PAID IN FULL

A country doctor called upon a widow, soon after the death of her husband, and announced his intentions of cutting his bill, for services rendered, in half. With tears in her eyes, the old lady reached out and clasped the doctor's hand and in a trembling voice said, "God bless you, my good friend. I'll be as good as you and knock off the other half."

1157   GIVE 'EM MORE TIME

"Have you any children, Mr. Smith?"
"Yes—three."
"Do they live at home with you?"
"Not one of them—They are not married, yet."

1158   WHY IT CAN'T BE DONE

Boy: "But they say, dear, that two can live as cheaply as one."
Girl: "That may be so, darling, but it'll take something for mother."

1159   GOOD PHILOSOPHY

One day on my asking him why he took such long steps in walking a Scotch friend of mine replied: "Whin I was a wee lad me Mither used to say to me, 'Laddie, whin ye're a walkin' ye should take longer steps an' wear yer brogs the less the mile.'"

1160   CLOCK WATCHER

Mr. Jones: Say, did you hear about Jim getting drowned?
Mrs. Jones: No, couldn't he swim?
Mr. Jones: Yes, but he belonged to the union. He swam eight hours and then quit.

1161   MAGIC

A little girl went into a large business establishment, and had her first ride in an elevator. "How did you like it?" asked her father.
"Why, it was so funny," answered the child. "We went into a little house, and the upstairs came down."

1162   ORDERS

Joe: "I traveled as a salesman the entire summer, and only received two orders."
Sympathetic one: "Too bad; who gave you those?"
Joe: "Every one—Get out, and stay out!"

1163   COMPLETELY OUTFITTED

Visitor (speaking of little boy): "He has his mother's eyes."
Mother: "And his father's mouth."
Child: "And his brother's trousers."

1164   JUST A SMALL ERROR

Three piano-movers knocked on the door of a house. A meek-looking man with an inferiority complex opened the door.

G

"Did you order a piano from the Flatnote Music Store?" asked the first piano-mover.

The tenant shook his head.

"Not a piano," he corrected. "I ordered a flute."

The piano-mover studied a slip of paper.

"Accordin' to this bill of ladin'," he grumbled, "you ordered a piano."

The gentleman with the inferiority complex studied the three husky piano movers.

"Very well," he said nervously, "move it in. But if your firm makes any more errors like that, I'll have to deal somewhere else!"

1165   HAD IT CORRECT

Teacher: "Johnny, can you tell me the name of a city in Alaska?"
Johnny: "Nome."

1166   WASTING GAS

Little George was visiting his aunt. He found the cat in a sunny window purring cheerfully.

"Oh, Auntie, come quick," said Little George, "the cat has gone to sleep and left his engine running."

1167   THE REASON

A servant asked her mistress if she would be good enough to advance her a few dollars out of her next month's wages, and gave the reason as follows:

"You see our minister is leaving and we are collecting money so that we can give him a little 'momentum.'"

1168   AMERICAN?

"Is he a typical American?"

"Yes, he likes baseball, has a fast car, owes a mortgage, pays alimony, and thinks moving pictures have grand opera beaten a mile."

1169   CONFUSED

"What parable in the Bible do you like best?" was the question asked of a little boy. And the answer was, "The one about the fellow that loafs and fishes."

1170   TRAFFIC COP

Traffic Cop (producing notebook): "Name, please."
Motorist: "Aloysius Alastair Cyprian."
Traffic Cop (putting book away): "Well, don't let me catch you again."

1171   EMPTY HEAD

"I have a cold or something in my head."
"A cold, undoubtedly."

1172   TACT

Young Husband: "Last night when I got home, my wife had my chair drawn up before the fire, my slippers ready for me to put on, my pipe all filled, and——"

Old friend: "How did you like her new hat?"

173 **FREE**

"How long in jail fo', Moses?"
"Two weeks."
"What am de cha'ge?"
"No cha'ge; everythin' am free."

174 **FREE TOWELS**

"Mother, was your name Pullman before you were married?"
"No dear, why do you ask?"
"Well, I just wondered. I see that name on a lot of our towels."

175 **ANCESTORS**

"Speaking of old families," said the aristocrat of the party, "one of my ancestors was present at the signing of the Magna Charta."
"And one of mine," said little Abe, who was one of the push, "vos present at the signing of the Ten Commandments."

176 **D.D. OR M.D.**

The temporary member of a golf club wished to fix up a game. The secretary introduced him to one Doctor Clark.
"Now, Doctor," said the stranger with a twinkle of the eye, "it is important for me to know whether you are a doctor who preaches or one who practices."

1177 **A LITTLE HOARSE**

Aunt Prudence: "Keep away from the loudspeaker, Denny. The announcer sounds as if he had a cold."

1178 **THE OTHER HALF POUND**

"I sent my little boy for two pounds of plums and you only sent a pound and a half. Are your scales correct?"
"My scales are all right, madam. Have you weighed your little boy?"

1179 **AIN'T WORTH IT**

Rastus: "Here's dat quarter Ah borrowed from you last year."
Sambo: "Yuh done kep' it so long dat Ah don't know if it's wuff while for me to change my 'pinion of yuh jes' fo' two bits."

1180 **EFFICIENCY**

The department store engaged an efficiency expert, whose obsession was to move the departments to different parts of the store every day. One day a section would be on the top floor, the next it would be in the basement, and on the third it would be placed where the restaurant had been.
After three weeks of this an old lady approached a harassed floorwalker and asked him if he could tell her where the draperies department was.
"No, madam," he said wearily; "but if you'll stand here for a few minutes I'm sure you'll see it go by!"

1181 **REINCARNATION**

She (thoughtfully): "Did you ever think much about reincarnation, dear?"
He (otherwise): "Think about it? I eat it nearly every day, only we call it hash."

1182   I Don't Know

Prof.: "What three words are used most among college men?"
Frosh: "I don't know."
Prof.: "Correct."

1183   Should Know Better

Mother: "Willie, why did you kick your little brother in the stomach?"
Willie: "It was his own fault. He turned around."

1184   Last Chance

Flying over the Bay of Naples, an air pilot turned to his passenger and said:
"Have you ever heard that phrase, 'See Naples and Die'?"
"Yes," said the passenger.
"Well," said the pilot, "take a good look—the propeller's come off."

1185   Usually the Case

Smith: "So your son is in college? How is he making it?"
Smithers: "He isn't. I'm making it and he's spending it."

1186   That for You!

Prospective Customer: "Do you keep fountain pens here?"
Clerk (brightly): "No, we sell them."
Prospective Customer: "Okay, but keep the one you might have sold me if
you hadn't been so smart."

1187   Half Educated

Over in a corner near the fireplace, Uncle Ezry had been working indus-
triously with a stub pencil and a piece of paper. Suddenly he looked up and
smiled. "Doggone!" he exclaimed. "If I ain't learned to write."
Maw got up and looked over his shoulder at the lines scrawled across the
paper. "What do it say?" she asked.
"I don't know," said Uncle Ezry, puzzled. "I ain't learned to read yet."

1188   Afraid

Mother: "Has William come in yet?"
Sister: "I think so. I haven't seen him, but the cat is hiding."

1189   Rural Free Delivery

A Kansas farmer stopped at a bank to see if he could get a loan on his farm.
"It might be arranged," said the banker. "I'll drive out with you and
appraise it."
"You don't need to bother," said the farmer, noticing a huge cloud of dust
rolling up the road. "Here it comes now."

1190   He Was First

Oliver was careless about his personal effects. When his mother saw clothing
scattered about on the chair and floor, she inquired: "Who didn't hang up his
clothes when he went to bed?"
A muffled voice from under the covers murmured, "Adam."

1191   MY MISTAKE

She: "Sorry, darling, I'm afraid I'm late."
He: "Humph! Only half an hour."
She: "Oh, I thought I was late."

1192   SIGN OF IMPROVEMENT

Doctor: "How's the patient this morning?"
Nurse: "I think he's regaining consciousness. He tried to blow the foam off his medicine."

1193   CONSERVATION

One Chinese bragged to another that he made a fan last twenty years by opening only a fourth section, and using this for five years, then the next section, and so on.

The other Chinese registered scorn.

"Wasteful!" he ejaculated. "I was better taught. I make a fan last a lifetime. I open it wide, and hold it under my nose quite motionless. Then I wave my head."

1194   SUBTRACTION

The school teacher was endeavoring to drum into her small pupils the fundamentals of arithmetic.

"Now, listen," she said rather desperately, "in order to subtract, things have to be the same denomination. This is what I mean. Now, you couldn't take three apples from four bananas, or six plums from eight peaches. It must be three apples from four apples, six plums from eight plums, and so on. Do you understand now?"

The majority of the children seemed to grasp the idea. One chubby-faced youngster very near the bottom of the class, however, raised a timid hand.

"Please, teacher," he said rather timidly, "you can take three quarts of milk from two cows."

1195   DRASTIC CHANGE

"Father," said the minister's son, "my teacher says that 'collect' and 'congregate' mean the same thing. Do they?"

"Perhaps, my son; perhaps they do," said the clergyman. "But there is a vast difference between a 'congregation' and a 'collection.'"

1196   HE KNEW

Hotel Guest: "Is there an Encyclopaedia Britannica in the hotel?"

Clerk (with polite attention and regret): "There is not, sir; but what is it you wish to know?"

1197   STYLE NOTE

"I see where a Chicago man proposes that a badge be given every person who pays all of his taxes promptly."

"Huh! A barrel would be more appropriate."

1198 FAIR OFFER

Suitor: "I would like to marry your daughter."

Business Man: "Well, sir, you can leave your name and address, and if nothing better turns up, we can notify you."

1199 QUALIFIED TO TALK

Mr. J. B. Forgan, in an address before a convention of the American Red Cross, indicated that he felt the members of the audience were more qualified to talk on the subject than he—"like the boy whose father thought he ought to be told something about the facts of life. It took considerable courage, but finally the father invited the boy into the living room after dinner, and after some hesitation said, 'Son, I should like to discuss with you some of the facts of life.' The boy said, 'Father, that is fine, what would you like to know?'"

1200 WHOSE REMARKS

Tony dropped a piece of heavy metal on his foot. His employer had to fill out a long blank under the workingmen's compensation plan. He filled everything out down to the last question, which simply said, "Remarks." He was stumped, and went out and asked the foreman, "What do they want in here—Tony's remarks, or mine?" (Can be used in asking an audience whose remarks they want on a specific subject.)

1201 HORTICULTURAL

Mrs. Newrich was fond of flowers and especially liked the salvia, but was not very reliable in getting the names right. She was giving directions to her gardener. "On this side of the walk," she said, "I want you to put out some salivas. Now what would you suggest for the other?"

"Well, madam," answered the gardener solemnly, "maybe it would be a good idea to put some spittoonias there."

1202 NOT SO ROMANTIC

Friend: "Did you get any replies to your advertisement that a lonely maiden sought light and warmth in her life?"

Spinster: "Yes, two from the electric light company and one from the gas company."

1203 A FEW REMARKS

If one wishes to make a few unrelated preliminary remarks, he may say in good humor, as Dr. Emory W. Luccock said at the beginning of an address: "I should like to make a few remarks before I say anything."

1204 NO LAUGHING MATTER

A married couple lived on the third floor: They were in financial difficulties and were unable to pay their rent. Finally they were put out. On the way down the stairs, she carried a lamp under one arm and a bird-cage in the other. He had the baby and a vacuum cleaner. The wife stopped and began to laugh. Finally, the husband said, "Mary, this is no laughing matter." She answered, "Yes, it is; this is the first time we have gone out together in nine years." And so—I am happy to see so many women here tonight with their husbands. (Told by Silas H. Strawn in beginning an address after a dinner.)

1205 UNACCUSTOMED AS I AM

When giving an address, many men appreciate the comment of the college student who was writing an examination and who had simply drawn the design of a tombstone in the upper right hand corner of his paper. On the tombstone he placed these words—"Sacred to the memory which leaves me on occasions like this."

1206 BEGINNING AN ADDRESS

In opening an address one might say: If I lived in this great city (state, splendid community) with its magnificent mountains, beautiful lakes, cultured people, etc., I know I could repeat what the fellow from Boston said. He said— "I live in Boston, so I never have to travel, because I am already there."

1207 CAMERA-ACTION

"Did they take an x-ray photo of your wife's jaw at the hospital?"
"They tried to, but they got a moving picture."

Chapter 5

WISE CRACKS AND EPIGRAMS

....

1208 When a woman motorist holds out her hand, you can be certain that she is going to turn to the right, to the left, or stop.

1209 In fairness, it ought to be conceded that the old-fashioned dime novel which is now selling for $2.50 is printed on better paper.

1210 Men are just opposite from guns; the smaller the caliber, the bigger the bore!

1211 Another good test of blood pressure is to watch a man being liberal with the money he owes you.

1212 If you build a big business, you're a sinister influence; if you don't, you re a darned failure.

1213 The modern idea of roughing it is to have no radio in the camp.

1214 Children have become so expensive that only the poor can afford them.

1215 What we need is a child labor law to keep them from working their parents to death.

1216 If all the college boys who slept in class were placed end to end, they would be much more comfortable.

1217 In every one of our universities, there are a number of aggressive, clean-cut young men who are diligently working their dads through college.

1218 The worst thing about football is that none of the cheer leaders ever get injured.

1219 If biologists are right in their assertion that there is not a perfect man today on the face of the globe, a lot of personal opinions here and there will have to be altered.

1220 It's easy to pick out the best people. They'll help you do it.

1221 Every man should remember that it is much easier to live within an income than to live without one.

1222 Back in our day the board of education was a shingle.

1223 A college education seldom hurts a man if he's willing to learn a little something after he graduates.

1224 The only thing that can keep on growing without nourishment is an ego.

1225 Many a man thinks he has an open mind when it's merely vacant.

1226 As a general rule, a man who doesn't know his own mind hasn't missed so much at that.

1227 Oftentimes, it's the mink in the closet that is responsible for the wolf at the door.

1228 Profits, not prophets, foretell the future.

1229 When a man "knocks" a town, he confesses he was a failure in it.

1230 Every day is Judgment Day—use a lot of it.

1231 Don't do so much conversational detouring before arriving at a point of interest.

1232 It doesn't matter whose pay roll you are on, you are working for yourself.

1233 When contentment enters, progress ceases.

1234 A crooked path is the shortest way to the penitentiary.

1235 You have heard of the old woman who said she always felt bad even when she felt good, for fear she would feel worse tomorrow.

1236 The joke was a Bob Feller—no hit.

1237 His coffee had been poured, saucered, and blown.

1238 No man in the world has more courage than the man who can stop after he has eaten one peanut.—*Channing Pollock*.

1239 Education is not given for the purpose of earning a living. Education is learning what to do with a living after you earn it.

1240 He found that what he wanted was always illegal, immoral, or fattening

G*

1241 I am the kind of a fellow who is always willing to give people the benefit of my inexperience in various lines. I saw a team of two donkeys stuck with a heavy load. I asked the farmer if he had tried twisting the tails of the donkeys. He said he knew all about that and was saving it for the next hill.—*Tom Collins.*

1242 The absent-minded professor rolled under the dresser and waited for his collar button to find him.

1243 The weaker the argument the stronger the words.

1244 We like a man that comes right out and says what he thinks, when he agrees with us.—*Ohio State Journal.*

1245 There are two sides to every question that we're not interested in.—*Ohio State Journal.*

1246 Many an argument is sound—merely sound.—*Tampa Daily Times.*

1247 A windshield that won't shatter is an improvement. Now give us rubber telephone poles.—*Washington Post.*

1248 Too much of the world is run on the theory that you don't need road-manners if you are a five-ton truck.—*El Paso Herald.*

1249 Occasionally you see a man driving a car so carefully that you conclude it must be paid for.—*Milwaukee Journal.*

1250 The automobile may be putting a few railroad trains out of business—but not when they meet on a grade crossing.—*Los Angeles Times.*

1251 According to Frank Case's "Tales of a Wayward Inn," the following saying originated with Wilson Mizner: "When you take stuff from one writer, it's plagiarism, but when you take it from many writers, it's called research."

1252 He is a ginger ale speaker—a good talker, but goes flat after he's uncorked a few minutes.

1253 He who laughs last is an Englishman.

1254 Very few people have the courage of my convictions.

1255 He had been dead long enough to be great.

1256 The region north of the ears is the greatest unemployed area in the world.

1257 About the time a man is cured of swearing, it's time to make up another income tax report.

1258 The way to return to Home Life from High Life is to put more paint on the house and less on the face.

1259 There is only one man living who can make a man out of you—that's you.

1260 It is a good idea not to believe more than half you hear and less than that of what you think.

1261 By the time father gets the vacation bills paid, it is time to think about Christmas presents.

1262 The first sandwich was said to have been made in the 17th century. Replicas of the original are exhibited in glass cases at all railway stations.

1263 Only possible reason we can see why old fools are the biggest fools is because they have had more practice.

1264 Nowadays a real football fan is one who knows the nationality of every man on the All-American team.

1265 Friends are folks who excuse you when you have made a fool of yourself.

1266 One view of an athletic man is the fellow who hires a small boy to cut the grass so he can play golf and obtain a little exercise.

1267 All the Constitution guarantees is the pursuit of happiness. You have to catch up with it yourself.

1268 An honest confession is good for the soul, but bad for the reputation.

1269 Humor, like history, repeats itself.

1270 If Adam came back to earth, the only thing he'd recognize would be the jokes.

1271 Note to hunters: If it stands on its hind legs, and has a pipe in its mouth, it isn't a squirrel.

1272 Trimming expenses is a Government's last resort when the tax-payers can stand no more trimming.—*Arkansas Gazette.*

1273 The fellow who thinks himself a wit is usually half right.

1274 There is a lot of history that isn't fit to repeat itself.—*Toledo Blade.*

1275 A lot of pity is wasted on animals. There are many contented cows, but who ever heard of a contented farmer?—*Buffalo Evening News.*

1276   Benjamin Franklin wrote: "Only two things in this life are certain—death and taxes." What the taxpayer resents is that they don't come in that order.—*Punch (London)*.

1277   When you see a married couple coming down the street, the one who is two or three steps ahead is the one that's mad.

1278   Headline: "Husband Leaves in Midst of Wife's Bridge Party; Disappears." Just a fugitive from the chin gang.—*Atlanta Journal*.

1279   *The Survey* tells of the young daughter of a radio announcer who, called upon to say grace at a family dinner, bowed her head and said in loud clear tones, "This food comes to us through the courtesy of Almighty God."—*Christian Register*.

1280   "An old fowl was recently discovered to have two hearts."—*News Item*. Sounds like the bridge partner I had last week.—*Smith's Weekly (Australia)*.

1281   Indians on a Western reservation are reported to be showing symptoms of uneasiness. Maybe some one has been telling them that the whites want to give the country back to them.—*Buffalo Evening News*.

1282   Lee Shippey, of the Los Angeles *Times*, has a head-line "How To Tell Ladies From Men Now that Both Wear Pants." That ought to be easy. The one that is listening is the man.—*Cincinnati Enquirer*.

1283   Liberalism may be coming into the churches, but it hasn't reached the contribution boxes yet.

1284   There's a bright side to everything, but there's no joy when it's on your blue serge suit.

1285   Among all the nations, we certainly play a loan hand.

1286   When people remove their bills from the envelopes, economic conditions are getting better.

1287   If the milk business ever becomes a public utility, we suppose that will make a cow a holding company.

1288   One nice thing about spending an evening at home is that you never have to redeem your hat after it's over.

1289   When men wear their Christmas neckties, business conditions are really bad.

1290   After the government takes enough to balance the budget, the citizen has the job of budgeting the balance.

1291   Nature is wonderful! A million years ago she didn't know we were going to wear spectacles, yet look at the way she placed our ears.—*Annapolis Log.*

1292   The only trouble with doing your Christmas shopping early is to get your wherewithal on the same schedule.

1293   You may get along at Christmas time without the holly, but you must have the berries.

1294   What the poets refer to as the touches of Spring aren't a marker to the touches of Christmas.

1295   Bragging may not bring happiness, but no man having caught a large fish goes home through an alley.

1296   Money is an article which may be used as a universal passport to everywhere except heaven, and as a universal provider of everything except happiness.

1297   If you can't make light of your troubles, keep them in the dark.

1298   A sharp tongue and a dull mind are usually found in the same head.

1299   The character of a man is his principles drawn out and woven into himself.

1300   It is better to remain silent and appear a fool, than to speak and remove all doubt.

1301   An optimist is one who makes the best of it when he gets the worst of it.

1302   Defeat is for those who acknowledge it.

1303   Get your happiness out of your work or you may never know what happiness is.—*Elbert Hubbard.*

1304   A failure is a man who is unable to cash in his experiences.—*Elbert Hubbard.*

1305   Don't feel sorry for yourself—feel sorry for the folks who have to live with you.—*Elbert Hubbard.*

1306   Common sense is the ability to detect values.

1307   The meanest habit in the world is that of self-pity.

1308   Our grandchildren are going to have a hard time paying for the good times we didn't have.

1309   Any idea a college professor has about money is almost certain to be theoretical.—*Grand Rapids Press*.

1310   You can't fool all of the people all the time, but somebody is trying it all the time.—*Savannah Morning News*.

1311   "It can be done" is good, but "it's done" is better.

1312   Talent knows *what* to do, tact knows *how* to do it.

1313   Talent makes a man *respectable*, tact makes him *respected*. Talent is *wealth*, tact is *ready money*.

1314   He is a well-known lecturer. In fact, he takes an annual boast to boast tour.

1315   The hen is the only animal in Nature that can lay around and make money.

1316   No sooner do they get the athletes off the gridiron than they begin putting the coaches on the pan.

1317   And now and then a collision occurs when two motorists go after the same pedestrian.

1318   A nickel isn't supposed to be as good as a dollar, but it goes to church more often.

1319   We are inclined to agree with the Connecticut newspaper which affirms that Barnum never said of suckers, "One is born every minute." The great showman seldom was guilty of understatement.

1320   What this country needs, in fact what the whole world needs, is to settle up and settle down.

1321   The main thing we have learned from our short-wave set is that nearly every country in the world is full of sopranos.

1322   Law gives the pedestrian the right of way, but makes no provision for flowers.

1323   You can't fool all the people all the time, but it isn't necessary. A majority will do.

1324   Physician recommends for the middle-aged light exercise and a siesta each day. Daily dozen and daily dozing.

1325   "Those who have hobbies rarely go crazy," asserts a psychiatrist. Yeah, but what about those who have to live with those who have hobbies?

1326   A lot of fellows who spout so profusely about capital and labor never had any capital and never did any labor.

1327   Science is resourceful. It couldn't pry open a day-coach window, so it air-conditioned the train.

1328   Human diseases are the same as they were a thousand years ago, says an authority. Yes, but doctors have selected more expensive names for them.

1329   While they're abolishing "isms," how about including that "ism mamma's iddle man," etc.

1330   Voice over the phone: "Pop, guess who just got kicked out of college?"

1331   The dramatic critic's meat is the ham actor.

1332   The trouble with a husband who works like a horse is that all he wants to do evenings is hit the hay.

1333   The fellow who gets on a high horse, is riding for a fall.

1334   The steps of the dining hall have become considerably worn by the treading of so many heels.—*Prof. Bott*, Notre Dame University.

1335   Many a fellow comes out of his shell when a wife eggs him on.

1336   One hitch hiker to the other—"That's right, just sit there and let me work my finger to the bone."

1337   Taking my economic theory course may not keep you off the bread-lines, but at least you'll know why you're there.—*Prof. Roberts-Michel*, Hunter (N. Y.) College.

1338   Never miss an opportunity to make others happy—even if you have to let them alone to do it.

1339   What a pity it is that a person can't dispose of his experience for as much as it cost him.

1340   You may write your term papers in any manner you choose—only, please observe the copyright laws.—*Prof. F. G. Marsh,* San Francisco Junior College.

1341   When she lost fifty pounds, it certainly was a weight off her mind.

1342   Modern advertising—This car is so fast it registers sixty in a parking place.

1343   Caution is a most valuable asset in fishing, especially if you're the fish.

1344 A dull person is one with too much polish.

1345 He who laughs last may laugh best, but he soon gets a reputation for being a dummy.

1346 Dad may not be able to appraise the worth of a college career, but he can tell you the cost.

1347 She was all will and a yard wide.

1348 Some college graduates I know ought to carry their diplomas with them to prove they've been to college.—*Prof. Israel J. Kapstein*, Brown University.

1349 The nice thing about a dull party is that you get to bed at a decent hour.

1350 Many of us spend half our time wishing for the things we could have if we didn't spend so much time wishing for them.

1351 Many a girl who spends all day splashing around in a swimming pool can put up an awful argument about water spoiling her hands when asked to bathe the dishes.

1352 Actually there is no distinct class trodden under foot except those who hold aisle seats.

1353 An Iowa professor says he finds five different kinds of dumbness. It seems incredible that a prominent man like that should have met so few people.

1354 The real problem concerning your leisure is how to keep other people from using it.

1355 Rip Van Winkle slept for twenty years, but, of course, his neighbors didn't have a radio.

1356 A sports-writer says there are 300 kinds of games played with balls. There are more than that many played with golf balls alone.

1357 But it would seem that it should be easy to make an honest living—there's so little competition.

1358 Many a woman who goes on a diet finds that she is a poor loser.

1359 The political pot never boils much. The old apple-sauce is only warmed over.

1360 There are two kinds of voters. Those who will vote for your candidate, and a lot of ignorant prejudiced fools.

1361 An ash tray is something to put cigarette ashes in when the room hasn't a fine table top or a floor.

1362 Often when a person starts to rest on his laurels he discovers they are poison ivy.

1363 Social tact is making your company feel at home, even though you wish they were.

1364 All kinds of social knowledge and graces are useful, but one of the best is to be able to yawn with your mouth closed.

1365 There isn't much practical advice to be given the hopeful young graduate, except to marry the first girl he finds who has a steady job.

1366 Generally speaking, a Communist is a person who has given up hope of becoming a capitalist.

1367 The reason father prefers a roast of beef to chicken when they are having guests for dinner is because with beef he can get what the guests do, instead of having to decorate his plate with the neck.

1368 We can't understand why goods sent by ship is called a cargo, while goods sent in a car is a shipment.

1369 If both sides make you laugh, you are broad-minded.

1370 When you sell yourself, be sure that you don't misrepresent the goods.

1371 Some folks would rather blow their own horn than listen to the Marine band.

1372 When you argue with a fool, be sure he isn't similarly engaged.

1373 The two most important muscles which operate without the direction of the brain are the heart and the tongue.

1374 "A vegetarian diet is best for those who would be beautiful," we read. Well, it does not seem to have done much for the elephant.—*Punch* (London).

1375 All we know about "hard" and "easy" money is that any kind is both—hard to get and easy to spend.—*Atlanta Journal*.

1376 Clothes don't make a man, but they can break a husband.

1377 The Smithsonian Institution reveals that there is 45 trillion dollars' worth of gold in the ocean, but we don't suppose it will comfort a seasick guy much to know he's rolling in wealth.—*Boston Herald*.

1378   What this country needs is a dollar which will be not so much elastic as it will be adhesive.

1379   It has been discovered that in giving till it hurts some people are extremely sensitive to pain.

1380   It is much more dignified to say we're moving in cycles rather than running around in circles, altho it comes to about the same thing.—*Arkansas Gazette.*

1381   Our idea of the meanest guy in the world is the guy who was deaf and never told his barber.

1382   Man is the only animal that laughs. He is the only animal that has a Legislature.

1383   A whale's tongue is found to contain 8 per cent of the oil in his system. In politicians the proportion is even heavier.

1384   It takes at least forty-eight rabbits to make a seal-skin coat for a woman.

1385   Ideas are such funny things; they never work unless you do.

1386   A woman who can spot a blonde hair on a man's coat across the room can't always see a pair of garage doors ten feet wide.

1387   The fact that silence is golden may explain why there is so little of it.

1388   Before marriage a man yearns for a woman. After marriage the "Y" is silent.

1389   A boy goes four years to college because it takes about that long to develop an all-American football player.

1390   Worry is the interest you pay on trouble before it comes.

1391   Experience is one thing you can't get on the easy payment plan.

1392   He called his wife Echo. She always had the last word.

1393   One touch of scandal makes the whole world chin.

1394   A speaker who does not strike oil in twenty minutes should stop boring.

1395   Time wounds all heels.

1396   What constitutes a living wage depends upon whether you are giving it or getting it.

1397   Doctors have discovered that hay fever can be either positive or nega-tive. Sometimes the eyes have it and sometimes the nose.

1398   A medical journal advances the theory that "man is slightly taller in the morning than he is in the evening." We have never tested this, but we have certainly noticed a tendency to become "short" toward the end of the month.

1399   One person in every eight has an accident. The other seven have accident insurance.

1400   There are two sides to every question, and a politician usually takes both.

1401   If a man takes off his hat in an elevator, it means he has good manners and hair.

1402   There are only two kinds of pedestrians—the quick and the dead.

1403   Restaurant Version—One man's meat is another man's croquette.

1404   The car to watch is the car behind the car in front of you.

1405   An article in an English journal tells how to start an amateur glee club. The real need, however, is an article telling how to stop one.

1406   A movie patron arose from his seat while viewing a picture and shot himself. We believe we have seen that picture.

1407   Everything in the modern home is controlled by switches except the children.

1408   Instruments have been invented that will throw a speaker's voice more than a mile. Now we need an instrument that will throw the speaker an equal distance.

1409   They call it the sea of matrimony because husbands have such a hard job keeping their heads above water.

1410   On a street-car a man gave his seat to a woman. She fainted. On recover-ing she thanked him. Then he fainted.

1411   Many a man who does not know his own mind would be surprised to learn how well his acquaintances know it.

1412   A correspondent declares that in many boarding houses eggs are not boiled long enough. Nor, we fear, soon enough.—*London Opinion*.

1413   And anything you tell a woman goes in one ear and over the back fence.

1414   Patent medicine ads are so attractive that it makes a man who has his health feel like he is missing something.

1415   The cost of living is always about the same—all a fellow has.

1416   An English neurologist says that a man who owns a car seldom walks in his sleep, but we bet, if he's got a family, he does it a lot when he's awake.

1417   It's hard to tell whether some people are walking to reduce—or reduced to walking.

1418   We've always believed that breaking a mirror is a good sign. It means that you're going to live at least another seven years.

1419   The best sense of humor is that which tells you what is not safe to laugh at.

1420   Home is where part of the family waits until the rest of them bring back the car.

1421   They say that every bride who is married isn't happy—just triumphant.

1422   When a man begins to realize the truth about himself, it frequently retards his program for reforming his neighbors.

1423   So much down usually means so much to keep up.

1424   A recent society bride had six bridesmaids in hyacinth blue silk and two pages in rich crimson velvet, with gold lace. A pale bridegroom completed the color scheme.

1425   We understand that tickets for a Hollywood garden party were issued to admit "Bearer and one wife."

1426   Thirty is a nice age for a woman, especially if she happens to be forty.

1427   According to a doctor, singing warms the blood. We have heard some that has made ours positively boil.

1428   Love at first sight is possible, but it is always well to wipe off your spectacles and take a second look.

1429   Now and then one picks up a magazine on the stands that makes one curious to see the stuff the editor rejected.

1430   So far, no modern has invented an intelligence test to equal matrimony.

1431   Modern woman's place seems to be in either the delicatessen store or the beauty parlor.

1432 This is the age when a child who is tied to his mother's apron-strings isn't tied to his mother.

1433 An optimist is a man who sees only the initial payment; the pessimist can't overlook the future installments and the upkeep.

1434 Let us not forget that a good deal of our prosperous appearance is due to driving a mortgaged car over a bonded road.

1435 Only Americans have mastered the art of being prosperous though broke.

1436 An advertisement for a lecturer says he "speaks straight from the shoulder." Too bad some of these talks can't originate a little higher up.

1437 Punctuality is the art of guessing how late the other fellow is going to be.

1438 One shudders to think what will be needed to constitute a radical fifty years from now.

1439 Reforms come from below. No man with four aces howls for a new deal.

1440 When a man says, "I run things at my house," he may mean the washing machine, the vacuum cleaner, and the furnace.

1441 Many a man stays home nights because he has the house to himself.

1442 A man who sits in a swamp all day waiting to shoot a duck will kick if his wife has dinner ten minutes late.

1443 There's no justice. If you make out your income tax correctly, you go to the poorhouse. If you don't, you go to jail.

1444 Probably the world's greatest humorist was the man who called "installments" "easy payments."

1445 The paramount question before the country today is, "How much is the down payment?"

1446 "To think," exclaimed the enthusiastic young husband, "that by the time we get all this furniture paid for we shall have genuine antiques!"

1447 What labor really needs in these days of installment payments is not a five-day week but a forty-day month.

1448 Our laundryman has the wisdom of a Solomon. When he can't decide to whom a certain shirt belongs, he splits it in half.

1449 A man left the bulk of his fortune to his lawyer. If everybody did this, a lot of time would be saved.

1450 Golf liars have one advantage over the fishing kind—they don't have to show anything to prove it.

1451 About the time one learns how to make the most of life, the most of it is gone.

1452 Some motorists are in such a hurry to get into the next county that they go right on into the next world.

1453 Among the things that seem to grow by leaps and bounds are the children in the apartment overhead.

1454 Many a man of Presidential timber turns out to be but another splinter.

1455 Be satisfied with a little. The atom has taken its split without beefing.

1456 What this country needs is a man who can be right and President at the same time.

1457 "An Eskimo woman is old at forty," says an explorer. An American woman is not old at forty. In fact, she's not even forty.

1458 The comic strips seem to amuse the younger generation, but it must wonder at times what other use a rolling-pin has.—*Jackson News.*

1459 It takes three generations or one good guess in the stock market to make a gentleman.—*Springfield Union.*

1460 A wizard is the person who can keep up with the neighbors and the installments, too.—*Chicago Times.*

1461 The timid girl who blushes and hesitates before marriage about accepting even a bunch of flowers or a box of candy will grab a man's pay envelope after marriage before he gets in the front door.

1462 What a world! To be a valedictorian and then get a job working for a fellow who dropped out at the eighth grade.—*San Francisco Chronicle.*

1463 Well, there's still a sucker being born every minute. The trouble is he hasn't got anything you can take away from him.

1464 It's nice to have four years between elections. It takes people that long to regain their faith.

1465 You can fool some of the people all of the time and all of the people some of the time and the rest of the time somebody else will fool them.

1466 We used to worry about future generations becoming soft, but no more. Not when we think of the bond issues they're going to have to pay off.—*Judge.*

1467 A college professor declares that contrary to scientific opinion, the interior of the earth is not so hot. In our opinion, the same thing is true of the exterior.

1468 One trouble with the world is that there are always more victors than spoils.

1469 Another change the game of bridge needs is a cross-bar under the table.

1470 If you want economy, never let an economic question get into politics.

1471 American women are so beautiful they can wear anything. The trouble is they won't.

1472 Problems in marriage often arise because a man too often shows his worst side to his better half.

1473 What any government almost invariably needs is more pruning and less grafting.

1474 A good many human dynamos are short-circuited in a few years.

1475 Some day we hope to be wise enough to get the vitamins that wild animals get by eating what they like.

1476 A politician doesn't stand on his record; he jumps on the other fellow's.

1477 The two agencies used to redistribute great fortunes are taxation and offspring.—*Muskogee Phoenix.*

1478 The human race seems to have improved everything except people.—*Easton Express.*

1479 The great leader is one who never permits his followers to discover that he is as dumb as they are.—*Rochester Times-Union.*

1480 We wonder if the eloquent founders of this nation would have talked so glowingly of posterity, if they had known we were going to be it.

1481 On the political menu, too, applesauce is served with pork.—*Philadelphia Inquirer.*

1482 A small town is one where the folks know all the news before the paper comes out, but merely take it to see whether or not the editor got the stories according to the way they heard them.

1483   "The first lie detector," says Sam Hill in the Cincinnati *Enquirer*, "wa
made out of the rib of a man." And no improvement has ever been made or
the original machine.

1484   It won't hurt us to discover that "roughing it" means more than ridin
with the sedan windows open.

1485   Man is like a car. Just so much mileage in him, whether he runs it ou
in 40 years or 80.—*Cedar Falls Record*.

1486   In some respects the idea of finger-printing children seems to be a goo
one. At least it will settle the question as to who used the guest towel in th
bathroom.

1487   A kiss is a peculiar proposition. Of no use to one, yet absolute bliss to
two. The small boy gets it for nothing, the young man has to lie for it, and
the old man has to buy it. The baby's right, the lover's privilege, and the
hypocrite's mask. To a young girl, faith; to a married woman, hope; and to
an old maid, charity.—*V. P. I. Skipper*.

1488   The great difficulty in amplifiers is that they amplify the speaker's
voice, but not his ideas.

1489   A past President of the United States was said to have written a history
of America in one sentence, reading as follows: "America was discovered in
1492, and now look at the darn thing."

1490   When a boy marries, two opinions prevail at the home he is leaving:
His mother thinks he is throwing himself away, and his sisters think the girl is.

1491   All work and no play makes jack for the nerve specialist.

1492   Some people are like French bread—little dough, but lots of crust.

1493   Nowadays a businessman is judged by the company he keeps solvent.

1494   And there was that dumb girl in the commodity house who thought
spot hides came from a leopard.

1495   Every man is a hero in his own home—until the company leaves.

1496   Contentment has one big advantage over wealth; friends don't try to
borrow it from you.

1497   The young man who worked so hard to graduate later wonders what
the hurry was.

1498   We send our actors to England and England sends her actors to us.
It's getting to be hams across the sea.

1499 In the very near future men will eat baked beans and say: "Ah, dear, these are just like those in the cans mother used to open."

1500 It's a good thing that politicians are generally paid by the year. They would starve to death on piecework.

1501 Whenever everybody tends to his own business, news is scarce.

1502 One reason we are a great nation is because we have been unable to exhaust our natural resources in spite of our best efforts.

1503 Pat a man on the back and you may make his head swell.

1504 Almost any time now we may expect to see the restaurants retaliate by putting in a line of drugs and toilet articles.

1505 The man who saves money nowadays isn't a miser; he's a wizard.

1506 You should try to save something while your salary is small. It is almost impossible to save after you begin earning more.

1507 The bigger the bankroll, the tighter the rubber band.

1508 The trouble with self-made men is that they quit the job too early.

1509 A sordid money-grabber is anybody who grabs more money than you can grab

1510 The subways are becoming so crowded that even the men can't all get seats.

1511 More times than not a woman is responsible for her husband's success because of the money she makes it necessary for him to make.

1512 The trouble with these "Do You Want Money?" ads is that when you read them you always discover you either have to work for it or mortgage something to get it.

1513 If all the autos in the world were laid end to end, it would be Sunday afternoon.

1514 Personally we are not very superstitious, but when we are crossing rail-road tracks we know it's a bad sign to see a train coming.

1515 Longfellow said that man must be either a hammer or an anvil. But he overlooked the fellow who is simply bellows.

1516 A cynic recently said of his wife: "At the end of the evening she was so tired she could hardly keep her mouth open."

1517   An average woman's vocabulary is said to be about 500 words. Small inventory, but think of the turnover.

1518   It's worth the taxi fare to feel you don't care what happens to the fenders.

1519   There are 17,000,000 telephones in the United States, so when a girl makes it in two guesses she isn't doing so badly at that.

1520   The broad general rule is that a man is about as big as the things that make him mad.

1521   A lot of nice, fat turkey gobblers would strut less if they could see into the future.

1522   The theater, at the present time, is not holding a mirror up to life, but a keyhole.

1523   It is said that the engineers of the faster trains eventually lose their nerve. The porters, of course, don't have to be up there in the cab.

1524   The camera never lies, and it takes a family album to convince some people that the truth is a terrible thing.

1525   The greatest consolation for many vacationists is that they have found, at least, where to stay away from next time.

1526   A resort is a place where the natives live on your vacation until next summer.

1527   The polls are places where you stand in line for a chance to decide who will spend your money.

1528   Man wants but little here below, but he usually gets along on less.

1529   The greatest paradox of them all is still civilized warfare.

1530   One trouble with the country is that it wants to raise nothing but cotton and wear nothing but silk.

1531   Maybe what's wrong with this generation is that too many parents' slippers are being worn out on the dancing floors.

1532   The poet, Heine, once said to a caller, "My head today is perfectly barren, and you will find me stupid enough; for a friend has been here, and we exchanged ideas."

1533   U. S. now stands for Unlimited Spending.—*Tampa Tribune*.

1534 If all the road-hogs were laid end to end, that would be Utopia.—*Greensboro (Ga.) Herald-Journal.*

1535 Scientists say that only one man in a hundred has a perfect voice. The rest of them, however, insist upon singing "Sweet Adeline."—*Grand Rapids Press.*

1536 In the approaching campaign, a Washington gossip note says, party-managers will concentrate their efforts only on promising candidates. What! Is there any other kind?—*Boston Herald.*

1537 Most of us go through life on a five-cent fare and then ask for a transfer.

1538 An optimist says his glass is still half full; a pessimist declares that his glass is already half empty.

1539 The bigger a man's head gets, the easier it is to fill his shoes.

1540 Evolution: Dress, $3.75; frock, $19.98; gown, $65; creation, $225.

1541 Don't be afraid of having too many irons in the fire, if the fire is hot enough.

1542 A man can't even blow his own horn nowadays until he completes all the payments.

1543 A fool and his money sooner or later wind up in college.

1544 Someone has observed that it takes a student 20 minutes longer to say what he thinks than to tell what he knows.

1545 When he gets into a taxi, they leave the "vacant" sign up.

1546 He was just one of the ciphers in the "400."

1547 That toastmaster is the living proof that all oil cans aren't in the toolbox.

1548 She was a woman of few words, but often.

1549 That farm is so muddy you have to jack up the cows to milk them.

1550 They call him Tonsillitis, because he's a pain in the neck.

1551 We call him Asthma—he's so full of old wheezes.

1552 A woman's tears are the greatest water-power known to man.—*Atchison County Mail.*

1553 All things come to him who waits, but they are apt to be pretty well shop-worn.

1554 The man's insomnia was so bad that the sheep were picketing him for shorter hours.

1555 Judging from the amount of the public debt, it is no longer much of a compliment to tell a lady she looks like a million dollars.—*Santa Fe New Mexican.*

1556 If you can spend a perfectly useless afternoon in a perfectly useless manner, you have learned how to live.—*Lin Yu Tang.*

1557 He made a nickel go so far the buffalo got sore feet.

1558 He's so stingy that when the boys give three cheers, he only gives two.

1559 A woman is a man's solace, but if it wasn't for her he wouldn't need any solace.

1560 According to a survey, the most dangerous traffic hour is between 7 and 8 o'clock at night. That's when everyone is through supper and hurrying to get nowhere.—*Ohio State Journal.*

1561 Hanging out the family wash to dry is a simple problem to the trailer housewife. If it rains, they move over into the next county.—*Christian Science Monitor.*

1562 To enjoy garden work, put on a wide hat and gloves, hold a little trowel in one hand, and tell the man where to dig.—*Grand Rapids (Mich.) Press.*

1563 There will always be a multitude who are congenitally unable to think straight.—*Charles Evans Hughes.*

1564 A golf player is a person who can drive 70 miles an hour in any traffic with perfect ease, but blows up on a two-foot putt if somebody coughs.—*Cleveland News.*

1565 Stout people usually claim they eat like a bird. Yeah, a peck at a time.

1566 Right is might, but a good left never hurt a fighter.

1567 Saving is a way of spending money without getting any fun out of it.

1568 Married life is just one undarned thing after another.

1569 A real friend will not visit you in prosperity unless he is invited, but when you are in adversity he will call without invitation.

1570 The cautious suitor who stays on the fence too long usually ends up getting the gate.

1571 The greatest inspiration is often born of desperation. The fellow who thinks he can't is probably right.

1572 And one guy who always goes to the top is a barber.

1573 When a fellow's too much in love with himself, he's not likely to have much competition.

1574 It's the fellow in the office who blows his horn the loudest who is generally in a fog.

1575 The United States Treasury has recently dug a big hole down in the hills of Kentucky and buried our gold in it. The next thing you know they'll be moving the mint down there to have it near the juleps.

1576 A drug store has decided to add one more line to make their service complete, so they're advertising, "Board and Rooms."

1577 When a wife explores a man's pockets, she generally gets what the average explorer does—enough material for a lecture.

1578 Lots of surgeons write books that are best sellers. It's the *opening* pages that make one nervous.

1579 The business man is always in a sweat. He never knows whether the period just ahead is going to be a new era or a new error.

1580 The corn in Illinois and Iowa grows so big they use the cobs for railroad ties.

1581 Sixty million people go to the movies every week, and almost all of them file past our seats just at the most exciting part of the picture.

1582 We seem always to move between extremes in this country. Either you can't buy a new car, or you have to wait four weeks for delivery.

1583 Remember you can't fall out of bed if you sleep on the floor.

1584 We've heard that college-bred means a four-year loaf made with dad's dough. Some crust, eh?

1585 It is going to be pretty tough when this country gets back to normal and the fellows who write those articles on economics have got to know what they're talking about again.

1586 It might be well to bear in mind that when Uncle Sam plays Santa Claus, it's the tax-payer who holds the bag.

1587 Professor Warren of Harvard Law School concedes modern youth a little: "An A.B. degree nowadays means that the holder has mastered the first two letters of the alphabet."

1588   A political leader's task is to keep ahead of four or five crowds, each going in a different direction.

1589   The trick in campaigning is to give them platitudes without fear or favor and straight-from-the-shoulder generalities.

1590   A senator tells us the average American is not tax conscious yet, and this is doubtless so. If he shows signs of coming to, he is struck by another.

Some Answers from Sophomores

1591   "James I claimed the throne of England through his grandmother because he had no father."

1592   "Benjamin Franklin produced electricity by rubbing cats backward. Benjamin Franklin was the founder of electricity."

1593   "America was discovered by the Spinach."

1594   "In 1685 the Pilgrims crossed the ocean, and this was known as Pilgrim's Progress."

1595   "An ibex is where you look at the back part of a book to find out anything you want."

1596   "A deacon is the lowest kind of a Christian."

1597   "A monastery is a place of monsters."

1598   "False doctrine is when a doctor gives wrong stuff to a man."

1599   When success turns a man's head, he faces failure.

1600   Weak knees come from a weak head.

1601   Some people have tact, others tell the truth.

1602   There are two kinds of fishermen; those who fish for sport and those who catch something.

1603   Buying what you do not need is an easy road to needing what you cannot buy.

1604   Riches are no menace if we do not divorce dollars from sense.

1605   At a certain age some people's minds close up. They live on their intellectual fat.—*W. L. Phelps.*

1606   The chief fault of American audiences is that they see the point before you get there, which is disconcerting.—*Jerome K. Jerome.*

1607   It will be time enough to talk about changing religion when men grow up to the present one.

1608   The man whose conscience never troubles him must have it pretty well trained.

1609 A wise man said the other day, "If people did no more than they had to, life would come to a standstill tomorrow."

1610 Where there's a will, there's a way—but where there are many wills, there's no way.

1611 At a banquet of firemen, recently, the chief proposed the toast: "The ladies! Their eyes kindle the only flame which we cannot extinguish, and against which there is no insurance."

1612 It is better to wear out than rust out.

1613 The real test of golf and in life is not keeping out of the rough . . . but getting out after we are in.

1614 Life has a way of evening up things. For every woman who makes a fool out of some man there's another who makes a man out of some fool.

1615 The difference between a groove and a grave is only a matter of depth.

1616 The only reason a great many American families don't own an elephant is that they have never been offered an elephant for a dollar down and a dollar a week.

1617 A politician thinks of the next election; a statesman, of the next generation.

1618 A swelled head, like an inflated balloon, is of no use on earth.

1619 To preserve peace, we need guns of smaller and men of larger caliber.

1620 Art, like morality, consists in drawing the line somewhere.

1621 All that stands between the college graduate and the top of the ladder is the ladder.

1622 It is stated that on an average a stout man lives longer than a thin man. Just a case of the survival of the fattest.

1623 Mosquitoes were unknown in England 500 years ago. Well, how would you like to be a mosquito trying to pick up a living in an age when everyone wore suits of armor?

1624 There are some who call it the Sock Market.

1625 No matter how bad prose is it might be verse.

1626 Every time he looks in the mirror he takes a bow.

1627 The difference between a prejudice and a conviction is that you can explain a conviction without getting mad.

1628   The average American works himself to death so he can live.

1629   Many marriages crack up when the installment collector cracks down.

1630   Someone wants to know if there is any cure for always waking up with a severe headache? We can only think of insomnia.—*Punch*.

1631   Scientists are now trying to find out the speed of light. Laymen say that it arrives too early in the morning.—*Punch*.

1632   When a girl reduces, she is going out of her weigh to please some man.

1633   By the streets of "by and by," one arrives at the house of "never."—*Cervantes*.

1634   If you wish to be miserable, you must think about yourself, what you want, what you like, what respect people ought to pay you, and what people think of you.

1635   Truth is the opinion that still survives.

1636   Minimize friction and create harmony. You can get friction for nothing, but harmony costs courtesy and self-control.

1637   The only things worth saying are those all men know, but which they have forgotten.

1638   Genius may have its limitations, but stupidity is not thus handicapped.

1639   The modern idea of roughing it is to do without a heater in the limousine.

1640   Another great danger of one-arm driving is that you're so likely to skid into a church.

1641   It should be easy for any government to please the people. All they want is lower taxes and larger appropriations.

1642   It is commendable, to be sure, for a college to offer a course in "What Contemporary Civilization Is," but a little information as to where it is would help a lot, too.

1643   A careful driver approached a railroad; he stopped, looked, and listened. All he heard was the car behind him crashing into his gas-tank.

1644   If you want to flatter somebody, just look serious and ask him what he thinks of the general situation.

1645   The Florida Supreme Court holds that the slot-machine is not a lottery. Certainly there is little of the element of chance about it.

1646 If the colleges continue to get more and more finicky, pretty soon an amateur won't be able to make a decent living in any sport.—*Boston Herald.*

1647 Sign at Library: Only low talk permitted here.

1648 Many a janitor would rather sleep than heat.

1649 Chili today and hot tomale.

1650 Man isn't so smart. Thousands of years before he began to have afternoon headaches from trying to think, the turtle had a stream-lined body, turret-top, retractable landing gear, and a portable house.

1651 There is nothing more difficult than the art of making advice agreeable.

1652 At twenty the will reigns, at thirty the wit, and at forty the judgment.

1653 A rabbit's foot is a poor substitute for horse sense.

1654 It is possible that the man who wakes up to find himself famous has been sleeping all the while with one eye open.

1655 A friend forgives your defects, and if he is very fond of you, he doesn't see any.

1656 Nowadays every man wants life, liberty and an automobile in which to pursue happiness.

1657 Broadmindedness is the ability to smile when you learn that the ten bucks you lent your roommate is taking your girl to the prom.

1658 Simile—R is silent as in Harvard.

1659 Our eyes are placed in front because it is more important to look ahead than look back.

1660 Said the raindrop to the particle of dust: "This settles you."

1661 If you can't think of any other way to flatter a man, tell him he's the kind that can't be flattered.

1662 Sign at Jonestown, Pa., store on New York to Harrisburg highway: "Modern Antiques."

1663 It certainly pays to advertise. There are twenty-six mountains in Colorado higher than Pike's Peak.

H

1664   And in the old days a bad man would go around with niches in his gun handle, instead of in his fenders.

1665   Some people just can't unbend and be human until misfortune has taken the starch out of them.

1666   You might as well do your Christmas hinting early.

1667   I had a little dog. I called him August. August was fond of jumping at conclusions, especially at the wrong conclusion. One day he jumped at a mule's conclusion. The next day was the first of September.—*North Carolina Buccaneer.*

1668   There are three applause periods in a speech. Applause by the audience at the beginning of a speech expresses faith. Applause in the middle of a speech expresses hope. Applause at the end of a speech expresses charity.

1669   A student makes his bed and has to lie in it; a professor makes his bunk and has to lie out of it.

1670   A recession is a period in which you tighten up your belt. A depression is a time in which you have no belt to tighten. When you have no trousers to hold up, it's a panic.—*Postage Stamp.*

1671   In some cities they tear down buildings to save taxes. They might try tearing down some taxes to save buildings.

1672   The government not only has the bad habit of living beyond its income, but also beyond ours.

1673   It's hard to keep up with the neighbors without falling behind with the creditors.

1674   Think of the different ways of saying "Good morning." Someone says it one way and they put a punch in you. They say it in another way, and you want to punch them.

1675   "Many of the compositions that have been handed in are trite—or should I say tripe!" (Professor in English class.)

1676   When a woman paints her face, she's sophisticated; when an Indian paints his face he's savage—but really it is the woman who is dressed to kill.

1677   Want Ad—"Young man who gets paid on Monday and is broke by Wednesday would like to exchange small loans with a young man who gets paid on Wednesday and is broke by Monday."

1678   Customer (to headwaiter): "Just for a point of information, did the waiter who took my order leave any family?"

1679   In June the boys and girls graduate from high school and college. The education won't hurt them if they learn a little something after they graduate. They'll find next to the sheepskin, shoe leather is most important. But nowadays, you really don't have to go to school. You can get your geography from the rumble seat of an old jallopy, your arithmetic from trying to get the numbers on a dial telephone, and the alphabet from the AAA, CCC, FHA, and TVA. All you have to know now to live to be a hundred is a green light from a red light, and be able to read the traffic signs.

There is one great thing about graduating from college. Later on you never have to buy bonds from a stranger; and if you ever get into one of those college fraternities, boy, you're "brother" afterwards to more birds in the insurance business than there are yodelers in the Swiss Army.

1680   If they ever close up the Metropolitan opera, where will society go to talk while opera is being sung?

1681   Men who are run down generally wind up in a hospital.

1682   Times are so bad with him he doesn't scratch matches on the bottom of his shoes any more because it tears his socks.

1683   Lots of people plan their vacations in June. With streamlined trains and automobiles, we've got things speeded up so you can take a two weeks' vacation in three days. Most people use this year's vacation to find out where to stay away from next year, but the best place to spend your vacation is just inside your income.

1684   Before putting on her hat, the chic dresser will make sure it is her hat. If it has money in it, it's her purse.—*Detroit News.*

1685   June is the month of weddings and cooing. In July the billing follows. The main difference in being married instead of single is that the grocer gets the pay check the tailor used to get. We used to marry for better or worse, now it's for more or less.

1686   According to reports in the papers we have far too many divorces. Too many women marry in haste and repeat at leisure. In fact a wedding is the only prerequisite for a divorce now. Divorces have become so common that the really smart folks are staying married in order to be different. Lots of the old folks are moving to Reno to be near the children. As the old-timer said to the newly married couple, "Cheer up! Divorce is yet to come!"

1687   The other day, the newspapers were showing the pictures of an old man who had reached the age of 98. But there is nothing so wonderful about that. Look at the time it took him to get there.

1688   "The surtax on any amount of surtax net income not shown in the table is computed by adding to the surtax for the largest amount shown which is less than the income, the surtax upon the excess over the amount at the rate indicated in the table." Instruction on income-tax blank. We contend that the government should supply a slide rule, prayer book, and ouija board with each income-tax return-form.—*Washington Post.*

1689   When you hear some folks you know blow and brag, you are reminded of the time the flea said to the elephant, "Boy, didn't we shake that new bridge when we crossed it?"—*Goodland News.*

1690   A thoughtful economist has just written a 100-page "Short History of Money." We could write a history of ours in six words: "Here it is! There it goes!"—*Boston Herald.*

1691   Found on a Freshman's registration card: Name of parents: "Mamma and Papa."—*Columbia Jester.*

1692   "A Toast," exclaimed the hobo lifting his tomato can. "Here's to de holidays! Bless de hull t'ree hundred and sixty-five of 'em!"

1693   Lloyd George, in one of his lighter moments, said that "tranquillity is never a philosophy or a policy. It is simply a great yawn."

1694   Most of us are confident we could move the mountains if somebody would clear the hills out of our way.

1695   Making love is like making pie. All you need is a lot of crust and some applesauce. (Then mix it with a spoon.)

1696   A famous old inn claims to own a sixty-year-old cheese. It is, of course, still going strong.

1697   Sign on a Scottish golf course: Members will refrain from picking up lost balls until they have stopped rolling.

1698   "Multiple births are more frequent in larger families," declares a statistician. It's mighty hard to fool these statisticians.

1699   In trying to convey an important idea to another person, the Irishman said, "If I can get this one idea into your head, you will have it in a nut shell."—*Dr. Emory W. Luccock.*

1700   A good speech has a good beginning and a good ending, both of which are kept very close together.

1701   Many a man keeps his nose to the grindstone so his wife can turn hers up at the neighbors.—*The Scandal Sheet, Graham, Texas.*

1702   Don't judge a man by his clothes. The door man at the movie who is dressed like an admiral probably does not even know how to row.

1703   There is nothing but ill-fortune in a habit of grumbling, which requires no talent, no self-denial, no brains, no character.—*O. S. Marden.*

1704   Samuel Johnson demolished a loquacious bore with: "You talk like a watch which ticks away minutes but never strikes the hour."

1705   A marital expert says that when you see a man polishing a woman's car you may be sure they are engaged; and when you see a woman polishing a man's car you may be sure they are married.

1706   A depression is a period when people do without the things their parents never had.

1707   One nice thing about a one-way street is that you can only be bumped in the rear.

1708   A sensible girl is not so sensible as she looks because a sensible girl has more sense than to look sensible.—*Wall Street Journal.*

1709   The reason a lot of people do not recognize an opportunity when they meet it, is that it usually goes around wearing overalls and looking like hard work!

1710   He can compress the most words into the smallest ideas of any man I ever met. Abraham Lincoln, of a fellow lawyer.—*"Lincoln's Own Stories."*

1711   One half of knowing what you want is knowing what you must give up before you get it.—*Sidney Howard.*

1712   A seventh grade pupil won first prize in his class for the best short baseball story: "Rain, no game."

1713   When prices are high, money doesn't talk; it whispers.

1714   Experience is what you get when you're looking for something else.—*Pathfinder.*

1715   Snobbery is the pride of those who are not sure of their position.—*Berton Braley.*

1716   Be pretty if you can, be witty if you must, be agreeable if it kills you.—*Elsie De Wolfe.*

1717   Some folk seem to get the idea they're worth a lot of money just because they have it.—*Seth Parker.*

1718   A young girl came into a member bank to buy some defense savings stamps. When the teller asked her what denomination, she replied, "Presbyterian."—*Savings Banks Bulletin.*

1719 The average fire is put out before any considerable damage is done by the fire department.

1720 A foreigner who killed himself because he was unable to learn English in New York seems to have thought it was spoken here.

1721 If we should lock up all the feeble-minded, who would write our song hits?

1722 Alarmists seemingly regard the rising generation as a falling one.

1723 Everybody should learn to drive a car. This is especially true of those who sit behind the steering wheels.

1724 Man is an able creature, but he has made 32,600,000 laws and hasn't yet improved on the Ten Commandments.

1725 The world never will be wholly civilized. Some outlying portions have no natural resources worth seizing.

1726 The members of the smart set never get that way by listening to one another.

1727 The evil that men do lives after them. The saxophone was made in 1846.

1728 Success is getting what you want; happiness is wanting what you get.

1729 The greatest service that could be rendered the Christian peoples would be to convert them to Christianity.

1730 How is it possible for women to understand politics when they have to depend almost entirely on their husbands for their political education?

1731 It is just as well that justice is blind; she might not like some of the things done in her name if she could see them.

1732 A doctor gives us the cheerless news that women are too weak for housework. Well, the men are not strong for it, either.

1733 On the first of the month there is no female or anything else more deadly than the mail.

1734 The habit of going to the bottom of things usually lands a man on top.

1735 The world has facilities enough now for transmitting intelligence rapidly—that is, until we get more intelligence to transmit.

1736 Somebody always backs down when the public gets its back up.

1737   Edison said college men object to work. College doesn't seem to change people so much, then.

1738   "The slow-thinkers live longest," says a prominent psychologist. Not if they cross the street.

1739   If a man wants his dreams to come true, he must wake up.

1740   The difficulty in turning immigrants into good Americans is to find a model to work by.

1741   A magazine writer says we need a new religion. But let's not do anything rash until we try the old one.

1742   If he dodges jitneys, he is a pedestrian; if he dodges taxes, he is a financier; if he dodges responsibility, he is a statesman.

1743   The modern girl may have her little weaknesses, but she isn't effeminate.

1744   Many a live wire would be a dead one if it weren't for his connections.

1745   The matrimonial bark is wrecked by the matrimonial barking.

1746   If you do housework at $10 a week, that's domestic service. If you do it for nothing, that's matrimony.

1747   Some so-called open minds should be closed for repairs.

1748   Scientists say we are what we eat. Nuts must be a commoner diet than we had thought.

1749   The reason ideas die quickly in some heads is because they can't stand solitary confinement.

1750   Queer that men should take up a life of crime when there are so many legal ways to be dishonest.

1751   Some are bent with toil, and some get crooked trying to avoid it.

Chapter 6

AMUSING DEFINITIONS

....

1752 *Acrobat*—The only person who can do what everyone else would like to do—pat himself on the back. The inventor of the rumble seat.

1753 *Adam*—The one man in the world who couldn't say, "Pardon me, haven't I seen you before?"

1754 *Advice*—What you take for a cold. The suggestions you give someone else which you believe will work to your benefit. Something most of us "give until it hurts."

1755 *Alibi*—An excuse that's cooked up, but is always half-baked.

1756 *Alimony*—A man's cash surrender value.

1757 *All-expense tour*—The perfect example of truth in advertising.

1758 *Amateur athlete*—An athlete who is paid in cash—not by check.

1759 *Amateur carpenter*—A carpenter who resembles lightning. He never strikes twice in the same place.

1760 *Amateur golfer*—The man who moves heaven and earth to play golf.

1761 *Antique collector's song*—"You take the highboy and I'll take the lowboy."

1762 *Apartment house bonds*—Flat failures.

1763 *Appendicitis and tonsillitis*—Two sicknesses that made famous the well-known medical saying, "There's gold in them thar ills."

1764 *Automobile*—A machine that eliminated horses but made horse sense necessary. Contains over 1,000 nuts—the biggest one often being in the driver's seat.

1765 *Bachelor*—A bachelor is a man who gives in when he is wrong; a married man gives in when he is right. A bachelor either lacks the sand to propose or the rocks to marry. He is the only man who never lied to his wife. The difference between a married man and a bachelor is that when a bachelor walks the floor with a baby at midnight he is dancing. The fellow who never says hasty things he has to regret afterward. It has been said, "Not all men are fools—some are bachelors." A man who, when he accomplishes something great, gets all the credit.

1766 *Bargain sale*—A sale at which a woman ruins a $25 street dress to get a house dress for 98 cents.

1767 *Beauty*—The one thing a woman may lose and never know it's gone.

1768 *Beginner's luck*—A college freshman with an idea.

1769 *Big game hunter*—A man who can spot a leopard.

1770 *Blessed event*—When a man's mother-in-law goes home.

1771 *Block*—The distance between some people's ears.

1772 *Blotter*—A porous substance you spend your time looking for while the ink is drying.

1773 *Boarding school*—The place where the father sent his son who wanted to be a carpenter.

1774 *Bottoms up to you!*—A toast you never make to the crew in a boat race.

1775 *Bridge*—Next to hockey the most dangerous shin-bruising game in America.

1776 *Buffer state*—One that's between two biffer states.

1777 *Business economy*—A reduction in some other employee's salary.

1778 *Busy doctor*—The doctor who has so many patients that when there is nothing the matter with you, he will tell you so. Write your own daffynition for a busy dentist.

1779 *Caesar*—A man of great nerve and a wonderful Gaul.

1780 *Canoe*—An object that acts like a small boy—it behaves better when paddled from the rear.

1781 *Careful driver*—The fellow who has made the last payment on his car. A careful driver is one who can wear out a car without the help of a railroad engine and a crossing.

H*

1782 *Centenarian*—A person who has lived to be 100 years old. He never smoked or he smoked all his life. He used whisky for eighty years or he never used it. He was a vegetarian or he wasn't a vegetarian. Follow these rules carefully and you, too, can be a centenarian.

1783 *Cheap politician*—There isn't any such thing.

1784 *Chiropodist*—A fellow who, when given an inch, will take a foot. A man who is down at the heel even when he is prosperous.

1785 *Club secretary*—The person who keeps the minutes and wastes the hours.

1786 *Cold feet*—The ailment you get when you know what the consequences are going to be.

1787 *College*—The land of the midnight sons.

1788 *College English department*—The chamber of commas.

1789 *College football team*—An organization the American boy joins in order to see the United States.

1790 *College mixer*—A place where the coeds without dates meet the men without money.

1791 *College senior*—A young man with a raccoon coat and a black derby. He likes ties with dots, suits with stripes and letters with checks. He joins a fraternity so he doesn't have to buy his own clothes.

1792 *Conscience*—The sixth sense that comes to our aid when we are doing wrong and tells us that we are about to get caught.

1793 *Cow hide*—The thing that holds the cow together.

1794 *Crooked dough*—Something handled by counterfeiters and pretzel manufacturers.

1795 *Dangerous surgical operation*—Nothing that costs less than $150.

1796 *Deaf and dumb couple*—The only married people who can settle a quarrel at night by turning out the lights.

1797 *Defeated politician*—The candidate who never has to explain why he is unable to keep his campaign promises.

1798 *Delegate-at-large*—A man who goes to a convention without his wife.

1799 *Delicatessen operator*—A man who has women eat out of his hand.

1800 *Dentist*—A man who runs a filling station. A collector of old magazines.

1801 *Depression*—A period when you can't spend money you don't have.

1802 *Detour*—The roughest distance between two points.

1803 *Diplomat*—An honest man sent abroad to lie for his country. A man who pours banana oil on troubled waters.

1804 *Discretion*—When you are sure you are right and then ask your wife.

1805 *Doctor*—A man who has his tonsils, adenoids and appendix.

1806 *Dog*—The same as bill collector. Both will stick to a fellow when he hasn't got a cent.

1807 *Dough*—A misnomer for money; dough sticks to your fingers.

1808 *Dramatic critic*—A man who gives the best jeers of his life to the theater.

1809 *Draw*—A term used to describe the result of a battle between a dentist and a patient.

1810 *Dumb Dora*—A coed who is so dumb she brings her cosmetics for a make-up exam.

1811 *Economist*—One who tells you what to do with your money after you have done something else with it.

1812 *Education*—"The inculcation of the incomprehensible into the ignorant by the incompetent."—*Sir Josiah Stamp*. The only thing a man is willing to pay for, and hopes he doesn't get. Training that helps one to make more money unless he becomes an educator.

1813 *Election year*—One year in four when the great national dish is tripe.

1814 *Electrician*—A man who wires for money.

1815 *Elephant*—A useful animal with a vacuum-cleaner in front and a rug-beater at the back.

1816 *Error*—Something wrong—a mistake. To illustrate: First Tramp: "Is this right? I have et." Second Tramp: "No. That's an error. It's wrong." First Tramp: "What's the mistake?" Second Tramp: "You ain't et yet."

1817 *Error in judgment*—A man who thinks he has an open mind when it's merely vacant.

1818 *Example*—To give an illustration. The teacher asked the student to give an example of the word "boycott." The student said, "The wind blew down my brother's neck and the boycott an awful cold."

1819 *Executive ability*—The faculty of earning your bread by the work of other people.

1820 *Faithful*—An adjective which describes a man's mother-in-law. She never leaves him no matter what he does.

1821 *Farm*—A portion of land entirely covered by a mortgage.

1822 *Farsighted*—A term used to describe a man who wouldn't take a chance on an auto raffle because he didn't have a garage. When one buys three lawn mowers—two for the neighbors to use. To order three eggs in a restaurant— one for your vest.

1823 *Father*—A fellow who is put on the pan if he doesn't bring home the bacon.

1824 *Female archer*—A girl who works on eyebrows in a beauty parlor.

1825 *Flaw*—What the Harvard graduate thinks you walk on in a house.

1826 *Floating debt*—A 1929 yacht that hasn't been paid for.

1827 *Football coach*—A fellow who is willing to lay down your life for his school.

1828 *Frog*—The only living thing that has more lives than a cat. It croaks every night.

1829 *Gentleman*—Any man who wouldn't hit a woman with his hat on.— *Fred Allen.*

1830 *Gold-digger*—A woman who doesn't marry a man for his money, but divorces him for it. A woman who will be five years older twenty years from now. The difference between a millionaire and her is that he's got what it takes, and she takes what he's got.

1831 *Golf optimist*—The fellow who said he made fifteen on the first hole, fourteen on the second, thirteen on the third, and then blew up.

1832 *Grammatical error*—The use of poor English. Illustration: Lady (to tramp): "Did you notice that pile of wood?" Tramp: "Yes'm, I seen it." Lady: "You have made a grammatical error. You mean you saw it." Tramp: "No'm. You saw me see it, but you haven't seen me saw it."

1833 *Grapefruit*—The most frequently used American eye tonic.

1834 *Guest towel*—A towel you look at but never use.

1835 *Hamburger*—The last round-up.

1836 *Harness manufacturer*—The only man in the world who can put what he makes on the horses and not go broke.

1837 *Havana tobacco*—A product you find in Cuba and in a few cigars.

1838 *Hide and sick*—A game played on any ocean liner by a large number of the passengers.

1839 *Hitch-hiker*—The only person who could be completely incapacitated by the loss of his thumb.

1840 *Home*—The only place where you can enjoy corn on the cob and soup.

1841 *Hospital*—A place where people who are run down, wind up.

1842 *Human nature*—The thing which makes some men hewers of wood and others drawers of dividends.

1843 *Humor-in-advertising*—"We welcome complaints." "We Trust You." "Home Cooking."

1844 *Husband*—A man of few words.

1845 *I owe it all to*—An expression commonly used in connection with one's wife, landlord, or pawn broker.

1846 *In the money*—A condition many men hope for, but only a bank teller experiences.

1847 *Indigestion*—The failure to adjust a square meal to a round stomach.

1848 *Insomnia*—A sad condition in which you can't sleep when it's time to get up. When you keep a lot of innocent sheep jumping over a fence all night because one man can't go to sleep.

1849 *Ireland*—A great copper-producing country.

1850 *Jack*—A thing that lifts a car and also keeps it going.

1851 *Janitor*—A man who never puts out any excess hot air.

1852 *Jump*—The last word in airplanes.

1853 *June*—The month for weddings—when you have perfect daze.

1854 *Jury*—The only thing that doesn't work right when it's fixed. When the jury disagrees, the defendant can say, "No noose is good news."

1855 *Kangaroo*—Nature's initial effort to produce a cheer leader.

1856 *Kibitzer*—A guy with an inferiority complex.

1857 *Kitchenette couples*—Married folks who can say, "Now, Helen, you take the can opener and I'll take the poodle, and we'll move again."

1858 *Lame duck*—A politician whose goose has been cooked.

1859 *Law of diminishing returns*—An economic law familiar to laundrymen.

1860 *Lean years ahead*—What every woman hopes for.

1861 *Lend me your ears*—A phrase used by Marc Antony and by the mothers of ten million six-year-olds.

1862 *Life insurance*—A plan that keeps you poor all your life so you can die rich.

1863 *Limburger cheese business*—A business that always goes strong.

1864 *Love at first sight*—The world's greatest time-saver.

1865 *Lucky*—To have things go your way—illustrated in the conversation of two colored men playing cards: "Ah wins." "What yuh got?" "Three aces." "No yuh don't. Ah wins." "What yuh got?" "Two nines an' a razor." "Yuh sho win. How come yuh so lucky?"

1866 *Major general*—The army officer who has his men behind him before the battle and ahead of him during it.

1867 *Man*—The only animal with brains enough to find a cure for the diseases caused by his own folly.

1868 *Man of few words*—One who takes three hours to tell you he is a man of few words. Husband.

1869 *Manager of doughnut factory*—A fellow who has charge of the hole works.

1870 *Married life*—A period when you make progress if you break even. The most dangerous year in married life is the first; then comes the second, third, fourth, fifth, etc. Has three stages—cooing—wedding—billing.

1871 *Married man's razor*—His wife's pencil sharpener.

1872 *Microscope expert*—A person who magnifies everything.

1873 *Modern girl*—A girl who wants to go with every Tom, Dick and marry. She marries for money in order to make her dream come through. She demands the troth, the whole troth, and nothing but the troth. She is not so much concerned with what a man stands for, as what he will fall for. She loves a man for all he is worth.

1874 *Monkey business*—A lecture on evolution.

1875 *Monologue*—A conversation between a man and his wife.

1876 *Mussolini*—Looks like a case of duces wild.

1877 *Mystery*—How the Joneses do it on that salary.

1878 *Naïve person*—Anyone who thinks you are interested when you ask how he is.

1879 *New York*—The city where the people from Oshkosh look at the people from Dubuque in the next theater seats and say, "Humph, these New Yorkers don't dress any better than we do."

1880 *Oculist*—A man with an eye for business.

1881 *Oleomargarine*—A food bought by people who have seen butter days.

1882 *On the rocks*—A phrase meaning a person is either bankrupt or working in jail. The difference is inconsequential.

1883 *One set of dinner dishes*—A measure for the time the average maid lasts in an American home. If it's Woolworth china, it takes six weeks to break a set; Wedgwood, two weeks.

1884 *Open mind*—The mind of a man who has the will power to get rid of his present prejudices and take on a new set of prejudices. Sometimes, a case of a man merely rearranging his prejudices.

1885 *Opportunity of a lifetime*—A second-hand car. You can always hear it knocking.

1886 *Optimist*—One who looks in a cuckoo clock for eggs—or who takes a frying pan on a fishing trip.

1887 *Overworked*—To be busy continually. Example: a can opener in a kitchenette.

1888 *Parking space*—An unoccupied space about seven feet wide and fifteen feet long next to the curb—on the other side of the street. Ed Wynn says a parking space is the place where you take your car to have those little dents put in the mudguards.

1889 *Perfection*—An alarm clock that doesn't ring.

1890 *Pessimist*—A person who would commit suicide if he could do it without killing himself.

1891 *Pickpocket*—A man who generally lives alone, but occasionally goes out in a crowd for a little change. The optimist in a crowd.

1892 *Playing by note*—To learn to play the piano by note instead of by ear. Twelve payments on the note and the piano is yours to learn to play.

1893 *Politician*—A person who never duels, but certainly can fence. He never uses anti-knock gas.

1894 *Political plum*—One result of careful grafting.

1895 *Polka*—An old-fashioned dance, but now seen in almost any prize fight ring.

1896 *Precocious child*—The child who took his nose apart to see what made it run.

1897 *Premonition*—A warning of something to happen. Illustrations: An itching palm indicates you are about to receive something. An itching head shows that you already have something.

1898 *Prison warden*—A person who makes his living by his pen.

1899 *Profanity*—A way of escape for the man who runs out of ideas.

1900 *Prosperity*—A period when there are a lot of after-dinner speakers after dinners to speak after.

1901 *Proverb*—Any short saying that states a great truth. Examples: "A soft answer turneth away wrath, but hath little effect on a door-to-door salesman." "Birds of one feather catch a cold." "Uneasy is the tooth that wears a crown." "A thing of beauty keeps you broke forever."

1902 *Public library building*—The tallest building in town—it has more stories than any other.

1903 *Rabbit*—A little animal that grows the fur other animals get credit for when it's made into a lady's coat.—*Cincinnati Enquirer*.

1904 *Raccoon coats*—The earmarks of collegians. They cover a multitude of sons.

1905 *Reckless driver*—The other motorist. When you have two of these at an intersection at the same time, it's a case of the "survival of the hittest." Do not confuse a reckless driver with a wreckless driver.

1906 *Reckless driving*—A woman with a hammer and some nails working on a freshly painted, living room wall.

1907 *Reducing machine*—A machine that costs so much you have to starve yourself to keep up the payments.

1908 *Reformer*—One who insists on his conscience being your guide. One who makes his associates feel miserable about their pleasures.

1909 *Rejected play manuscript*—A case of all work and no play.

1910 *Repartee*—Clever conversation. To illustrate: "My ancestors came over on the Mayflower." "You're lucky. The immigration laws are stricter now."

1911 *Retraction*—To make one take back a statement. For example: A newspaper headline said—"Half of the city council are crooks." The city council demanded a retraction. The next day the headline said—"Half of the city council are not crooks."

1912 *Rich man*—A man who has so much money he doesn't even know his son is in college.

1913 *Rounder*—The fellow who can't look his wife squarely in the eye.

1914 *Rundown*—Not to feel well. When in this condition, always take the license number.

1915 *Scissors grinding*—A business that goes ahead when things are dull.

1916 *Scotchman*—The only golfer who wouldn't knock a golf ball out of sight.

1917 *Self-made man*—An individual who might have done better by letting out the contract. An admission that one is a self-made man makes one a martyr; it relieves the conscience of the rest of the world.

1918 *Sense of humor*—It's a gift—every Scotchman has it.

1919 *Settlement work*—Bill collecting.

1920 *Shoehorn*—An instrument that only plays foot notes.

1921 *Sickness*—Means not to feel well. There are three stages: 1. Ill; 2. Pill; 3. Bill. Sometimes there is another: 4. Will.

1922 *Silence*—What would follow if the average politician spoke his mind.

1923 *Sixth marriage*—The triumph of hope over experience.

1924 *Slogan*—Phrase used by businessmen to sell their products. Illustrations: "Good to the last drop" for Nookwood Pottery and also Arden Elevators; "The Hams What Am"—good for any amateur theatrical group.

1925 *Small town*—A place where everybody knows whose check is good.

1926 *Smallest man in history*—The soldier who went to sleep on his watch.

1927 *Smart fellow*—A man who says what he thinks, provided of course he agrees with us.

1928 *Smoking lounge*—A place that is usually crowded, but there is always room for one bore.

1929 *Snorer*—Just a sound sleeper.

1930 *Snoring*—The last of the personal liberties.

1931 *Sophistication*—To be too "smart" to feel guilty about anything you do.

1932 *Sound effects man*—The fellow in the radio station who can wreck a train, shoot a policeman and burn a house all in an evening's work.

1933 *Spaghetti*—A food that should not be cooked too long—at least, not over 18 inches for most of us.

1934 *Statistician*—A man who can go directly from an unwarranted assumption to a preconceived conclusion.

1935 *Strap hanger*—A person who has a complaint of long-standing.

1936 *Street car conductor*—The gent who tells them all where to get off at.

1937 *Success*—To get as much money as the other fellow wishes he could have got. A country retail merchant retired with a fortune of $100,000. That was success. His ability to retire with $100,000 after 40 years, was due to hard work, strict attention to duty, absolute honesty, economical living, and to the recent death of his uncle who left him $98,500.

1938 *Successful man*—One who can earn more than his wife can spend.

1939 *Successful wife's motto*—If at first you don't succeed, cry, cry again.

1940 *Sugar daddy*—A fellow who calls his sweetie a little sugar and later pays her a lump sum.

1941 *Summer resort*—A town where the inhabitants live on your vacation money until the next summer.

1942 *Synonym*—A word to use when you can't spell the other word.

1943 *Tactful*—To say the right thing at the right time. Example: Information man at zoo to fat lady—"The elephant is right over there lady; you haven't far to go."

1944 *Teeth*—The little white things you have pulled just before the doctor says: "Guess it must be the tonsils, then."

1945 *The meek*—The people who are going to inherit the earth and pay off the mortgage we leave them.

1946 *Thirty years old*—The age of a woman who is forty.

1947 *Toot ensemble*—Two hundred cars waiting for a green light at a busy intersection on a Sunday afternoon.

1948 *Tragedy*—A bride without a can opener. A California citizen dying in Florida. The man who wanted to become a great public speaker and wound up as toast master in a restaurant.

1949 *Traveling man's estate*—Five hundred towels, one thousand cakes of soap, one hundred spoons and eighty-five hotel keys.

1950 *Truth-in-advertising*—Examples: "They Groaned When I Reached for my Saxophone." "Nobody Laughed When He Stepped to the Piano. He was the Agent Who Had Come for the Second Installment."

1951 *Truthful woman*—A woman who does not lie about anything except her age, her weight, and her husband's salary.

1952 *Typographical error*—A misstatement. Illustration: A newspaper carried the notice that John Doe was a "defective" on the police force. This was a typographical error. It should have said, "Mr. John Doe is a detective on the police farce."

1953 *Umbrella*—Common property. One man's loss is another man's umbrella. Synonyms: Hotel spoons or towels, the former, like medicine, being taken after meals.

1954 *Umpire*—A retired baseball player whose eyesight begins to fail him.

1955 *Vacation resort*—A place that overlooks a lake, and also overlooks comfortable beds, good food and running water.

1956 *Velocity*—What a person puts a hot plate down with.

1957 *Vice-president*—A title given to a bank officer in place of a raise in salary. Any good golf player.

1958   *Noah Webster*—The author who had the biggest vocabulary.

1959   *Wife*—A man's booin' companion. The old-fashioned wife darned her hubby's socks, but the modern wife socks her darned hubby. A continual buzzing in a man's ears.

1960   *Woman's ambition*—To be weighed and found wanting.

1961   *Woman's crowning glory*—A rich man's scalp.

1962   *Yellow peril*—A banana skin on the front steps.

1963   *Yes*—The answer to any question the boss asks. A married man's last word.

Chapter 7

INTERESTING LIVES AND
INTERESTING FACTS

....

1964   MARK TWAIN

Mark Twain once asked a neighbor if he might read a set of his books. The neighbor replied ungraciously that he was welcome to read them in his library, but he had a rule never to let a book leave the house. Some weeks later the same neighbor sent over to ask for the loan of his lawn-mower.

"I shall be very glad to lend you my lawn-mower," said Mark Twain, "but since I made it a rule never to let it leave my lawn, you will be obliged to use it there."

1965   DISRAELI

Disraeli, when Prime Minister of England, was known among many other things, as having an excellent memory. One day he was asked how he managed to remember all those names and never offend anyone by appearing not to recognize members of Parliament on sight. The prime minister replied: "When I meet a man whose name I cannot remember, I give myself two minutes; then if it is a hopeless case, I always say: 'And how is the old complaint'?"

1966   DARROW

The late Clarence Darrow, eminent Chicago criminal lawyer, was one evening the principal speaker at a meeting of a Women's Club in a middle western city. After his speech, which had been greeted with salvos of applause, the lawyer found himself engaged in conversation with a couple of ladies who insisted on discussing birth control.

"Now, Mr. Darrow," said one, "what do you think of birth control for the masses?"

"My dear lady," replied the famous lawyer, "whenever I hear people discussing birth control, I always remember that I was the fifth."

1967   SCHUBERT

Schubert's C-Major Symphony, familiarly known as the Sixth Symphony, is conceded by many musicians to be his masterpiece. This work was first performed in Vienna in 1828, but London and Paris did not hear it until thirty years later. The Paris Orchestra, under Habeneck, refused to play it, and the

London Philharmonic laughed at the composition. The conductor withdrew it from rehearsal. Sir August Manns placed it on a program in London in 1856, and after the first movement was finished the horn player called to the first violin sitting close to him:

"Tom, have you been able to discover a tune yet?"

"Heck, no. This hasn't any tune," the violinist replied.

1968   PATIENCE

Infinite patience is the price that many a man has paid for success. Gibbon worked twenty years on his "Decline and Fall of the Roman Empire." Noah Webster spent thirty-six years on his dictionary. George Bancroft spent twenty-six years on his "History of the United States."

1969   HAWTHORNE

The greatest literary artist in American history, our foremost novelist, Nathaniel Hawthorne, not only owed his success to the daily inspiration of his wife, but also his only opportunity to compose first his mind, and then his masterpiece. If it had not been for Sophia, perhaps we should not now remember Nathaniel. He lost his job in the custom house. A broken-hearted man, he went home to tell his wife that he was a failure. To his amazement, she beamed with joy, and said: "Now you can write your book!" To his bitter rejoinder, "Yes, and what shall we live on while I am writing it?" the astounding woman opened a drawer and took out an unsuspected hoard of cash. "Where on earth did you get that?" She answered, "I have always known that you were a man of genius. I knew that some day you would write an immortal masterpiece. So every week, out of the money you have given me for housekeeping, I have saved something; here is enough to last us one whole year." Hawthorne sat down and wrote one of the finest books ever written in the western hemisphere—"The Scarlet Letter."

1970   LINCOLN

The battle of Gettysburg had just been fought. Lincoln sensed an opportunity to end the war by driving hard against Lee's rear in retreat. A swift, daring attack might do it. As commander-in-chief of the army, he ordered General Meade to pursue. A friendly note in the president's handwriting accompanied the instructions:

"The order I enclose is not of record. If you succeed, you need not publish the order. If you fail, publish it. Then, if you succeed, you will have all the credit of the movement. If not, I'll take all the responsibility."

That was Abraham Lincoln, brave, self-effacing, a nobleman in thought and deed.

1971   BENJAMIN FRANKLIN

Printer, editor, publisher, business man, financier, economist and teacher of thrift, philosopher, moralist, and advocate of the simple life, scientist and patron of education, philanthropist, statesman, diplomat—and above all a man and a patriot, he is claimed as their own by more groups than any other person in our history. With truth he has been characterized as: "A Man" so various, that he seemed not one but all mankind's epitome. Someone has called him a typical American; rather might we think of him as a composite

American. Born in poverty, he was apprenticed in a print shop and always thought of himself as a printer. "He that hath a trade, hath an estate" is one of his famous maxims. By thrift and industry he accumulated a competency which enabled him to devote the latter half of his life to public service. By one fitted to judge, Franklin has been referred to as "the greatest of all diplomatic representatives of this country." As the collector of funds for the Revolutionary War, he might be known as the originator of the "Liberty Loan." He has been called the Father of our Navy; and as Postmaster General of the Colonies founded the first adequate postal system here. Not only does our government recognize his great services, but more and more are we coming to realize how much we owe to Benjamin Franklin's genius in all manner of human relationships and endeavors.—*Calvin Coolidge.*

1972   TACT

Charles Schwab walked through a factory. He saw three men smoking. He did not reprimand them. He merely reached in his pocket, took out three cigars and said, "Boys, have a cigar on me, but I should appreciate it if you would not smoke it during working hours."

1973   BENJAMIN FRANKLIN

Did you ever stop to wonder who invented the old-fashioned stove—or bifocal glasses—who first advocated the use of copper for roofs—who conceived of a damper for chimneys—who first pointed out that white is the coolest thing to wear in summer—who invented the long pole that is now used in grocery stores to reach articles on top shelves—who thought of a combined chair and step-ladder—who was responsible for the paving and lighting of streets—who thought it would be nice to have trees bordering both sides of streets—who formed the first library company—the first fire company—the first American fire insurance company—who founded the dead letter office and the penny post—who was responsible for American university education? Well, it was Benjamin Franklin, who incidentally was the first president of America's oldest university—the University of Pennsylvania.—*The Fusion Point.*

1974   WINSTON S. CHURCHILL

A story of Winston S. Churchill—told by Gertrude Atherton:

"Shortly after he left the Conservative side of the House (of Commons) for the liberal, he was taking a certain young woman down to dinner, when she looked up at him coquettishly, and remarked with the audacity of her kind:

" 'There are two things I don't like about you, Mr. Churchill.'

" 'And what are they?'

" 'Your new politics and mustache.'

" 'My dear madam,' he replied suavely, 'pray do not disturb yourself. You are not likely to come in contact with either.' "—*Atlanta Journal.*

1975   LORD CHESTERFIELD

Lord Chesterfield, attending an entertainment in France, appeared to be gazing about at the brilliant circle of ladies which surrounded him, when he was approached by Voltaire.

"My Lord," laughingly remarked the great Frenchman, "I know **you are** a well-qualified judge. Tell me, who are more beautiful—the English or the French ladies?"

In the face of such a ticklish question most men might have quailed; but not the adroit Chesterfield. Looking about at the sea of feminine faces made lovely by the liberal use of rouge and other artificial colorings, he replied, "Upon my word, I cannot tell. I am really no connoisseur of paintings."

1976   CHARLES I

Although it was Ferdinand V of Spain who dispatched Hernando Cortez on an exploration of the New World, it was to his son, Charles I, that the redoubtable explorer returned to make his report. Cortez recommended that a passage to India be effected by digging a canal across the Isthmus of Panama.

Charles consulted his advisers and then rejected the recommendation. Asked to explain the reason for his decision, the King sternly replied, "It would be a violation of the Biblical injunction: 'What God hath joined together let no man put asunder.' "

1977   LAFAYETTE

One day at a public function, the admirers of General Lafayette, desiring to show the love and admiration they felt for their idol, unhitched his horses from the carriage and pulled the vehicle to the hotel themselves.

Some weeks later, a friend of the General, recalling the stirring event, remarked, "You must have been very much pleased."

Lafayette regarded him quietly for a moment, then, with a whimsical smile, replied, "Yes, it was delightful, delightful; but one thing disturbs me a little—I never saw anything more of my horses."

1978   SIR WALTER SCOTT

Long after Sir Walter Scott had gained renown as a writer he endeavored to conceal his literary fame from his children, even attempting to keep them from reading his works.

One day his publisher, Ballantyne, came to congratulate him upon the success of his "Lady of the Lake," and, seeing the author's 12-year-old daughter alone in the library, said, "And how do you like 'The Lady of the Lake'?"

"Oh," she replied, "I haven't read it. Father says that nothing is so harmful for young people as reading bad books."

1979   SAMUEL F. B. MORSE

Samuel F. B. Morse was an eminent painter before he invented telegraphy. He painted a scene showing a man in death-agony once, and asked a physician friend to examine it. "Well?" Morse inquired after the doctor had scrutinized the picture. "What's your opinion?"

The physician removed his spectacles, turned to Morse and commented: "Malaria!"

1980   RESPECT

Charles V admired and respected the great Titian. One day when the brush dropped from Titian's hand, Charles V picked it up for him, saying, "You deserve to be served by an emperor."

1981   MOZART AND HAYDN

Mozart once said to a critic, "If you and I were both melted down together,
we should not furnish materials for one Haydn."

And Haydn said of Mozart that if every friend of music, and great men
in particular, appreciated Mozart's genius as he did, "nations would vie with
each other to possess such a jewel within their frontiers."

1982   RESPECT A BURDEN

One time when Napoleon was walking at St. Helena with Mrs. Balcombe,
some servants approached carrying a load. Mrs. Balcombe ordered them out
of the way, but Napoleon interrupted and said, "Respect the burden, madam."

1983   A LIVELIHOOD AND LETTERS AND ARTS

Many writers, scientists and distinguished men have had to make a living
in business, government and various fields while they pursued their other
interests as time permitted. Chaucer was a soldier and later comptroller of
petty customs. Spencer was secretary to the Lord Deputy of Ireland; Bacon
was a lawyer before he became lord keeper and lord chancellor. Addison was
secretary of state. Shakespeare managed a theater and was but an ordinary
actor. Dante and Boccaccio were in embassies. Galileo was a physician; Schiller
a surgeon. De Foe was a brick and tile maker and a shop keeper. John Stuart
Mill was an examiner in the East India House, and Charles Lamb also
worked there. Macaulay wrote the "Lays of Ancient Rome" while holding
the position of secretary of war. Ricardo was a banker. Sir Isaac Newton was
a Master of the Mint.

1984   AN ESTIMATE OF THE VALUE OF CHARACTER AND LEADERSHIP

In 1798, Washington was an old man living in retirement at Mount Vernon.
It seemed possible that France might declare war against us. President Adams
wrote Washington, "We must have your name, if you will permit us to use
it; there will be more efficacy in it than in many an army." Here was an estimate of the great esteem in which the people held Washington's character and
leadership.

1985   MEN AND MOVEMENTS

Great institutions and movements grow out of men of great character. So
we think of Quakerism and Fox, Methodism and Wesley, Puritanism and
Calvin, Jesuitism and Loyola.

1986   MOTHERS

George Herbert said a good mother equaled a hundred school masters.
George Washington, the eldest of five children, was only eleven years old
when his father died. His mother was a woman of extraordinary ability who
handled her responsibilities with such success that her children grew up to
reflect honor upon themselves and upon her. Goethe, Scott, Gray, Schiller,
Wesley, Bacon, Erskine all were particularly influenced by the intelligent
guidance of their mothers.

1987   ABSENT-MINDED

Henry Erskine, Lord Advocate of Scotland toward the close of the eighteenth century, had a tutor who was very absent-minded. So much so that Erskine, who thought a great deal of the old man, was one day flabbergasted to hear him say: "I was very sorry, my dear boy, you have had the fever in your family; was it you or your brother who died of it?" "It was I," Erskine replied. "Ah, dear me, I thought so—very sorry for it—very sorry for it." And the old man walked away.

1988   DETAILS

Shortly after the entry of the United States into the World War, General John J. Pershing was equally praised and criticized by those who thought they knew as much about running the army as he did. As is the case with most public figures, he had a hard time pleasing everyone. One of his chief critics called him to task for spending so much time on small details. Pershing replied:

"I am doing this now, while I have the time, in order that those under me will know how my mind works when I have not the time to spend on minor details."

1989   NO REASON FOR DISLIKE

Years on Wall Street failed to rob the late Dwight Morrow of a shy, whimsical humor. Being told that a certain business acquaintance had acquired a marked dislike for him, Mr. Morrow lapsed into a puzzled silence, then plaintively exclaimed, "I don't see why he should feel hard toward me. I don't remember ever doing anything for him."

1990   INSPIRATION

Boswell and Johnson were at Drury Lane Theatre together watching the great actor, Garrick. Boswell said to Johnson, "Garrick is not himself tonight," and the great man replied, "No."

All at once Garrick commenced to act superbly, and Boswell remarked, "Do you notice how he has changed and changed for the better?" "Yes," said the old sage, "and did you notice at what point he changed? He took a higher style when Edmund Burke came into the theater."

1991   YOUTH

Alfred Tennyson wrote his first volume at eighteen.

Alexander was a mere youth when he rolled back the Asiatic hordes that threatened to overwhelm European civilization almost at its birth.

Napoleon had conquered Italy at twenty-five.

Byron, Raphael and Poe died at thirty-seven after writing their names among the world's immortals.

Newton made some of his greatest discoveries before he was twenty-five.

It is said that no English poet ever equaled Chatterton at twenty-one.

Victor Hugo wrote a tragedy at fifteen. Many of the world's greatest geniuses never saw forty years.

1992   DANIEL WEBSTER

Gray's "Elegy" was Daniel Webster's favorite poem, and he delighted to repeat it with great emphasis.

1993   BENJAMIN FRANKLIN

Famous was the toast given by Benjamin Franklin when he was dining, as the American emissary, with the English Ambassador and the French Minister, at Versailles. The story was first published in 1797.

"George the Third," proposed the British Ambassador, "who, like the sun in its meridian, spreads a luster throughout and enlightens the world."

"The illustrious Louis the Sixteenth," proposed the French Minister, "who, like the moon, sheds his mild and benignant rays on and influences the globe."

"George Washington," thereupon proposed witty Benjamin Franklin, "commander of the American armies, who, like Joshua of old, commanded the sun and the moon to stand still, and they obeyed him."

1994   MARK TWAIN

Mark Twain, as Samuel Langhorne Clemens (1835-1910) chose to call himself, was known to be eccentric—Mrs. Clemens called him "careless"—in his dress. As many a man did before him, and many another has done since, Mark Twain went calling one day without his necktie. He had been visiting Harriet Beecher Stowe, of "Uncle Tom" fame, and he was not aware of his lack of haberdashery until Mrs. Clemens called attention to it on his return.

A little later Mrs. Stowe answered her door to find a messenger, who gave her a small package. Opening it, she found a black silk necktie inside, and a brief note:

"Here is a necktie. Take it out and look at it. I think I stayed half an hour this morning without this necktie. At the end of that time, will you kindly return it, as it is the only one I have. MARK TWAIN."

1995   WEBSTER AND CROCKETT

After hearing Daniel Webster speak, David Crockett said to him: "I had heard that you were a very great man, but I don't think so. I heard your speech and understood every word you said."

1996   RUDYARD KIPLING

When the report went around that Rudyard Kipling was getting a shilling a word for his writings, some Oxford students set about a "rag." They sent him a shilling, accompanied by this message:

"Please send us one of your words."

And right back came the unexpected answer:

"Thanks."

1997   HOUDINI

Florenz Ziegfeld and Charles Dillingham, the great Broadway producers, were pallbearers at Houdini's funeral. As they carried the coffin of the famed handcuff and escape wizard out of the church, Dillingham leaned over and said, "Ziggie, I bet you a hundred dollars he ain't in here!"—*Ladies' Home Journal.*

1998   A DIFFERENCE

A musical student visited Mozart one day and said, "I want to write a concerto. Will you tell me how to go about it?"

"You are too young," replied the great composer. "Wait until you are a few years older."

"But," objected the young man, "you composed when you were seven or eight."

"Yes," agreed Mozart, "but I didn't have to ask anyone how to do it."

1999   NOT HIS ATTIRE

For some reason Bret Harte frequently found himself credited with the authorship of the popular poem, "Little Breeches," a distinction properly belonging to John Hay.

"My dear Mr. Harte, I am so delighted to meet you," exclaimed a gushing young lady. "I want to tell you how much I enjoyed reading your 'Little Breeches.'"

"I thank you very kindly, madam," replied Harte, "but permit me to say —you have put the little breeches on the wrong man."

2000   FREDERICK THE GREAT

Frederick the Great was a master diplomat, and able to compliment those whom he wished to please. In 1770, when the interviews were being held at court, he noticed General Laudohn, one of his most able adversaries seated across the table. Speaking up in a loud voice, he said: "Pray, sir, take place here at my right; I do not feel at ease to have you opposite me even at the table."

2001   BRANDEIS

Louis D. Brandeis, Associate Justice of the United States Supreme Court, was one evening attending a dinner party, and a discussion of lawsuits and trials came about. After listening for several minutes to the discussion, which centered on the causes of arguments which wound up in the court for termination, the Justice said:

"Arguments seem so futile to me, for behind every argument I have ever heard lies the astounding ignorance of someone."

2002   WELLINGTON

At the battle of Waterloo, the colonel commanding the British artillery observed to the Duke of Wellington: "I have got the exact range of the spot where Bonaparte and his staff are standing. If your grace will allow me, I think I can pick some of them off." "No, no," replied Wellington, "Generals-in-chief have something else to do in a great battle besides firing at each other."

2003   BEING DIFFERENT

Woolworth conceived the idea of the Five and Ten Cent store.

That was *different.* His fortune was measured by millions when he passed away.

Wanamaker conceived the idea of one-price to everybody in his retail stores.
That was *different*, for at the time he put this policy into effect it was directly contrary to the accepted practice throughout the country.

Ford determined to build a light, cheap car for the millions.
That was *different*. His reward came in the greatest automobile output in the world.

Human progress has often depended on the courage of a man who dared to be different.

2004   FAILURES

Lord Bulwer's life was a succession of failures, crowned with final triumph. His first novel was a *failure*; his first drama was a *failure*; so were his first speeches and poems. But he fought both defeat and ridicule and finally won a place with Thackeray and Dickens.

Savonarola's first efforts were dismal *failures*. His brave heart eventually made him Italy's greatest orator.

Daniel Webster could not make a speech until after years of persistent effort. Finally, he became one of America's greatest orators.

Washington lost more battles than he won. But he triumphed in the end.

Franklin, Patrick Henry, Clay, Jackson, Douglas, Lincoln, Grant, were all sons of poor parents. They faced many obstacles, but they finally surmounted them successfully.

2005   TIME

Voltaire, the famous Frenchman, was a dwarf in body and a giant in intellect.

In his "Zadig, a Mystery of Fate," is found the following question put to Zadig by the Grand Magi:

"What, of all things in the world, is the longest and the shortest, the swiftest and the slowest, the most divisible and the most extended, the most neglected and the most regretted, without which nothing can be done, which devours all that is little, and enlivens all that is great?"

Here is Zadig's answer:

"Time."

"Nothing is longer, since it is the measure of eternity."

"Nothing is shorter, since it is insufficient for the accomplishment of your projects."

"Nothing is more slow to him that expects; nothing more rapid to him that enjoys."

"In greatness it extends to infinity, in smallness it is infinitely divisible."

"All men neglect it; all regret the loss of it; nothing can be done without it."

"It consigns to oblivion whatever is unworthy of being transmitted to posterity, and it immortalizes such actions as are truly great."

Time is man's most precious asset.

2006   NO PASSES

In the days when the late Col. Edward H. R. Green, railroad industrialist and banker, was managing the Texas Midland Railroad for his mother, the

astute Hetty Green—known to fame as the "richest woman in America"—
he was having a lot of trouble with applicants for passes over the line, and
so consulted his mother about it. She mentioned the matter to her friend
Chauncey M. Depew, who knew all about railroads, being a high official
of the New York Central. Depew gave her a list of Biblical quotations, which
she forwarded to her son.

The list was arranged as a calendar in this manner:
Monday—"Thou shalt not pass." (Num. 20:18.)
Tuesday—"Suffer not a man to pass." (Judg. 3:28.)
Wednesday—"The wicked shall no more pass." (Nah. 1:15.)
Thursday—"This generation shall not pass." (Mark 13:30.)
Friday—"By a perpetual decree it cannot pass." (Jer. 5:22.)
Saturday—"None shall pass." (Isa. 34:10.)
Sunday—"So he paid the fare thereof and went." (Jonah 1:3.)

2007   PARENTAL PRAISE

When Edward Bok asked Lockwood Kipling, the father of Rudyard Kipling, what he thought of his son's work, the elder Kipling replied, "Creditable."

Surprised, Bok persisted, "But surely you must consider that Rud has done
some great work?" He was thinking of "The Jungle Book," "If," "Captains
Courageous" and other immortal works.

"Creditable," repeated Kipling's father briefly.

Bok was almost ready to give up. "But you think him capable of great
work, do you not?"

"He has a certain grasp of the human instinct," Lockwood Kipling admitted. "That some day will lead him to write a great work."

Kipling was never in danger of meaningless praise from his father.

Christian Science Monitor

2008   A GOOD ADDRESS

Lord Balfour was guest of honor at a banquet where many speeches were
made. When it came time for him to deliver his own remarks, the hour was
late and he was exceedingly weary.

"I have been asked to give an address," he said, "and I shall beg the privilege of giving my own. It is No. 40, Carlton Garden, and, with your kind
permission, I will go there at once."

2009   ONE MUST EAT

Daniel Webster, the great American statesman, was once sued by his
butcher for a bill of long standing. Before the suit was settled he met the
butcher on the street, and to that worthy's embarrassment said: "Why have
you not sent around for my order?" "Why, Mr. Webster," said the man. "I
did not think you wanted to deal with me when I brought this suit."

"Tut, tut," said Webster, "sue all you wish, but for heaven's sake, don't
try to starve me to death."

2010   A LONG SPEECH

In an early American Congress, General Alexander Smythe, of Virginia,
and Henry Clay were members. Smythe was a studious man, but a very la-

borious speaker, who worried the House with prolonged speeches. One day, in particular, he was being very tedious, and turning to Mr. Clay, said: "You, sir, speak for the present generation; but I speak for posterity." Clay, without smiling, retorted: "Yes, and you seem resolved to speak until the arrival of your audience."

2011   JOSEPH CHOATE

When Joseph Choate was American ambassador to Great Britain, many amusing incidents arose. For one, he had gained quite a lot of weight while in England. When he returned to this country, some of his friends, remembering his slight build, remarked about his corpulence. "Why, Mr. Choate," said one, "you have been getting stout since you went abroad." "Oh, yes," replied he, "I found it necessary to meet the Englishmen half way."

2012   WESTINGHOUSE

Two freight trains collided and a young man set to work to prevent a repetition of such an accident. The result was the invention of the air brake and the beginning of a great industry.

Railroad executives took the attitude of Commodore Vanderbilt, who, when George Westinghouse explained the superiority of the air brake over the dangerous hand brakes, exclaimed, "Do you mean to tell me that you expect to stop a train with wind? I have no time to waste on damn fools."

Westinghouse did not give up and complain that his ability was not appreciated. He invented a railroad frog which appealed to the railroad officials and eventually gave him an opportunity to have the air brake tested. It is that air brake and Westinghouse's system of railway signaling which makes all travel safer.

2013   OLE BULL

When Ole Bull, the famous Norwegian violinist, came to play in America, there were some jealous musicians here who attacked him through the press. Mr. James Gordon Bennett very graciously offered him the columns of the Herald, so that he might make his reply. But wise Ole Bull knew that he possessed a far better weapon than a printing press.

"I tink, Mr. Bennett," he replied in his broken English, "it is best tey writes against me, and I plays against tem."

The great acclaim he received at the hands of the American public proved that he was right.

2014   WILLIAM E. BORAH

During the administration of the late President Warren G. Harding, the late Senator William E. Borah, one of the so-called "insurgents" of the Republican party, was sought as an administration leader. The President's advisers hoped, in this manner, to keep Borah more or less in "line" with the party. The senator listened with interest until the President had finished speaking, then said:

"Mr. President, you can get along without me, but I cannot get along without my political views. Thanks just the same."

2015 EINSTEIN

Professor Albert Einstein gave recently what he considered the best formula for success in life. "If a is success in life, I should say the formula is a equals x plus y plus z, x being WORK and y being play."

"And what is z?" inquired the interviewer.

"That," he answered, "is keeping your mouth shut."

Christian Register

2016 NAPOLEON III

The brilliant and beautiful Irish lady, the Countess of Blessington, had befriended Louis Napoleon, later Napoleon III, when he was a fugitive, exiled in England.

After his rise to power, having never invited her to the Tuileries Palace, he met her one day accidentally in Paris and said: "Do you expect to remain long in Paris?"

She gazed at him coldly and replied: "And you?" walking on. Later Bismarck drove him from the throne.

2017 MADAME DE STAEL

Madame de Stael, whose plain features and blunt manner caused many men discomfiture, one night was dining at the home of the beautiful Madame Recamier. The astronomer, Lalande, found himself seated between these two women. Thinking he would please both, he exclaimed: "How happy I am to find myself between wit and beauty."

Not lacking in spirit was Madame de Stael, whose prompt reply was: "And without possessing either."

2018 MARK TWAIN

Mark Twain once told a story of his early lecturing days. Arriving in a town where he was to speak in the early afternoon and seeing that the evening lecture was poorly billed, he stopped in at the general store and addressing the proprietor, said:

"Good afternoon, friend, any entertainment here tonight to help a stranger while away his evening?" The storekeeper straightened up, wiped his hands on his apron and said: "I expect there is going to be a lecture—I have been sellin' eggs all day."

2019 ROYALTY

Nicholas I of Russia had asked Liszt, the great pianist, to play at court. Right in the middle of the opening number, the great musician looked at the Czar and saw him talking to an aide. He continued playing, but was very much irritated. As the Czar did not stop, Liszt finally quit playing. The Czar sent a messenger to ask why he was not playing and Liszt said: "When the Czar speaks, everyone should be silent." Thereafter there was no interruption in the concert.

2020 QUEEN VICTORIA

Her exalted rank did not give Queen Victoria immunity from the trials of a grandmother. One of her grandsons, whose recklessness in spending money provoked her strong disapproval, wrote to the Queen reminding her of his approaching birthday and delicately suggested that money would be the most acceptable gift. In her own hand she answered, sternly reproving the youth for the sin of extravagance and urging upon him the practice of economy. His reply staggered her:

"Dear Grandma," it ran, "thank you for your kind letter of advice. I have sold the same for five pounds."

2021   Dr. Everett's Advice

An indignant Bostonian once rushed to Dr. Everett's house. One of the local papers had published an article severely criticizing this man. Should he demand a public apology, or file a suit for damages?

Dr. Everett listened quietly, then interrupted. "What should you do? My dear sir, do nothing. Half the people who read that paper never saw that article. Half of those who read it do not understand it. Half of those who did understand it did not believe it. Half of those who believed it were of no consequence anyway."

Christian Science Monitor

2022   Marconi

Signor Marconi, in an interview in Washington many years ago, praised American democracy.

"Over here," he said, "you respect a man for what he is himself—not for what his family is—and thus you remind me of the gardener in Bologna who helped me with my first experiments.

"As my mother's gardener and I were working on my apparatus together, a young count joined us one day and while he watched us work the count boasted of his lineage.

"The gardener, after listening a long while, smiled and said:

"'If you come from an ancient family, it is so much the worse for you, sir; for, as we gardeners say, the older the seed the worse the crop.'"

2023   Research

Scientific research has opened up new avenues of employment for countless thousands through the development of new products which gave birth to new industries. . . . In 1900, the horse and buggy business gave jobs to around 1,000,000 persons. But in 1937, the automobile industry furnished employment, in making, selling, and servicing cars to over 6,000,000 persons. Fifteen of our major manufacturing industries of today have been developed since 1879, and it has been estimated that these 15 industries have created, directly and indirectly, 15,000,000 new jobs. On the basis of these figures, at least one out of every four persons gainfully employed today owes his job to one of these 15 industries having their origin wholly or in part in developments resulting from scientific research.

In the Du Pont Company, 12 new lines accounted for about 40 per cent of the total sales during 1937, and these have been developed largely during the past ten years. During this period, 7,000 additional employees were required for the production and sale of the new items. Incidentally the average price of these products was reduced 40 per cent during this period of ten years.

Dr. Ernest B. Benger, Assistant Chemical Director, Du Pont Company

2024   THRIFT

One hundred average men start their productive life at age 25. At age 65 one is wealthy; four are well-to-do; 54 are not self-supporting; 36 have died. At age 75, 33 of the 100 are still living, and of these, three are entirely self-supporting and thirty are dependent.—*U. S. Treasury Dept. Textbook on Thrift.*

2025   SIMPLE OR COMPLEX ECONOMY

We are told that, when Washington, Jefferson and company originally assigned tasks to governmental and business leaders, we had in this country a "simple economy" and that now we have a "complex economy," though I have never been able to see why one is complex and the other is simple. When my grandmother had to build a fire out of buffalo chips and make a pot of soup out of nothing, that wasn't so simple. My daughter can turn on the gas, open up a tin can and there is the soup. I would like to know which is the complex and which is the simple.—*B. E. Heacock, President, Caterpillar Tractor Company.*

2026   COMPOUND INTEREST

Here are four rules that will help anyone who wants to know just what money will do:

At 4 per cent compound interest, money will double itself in a little less than eighteen years.

At 5 per cent compound interest, money will double itself in approximately fourteen years.

At 6 per cent compound interest, money will double itself in approximately twelve years.

At 8 per cent compound interest, money will double itself in about nine years.

When these facts are understood, large fortunes are not so wonderful after all, and a person only wonders that more families do not possess them.

2027   CODE OF CONDUCT

Written in 1858 for the four employees of Carson, Pirie & Company, now Carson, Pirie, Scott & Company, Chicago.

"Store must be open from 6 a. m. to 9 p. m. the year round. Store must be swept; counter base and showcases dusted, lamps trimmed, filled and chimneys cleaned; pens made; doors and windows opened; a pail of water, also a bucket of coal brought in before breakfast (if there is time to do so and attend to customers who call).

"Store must not be opened on the Sabbath, *unless necessary to do,* and then only for a few minutes.

"The employee who is in the habit of smoking Spanish cigars, being shaved at the barber shop, going to dances and other places of amusement, will surely give his employer reason to be suspicious of his integrity and honesty.

"Each employee must pay not less than $5 per year to the church and must attend Sunday school regularly.

"Men employees are given one evening a week for courting and two if they go to prayer meeting.

"After fourteen hours of work in the store, the leisure hours should be spent mostly in reading."

Some of these rules may seem a bit humorous now, but there are great lessons in this code for all of us.

2028   WORDS

Of the 400,000 words in the English language, the working journalist is accredited with use of the largest number, something less than 20,000. Clergymen, lawyers and doctors use an average of about 10,000 words. Skilled workers of ordinary education know about 5,000, farm laborers about 1,600. The sciences and professions have large numbers of words the layman never hears of. For instance, medical men and women must know the names of 433 muscles, 193 veins, 707 arteries, 500 pigments, 295 poisons, 109 tumors, 700 tests, over 200 diseases, and over 1,300 bacteria.

Yet with all these words, think of the people who still have trouble expressing themselves. Think of the people who constantly wonder what they are all about.

2029   EPITAPH

A tombstone in an English village cemetery has the following inscription
      "Here lies a miser who lived for himself,
      And cared for nothing but gathering pelf,
      Now, where he is or how he fares,
      Nobody knows and nobody cares."

2030   AMERICA IN THE EARLY NINETEENTH CENTURY

There was not a public library in the United States.
Almost all the furniture was imported from England.
An old copper mine in Connecticut was used as a prison.
There was one hat factory, and that made cocked hats.
Every gentleman wore a queue, and powdered his hair.
Crockery plates were objected to because they dulled the knives.
Virginia contained a fifth of the whole population of the country.
A gentleman bowing to a lady always scraped his foot on the ground.
The Whipping Post and Pillory were still standing in Boston and New York.
Beef, pork, salt fish, potatoes and hominy were the staple diet all the year round.
Buttons were scarce and expensive, and the trousers were fastened with pegs or laces.
When a man had enough to eat he placed his spoon across his cup, to indicate that he wanted no more.
The church collection was taken in a bag at the end of a pole, with a bell attached to arouse sleepy contributors.

2031   EPITAPH—1827

A seventeenth century tombstone in an English churchyard contains this inscription:

> "Here lies the body of Ethan Bevan,
> Killed by lightning sent from heaven
> For trading horses on Sunday, June eleven,
> In the year Eighteen Hundred Twenty-seven."

2032   GIVING

The grave of Christopher Chapman in Westminster Abbey, bearing the date of 1680, says:

> "What I gave, I have,
> What I spent, I had,
> What I left, I lost
> By not giving it."

2033   END MISSING

Benjamin Franklin was invariably prompt in the performance of his public duties, and grew weary when they could not be consummated with reasonable dispatch.

Once after giving a great deal of time to a public matter, with no end in sight, he remarked, "I begin to be a little of the sailor's mind when they were handing a cable out of the store into a ship, and one of 'em said: ' 'Tis a long, heavy cable. I wish we could see the end of it.' 'Bless my soul,' said another, 'if I believe it has any end; somebody has cut it off.' "

2034   COLD FEET

Measuring six feet four himself, Lincoln once met a soldier several inches taller than himself. "Say, friend," said the president, looking up in admiration, "does your head know when your feet are cold?"

2035   SECOND CHOICE

Carlos of Portugal once paid a visit to England, where he was given the opportunity of observing phases of English life. At the conclusion of his stay, King Edward asked the young sovereign what of all things in England he liked best.

Carlos, who was something of a gourmand, replied, "The roast beef."

"Is that all that impressed you?" inquired the English sovereign.

Carlos reflected a moment, and then replied, "Well, the boiled beef is not so bad."

2036   THE END IN VIEW

Thackeray knew how to puncture the ego of a snob as well with his tongue as with his famous pen.

One day, at his club, he was accosted by an officer of the Guards notorious for both his vanity and his pomposity, who, in a tone of patronizing familiarity, exclaimed, "Haw, Thackeray, old boy, I hear Lawrence has been painting your portrait!"

"So he has," replied Thackeray.

"Haw! Full length?"

"No. Full-length portraits are for soldiers that we may see their spurs. But with authors, the other end of the man is the principal thing."

Wall Street Journal

2037   OUTWITTED

Rufus Choate, in association with Daniel Webster, was handling an important case for a Boston shipping house. Before him in the witness box was an Irish shipowner, whom he was trying to confuse by asking him a long and involved question. According to a spectator, the question wound all round the case and straggled through every street in Boston. But the witness remained calm and unruffled.

When Mr. Choate had finished, the Irishman leaned forward and quietly asked, "Mr. Choate, will ye be afther repating that question again?"

Wall Street Journal

2038   LINCOLN'S MEASURE

At a White House reception the Russian Ambassador was talking to President Lincoln, when the Chief Executive asked, "Would you have taken me for an American if you had met me anywhere else than in this country?"

The Muscovite, who was something of a wag, surveyed the President's tall frame, and replied, "No, I should have taken you for a Pole."

"And so I am," exclaimed Lincoln, drawing himself up to his full height, "and a Liberty Pole at that."

Wall Street Journal

2039   SYMPATHETIC HAMMERSTEIN

When Oscar Hammerstein seemed to be encountering financial difficulties in his grand opera undertaking at the Metropolitan Opera House it was his habit to go to other theaters and console himself for his own trouble by gazing on the spectacle of the empty seats in the other fellow's playhouse.

One night he hied himself over to a theater where a prominent star was holding forth; Hammerstein began to sympathize with the manager of the star, saying, "Really it is too bad you are not drawing better houses."

"I don't need your sympathy; why there's just twelve hundred dollars in this house tonight," said the house manager.

"Whew!" exclaimed Oscar, "that's an honest usher you have here."

"What do you mean?" demanded the manager.

"I mean that if there is twelve hundred dollars in the house tonight someone has dropped a thousand on the floor"—and Oscar departed in triumph.

2040   EQUIPPED FOR A LECTURE TOUR

A good story concerns Herr Remarque, the author of "All Quiet on the Western Front," and a pretty American girl to whom he was introduced in Berlin.

The American, speaking in German, asked Remarque why he had never visited the United States. His answer was that he knew only a few sentences in English.

"What are the sentences?" inquired the girl.

Whereupon Remarque, speaking slowly in somewhat guttural English, said: "How do you do? I love you. Forgive me. Forget me. Ham and eggs, please."

"Sakes alive!" ejaculated the girl. "Why, with that vocabulary you could tour my country from Maine to California."

2041   DEPEW'S CHOICE

At a dinner given in his honor Chauncey Depew was the recipient of many compliments from various speakers.

Replying, Mr. Depew began, "It's pleasant to hear these nice words while I'm still alive. I'd rather have the taffy than the epitaphy."

2042   MISPLACED

Bernard Shaw is a past master at the ready retort. A young woman sitting next to him at dinner remarked: "What a wonderful thing is youth!"

"Yes—and what a crime to waste it on children," G. B. S. replied sagely.

2043   DISENGAGED

At one time during the American Civil War, Gen. George B. McClellan, then in command of the Union forces, was conducting a waiting campaign. He was so careful to avoid mistakes that little headway was evident. President Lincoln thereupon wrote him a letter:

"My dear McClellan: If you don't want to use the Army, I should like to borrow it for a while. Yours respectfully, A. Lincoln."

2044   CHARLES LAMB AND WHIST

Charles Lamb tells of a chronic grumbler who always complained at whist because he had so few trumps. By some artifice his companions managed to deal him the whole thirteen, hoping to extort some expression of satisfaction, but he only looked more wretched than ever as he examined his hand. "Well, Tom," said Lamb, "haven't you trumps enough this time?" "Yes," grunted Tom, "but I've no other cards."

2045   FULTON AND NAPOLEON

An American inventor had come to Paris and had offered the French Admiralty two new inventions: one of them a ship to be propelled by steam power instead of by the wind; the other, a submarine boat which was to sink ships by the discharge of a kind of torpedo. "The man is a charlatan," was Napoleon's comment on Fulton, after an experiment in which the inventor's "plunging boat" had had a partial success; and he brushed the whole matter aside. If the American had brought him models of a machine gun and field telegraph, he would have opened his purse.—*Emil Ludwig, "Napoleon."*

2046   WOODROW WILSON

Someone asked Woodrow Wilson how long he would prepare for a ten-minute speech. He said, "Two weeks." "How long for an hour speech?" "One week." "How long for a two-hour speech?" "I am ready now."

2047   SIR JOSIAH STAMP

The late Sir Josiah Stamp, in a speech at the Chicago Club, expressed a hope that he wasn't talking too long. "I shouldn't like to be in the position of the parson," he explained, "who, in the midst of an interminable sermon, suddenly broke off his discourse to chide: 'You know I don't mind a bit having you look at your watches to see what time it is, but it really annoys me when you put them up to your ears to hear if they are still running!' "

2048   POWER OF THE PRESS

When Sarah Bernhardt was traveling through California, Sam Davis, of the Carlson Appeal and the San Francisco Examiner, accompanied her as publicity agent. He was an enchanting companion and pleased the actress so much that on the trip she would give no interviews to any other publications.

When the moment of her return to New York arrived and the train was about to leave the station, she put her arms around Sam's neck, kissed him on each cheek and on the mouth, and said: "The right cheek for the Carlson Appeal, the left for the Examiner and the mouth for you."

"Madame," said the reporter, visibly affected, "may I remind you that I also represent the Associated Press, which serves 380 newspapers west of Kansas."

2049   A DIFFERENCE OF ONLY TWO COMMAS

Margaret Anglin, the story goes, left this message stuck in the mirror of Mrs. Fiske's dressing room:

"Margaret Anglin says Mrs. Fiske is the best actress in America."

Mrs. Fiske read it, added two commas, stuck it in an envelop, and sent it back to Miss Anglin. It read: "Margaret Anglin, says Mrs. Fiske, is the best actress in America."

Chapter 8

SIMILES

....

2050 He had crumbled like an old ruin.

2051 Awkward as a bull in a china shop.

2052 Bashful as a ten-year-old girl.

2053 Beautiful as a drug store blonde.

2054 Beautiful as a rustic bridge over a mountain stream.

2055 Bent over like a flagpole in a hurricane.

2056 Black as a coal shaft.

2057 He went through things like a customs inspector.

2058 Quiet as a monastery.

2059 As inert as an oyster on the beach in August.

2060 Cautious as a flag-pole climber.

2061 A man of oak and rock.

2062 He is as cosmopolitan as a comet.

2063 He was a man with a mind like an accounting ledger.

2064 He had all the qualities of a fireplace poker except its occasional warmth.

2065 He talks like a man who is unable to keep up with his thoughts no matter how rapidly he speaks.

2066 He is a steam roller in a pair of pants.

2067 Coolidge's perpetual expression was of smelling something burning on the kitchen stove.—*Sherwin L. Cook.*

2068   A rude man of the open.—*Lynn H. Hough.*

2069   Civilization ran into a cyclone of reform.

2070   Time is a threshing floor.—*Newell Dwight Hillis.*

2071   Criticism is a flail, and discussion is the wind that drives the chaff away.—*Ibid.*

2072   A face with lines as fine as old parchment.

2073   Government by stampede.

2074   Her face was as white and colorless as an icicle.

2075   As uncompromising as a policeman's club.

2076   As companionable as a cat and a goldfish.

2077   An unambitious snore, like a slow leak in an old tire.

2078   As never ending as a brook.

2079   He was as welcome as a monthly bill.

2080   As cynical as Diogenes.

2081   As desolate as a cemetery.

2082   Absence, like death, sets a seal on the image of those we have loved.—*Goldsmith.*

2083   Could tell the hour by his movements as accurately as by a sun-dial.—*Washington Irving.*

2084   Advancing like the shadow of death.—*Ruskin.*

2085   Sweet are the uses of adversity,
            Which, like the toad, ugly and venomous,
            Wears yet a precious jewel in his head.
                                    —*Shakespeare*

2086   Aimless as an autumn leaf
            Borne in November's idle winds afar.
                                    —*P. H. Hayne*

2087   Ambition is like hunger; it obeys no law but its appetite.—*Josh Billings.*

2088   Ancient as the stars.—*Voltaire.*

2089   An army, like a serpent, goes upon its belly.—*Frederick the Great.*

2090   Attracted about as much attention in the artistic world as the advent of another fly in a slaughter house.—*James L. Ford.*

2091   Blighted and forlorn, like Autumn waiting for the snow.—*Whittier.*

2092   Bright as mountain snow.—*Southey.*

2093   Calm as a child to slumber soothed,
               As if an Angel's hand had smoothed
               The still, white features into rest.
                                          —*Whittier.*

2094   Changeless as heaven.—*Ibid.*

2095   Childhood shows the man, as the morning shows the day.—*Milton.*

2096   Clear as a bell.—*Chaucer.*

2097   Contagious, like the gladness of a happy child.—*Bulwer-Lytton.*

2098   Cool as a snow bank.—*Louisa M. Alcott.*

2099   Countless as the desert sands.—*Bayard Taylor.*

2100   The court is like a marble statue, I mean, it may be finely polished but it is very hard.—*M. de LaBruyere.*

2101   Crisp as new bank notes.—*Dickens.*

2102   A critic is a legless man who teaches running.—*Channing Pollock.*

2103   Critics are like brushers of noblemen's clothes.—*Sir Henry Wotton.*

2104   Cry of anguish, like the last dying wail of some dumb, hunted creature.—*Adelaide A. Procter.*

2105   Cunning as Satan.—*Philip Freneau.*

2106   Dark as the grave.—*Cowley.*

2107   Dead as a herring.—*Samuel Butler.*

2108   She was delicate and fair as moonlight.—*Hans Christian Andersen.*

2109   His speech was like a tangled chain; nothing impaired, but all disordered.—*Shakespeare.*

2110 Driven . . . like leaves before the autumnal wind.—*Southey.*

2111 The slow mists of the evening dropped,
Dropped as a cloth upon a dead man's face.
—*Kipling*

2112 As modest as a violet.

2113 It is as dignified and beautiful as a Beethoven Sonata.—*I. Zangwill.*

2114 Eyes, brilliant and humid like the reflection of stars in a well.—*Edmondo de Amicis.*

2115 These lovely lamps, these windows of the soul.—*Du Bartas.*

2116 As hollow as a villain's laugh.—*Herbert V. Prochnow.*

2117 Her eyes are blue and dewy as the glimmery Summer-dawn.—*James Whitcomb Riley.*

2118 In her hazel eyes her thoughts lay clear
As pebbles in a brook.
—*Alexander Smith*

2119 He was oilier than a kerosene lamp.

2120 He had a face like a benediction.—*Cervantes.*

2121 His face looked like a face that had refused to jell and was about to run down on his clothes.—*Irvin S. Cobb.*

2122 'Tis not that she paints so ill but, when she has finished her face, she joins so badly to her neck, that she looks like a mended statue, in which the connoisseur may see at once that the head is modern, though the trunk's antique.—*R. B. Sheridan.*

2123 His face had as many wrinkles as an old parchment.—*Herbert V. Prochnow.*

2124 Faded like a dream of youth.—*O. W. Holmes.*

2125 Faint as a glimmering taper's wasted light.—*Sir William Jones.*

2126 As welcome as a collect telegram.

2127 As fair a thing as e'er was form'd of clay.—*Byron.*

2128 A face as fair as the summer dawn.—*James Whitcomb Riley.*

2129   Fall off, like leaves from a withered tree.—*Voltaire.*

2130   Faultless as blown roses in June days.—*Edward Dowden.*

2131   It is with feelings as with waters: the shallow murmur, but the deep are dumb.—*Sir Walter Raleigh.*

2132   His face fell like a cookbook cake.—*Joseph C. Lincoln.*

2133   My head rang like a fire station gong.

2134   Like the mower's grass at the close of day.—*Byron.*

2135   Fits as a shell fits a crab.—*Sir A. Conan Doyle.*

2136   As flabby as a sponge.—*Guy de Maupassant.*

2137   Flexible as figures in the hands of the statistician.—*Israel Zangwill.*

2138   Follow, as the night the day.—*Shakespeare.*

2139   Folds up like a crush hat or a concertina.—*Irvin S. Cobb.*

2140   Shall fold their tents like the Arabs and as silently steal away.—*Longfellow.*

2141   A forehead more pure than the Parian stone.—*Whittier.*

2142   Poor and forgotten like a clod upon the field.—*Hugo.*

2143   Good fortune, like ripe fruit, ought to be enjoyed while it is present.—*Epictetus.*

2144   Rattled like window shutters in a cyclone.

2145   The fragrance of her rich and delightful character still lingered about the place where she had lived, as a dried rosebud scents the drawer where it has withered and perished.—*Hawthorne.*

2146   Free as mountain winds.—*Shakespeare.*

2147   The feeling of friendship is like that of being comfortably filled with roast beef.—*Dr. Johnson.*

2148   As frightened as Macbeth before the ghost of Banquo.—*Louis Veuillot.*

2149   Fruitless as the celebrated bee who wanted to swarm alone.—*G. K. Chesterton*

2150 Futile as a tenor in a boiler shop.—*Henry Irving Dodge.*

2151 She had more ornaments than a circus band wagon.—*Herbert V. Prochnow.*

2152 Genius, like a torch, shines less in the broad daylight of the present than in the night of the past.—*J. Petit Senn.*

2153 Ghastly as a laugh in hell.—*Thomas Hardy.*

2154 As regular as the roll of an army drum.

2155 Gleamed upon the water like a bride at her looking-glass.—*R. D. Blackmore.*

2156 His eyes dilated and glistened like the last flame that shoots up from an expiring fire.—*Guy de Maupassant.*

2157 Glitter . . . like the bayonets of a regiment on parade.—*John C. Van Dyke.*

2158 Going as if he had trod upon eggs.—*Robert Burton.*

2159 Gossip, like ennui, is born of idleness.—*Ninon de Lenclos.*

2160 Graceful as a faun.—*Samuel Rogers.*

2161 Grasps, like death.—*Ebenezer Elliott.*

2162 Her eyes are grey like morning dew.—*W. B. Yeats.*

2163 Genuine grief is like penitence, not clamorous, but subdued.—*Josh Billings.*

2164 Gush like a fountain at its source.—*Donald G. Mitchell.*

2165 His speech came in gusts, like linnets in the pauses of the wind.—*William De Morgan.*

2166 He returned as often as the postman.

2167 Hairless as an egg.—*Robert Herrick.*

2168 He had a hand like a bunch of bananas.—*R. F. Outcault.*

2169 Happy as birds in the spring.—*William Blake.*

2170 Fingers, hard as a lobster's claws.—*Guy de Maupassant.*

2171   Hard as a pine-knot.—*James K. Paulding.*

2172   As hard as for an empty sack to stand upright.—*Benjamin Franklin.*

2173   The head of a woman is like a weather cock on the top of a house, which turns with the slightest wind.—*Molière.*

2174   The head, like the stomach, is most easily infected with poison when it is empty.—*Richter.*

2175   As shallow as a pie pan.

2176   A noble heart, like the sun, showeth its greatest countenance in its lowest estate.—*Sir Philip Sidney.*

2177   Heaves . . .
             Like a mighty ship in pain,
             Facing the tempest with struggle and strain.
                                    —*E. B. Browning*

2178   Lies heavy . . . like murder on a guilty soul.—*Schiller.*

2179   The sea hissed like twenty thousand kettles!—*Joseph Conrad.*

2180   Hissing like a snake.—*Hugo.*

2181   He stuck to it about as long as a drug store cowboy on a broncho.

2182   Holds . . . together as the shell does the egg.—*John C. Van Dyke.*

2183   As much at home . . . as a fish in water.—*Balzac.*

2184   Our hopes, like withered leaves, fall fast.—*Longfellow.*

2185   Hopeful as the break of day.—*T. B. Aldrich.*

2186   Hot as hell-fire.—*Dryden.*

2187   Hover—like a moth intoxicated with light.—*John Galsworthy.*

2188   Howlings, like a herd of ravenous wolves disappointed of their prey.—*William H. Prescott.*

2189   Huddled like beasts beneath the drovers' whips.—*John Masefield.*

2190   Humility like darkness reveals the heavenly lights.—*Henry D. Thoreau.*

2191   Hungry as the chap that said a turkey was too much for one, not enough for two.—*O. W. Holmes.*

2192 Hungry as a wolf.—*John Palgrave.*

2193 Hysterical as a tree full of chickens.—*Irvin S. Cobb.*

2194 As frivolous as April.—*Herbert V. Prochnow.*

2195 As idle as a painted ship upon a painted ocean.—*Coleridge.*

2196 He makes his ignorance pass for reserve, and, like a hunting-nag, leaps over what he cannot get through.—*Samuel Butler.*

2197 Immortal as the stars.—*Mathilde Blind.*

2198 Impersonal as the justice of God.—*Hugo.*

2199 Imposing as a set of solid gold teeth.—*Rex Beach.*

2200 Indolent as an old bachelor.—*Goethe.*

2201 The highest intellects, like the tops of mountains, are the first to catch and reflect the dawn.—*Macaulay.*

2202 Irrevocable as death.—*Charlotte Brontë.*

2203 Ended abruptly like a rabbit's tail.

2204 As languid as a lilied pond.—*Norman Gale.*

2205 A lie is like a snow-ball; the longer it is rolled, the larger it is.—*Luther.*

2206 Life is like a tale ended ere 'tis told.—*T. B. Aldrich.*

2207 Lifeless as a string of dead fish.—*G. K. Chesterton.*

2208 Light and feathery as squirrel-tails.—*John Muir.*

2209 A face as wrinkled as a dried plum.

2210 Lingering like an unloved guest.—*Shelley.*

2211
I wandered lonely as a cloud
That floats on high o'er vales and hills.

—*Wordsworth*

2212 He looked like a composite picture of five thousand orphans too late to catch a picnic steamboat.—*O. Henry.*

2213 He was as wise as Solomon, but as humble as Uriah Heep.—*Herbert V. Prochnow.*

2214   Majestic in its movement as a sonnet of Milton.—*Israel Zangwill.*

2215   Men, like peaches and pears, grow sweet a little while before they begin to decay.—*O. W. Holmes.*

2216   Great men are like meteors: they glitter and are consumed to enlighten the world.—*Napoleon.*

2217   Marriage is not like the hill of Olympus, wholly clear, without clouds. —*Thomas Fuller.*

2218   As restless as the wind.

2219   Melancholy sound . . . like the weeping of a solitary, deserted human heart.—*Guy de Maupassant.*

2220   Swell menacingly like the first whisper of a rising wind.—*Joseph Conrad.*

2221   Merciless as ambition.—*Joubert.*

2222   As freely as the firmament embraces the world, so mercy must encircle friend and foe.—*Schiller.*

2223   Monotonous as mutton.—*Richard Le Gallienne.*

2224   Motionless as a king's mummy in a catacomb.—*Flaubert.*

2225   A voice as mournful as the dying light in the west—for a vague reminder of Death is divinely set in the heavens, and the sun above gives the same warning that is given here on earth by the flowers and the bright insects of the day.—*Balzac.*

2226   Moved one like the finest eloquence.—*Alexander Smith.*

2227   Multitudinous tongues, like the whispering leaves of a wind-stirred oak. —*Hawthorne.*

2228   Murmurs . . . like a bell that calls to prayer.—*John Ruskin.*

2229   Muscular as dogmeat.—*Rex Beach.*

2230   As mute as the tomb.—*Dumas, Père.*

2231   As mute as Pygmalion.—*James Smith.*

2232   The nations narrow and expand,
               As tides that ebb, or tides that flow.
                                                    —*Lord De Tabler*

2233 As hopeful as a Spring morning.

2234 Natural to die as to be born.—*Bacon.*

2235 Neglected, as the moon by day.—*Swift.*

2236 Obstinate as death.—*Dryden.*

2237 Opportunitays, like eggs, don't kum but one at a time.—*Josh Billings.*

2238 Pains like a horrible vulgarism.—*Lafcadio Hearn.*

2239 He was as polished, and as hard, as the brass plate upon which his name was etched.—*Herbert V. Prochnow.*

2240 God pardons like a mother who kisses away the repentant tears of her child.—*Henry Ward Beecher.*

2241 Panted like a forge bellows.—*Hugo.*

2242 Pathetic as an autumn leaf.—*George Moore.*

2243 Patiently as the spider weaves the broken web.—*Bulwer-Lytton.*

2244 As innocent as a child.

2245 Pleading like a frightened child.—*Robert Louis Stevenson.*

2246 Pliable as wax.—*James Shirley.*

2247 Poignant and silent like the terrible questioning of one's conscience. —*Joseph Conrad.*

2248 A woman preacher is like a dog walking on his hind legs. It is not done well; but you are surprised to find it done at all.—*Dr. Johnson.*

2249 She was as pretty as the spring time.—*Balzac.*

2250 Prim as a Quaker.—*G. P. Morris.*

2251 Kings will lose their privilege, as stars which have completed their time lose their splendor.—*Dumas, Père.*

2252 Puffed himself up like a ship in full sail.—*Hans Christian Andersen.*

2253 As soft as a Southern wind.

2254 Punctual—like morning.—*James Whitcomb Riley.*

2255   She is as pure, as good, and as beautiful as an angel.—*Guy de Maupassant.*

2256   Receded, as mists fade before a morning sun.—*Barrett Wendell.*

2257   Red as the Baldinsville skool-house.—*Artemus Ward.*

2258   Ruddy and fresh as the waking morn.—*Eugene Field.*

2259   Fell slowly into ruin, like all dwellings to which the presence of man no longer communicates life.—*Hugo.*

2260   As illusive as a dream.

2261   Sad as twilight.—*George Eliot.*

2262   Saunters . . . like an idle river very leisurely strolling down a flat country to the sea.—*Dickens.*

2263   In scandal, as in robbery, the receiver is always as bad as the thief.—*Chesterfield.*

2264   Sealed as the voice of a frost-bound stream.—*Swinburne.*

2265   Serene as night.—*Byron.*

2266   Set, as a piece of sculpture.—*Dickens.*

2267   It stuck tighter than bark on a tree.

2268   Shone like the evening star.—*O. W. Holmes.*

2269   Shrink as though Death were passing in his shroud.—*John Masefield.*

2270   Shun him like the plague.—*Robert Browning.*

2271   Sifted like great snowdrifts o'er the landscape.—*Longfellow.*

2272   Sighed with such a sigh as drops from agony to exhaustion.—*E. B. Browning.*

2273   Sighs as men sigh relieved from care.—*Lowell.*

2274   Silent as a country churchyard.—*Macaulay.*

2275   Silent as the grave.—*Schiller.*

2276   As greedy as the jaws of hell.

2277 Sobbing, as if the body and soul were torn.—*Bulwer-Lytton*.

2278 Society, like the Roman youth at the circus, never shows mercy to the fallen gladiator.—*Balzac*.

2279 Soft as is the falling thistle downe.—*Joseph Hall*.

2280 Soft and still, like birds half hidden in a nest.—*Longfellow*.

2281 Walked as softly as the ghost in Hamlet.—*Dickens*.

2282 As hard-boiled as an Easter egg.

2283 Sparkle like brooks in the morning sun.—*William Cullen Bryant*.

2284 Stood spellbound, like a child to whom his nurse is telling some wonderful story.—*Balzac*.

2285 As shriveled as an old prune.

2286 Staggered away as a defeated man staggers away from the field of battle.—*Joseph Conrad*.

2287 Stealthily like rocks that tear a ship's life out under the smooth sea.—*Ibid*.

2288 He stood . . . stiff as a marble statue.—*Goethe*.

2289 As harmless as a meadow lark.

2290 Struggling like a man led towards death and crucifixion.—*Carlyle*.

2291 Swayed like a bird on a twig.—*Arnold Bennett*.

2292 Hesitating like an animal at bay.

2293 Talent, like gout, sometimes skips two generations.—*Balzac*.

2294
Tenderly, as round the sleeping infant's feet,
We softly fold the cradle-sheet.
—*William Cullen Bryant*

2295 Terrifying as the monologue of a storm.—*Hugo*.

2296 He was as short and stubby as a hedge fence.

2297 Human thought is like a monstrous pendulum: it keeps swinging from one extreme to the other.—*Eugene Field*.

2298 Tossed . . . like a cork on the waves.—*Thomas Hardy*.

2299 As frank as a mirror.

2300 Turned like a weather cock with every wind.—*Guy de Maupassant*.

2301 As inflexible as a marble pillar.

2302 Unconquerable as chewing gum.—*Arnold Bennett*.

2303 Stand unmoved, like a rock 'mid raging seas.—*Calderon*.

2304 As inseparable as a baseball fan and a bag of peanuts.

2305 Upright as a wooden sentinel at the door of a puppet-show.—*Sir Walter Scott*.

2306 Vagrant as the wind.—*John Ford*.

2307 Pranced around like a colt in a pasture.

2308 Vanished altogether, like the last spark on a burnt piece of paper.—*Hans Christian Andersen*.

2309 Vanished like the furrow cut by a ship's keel in the sea.—*Balzac*.

2310 Vices, like beasts, are fond of none but those that feed them.—*Samuel Butler*.

2311 Lies like a man with a second-hand car to sell.

2312 Virtue is like the polar star, which keeps its place, and all stars turn towards it.—*Confucius*.

2313 Void of sense as the movement of the trees and the sound of the winds —*Hugo*.

2314 A wail, as of a babe new-born.—*George Meredith*.

2315 She walked with a proud, defiant step, like a martyr to the Coliseum. —*Balzac*.

2316 Wandered up and down there like an early Christian refugee in the catacombs.—*Joseph Conrad*.

2317 Wandered about at random, like dogs that have lost the scent.—*Voltaire*.

2318 His purse was as full as his head was empty.

2319 Warm as a sunned cat.—*Thomas Hardy.*

2320 Watchful as a spider sits in his web.—*Bulwer-Lytton.*

2321 As faultless as a spring flower.

2322 Withered and pale as an old pauper.—*Dickens.*

2323 His words, like so many nimble and airy servitors, trip about him at command.—*Milton.*

2324 The world is like a great staircase, some go up and others go down.—*Hipponax.*

2325 He floundered around like a fish on the beach.

2326 Yawns like a grave in a cemetery.—*Hugo.*

2327 Zeal without knowledge is like expedition to a man in the dark.—*Newton.*

2328 As fresh as the dawn.

2329 Adroit as a rhinoceros.—*Franklin P. Adams.*

2330 His cheek was like a rose in the snow.—*O. W. Holmes.*

2331 His head was as empty as a politician's speech.

2332 No more conscience than a fox in a poultry farm.—*G. B. Shaw.*

2333 Desolate looking as a summer resort in midwinter.—*Richard Harding Davis.*

2334 He stood as erect as a Grecian pillar.

2335 Her eyes looked like two rainy autumn moons.—*Henry James.*

2336 He felt like the symptoms on a medicine bottle.—*George Ade.*

2337 He was as exacting as a top sergeant.

2338 Freckles, like rust spots.—*Willa Cather.*

2339 The human mind should be like a good hotel—open the year around.—*William Lyon Phelps.*

2340 His face was as expressionless as a smoked herring.

2341   A white mustache, cut short like a worn-out brush.—*Henry James.*

2342   Unremembered as old rain.—*Edna St. Vincent Millay.*

2343   As changeable as a woman's mood.

2344   Vanish as raindrops which fall in the sea.—*Susan Coolidge.*

2345   I could see the man's very soul writhing in his body like an impaled worm.—*Joseph Conrad.*

2346   His joints creaked like those of an old weather-beaten wooden farm gate.—*Herbert V. Prochnow.*

2347   As unemotional as a baseball umpire.

2348   As unsatisfied as a boy's appetite.

2349   He was as patient as a cigar store Indian.

Chapter 9

COLORFUL PHRASES FOR
SPARKLING SPEECH

....

2350 *Abraham's bosom*—A figure of speech from the Bible. To rest in Abraham's bosom. A place of reward after death for the blessed and righteous. There was an old custom of allowing a good friend to recline at dinner on one's bosom. John reclined on the bosom of Jesus. The beggar died and was taken by the angels into Abraham's bosom.

2351 *Achilles' heel*—A vulnerable spot. Achilles' mother, to make him invulnerable, dipped him into the Styx river. She failed to immerse the heel by which she held him. Paris wounded him mortally by striking him in the heel with an arrow. Everyone may be said to have his Achilles' heel—his weakness.

2352 *A sulking Achilles*—One who withdraws from a part in an important enterprise or undertaking because he holds a personal grievance. In mythology it is said that Achilles sulked in his tent because of an argument with Agamemnon and declined for some time to take part in the battle of the Greeks against the Trojans.

2353 *An Adonis*—An exceptionally handsome man. In mythology he was a handsome young man loved by Venus.

2354 *After me, the deluge*—Means that "I shall keep on doing what pleases me regardless of what happens and even if I am overcome; after me, the deluge." The origin of the phrase is uncertain. Madame Pompadour, a favorite of Louis the Fifteenth, was one among several who were credited with having used this phrase. She was extravagant and refused to listen to her counselors who said she would ruin the country. She made light of their warnings, saying in French, "After us, the flood."

2355 *All my swans are geese*—To have your plans fail you. To be disappointed. If one says, "All her swans are turned to geese," it means her plans or boasts have failed her. The swan is beautiful; the goose far less attractive.

2356 *Alpha and Omega*—The beginning and the end of anything. In the Greek alphabet, alpha is the first letter, and omega the last. In the Bible the Lord said, "I am Alpha and Omega, the beginning and the ending."

269

2357   *He cannot bend Ulysses' bow*—The person is not equal to the task. Ulysses had a bow so great ordinary men could not bend it.

2358   *An Odyssey*—A story of great adventure. An epic attributed to Homer describing the ten years' wanderings of Ulysses in returning home after the siege of Troy.

2359   *An Amazon*—A woman of unusual physical strength. Sometimes also used to describe a woman of masculine boldness. The Amazons in mythology were a nation of fighting women.

2360   *Greek gifts or a case of the Greeks bearing gifts*—This means a fatal gift which is presented under friendly guise. In Virgil's *Aeneid* there is a line which says, "I fear the Greeks even when they bear gifts." This refers to the well-known "gift" of the wooden horse which the Trojans offered to the gods. The Greeks had left it outside of the city of Troy and apparently had departed. The Trojans took it within the city's walls and at night Greek soldiers hidden within the horse came out, capturing the city by morning.

2361   *To feed on ambrosia and nectar*—To have excellent food and drink. To the ancient Greeks "ambrosia" meant the food which the gods ate. Now it means anything delicious to taste or fragrant in perfume. "Nectar" is the drink of the gods.

2362   *To make the amende honorable*—According to *Webster's Collegiate Dictionary*, this term means "a formal and humiliating acknowledgment of offense and apology made to another, originally in reparation of his injured honor." The punishment was used under the Roman, Dutch, French and other legal systems. An apology in church or court might require the person to appear with bare feet and head, dressed in white, and carrying a torch.

2363   *An Ulysses*—A person who is clever in developing schemes. Ulysses was one of the Greek heroes in the Trojan War, famous for his craft, intelligence and eloquence.

2364   *To work or fight like a Trojan*—To fight with great courage or to work with exceptional energy. The ancient Trojans were noted for endurance and pluck.

2365   *A Cassandra utterance*—A prophecy foretelling evil which is not heeded. Cassandra, a daughter of King Priam, was given the power to prophesy by Apollo, according to Greek mythology. Becoming displeased with her, Apollo changed the power Cassandra had to prophesy so she could still prophesy truly, only to be laughed at by those who heard her.

2366   *To hector someone*—To annoy a person. Hector was greatly concerned over the shame brought upon his family and city by his brother, Paris, according to Greek legend, and consequently found fault with him.

2367 *An apple of discord*—A reason for dispute. According to mythology, Discord threw a golden apple on the table "for the most beautiful." Juno, Minerva, and Venus claimed it. Paris awarded it to Venus, thus bringing upon him the vengeance of Juno and Minerva which helped to cause the Trojan War.

2368 *Argonaut*—One of those who sailed with Jason, in the ship Argo, to Colchis to search for the Golden Fleece, according to Greek mythology. An adventurer who seeks fame or fortune in unexplored lands.

2369 *Argus-eyed*—Extraordinarily watchful. An Argus-eyed committee may watch the counting of the money or the ballots. Argus, a monster in Greek mythology, had one hundred eyes, only two of which were said to sleep at once. Argus-eyed means to see a great deal.

2370 *Halcyon days*—Days of peace and happiness. Greek legends tell of a girl named Halcyone whose husband perished. Juno, a goddess, did everything in her power to lessen Halcyone's grief and give her serenity of mind and happiness.

2371 *Ark of the covenant*—According to Jewish history, the chest in the most sacred place in the temple in which were placed the two tables of stone with the Ten Commandments written upon them. Anything which is exceptionally sacred. The Constitution of the United States and the Declaration of Independence might each be spoken of as an American ark of the covenant.

2372 *Armageddon*—The place where a titanic battle will be fought on "the great day of God," between the powers of good and evil, according to the Bible. Any great battle, political contest, or climactic conflict.

2373 *To work the oracle*—To attempt to influence some powerful agency so it will bestow a favor upon you.

2374 *Janus-headed*—An early Italian god, Janus, had two faces—one in front and one behind. Presumably he could see backward and forward at the same time. One may say of a committee with two heads that it is Janus-headed.

2375 *Janus-faced*—Means two-faced or deceptive. Janus-faced facts might be interpreted two ways.

2376 *A saturnine smile*—A smile which is not cheerful, perhaps because the idea of gloominess is connected with the planet Saturn.

2377 *A mercurial temperament*—The Greek god Mercury was light-hearted, clever, changeable, and even a little deceptive; so a mercurial temperament would be of that character.

2378 *Apollo*—In Greek mythology, the god of manly beauty and youth. An unusually handsome man

2379　*Palladium of our liberty*—A safeguard. The safety of the ancient city of Troy was supposed to depend upon the preservation of a certain wooden statue of Pallas Athena. "Our constitution is the palladium of our liberty."

2380　*Extending the olive branch of peace*—The goddess Minerva was closely connected with the olive tree, having given it to Greece as a gift. She ruled over the arts of peace. An olive-branch policy is a policy of peace.

2381　*A Bacchanalian revel*—Bacchus was the god of wine. Bacchanalian means riotous merriment resulting from the use of too much liquor. A wild orgy. Frenzied dancing, singing and revelry.

2382　*A mere bagatelle*—The word bagatelle comes from the French who took it from the Italian "bagattella" meaning a trifle. A man may spend his money on bagatelles.

2383　*Mounting Pegasus*—Describes the efforts of a person who hopes or attempts to write poetry or deliver orations. Pegasus was the winged horse of the Muses. With a blow of his hoof he caused Hippocrene, the fountain of the Muses, to spring from Mount Helicon. Therefore, poetic inspiration. Sometimes the airplane is called a modern Pegasus.

2384　*Is there no balm in Gilead?*—This means "Is there no remedy or consolation, even in religion, for our troubles?" In the Book of Jeremiah in the Bible, the prophet, sorrowing over the sins and troubles of his people asked, "Is there no balm in Gilead; is there no physician there? Why then is not the health of the daughter of my people recovered?"

2385　*Stygian darkness*—Gloomy darkness or deep night. It may also mean infernal darkness. The Styx in mythology was the river of the dark underworld. It flowed seven times around Hades.

2386　*Barkis is willin'*—When an individual especially desires to do something, we may say of him, "Barkis is willin'." In the story, *David Copperfield*, by Charles Dickens, Barkis loved Clara Peggotty. He asked young David to tell Clara Peggotty, after David had said she had no sweethearts, that "Barkis is willin'."

2387　*An Elysium*—In classical mythology, the place where the good dwelt after death. A state of delight and happiness.

2388　*A task of Sisyphus*—A task that is never completed. In Greek mythology, Sisyphus was a crafty king who was condemned in Hades to roll up a hill a huge stone, which constantly rolled back.

2389　*Beggar on horseback*—A person who has risen to wealth and position, forgets his previous poverty, and lords it over his former poorer friends.

2390 *The waters of Lethe*—Implies forgetfulness. An experience that makes one forget care. In mythology, a river of Hades whose waters when drunk caused forgetfulness of the past.

2391 *To beg the question*—To assume the truth of something in question. To assume as true something you are supposed to prove, and to argue from that point. Aristotle first used the phrase.

2392 *A Danaidean task*—An impossible task. King Danaus had fifty daughters (the Danaides) of whom forty-nine slew their husbands at their father's request. The forty-nine were doomed forever to draw water with a sieve in Hades, according to mythology.

2393 *A Pandora's box*—Surprises which are generally unpleasant and in the form of trouble, but sometimes are pleasant. A legislative act may turn out to be a Pandora's box of surprises, unpleasant and pleasant. In Greek mythology, Pandora was a woman sent by Zeus as punishment for the human race because Prometheus had stolen fire from heaven. Zeus gave her a box in which were all human ills; they escaped when she opened the box. In the box also was hope, which remained.

2394 *Belling the cat*—To take it upon one's self to undertake a great risk for friends and associates. The expression comes from the old story in which a mouse suggested that someone should hang a bell on the cat so the mice would know when she was coming. The only problem was "who is to bell the cat?"

2395 *Belshazzar's Feast*—When one takes part in a "feast of Belshazzar," he does so in the spirit of "eat, drink and be merry, for tomorrow we die." The feast of Belshazzar is described in the fifth chapter of the Book of Daniel in the Bible. "In that night was Belshazzar the king of the Chaldeans slain." At that feast Belshazzar saw the fateful "handwriting on the wall" which told him that the days of his kingdom were numbered, that he had been found wanting, and that his kingdom would be divided and assigned to others.

2396 *To yearn for the flesh pots*—Means to long for the material things of life. In the Book of Exodus in the Bible, it is related how the children of Israel regretted their deliverance from Egypt and the hardships of the wilderness. They wished they could have died in Egypt when they "sat by the flesh pots" and "did eat bread to the full."

2397 *A Cadmean victory*—A victory which involves the victor in even greater danger than that from which he escaped. In Greek mythology, Cadmus slew a dragon and sowed its teeth, but armed warriors sprang from the teeth and attacked him.

2398 *To sow dragon's teeth*—To do things out of which troubles are certain to spring. Cadmus sowed dragon's teeth and warriors sprang up threatening trouble for him. People may do things out of which troubles for themselves will almost certainly spring.

2399 *A bonanza*—Anything yielding a large return in money. There were several Americans in our earlier history who made great fortunes from the gold and silver mines of the West. They were the original "Bonanza Kings."

2400 *A herculean task*—A task which only Hercules could accomplish. We sometimes speak also of a herculean feat, or herculean labors; these are extraordinary exertions. Hercules was a Grecian hero noted for unusual strength and for achieving twelve great tasks or "labors" imposed on him as the result of the hatred of Juno.

2401 *Hydra-headed difficulties or evils*—A hydra-headed evil is one which, if it is overcome in one case, breaks out in several places. An evil having many sources, which cannot be overcome by a single effort. In Greek mythology, Hydra was a nine-headed monster slain by Hercules. When any one of its nine heads was cut off, it was succeeded by two others, unless the wound was cauterized.

2402 *Born to the purple*—To be born to a position of great wealth or to an exalted station. In Cicero's time, wool dyed purple was very expensive because the dye came in small quantities from a Mediterranean fish. Purple was, therefore, a highly sought after color and symbolized royal power. Today, purple dye has become inexpensive, but the phrase is still used.

2403 *Buncombe*—Anything said or written for mere show; hence, nonsense. "Bunk" is an abbreviation. In the early days of this country there was a member of Congress from the part of North Carolina including Buncombe county. The representatives were anxious to vote on an issue, but the member from Buncombe insisted on speaking. He refused to stop speaking when urged by members of Congress and said he was "bound to talk for Buncombe."

2404 *An Augean task*—A seemingly impossible task. An enormous job. In Greek mythology, King Augeas was said to have had an enormous stable containing many oxen. The stable had not been cleaned for years. Hercules cleaned it by diverting two rivers through it.

2405 *One cannot seize the club of Hercules*—It is impossible to steal the power and ability of one who is great. Hercules was noted for his strength.

2406 *Byzantine luxury*—A lavish and almost barbaric display of wealth and riches. Pertains to the Byzantine empire, Byzantium being the former name of Constantinople, now Istanbul. The Byzantine empire was rich and powerful.

2407 *To wear the cap and bells*—To play the part of a jester. Many years ago the court jesters wore bells attached to their caps.

2408 *A shirt of Nessus*—A gift which is harmful or causes trouble. According to mythology, Dejanira sent her husband, Hercules, a garment dipped in blood which had been given to her in a bottle by a centaur named Nessus. The garment poisoned Hercules.

2409 *Caviar to the general*—"General" means the "common run" of human beings. "Caviar to the general" means anything above the taste or appreciation of "ordinary" people. Caviar is roe of the sturgeon and other fish. It is a delicacy, an expensive appetizer, desired by those who acquire a taste for it. Shakespeare says in *Hamlet*, "The play, I remember, pleased not the million; 'twas caviar to the general." One could say also, "It was caviar to the masses."

2410 *Cheating the devil*—To believe that you can follow evil methods, particularly in making money unscrupulously, and then compromise with your conscience by giving part of your monetary gain to charity, the church, or some other worthy objective. That is an attempt to "cheat the devil."

2411 *A Cincinnatus*—One who puts aside his regular work to serve his country. Indicates unselfish patriotism. Cincinnatus was a Roman who was called from the field he was plowing to lead the Roman army. After the enemy was overcome, he put aside any personal ambition and returned to the plow. George Washington might be called an American Cincinnatus.

2412 *Hoc opus, hic labor est* (Latin)—This is the real difficulty; this is the task; there's the rub.

2413 *A Minotaur*—One who will sacrifice youths for his personal ambition. A ruler who will lead young men to death to satisfy his own ambition. In mythology, the Minotaur was a monster that devoured young men and women.

2414 *A Circe*—A beautiful woman whose charms are so great they cannot be resisted. In the *Odyssey*, Circe was a sorceress who turned her victims by magic into beasts, but she was thwarted by Odysseus with the herb moly given to him by Hermes.

2415 *A stentorian voice*—A very loud voice. Stentor was a herald in the *Iliad* with a very loud voice.

2416 *A Helen or a Helen of Troy*—A woman of extraordinary beauty. In mythology, Helen was the beautiful daughter of Jupiter and Leda.

2417 *Cordelia's gift*—A soft voice. Cordelia was the youngest of King Lear's three daughters in Shakespeare's play, *King Lear*. Shakespeare says in that play, "Her voice was ever soft, gentle and low; an excellent thing in woman."

2418 *Cornelia's jewels*—Children. Cornelia was the mother of the famous Gracchi. An old Roman story relates that a woman was displaying her jewels to Cornelia and asked to see the latter's jewels. Cornelia called her two sons and said, "These are my jewels, in which alone I delight."

2419 *A lotus-eater*—A person who lives a life without ambition or effort and in ease and idleness. In the *Odyssey*, one of a people who subsisted on the lotus and lived in the dreamy indolence it induced.

2420 *To give a sop to Cerberus*—To give a gift to some person who might make trouble, in order to keep him quiet. In mythology, Cerberus was a three-headed dog which guarded the entrance to Hades fiercely.

2421 *Rich as Croesus*—A very rich person. Croesus was a king of Lydia in the 6th Century B.C., and had vast wealth.

2422 *Under the aegis of*—To have the power or authority of some strong person or institution back of one. In Greek mythology, Jupiter was said to have permitted Minerva to wear his terrible aegis, a covering for the breast with the head of Medusa in the center, which was so awful to behold that even the strong were terrified upon seeing it.

2423 *Between Scylla and Charybdis*—When a person must choose between two great dangers. Scylla is a rock on the Italian coast opposite the whirlpool Charybdis off the Sicilian coast. In early legends Scylla and Charybdis were monsters who lived in caves in the strait between Italy and Sicily. They preyed upon vessels which passed and wrecked them.

2424 *A protean artist*—One who can take various roles successfully. In mythology, Proteus was a sea-god who could assume various shapes.

2425 *A Penelope*—A wife who remains faithful to her husband. Penelope was the wife of Ulysses. During his absence she was importuned by suitors, but postponed her decision until she had finished weaving a funeral pall for her father-in-law. Every night she unraveled what she had woven by day, and so deferred making any choice until Ulysses returned, when the unwelcome suitors were sent away.

2426 *An Icarian adventure*—A bold adventure which comes to a fatal end. In Greek mythology, Icarus fell into the sea when he attempted to escape from the Cretan Labyrinth by means of wings made from feathers. He flew too near the sun, the wax of his wings melted, and he fell into the sea.

2427 *To cut up didoes*—To make mischief; to cut up; to play tricks. Dido was a queen of Carthage. When Dido was obtaining land for her city, she was told she could have as much land as an ox hide would cover. She cut the hide into pieces so it would cover more ground.

2428 *Suffering the punishment of Tantalus*—To come close to attaining one's objectives and yet never reach them. According to mythology, Tantalus was punished in Hades by the sight of food and water which he could never quite reach.

2429 *To look to one's laurels*—To be careful that one's position or rank be not lost. The ancient Greeks used the foliage of the laurel to crown victors in the Pythian games and as a mark of distinction for certain offices. Later a crown of laurels was used for academic honors.

2430   *To win laurels*—To secure fame as a result of some significant accomplishment.

2431   *Coup de grace*—In French, a blow of mercy. The death blow by which the executioner ended the suffering of the condemned. A decisive, finishing stroke which mercifully puts an end to the sufferings of a victim.

2432   *A siren*—A fascinating woman who entices one to destruction. In mythology, the Sirens were beautiful women who lured mariners to their destruction by singing.

2433   *A Triton among minnows*—One who excels his competitors. The Tritons, in mythology, were sea-gods.

2434   *A fidus Achates*—A faithful friend. Achates was a faithful companion of Aeneas in Virgil's *Aeneid*.

2435   *Coup d'état*—A sudden decisive use of force by which an existing government is subverted. Power is seized and an existing government is overthrown. Napoleon III in 1851 dissolved the French Assembly by force and seized the supreme rule over France, becoming emperor; that was a coup d'état.

2436   *A Ganymede*—A handsome boy. In mythology, Ganymede was a beautiful Trojan boy who took the place of Hebe as a cup-bearer of the gods.

2437   *Crossing the Rubicon*—To take an important or decisive step. At the beginning of the civil war with Pompey, Caesar crossed a river called the Rubicon, and exclaimed, "the die is cast." By crossing this river contrary to government orders, Caesar precipitated the war.

2438   *Apollo serving Admetus*—A person of special ability who is compelled by necessity to do a menial task. Admetus was a king in Thessaly whom Apollo at one time served as a shepherd.

2439   *To feel the sword of Damocles hanging over one's head*—A sense of impending disaster. Damocles was a flatterer at the court of Dionysius of Syracuse. Damocles constantly called attention to the happiness of kings, so Dionysius invited him to a banquet, seating him under a sword hung by a single hair to show what dangers were present in the fancied happiness of kings. It showed how foolish it was to long for happiness which might end so soon.

2440   *The man is Midas-eared*—A person of poor judgment. According to mythology, King Midas was asked to judge a music contest between Apollo and Pan. He awarded the prize to Pan. As punishment, Apollo changed the ears of Midas into those of a donkey.

2441   *A pactolian flood*—A flood or a river of gold. For a time in the life of Midas, everything he touched turned to gold. He washed in the river Pactolus and the sands of the stream turned to gold.

2442 *To drink from the fountain of Hippocrene*—To obtain inspiration for a literary work. Hippocrene was a fountain on Mount Helicon in Boeotia whose water was said in Greek mythology to impart poetic inspiration.

2443 *A titanic effort*—An exceptional effort. The Titans in mythology were deities of enormous strength.

2444 *The Dark Ages*—One may say that a terrible war will drive civilization back into the Dark Ages. The Dark Ages represent a period in the history of the world characterized by the decline or eclipse of the arts, letters and sciences. The Dark Ages are considered as the period between ancient and modern times, as between the fall of the Roman Empire and the revival of letters; the period from about 400 to 1400 A.D.

2445 *Olympian anger*—Anger such as the gods might display. In Greek mythology, the gods were supposed to dwell upon a mountain called Olympus; Olympian implies something that is godlike.

2446 *A harpy*—A very greedy person who will do anything to obtain wealth. In Greek mythology, a Harpy was one of a group of foul creatures, part woman, part bird, that snatched away the souls of the dead or seized or defiled the food of their victims.

2447 *In the doldrums*—State of listlessness, boredom, or indifference. The doldrums are a part of the ocean near the equator, abounding in calms, squalls and baffling winds, making it difficult for a sailing vessel to make progress. A person may be "in the doldrums"—bored and listless, uninterested in progress.

2448 *As riotous as Donnybrook Fair*—A riotous disorder or occasion. Donnybrook Fair was an annual fair, noted for fighting and disorder, formerly held in Donnybrook, Ireland.

2449 *To dragoon someone*—To compel one, or try to force one, to follow a certain course by harsh means. To harass by, or as if by, dragoons. A dragoon was formerly a mounted infantryman heavily armed; and the name dragoon came from the dragons, or short muskets, which were said to spout fire like dragons.

2450 *To draw a red herring across the track*—To draw attention from the principal question to some secondary matter. To divert one's attention. The phrase is said to have arisen two or three centuries ago when a red herring or a dead cat or animal was drawn across the track to train dogs in hunting.

2451 *To play ducks and drakes*—To throw away heedlessly or squander foolishly. May be used in connection with money; for example, to show how an unworthy heir squanders his estate. Ducks and drakes refers to the sport of throwing flat stones or shells so that they will skim or bound along the water.

2452   *A Dulcinea*—A sweetheart. Dulcinea was one of the most famous sweethearts in all literature, being Don Quixote's lady-love in Cervantes' novel of that name.

2453   *A Xanthippe*—Xanthippe was Socrates' wife. Her peevish scolding and quarrelsome temper have become proverbial. A woman with these characteristics is a Xanthippe.

2454   *Utopia*—Any place of ideal perfection. In a book written in 1516, Sir Thomas More described an imaginary ideal commonwealth, enjoying perfection in politics, law and in every way. The word "Utopia" comes from two Greek words meaning "no place." Utopian schemes are impractical and impossible of realization.

2455   *To cut the Gordian knot*—To solve a problem or to get rid of a difficulty in a fearless, determined manner. Gordius, the king of Phrygia, tied a knot no one could loosen. An oracle declared that whoever untied the knot would be master of Asia. Alexander the Great cut it with his sword.

2456   *To eat crow*—To be forced to eat one's own words; to confess one was wrong; to accept what one has fought against. The crow is not considered fit for human food; one would only eat it against his will.

2457   *An El Dorado*—A place of fabulous richness. El Dorado refers to a legendary rich king of a South American tribe or his imaginary kingdom, having a great deal of gold.

2458   *To tilt at windmills*—To fight against imaginary wrongs, evils or opponents. The phrase comes from *Don Quixote* by Cervantes. Don Quixote declared thirty or forty windmills were giants and, riding his horse, he drove at one of the windmills with his lance.

2459   *On tenterhooks*—In suspense, or under a distressing strain. Cloth may be stretched or tenterhooked, a tenterhook being a sharp hooked nail used for fastening cloth on a tenter. A tenter is a frame for stretching cloth.

2460   *A stormy petrel*—A harbinger of trouble. One who may cause trouble. The petrel is a bird which it is believed is active before a storm at sea and so foretells the storm.

2461   *She is stately as Juno*—A complimentary remark to a woman. Juno in mythology was the wife of Jupiter and the queen of heaven.

2462   *Eureka*—An expression of triumph over a discovery. To cry out "Eureka" means one has found something after much effort, or that is greatly desired. "I have found it" is the exclamation attributed to Archimedes upon discovering a method of determining the purity of gold.

2463   *To speak or write ex cathedra*—To speak from the chair—the chair of power and knowledge; to speak with authority. Sometimes used to comment

K

sarcastically on the remarks of a dogmatic writer or speaker as "Mr. Jones certainly spoke in an ex cathedra manner on a subject about which he was little informed." In the Roman Catholic church, the Pope may speak ex cathedra in his pontifical character—from his throne as the representative of Saint Peter.

2464   *Star chamber proceedings*—A secret or irresponsible tribunal. In early English history, the star chamber was a high court exercising wide civil and criminal jurisdiction; it could proceed on mere rumor and could apply torture. One might say, "The committee applied star chamber methods in its examination of witnesses."

2465   *Neither fish, flesh nor good red herring*—Means not one thing or another—no particular thing—nothing at all. Many years ago, "not fish" meant not food for monks; "not flesh" meant not food for people; not "good red herring" meant not food for the poor. So anything that didn't fit one of these groups was nothing.

2466   *He can hear the pipes of Pan*—He is sensitive to the wind, the waves and nature. He is at one with nature. In mythology, Pan was the god of pastures, forests and their wild life, and patron of shepherds and hunters.

2467   *A stalking horse*—A mask or pretense. Something put forward as the apparent reason of a person or group whereas the real purpose remains hidden, temporarily at least. In politics, a candidate put forward to divide the opposition or to conceal someone's real candidacy.

2468   *Sons of Belial*—Wicked, evil, immoral or corrupt persons. In the New Testament the name "Belial" became identified with Satan; in Milton's *Paradise Lost*, one of the fallen angels.

2469   *In the Slough of Despond*—In the depths of despair or discouragement. In *Pilgrim's Progress* the Slough of Despond was a deep quagmire which Christian, the pilgrim, had to cross.

2470   *A fool's paradise*—A condition of illusive happiness. A person who indulges in vain hopes lives in a fool's paradise.

2471   *A fool's errand*—A ridiculous, profitless undertaking.

2472   *The fourth estate*—Newspapers; the public press. It has been said that Burke originated the term when he spoke of three estates in Parliament and then added that the reporters' gallery was the fourth estate, the most important of all. Macaulay used it also. The first three estates were the lords spiritual, the lords temporal and the commons.

2473   *An Iliad of ills or an Iliad of woes*—A long series of evils or woes. Many evils experienced at the same time. The *Iliad* is a Greek epic poem ascribed to Homer. It narrates events of the last year of the Trojan War, and is filled with many tragic experiences.

2474   *A Frankenstein's monster*—A work or agency that ultimately destroys its originator. Frankenstein was a student of physiology in Mrs. Shelley's romance of the same name. He constructed a monster and gave it a kind of life. The monster inflicted the most terrible retribution upon his creator. The name now is used to indicate someone destroyed by his own works.

2475   *A gay Lothario*—A man who trifles with women's affections. In Rowe's drama, *The Fair Penitent*, Lothario was a gay and unscrupulous seducer. The name is also found in stories by Cervantes and Goethe.

2476   *At sixes and sevens*—A condition when affairs, matters or things are in disorder and confusion. The origin of the phrase is not certain, but Shakespeare and other writers have used it.

2477   *Simon-pure*—Genuine; authentic. In the comedy, a *Bold Stroke for a Wife* (1718) by Mrs. S. Centlivre, a Colonel Feignwell poses as Simon Pure, a Pennsylvania Quaker. He wins the heart of Miss Lovely and when Simon Pure himself arrives, he is at first treated as an impostor until he identifies himself as the true Simon Pure.

2478   *A Scrooge or an Ebenezer Scrooge*—A hard, greedy person. In the *Christmas Carol* by Dickens, Ebenezer Scrooge was an avaricious man visited by spirits on Christmas Eve and made kindly when they showed him the meaning of consideration and generosity to others.

2479   *To find a Golconda*—To discover a source of great wealth. Golconda is the name of a city in India which was famous for its great riches.

2480   *A Sinon*—A skillful liar. Sinon was a Greek through whose lies the Trojans were led to take the wooden horse, in which were concealed Greek warriors, into the city of Troy.

2481   *A Golgotha*—A place of torment or martyrdom; a cemetery. In the New Testament, the place where Christ was crucified.

2482   *A Saturnalia of crime*—An unusually large number of crimes. Saturnalia was the old Roman festival beginning December 17 in honor of the god Saturn. It was a time of much rejoicing, but was also marked by excesses and periods of general license.

2483   *A round robin*—A written petition or protest with the signatures in a circle so as not to indicate who signed first. The origin of the phrase is not certain, some believing that it came from the French.

2484   *A Rosetta stone*—A key by which a mystery or difficult problem may be solved. The Rosetta stone was found in 1799 near the Rosetta mouth of the

Nile. It contains an inscription in hieroglyphic characters which gave the first clue for deciphering the Egyptian hieroglyphics.

2485 *To commit political hara-kiri*—To commit political suicide. Hara-kiri was formerly a Japanese method of suicide practiced in cases of disgrace or by government order.

2486 *Hobson's choice*—A choice in which one has no alternative; one must take the thing offered or nothing. Thomas Hobson was an Englishman (1631) who let out horses in Cambridge; he had many horses, but every customer had to take the horse nearest the door.

2487 *Wealthy as a nabob*—to have great riches. A nabob is a native deputy or viceroy in India, or a Mogul provincial governor. These men have great wealth.

2488 *To be proud as Lucifer*—To be proud or rebellious in spirit even in the face of power that may not be challenged. Lucifer is the name sometimes used for Satan as identified with the rebel archangel before his fall.

2489 *Homeric laughter*—Loud and uncontrolled laughter. The Greek epic poet Homer is said to have written the famous *Iliad*, and this phrase refers to a passage in that poem.

2490 *On the hustings*—Any place where political speeches are being made. The hustings is the platform from which candidates for Parliament were formerly nominated.

2491 *On the horns of a dilemma*—A dilemma is an argument which gives an antagonist two or more alternatives (or horns), but equally against him. One has a choice between equally undesirable and unsatisfactory alternatives. The horns probably refer to a bull which may toss an object from one horn to the other.

2492 *Pons Asinorum*—A Latin phrase meaning an asses' bridge. The phrase is used to mean some obstacle to be overcome which is difficult for beginners to comprehend. The asses' bridge is a proposition from geometry which it is not always easy for beginners to understand. To illustrate the phrase: the pons asinorum that worried the sidewalk onlookers was how engineers could build a subway under streets over which heavy traffic was moving.

2493 *A jackanapes*—A conceited or impertinent person. The word is said to have come from a jack (monkey or ape) from napes (Naples in Italy).

2494 *The Pierian spring*—A source of knowledge. The poet Pope wrote: "A little learning is a dangerous thing; drink deep, or taste not the Pierian spring." To drink from the Pierian spring, according to Greek legends, was to obtain knowledge. The spring was in Pieria, a region of ancient Macedonia, one of the earliest seats of the worship of the Muses, who were the goddesses of the arts, history and music.

2495 *From Dan to Beersheba*—From limit to limit. From one end of the land to the other. A candidate for office might carry the election from Dan to Beersheba, that is, from one end of the state or nation to the other. Dan and Beersheba were formerly the northern and southern limits of Palestine.

2496 *A Jason's quest*—A difficult search. According to Greek mythology, Jason was sent by Pelias in search of the Golden Fleece. Jason met very difficult conditions, but obtained the fleece. To be asked to find a Shakespeare among today's playwrights might be said to be a Jason's quest. When one goes in search of the golden fleece, it may also mean to try to find one's fortune.

2497 *Quid pro quo*—A Latin phrase meaning something for something. *Webster's Collegiate Dictionary, Fifth Edition,* defines it as "one thing for, or in place of, another; tit for tat."

2498 *Job's comforter*—One who maliciously injures with words which supposedly are meant to comfort. A person who pretends he feels sorry for you and sympathizes with you, but who blames you for your troubles. The phrase comes from the experience Job had, as related in the Bible, with his friends when he was in great trouble.

2499 *Robbing Peter to pay Paul*—To pay one person with something to which another person has a prior right. To satisfy one obligation by leaving another unsatisfied. The expression is said to have originated as follows: About 300 years ago the Abbey Church of St. Peter, Westminster, London, was made a cathedral; a decade later it became a part of the diocese of London and a large part of its property was taken over by St. Paul's Cathedral. Someone writing at the time implied it was not right to rob St. Peter's altar to build one for St. Paul's Cathedral.

2500 *Namby pamby*—Weakly sentimental; insipid. One may speak, for example, of namby pamby writing or talk. Ambrose Phillips was an English poet whose verses for children were ridiculed. Namby came from a baby way of pronouncing Ambrose and pamby merely rhymed with namby.

2501 *Peripatetic*—The word comes from the Greek and means to walk about. Aristotle and his followers were called peripatetics because they taught or discussed matters while walking or moving about.

2502 *Kilkenny cats*—Two persons, groups or nations who fight each other until both are destroyed. There is a legend that two Kilkenny cats fought until nothing was left but their tails.

2503 *Knight-errant*—One who travels looking for opportunities to exhibit skill, prowess and generosity. May also be used to indicate one who goes about attempting to correct conditions or actions he believes are wrong. In ancient legends the knights-errant went about seeking to set free imprisoned kings, right wrongs and aid the oppressed as they saw the need. They are mentioned in Don Quixote. A tourist from this country in a Central American country might be considered a knight-errant if he expressed his opinion about correcting what he thought was wrong in the social life and customs of the people of the foreign country.

2504   *Pickwickian*—An adjective relating to or characteristic of Mr. Pickwick of Dickens' *Pickwick Papers*. Mr. Pickwick was simple and goodhearted.

2505   *A jingo*—One who is in favor of a belligerent or warlike policy in foreign affairs. A chauvinist. The phrase was used in England about 1877 when some people wanted England to assist Turkey against Russia. A popular song at that time said,

"We don't want to fight; but, by jingo, if we do,
"We've got the ships, we've got the men, and got the money too."

2506   *A patriarch*—A father, leader, chief. A venerable old man. In Biblical history before Moses, the father and ruler of a family or tribe. A person regarded as the father or founder, as of a race, science, religion. Adam Smith might be called a patriarch of political economy. The monarch oak might be called the patriarch of the trees.

2507   *Pecksniffian*—To resemble the hypocrisy or suave insincerity of Pecksniff who was a canting rascal in Dickens' story *Martin Chuzzlewit*.

2508   *To hunt with the lantern of Diogenes*—Diogenes was a Greek Cynic philosopher who was said to have gone about the streets of Corinth in broad daylight with a lighted lantern looking for an honest man. To illustrate the expression: It would take a Diogenes hunting with a lantern to find an honest man in a graft-ridden municipal government.

2509   *A Macedonian cry*—A call for help or assistance. The expression is of Biblical origin. In the Book of Acts in the Bible, chapter sixteen and verses nine and ten, it is recorded that a vision appeared to Paul by night, the vision of a Macedonian standing and appealing to him with the words, "Cross over to Macedonia and help us," from which it was inferred that "God had called us to preach the gospel to them." As soon as Paul saw the vision, "we made efforts to start for Macedonia."

2510   *Patient as Griselda*—A very patient woman. In romantic stories of medieval days, Griselda was a lady who was proverbial for virtue and patience. Her husband put her to severe trials, and she became a model of patience.

2511   *Out-Herod Herod*—To surpass in violent treatment or in wickedness. Shakespeare uses the expression in *Hamlet*. Herod was the king of Judea (37 B.C.) who destroyed the infants of Bethlehem.

2512   *Machiavellian*—Political cunning or bad faith; unscrupulous. Machiavelli was a Florentine statesman (1469-1527) who believed that any means, however unscrupulous, may be properly employed by a ruler in order to maintain a strong central government.

2513 *A Mugwump*—An independent in politics; one who reserves the right to bolt the candidate or platform of his party. The term was originally used to describe a bolter from the Republican party in the presidential campaign of 1884.

2514 *A Mississippi bubble*—A visionary and fantastic financial scheme in which many people are financially interested and which later collapses. The reference is to a scheme a Scotsman, John Law, had for colonizing along the Mississippi River. Law lived in Paris. Ridiculous stories of gold mines were circulated. The mint of France was even involved in Law's schemes. The shares of his company increased greatly, but eventually the whole financial structure crashed.

2515 *To pile Ossa upon Pelion*—To pile one problem or difficulty upon another. In Greek mythology, the giants, striving to attack the Olympians, piled Pelion, a high wooded mountain, on Mount Olympus and Ossa, a steep mountain, on Pelion.

2516 *A Munchausen*—One who tells fantastic and impossible stories; a liar. Baron Munchausen was the pretended author of a book of travels (by Rudolph Eric Raspe, 1785) filled with extravagant fictions.

2517 *A Mrs. Malaprop*—One who makes blunders in the use of words. "Malapropism" means the ridiculous misuse of a word. Mrs. Malaprop was a character in Sheridan's *Rivals*, noted for her blunders in the use of words.

2518 *Aliquando bonus dormitat Homerus* (Latin)—Sometimes even the good Homer nods, that is, the greatest are sometimes caught napping. Homer, the Greek poet, was said to be the author of the famous *Iliad*.

2519 *A mare's nest*—According to *Webster's Collegiate Dictionary*, a mare's nest is something believed to be wonderful, but turning out to be imaginary or a hoax. To find a mare's nest is to make what you think is an important discovery, but which actually turns out to be a hoax.

2520 *A mess of pottage*—A mess is a confused or disagreeable mixture; a muddle or hodge-podge. A pottage is a thick soup or a dish of vegetables, sometimes including meat. The reference is to the book of Genesis in the Bible where it is related that Esau sold his birthright to Jacob for bread and pottage. To sell something of value for a mess of pottage would obviously be very unwise. A mess of pottage would be something of little value.

2521 *The mills of God*—In literature the idea has often been conveyed of God ruling over a great mill which grinds out the destinies of men. One finds the expression, "The mills of God grind slowly, yet they grind exceeding small." One may escape punishment for a time for wrongdoing, but eventually it comes. Justice may be a long time coming, but its coming is inevitable.

2522 *Bourgeois* (French)—Middleclass; ordinary; humdrum.

2523 *Cliché* (French)—Stereotyped expression; hackneyed phrase.

2524 *Commencement de la fin* (French)—Beginning of the end.

Chapter *10*

BIBLICAL QUOTATIONS

....

OLD TESTAMENT

GENESIS

2525 It is not good that man should be alone.—*2, 18.*

2526 In the sweat of thy face shalt thou eat bread.—*3, 19.*

2527 For dust thou art, and unto dust shalt thou return.—*3, 19.*

2528 Am I my brother's keeper?—*4, 9.*

2529 There were giants in the earth in those days.—*6, 4.*

2530 Whoso sheddeth man's blood, by man shall his blood be shed.—*9, 6.*

2531 The voice is Jacob's voice, but the hands are the hands of Esau.—*27, 22.*

EXODUS

2532 Who made thee a prince and a judge over us?—*2, 14.*

2533 A land flowing with milk and honey.—*3, 8.*

2534 The land of Egypt, when we sat by the flesh-pots, and when we did eat bread to the full.—*16, 3.*

THE TEN COMMANDMENTS—*20, 3-17*

2535 I. Thou shalt have no other gods before me.

2536 II. Thou shalt not make unto thee any graven image, or any likeness of any thing that is in heaven above, or that is in the earth beneath, or that is in the water under the earth: thou shalt not bow down thyself to them, nor serve them: for I the Lord thy God am a jealous God, visiting the iniquity of the fathers upon the children unto the third and fourth generation of them that hate me; and shewing mercy unto thousands of them that love me, and keep my commandments.

2537 III. Thou shalt not take the name of the Lord thy God in vain; for the Lord will not hold him guiltless that taketh his name in vain.

2538 IV. Remember the sabbath day, to keep it holy. Six days shalt thou labor, and do all thy work; but the seventh day is the sabbath of the Lord thy God: in it thou shalt not do any work, thou, nor thy son, nor thy daughter, thy manservant, nor thy maidservant, nor thy cattle, nor thy stranger that is within thy gates: for in six days the Lord made heaven and earth, the sea, and all that in them is, and rested the seventh day: wherefore the Lord blessed the sabbath day, and hallowed it.

2539 V. Honor thy father and thy mother: that thy days may be long upon the land which the Lord thy God giveth thee.

2540 VI. Thou shalt not kill.

2541 VII. Thou shalt not commit adultery.

2542 VIII. Thou shalt not steal.

2543 IX. Thou shalt not bear false witness against thy neighbor.

2544 X. Thou shalt not covet thy neighbor's house, thou shalt not covet thy neighbor's wife, nor his manservant, nor his maidservant, nor his ox, nor his ass, nor any thing that is thy neighbor's.

DEUTERONOMY

2545 Man doth not live by bread only.—*8, 3.*

2546 Eye for eye, tooth for tooth, hand for hand, foot for foot.—*19, 21.*

2547 Thou shalt not muzzle the ox when he treadeth out the corn.—*25, 4.*

JOSHUA

2548 I am going the way of all the earth.—*23, 14.*

JUDGES

2549 The stars in their courses fought against Sisera.—*5, 20.*

FIRST SAMUEL

2550 Be strong, and quit yourselves like men.—*4, 9.*

2551 A man after his own heart.—*13, 14.*

SECOND SAMUEL

2552 How are the mighty fallen! Tell it not in Gath, publish it not in the streets of Askelon.—*1, 19 and 20.*

2553 And Nathan said to David, Thou art the man.—*12, 7.*

FIRST KINGS

2554 How long halt ye between two opinions? if the Lord be God, follow him: but if Baal, then follow him.—*18, 21.*

2555 A still small voice.—*19, 12.*

K

FIRST CHRONICLES

2556 Our days on the earth are as a shadow.—*29, 15.*

2557 And he died in a good old age, full of days, riches, and honour.—*29, 28.*

JOB

2558 One that feared God, and eschewed evil.—*1, 1.*

2559 The Lord gave, and the Lord hath taken away; blessed be the name of the Lord.—*1, 21.*

2560 Skin for skin, yea all that a man hath will he give for his life.—*2, 4.*

2561 Shall a man be more pure than his Maker?—*4, 17.*

2562 Although affliction cometh not forth of the dust, neither doth trouble spring out of the ground: yet man is born unto trouble as the sparks fly upward.—*5, 6 and 7.*

2563 Man that is born of a woman is of few days, and full of trouble.—*14, 1.*

2564 I am escaped with the skin of my teeth.—*19, 20.*

2565 The price of wisdom is above rubies.—*28, 18.*

2566 Behold, my desire is . . . that mine adversary had written a book.—*31, 35.*

2567 He was righteous in his own eyes.—*32, 1.*

2568 He multiplieth words without knowledge.—*35, 16.*

2569 He saith among the trumpets, Ha, ha; and he smelleth the battle afar off.—*39, 25.*

PSALMS

2570 Yea, though I walk through the valley of the shadow of death, I will fear no evil: for thou art with me; thy rod and thy staff they comfort me.—*23, 4.*

2571 Many are the afflictions of the righteous: but the Lord delivereth him out of them all.—*34, 19.*

2572 The wicked borroweth, and payeth not again: but the righteous showeth mercy, and giveth.—*37, 21.*

2573 He heapeth up riches, and knoweth not who shall gather them.—*39, 6.*

2574 Blessed is he that considereth the poor.—*41, 1.*

2575 As the hart panteth after the water brooks.—*42, 1.*

2576 Deep calleth unto deep.—*42, 7.*

2577 Oh that I had wings like a dove! for then would I fly away, and be at rest.—*55, 6.*

2578 We took sweet counsel together.—*55, 14.*

2579 The words of his mouth were smoother than butter, but war was in his heart; his words were softer than oil, yet were they drawn swords.—*55, 21.*

2580 Cast thy burden upon the Lord, and he shall sustain thee: he shall never suffer the righteous to be moved.—*55, 22.*

2581 Vain is the help of man.—*60, 11.*

2582 For a thousand years in thy sight are but as yesterday when it is past, and as a watch in the night.—*90, 4.*

2583 As for man, his days are as grass: as a flower of the field, so he flourisheth.—*103, 15.*

2584 They that go down to the sea in ships, that do business in great waters; these see the works of the Lord, and his wonders in the deep.—*107, 23 and 24.*

2585 The stone which the builders refused is become the head stone of the corner.—*118, 22.*

2586 Lo, children are an heritage of the Lord: happy is the man that hath his quiver full of them.—*127, 3 and 5.*

2587 Behold, how good and how pleasant it is for brethren to dwell together in unity!—*133, 1.*

2588 If I forget thee, O Jerusalem, let my right hand forget her cunning.—*137, 5.*

2589 I am fearfully and wonderfully made.—*139, 14.*

PROVERBS

2590 Surely in vain the net is spread in the sight of any bird.—*1, 17.*

2591 Whom the Lord loveth he correcteth.—*3, 12.*

2592 Go to the ant, thou sluggard; consider her ways, and be wise.—*6, 6.*

2593 As an ox goeth to the slaughter.—*7, 22;* Jer. *11, 19.*

2594 A wise son maketh a glad father.—*10, 1.*

2595 In the multitude of counsellors there is safety.—*11, 14; 24, 6.*

2596 He that is surety for a stranger shall smart for it.—*11, 15.*

2597 A virtuous woman is a crown to her husband.—*12, 4.*

2598 The way of the transgressors is hard.—*13, 15.*

2599 He that walketh with wise men shall be wise: but a companion of fools shall be destroyed.—*13, 20.*

2600 He that spareth his rod hateth his son.—*13, 24.*

2601 Righteousness exalteth a nation.—*14, 34.*

2602 A soft answer turneth away wrath: but grievous words stir up anger.—*15, 1.*

2603 A merry heart maketh a cheerful countenance.—*15, 13.*

2604 Pride goeth before destruction, and an haughty spirit before a fall.—*16, 18.*

2605 The hoary head is a crown of glory, if it be found in the way of righteousness.—*16, 31.*

2606 He that is slow to anger is better than the mighty: and he that ruleth his spirit than he that taketh a city.—*16, 32.*

2607 He that repeateth a matter separateth very friends.—*17, 9.*

2608 He that hath knowledge spareth his words.—*17, 27.*

2609 Even a fool, when he holdeth his peace, is counted wise.—*17, 28.*

2610 A man's gift maketh room for him, and bringeth him before great men.—*18, 16.*

2611 He that hath pity upon the poor lendeth unto the Lord.—*19, 17.*

2612 Wine is a mocker, strong drink is raging.—*20, 1.*

2613 It is naught, it is naught, saith the buyer: but when he is gone his way, then he boasteth.—*20, 14.*

2614   A good name is rather to be chosen than great riches.—*22, 1.*

2615   Train up a child in the way he should go: and when he is old, he will not depart from it.—*22, 6.*

2616   The rich ruleth over the poor, and the borrower is servant to the lender.—*22, 7.*

2617   Seest thou a man diligent in his business? he shall stand before kings; he shall not stand before mean men.—*22, 29.*

2618   Drowsiness shall clothe a man with rags.—*23, 21.*

2619   If thou faint in the day of adversity, thy strength is small.—*24, 10.*

2620   Rejoice not when thine enemy falleth, and let not thine heart be glad when he stumbleth.—*24, 17.*

2621   Debate thy cause with thy neighbor himself; and discover not a secret to another.—*25, 9.*

2622   A word fitly spoken is like apples of gold in pictures of silver.—*25, 11.*

2623   Whoso boasteth himself of a false gift is like clouds and wind without rain.—*25, 14.*

2624   Seest thou a man wise in his own conceit? there is more hope of a fool than of him.—*26, 12.*

2625   The sluggard is wiser in his own conceit than seven men that can render a reason.—*26, 16.*

2626   As coals are to burning coals, and wood to fire; so is a contentious man to kindle strife.—*26, 21.*

2627   Boast not thyself of tomorrow; for thou knowest not what a day may bring forth.—*27, 1.*

2628   The wicked flee when no man pursueth: but the righteous are bold as a lion.—*28, 1.*

2629   He that maketh haste to be rich shall not be innocent.—*28, 20.*

2630   He that giveth unto the poor shall not lack: but he that hideth his eyes shall have many a curse.—*28, 27.*

2631   A fool uttereth all his mind: but a wise man keepeth it in till afterward.—*29, 11.*

2632 The ants are a people not strong, yet they prepare their meat in the summer.—*30, 25.*

2633 Favor is deceitful, and beauty is vain.—*31, 30.*

ECCLESIASTES

2634 One generation passeth away, and another generation cometh; but the earth abideth forever.—*1, 4.*

2635 All the rivers run into the sea; yet the sea is not full.—*1, 7.*

2636 In much wisdom is much grief.—*1, 18.*

2637 Better is an handful with quietness, than both hands full with travail and vexation of spirit.—*4, 6.*

2638 A living dog is better than a dead lion.—*9, 4.*

2639 The race is not to the swift, nor the battle to the strong, neither yet bread to the wise, nor yet riches to men of understanding, nor yet favour to men of skill; but time and chance happeneth to them all.—*9, 11.*

2640 He that diggeth a pit shall fall into it.—*10, 8.*

2641 Cast thy bread upon the waters: for thou shall find it after many days.—*11, 1.*

2642 Remember now thy Creator in the days of thy youth, while the evil days come not.—*12, 1.*

2643 Of making many books there is no end; and much study is a weariness of the flesh.—*12, 12.*

SONG OF SOLOMON

2644 Many waters cannot quench love.—*8, 7.*

ISAIAH

2645 The ox knoweth his owner, and the ass his master's crib.—*1, 3.*

2646 Bring no more vain oblations; incense is an abomination unto me.—*1, 13.*

2647 They shall beat their swords into ploughshares, and their spears into pruning hooks.—*2, 4.*

2648 Grind the faces of the poor.—*3, 15.*

2649 Woe unto them that are wise in their own eyes!—*5, 21.*

2650 The wolf also shall dwell with the lamb, and the leopard shall lie down with the kid.—*11, 6.*

2651 How art thou fallen from heaven, O Lucifer, son of the morning!—*14, 12.*

2652 Babylon is fallen, is fallen.—*21, 9.*

2653 Watchman, what of the night?—*21, 11.*

2654 Let us eat and drink; for tomorrow we shall die.—*22, 13.*

2655 We have made a covenant with death.—*28, 15.*

2656 Behold, the nations are as a drop of a bucket, and are counted as the small dust of the balance.—*40, 15.*

2657 Shall the clay say to him that fashioneth it, What makest thou?—*45, 9.*

2658 A man of sorrows, and acquainted with grief.—*53, 3.*

2659 We all do fade as a leaf.—*64, 6.*

JEREMIAH

2660 Saying, Peace, peace; when there is no peace.—*6, 14.*

LAMENTATIONS

2661 She that was great among the nations, and princess among the provinces, how is she become tributary!—*1, 1.*

HOSEA

2662 For they have sown the wind, and they shall reap the whirlwind.—*8, 7.*

JOEL

2663 Your sons and your daughters shall prophesy, your old men shall dream dreams, your young men shall see visions.—*2, 28.*

ZECHARIAH

2664 Prisoners of hope.—*9, 12.*

2665 I was wounded in the house of my friends.—*13, 6.*

NEW TESTAMENT

THE GOSPEL ACCORDING TO ST. MATTHEW

2666 And now also the axe is laid unto the root of the trees.—*3, 10.*

2667 Man shall not live by bread alone.—*4, 4 (also* Luke *4, 4).*

2668   Blessed are the poor in spirit: for theirs is the kingdom of heaven.

2669   Blessed are they that mourn: for they shall be comforted.

2670   Blessed are the meek: for they shall inherit the earth.

2671   Blessed are they which do hunger and thirst after righteousness: for they shall be filled.

2672   Blessed are the merciful: for they shall obtain mercy.

2673   Blessed are the pure in heart: for they shall see God.

2674   Blessed are the peacemakers: for they shall be called the children of God.

2675   Blessed are they which are persecuted for righteousness' sake: for theirs is the kingdom of heaven.

2676   Blessed are ye, when men shall revile you, and persecute you, and shall say all manner of evil against you falsely, for my sake.

2677   Rejoice, and be exceeding glad: for great is your reward in heaven: for so persecuted they the prophets which were before you.—*5, 3 to 12.*

2678   Ye are the salt of the earth: but if the salt have lost his savour, wherewith shall it be salted? (*See* Mark *9, 50*; Luke *14, 34.*)—*5, 13.*

2679   Ye are the light of the world. A city that is set on an hill cannot be hid.—*5, 14.*

2680   Neither do men light a candle, and put it under a bushel. (*See* Mark *4, 21.*)—*5, 15.*

2681   Whosoever is angry with his brother without a cause shall be in danger of the judgment.—*5, 22.*

2682   An eye for an eye, and a tooth for a tooth.—*5, 38.*

2683   Whosoever shall smite thee on thy right cheek, turn to him the other also. (*See* Luke *6, 20.*)—*5, 39.*

2684   Give to him that asketh thee, and from him that would borrow of thee turn not thou away.—*5, 42.*

2685   Love your enemies. (*See* Luke *6, 27.*)—*5, 44.*

2686   Let not thy left hand know what thy right hand doeth.—*6, 3.*

2687   Use not vain repetitions.—*6, 7.*

2688   Where moth and rust doth corrupt, and where thieves break through and steal.—*6, 19.*

2689   For where your treasure is, there will your heart be also. (*See* Luke *12, 34.*)—*6, 21.*

2690   No man can serve two masters. (*See* Luke *16, 13.*)—*6, 24.*

2691   Ye cannot serve God and mammon. (*See* Luke *16, 13.*)—*6, 24.*

2692   Consider the lilies of the field, how they grow; they toil not, neither do they spin: And yet I say unto you, That even Solomon in all his glory was not arrayed like one of these. (*See* Luke *12, 27.*)—*6, 28 and 29.*

2693   Take therefore no thought for the morrow: for the morrow shall take thought for the things of itself. Sufficient unto the day is the evil thereof.—*6, 34.*

2694   Judge not, that ye be not judged. (*See* Luke *6, 37.*)—*7, 1.*

2695   Ask, and it shall be given you; seek, and ye shall find; knock, and it shall be opened unto you: for every one that asketh receiveth; and he that seeketh findeth; and to him that knocketh it shall be opened.—*7, 7 and 8.*

2696   What man is there of you, whom if his son ask bread, will he give him a stone? (*See* Luke *11, 11.*)—*7, 9.*

2697   Therefore all things whatsoever ye would that men should do to you, do ye even so to them. (*See* Luke *6, 31.*)—*7, 12.*

2698   Wide is the gate, and broad is the way, that leadeth to destruction.—*7, 13.*

2699   Beware of false prophets, which come to you in sheep's clothing, but inwardly they are ravening wolves.—*7, 15.*

2700   Ye shall know them by their fruits.—*7, 16.*

2701   A foolish man, which built his house upon the sand. (*See* Luke *6, 49.*)—*7, 26.*

2702   I am a man under authority, having soldiers under me: and I say to this man, Go, and he goeth; and to another, Come, and he cometh.—*8, 9.*

2703   The foxes have holes, and the birds of the air have nests; but the Son of man hath not where to lay his head.—*8, 20.*

2704   Follow me; and let the dead bury their dead. (*See* Luke *9, 60.*)—*8, 22.*

2705 No man putteth a piece of new cloth unto an old garment. (*See* Mark *3, 21.*)—*9, 16.*

2706 The harvest truly is plenteous, but the labourers are few. (*See* Luke *10, 2.*)—*9, 37.*

2707 The very hairs of your head are all numbered. (*See* Luke *21, 18.*)—*10, 30.*

2708 A man's foes shall be they of his own household.—*10, 36.*

2709 Come unto me, all ye that labour and are heavy laden.—*11, 28.*

2710 He that is not with me is against me. (*See* Mark *9, 40*; Luke *9, 50*; *11, 23.*)—*12, 30.*

2711 The tree is known by his fruit. (*See* Luke *6, 44.*)—*12, 33.*

2712 Out of the abundance of the heart the mouth speaketh. (*See* Luke *6, 45.*)—*12, 34.*

2713 Whosoever hath, to him shall be given, and he shall have more abundance: but whosoever hath not, from him shall be taken away even that he hath.—*13, 12.*

2714 When he had found one pearl of great price.—*13, 46.*

2715 If the blind lead the blind, both shall fall into the ditch.—*15, 14.*

2716 Get thee behind me, Satan. (*See* Mark *8, 33.*)—*16, 23.*

2717 For what is a man profited, if he shall gain the whole world and lose his own soul? (*See* Mark *8, 36*; Luke *9, 25.*)—*16, 26.*

2718 What therefore God hath joined together, let not man put asunder. (*See* Mark *10, 9.*)—*19, 6.*

2719 It is easier for a camel to go through the eye of a needle, than for a rich man to enter into the kingdom of God. (*See* Mark *10, 25.*)—*19, 24.*

2720 But many that are first shall be last; and the last shall be first. (*See* Mark *10, 31*; Luke *13, 30.*)—*19, 30.*

2721 For many are called, but few are chosen.—*22, 14.*

2722 Render therefore unto Caesar the things which are Caesar's; and unto God the things that are God's. (*See* Mark *12, 17*; Luke *20, 25.*)—*22, 21.*

2723 And whosoever shall exalt himself shall be abased; and he that shall humble himself shall be exalted. (*See* Luke *14, 11.*)—*23, 12.*

2724 Ye blind guides, which strain at a gnat, and swallow a camel.—23, 24.

2725 Ye are like unto whited sepulchres, which indeed appear beautiful outward, but are within full of dead men's bones, and of all uncleanness.—23, 27.

2726 Wars and rumours of wars.—24, 6.

2727 Well done, thou good and faithful servant.—25, 21.

2728 Reaping where thou hast not sown, and gathering where thou hast not strawed. (See Luke 19, 21.)—25, 24.

2729 For unto everyone that hath shall be given. (See Mark 4, 25.)—25, 29.

2730 I was a stranger, and ye took me in.—25, 35.

2731 Inasmuch as ye have done it unto one of the least of these my brethren, ye have done it unto me.—25, 40.

2732 So the last error shall be worse than the first.—27, 64.

THE GOSPEL ACCORDING TO ST. MARK

2733 He that hath ears to hear, let him hear.—4, 9.

2734 Lord, I believe; help thou mine unbelief.—9, 24.

2735 Whosoever shall offend one of these little ones that believe in me, it is better for him that a millstone were hanged about his neck, and he were cast into the sea.—9, 42.

2736 Suffer the little children to come unto me, and forbid them not: for of such is the kingdom of God. (See Matt. 19, 13; Luke 18, 15.)—10, 14.

2737 Which devour widows' houses, and for a pretence make long prayers. (See Matt. 23, 14.)—12, 40.

THE GOSPEL ACCORDING TO ST. LUKE

2738 On earth peace, good will towards men.—2, 14.

2739 Be content with your wages.—3, 14.

2740 Physician, heal thyself.—4, 23.

2741 The labourer is worthy of his hire.—10, 7.

2742 He passed by on the other side.—10, 31.

2743 Go, and do thou likewise.—10, 37.

2744 Take thine ease, eat, drink, and be merry.—*12, 19.*

2745 Friend, go up higher.—*14, 10.*

2746 I have married a wife, and therefore I cannot come.—*14, 20.*

2747 Wasted his substance with riotous living.—*15, 13.*

2748 How hardly shall they that have riches enter into the kingdom of God!—*18, 24.*

2749 Father, forgive them; for they know not what they do.—*23, 34.*

2750 Father, into thy hands I commend my spirit.—*23, 46.*

2751 Why seek ye the living among the dead?—*24, 5.*

THE GOSPEL ACCORDING TO ST. JOHN

2752 He came unto his own, and his own received him not.—*1, 11.*

2753 Can there any good thing come out of Nazareth?—*1, 46.*

2754 Men loved darkness rather than light, because their deeds were evil.—*3, 19.*

2755 He was a burning and a shining light.—*5, 35.*

2756 Judge not according to the appearance.—*7, 24.*

2757 The truth shall make you free.—*8, 32.*

2758 The night cometh, when no man can work.—*9, 4.*

2759 Let not your heart be troubled.—*14, 1.*

2760 In my father's house are many mansions.—*14, 2.*

2761 Greater love hath no man than this, that a man lay down his life for his friends.—*15, 13.*

2762 What I have written I have written.—*19, 22.*

ACTS OF THE APOSTLES

2763 Your sons and your daughters shall prophesy, and your young men shall see visions; and your old men shall dream dreams.—*2, 17.*

2764 Of a truth I perceive that God is no respecter of persons: but in every nation he that feareth him, and worketh righteousness, is accepted with him.—*10, 34 and 35.*

2765   It is more blessed to give than to receive.—*20, 35.*

2766   Much learning doth make thee mad.—*26, 24.*

EPISTLE TO THE ROMANS

2767   To be carnally minded is death.—*8, 6.*

2768   He that giveth, let him do it with simplicity; he that ruleth, with diligence; he that sheweth mercy, with cheerfulness.—*12, 8.*

2769   Abhor that which is evil; cleave to that which is good.—*12, 9.*

2770   Mind not high things, but condescend to men of low estate. Be not wise in your own conceits.—*12, 16.*

2771   Vengeance is mine; I will repay, saith the Lord.—*12, 19.*

2772   In so doing thou shalt heap coals of fire on his head. (*See* Proverbs 25, 22.)—*12, 20.*

2773   Owe no man anything.—*13, 8.*

2774   The night is far spent, the day is at hand: let us therefore cast off the works of darkness, and let us put on the armour of light.—*13, 12.*

2775   None of us liveth to himself, and no man dieth to himself.—*14, 7.*

FIRST EPISTLE TO THE CORINTHIANS

2776   Eye hath not seen, nor ear heard, neither have entered into the heart of man, the things which God hath prepared for them that love him.—*2, 9.*

2777   The wisdom of this world is foolishness with God.—*3, 19.*

2778   Absent in body, but present in spirit.—*5, 3.*

2779   A little leaven leaveneth the whole lump.—*5, 6.*

2780   The fashion of this world passeth away.—*7, 31.*

2781   Knowledge puffeth up, but charity edifieth.—*8, 1.*

2782   Let him that thinketh he standeth take heed lest he fall.—*10, 12.*

2783   The earth is the Lord's, and the fullness thereof.—*10, 26 and 28.*

2784   Though I bestow all my goods to feed the poor, and though I give my body to be burned, and have not charity, it profiteth me nothing.—*13, 3.*

2785   Charity suffereth long, and is kind; charity envieth not; charity vaunteth not itself, is not puffed up, doth not behave itself unseemly, seeketh not her own, is not easily provoked, thinketh no evil; rejoiceth not in iniquity, but rejoiceth in the truth; beareth all things, believeth all things, hopeth all things, endureth all things.—*13, 4 to 7.*

2786 Charity never faileth.—*13, 8.*

2787 When I was a child, I spake as a child, I understood as a child, I thought as a child: but when I became a man, I put away childish things.—*13, 11.*

2788 And now abideth, faith, hope, charity, these three; but the greatest of these is charity.—*13, 13.*

2789 Let us eat and drink; for tomorrow we die.—*15, 32.*

SECOND EPISTLE TO THE CORINTHIANS
2790 A thorn in the flesh.—*12, 7.*

EPISTLE TO THE GALATIANS
2791 Whatsoever a man soweth, that shall he also reap.—*6, 7.*

2792 Let us not be weary in well-doing: for in due season we shall reap, if we faint not.—*6, 9.*

EPISTLE TO THE EPHESIANS
2793 Carried about with every wind of doctrine.—*4, 14.*

2794 Let not the sun go down upon your wrath.—*4, 26.*

2795 Let no man deceive you with vain words.—*5, 6.*

2796 Children, obey your parents in the Lord: for that is right.—*6, 1.*

EPISTLE TO THE PHILIPPIANS
2797 For to me to live is Christ, and to die is gain.—*1, 21.*

2798 The peace of God, which passeth all understanding.—*4, 7.*

2799 Whatsoever things are true, whatsoever things are honest, whatsoever things are just, whatsoever things are pure, whatsoever things are lovely, whatsoever things are of good report; if there be any virtue, and if there be any praise, think on these things.—*4, 8.*

2800 I have learned, in whatsoever state I am, therewith to be content.—*4, 11.*

SECOND EPISTLE TO THE THESSALONIANS
2801 Be not weary in well-doing.—*3, 13.*

FIRST EPISTLE TO TIMOTHY

2802 Every creature of God is good.—*4, 4.*

2803 And having food and raiment let us be therewith content.—*6, 8.*
For the love of money is the root of all evil.—*6, 10.*

2804 Rich in good works.—*6, 18.*

SECOND EPISTLE TO TIMOTHY

2805 I have fought the good fight, I have finished the course, I have kept the faith.—*4, 7.*

EPISTLE TO THE HEBREWS

2806 Faith is the substance of things hoped for, the evidence of things not seen.—*11, 1.*

2807 Whom the Lord loveth he chasteneth, and scourgeth every son whom he receiveth. If ye endure chastening, God dealeth with you as with sons; for what son is he whom the father chasteneth not?—*12, 6 and 7.*

EPISTLE OF JAMES

2808 Let every man be swift to hear, slow to speak, slow to wrath.—*1, 19.*

2809 Faith without works is dead.—*2, 20.*

2810 For what is your life? It is even a vapour, that appeareth for a little time, and then vanisheth away.—*4, 14.*

FIRST EPISTLE OF PETER

2811 Love covereth a multitude of sins.—*4, 8.*

SECOND EPISTLE OF PETER

2812 The dog is turned to his own vomit again; and the sow that was washed to her wallowing in the mire.—*2, 23.*

FIRST EPISTLE OF JOHN

2813 The world passeth away, and the lust thereof: but he that doeth the will of God abideth forever.—*2, 17.*

THE REVELATION

2814 Be thou faithful unto death, and I will give thee a crown of life.—*2, 10.*

2815 I am Alpha and Omega, the beginning and the end, the first and the last.—*22, 13.*

Chapter 11

A RICH TREASURE HOUSE OF SELECTED QUOTATIONS

....

ABILITY

2816 He is always the severest censor of the merits of others who has the least worth of his own.—*E. L. Magoon.*

2817 The winds and waves are always on the side of the ablest navigators.—*Edward Gibbon.*

2818 Any one can hold the helm when the sea is calm.—*Publius Syrus.*

ACHIEVEMENT

2819 First say to yourself what you would be; and then do what you have to do.—*Epictetus.*

2820
>Heaven is not reached at a single bound;
>But we build the ladder by which we rise
>From the lowly earth to the vaulted skies,
>And we mount to its summit round by round.
>
>*Josiah Gilbert Holland*

2821
>Oh may I join the choir invisible
>Of those immortal dead who live again
>In minds made better by their presence.
>
>*Marian Evans Cross*

2822 It makes us or it mars us.—*Shakespeare.*

2823 An ill-favoured thing, sir, but mine own.—*Shakespeare.*

2824 Finish every day and be done with it. You have done what you could; some blunders and absurdities crept in; forget them as soon as you can. Tomorrow is a new day; you shall begin it well and serenely and with too high a spirit to be encumbered with your old nonsense.—*Emerson.*

2825 We judge ourselves by what we feel capable of doing; others judge us by what we have done.—*Longfellow.*

2826   Men at some time are masters of their fates:
The fault, dear Brutus, is not in our stars.
But in ourselves, that we are underlings.

Shakespeare

2827   Nothing will come of nothing.—*Shakespeare.*

2828   No great thing is created suddenly, any more than a bunch of grapes or a fig. If you tell me that you desire a fig, I answer you that there must be time. Let it first blossom, then bear fruit, then ripen.—*Epictetus.*

2829   My greatest inspiration is a challenge to attempt the impossible.—*Albert A. Michelson.*

2830   "Give me a standing place," said Archimedes, "and I will move the world"—Goethe has changed the postulate into the precept. "Make good thy standing place, and move the world."—*S. Smiles.*

2831   A brain is known by its fruits.—*H. G. Wells.*

ACTION

2832   Awake, arise, or be forever fallen!—*John Milton.*

2833   Thought is the seed of action.—*Emerson.*

ADVERSITY

2834   Happy those who knowing they are subject to uncertain changes, are prepared and armed for either fortune; a rare principle, and with much labor learned in wisdom's school.—*Massinger.*

2835   In this thing one man is superior to another, that he is better able to bear prosperity or adversity.—*Philemon.*

2836   Most of our comforts grow up between our crosses.—*Young.*

2837   The greater the difficulty, the more glory in surmounting it.—Skillful pilots gain their reputation from storms and tempests.—*Epicurus.*

2838   Let us be of good cheer, remembering that the misfortunes hardest to bear are those which never come.—*J. R. Lowell.*

2839   It has done me good to be somewhat parched by the heat and drenched by the rain of life.—*Longfellow.*

2840   Adversity has the effect of eliciting talents which in prosperous circumstances would have lain dormant.—*Horace.*

2841   How blunt are all the arrows of adversity in comparison with those of guilt!—*Blair.*

2842 Adversity's sweet milk, philosophy.—*Shakespeare.*

2843
        Sweet are the uses of adversity,
        Which like the toad, ugly and venomous,
        Wears yet a precious jewel in his head;
        And this our life, exempt from public haunt,
        Finds tongues in trees, books in the running brooks,
        Sermons in stones, and good in every thing.

                                       Shakespeare

AGE

2844 Age will not be defied.—*Francis Bacon.*

2845 Men of age object too much, consult too long, adventure too little, repent too soon.—*Francis Bacon.*

2846 Some men never seem to grow old. Always active in thought, always ready to adopt new ideas, they are never chargeable with fogyism. Satisfied, yet ever dissatisfied, settled, yet ever unsettled, they always enjoy the best of what is, and are the first to find the best of what will be.—*Shakespeare.*

2847 It is not by the gray of the hair that one knows the age of the heart.—*Bulwer.*

2848 It is usual to associate age with years only because so many men and women somewhere along in what is called middle age stop trying.—*Henry Ford.*

2849 A poor, infirm, weak, and despised old man.—*Shakespeare.*

2850 The ripest fruit first falls.—*Shakespeare.*

2851 Crabbed age and youth cannot live together.—*Shakespeare.*

2852 Nobody loves life like an old man.—*Sophocles.*

2853 Some smack of age in you, some relish of the saltness of time.—*Shakespeare.*

2854 We hope to grow old, yet we fear old age; that is, we are willing to live, and afraid to die.—*Bruyère.*

2855 I am declined into the vale of years.—*Shakespeare.*

2856
                Age is a quality of mind;
                If you've left your
                Dreams behind,
                If hope is cold,
                If you no longer look ahead

If your ambitious fires
Are dead,
Then, you are old!

AMBITION

2857 'Tis not what man does which exalts him, but what man would do!—*Browning.*

2858 Most people would succeed in small things if they were not troubled by great ambitions.—*Longfellow.*

2859 Hitch your wagon to a star.—*Emerson.*

2860 Ambition like a torrent ne'er looks back.—*Ben Jonson.*

2861 Ye know right well, how meek soe'er he seem, no keener hunter after glory breathes.—*Tennyson.*

2862 No man's pie is freed from his ambitious finger.—*Shakespeare.*

2863 When that the poor have cried, Caesar hath wept: Ambition should be made of sterner stuff.—*Shakespeare.*

ANTICIPATION

2864 Nothing is so good as it seems beforehand.—*George Eliot.*

2865 Uncertainty and expectation are the joys of life. Security is an insipid thing, though the overtaking and possessing of a wish discovers the folly of the chase.—*Congreve.*

2866 All earthly delights are sweeter in expectation than enjoyment; but all spiritual pleasures more in fruition than expectation.—*Feltham.*

APPRECIATION

2867 Next to excellence is the appreciation of it.—*Thackeray.*

2868 I have yet to find the man, however exalted his station, who did not do better work and put forth greater effort under a spirit of approval than under a spirit of criticism.—*Charles Schwab.*

BEAUTY

2869 A thing of beauty is a joy for ever.—*John Keats.*

2870 There is no beautifier of complexion, or form, or behavior, like the wish to scatter joy and not pain around us. Even virtue is more fair when it appears in a beautiful person.—*Virgil.*

2871 In all ranks of life the human heart yearns for the beautiful; and the beautiful things that God makes are his gift to all alike.—*H. B. Stowe.*

BREVITY

2872   This is the short and the long of it.—*Shakespeare.*

2873   Brevity is the soul of wit.—*Shakespeare.*

BUSINESS

2874   The greatest meliorator of the world is selfish, huckstering trade.-*Emerson.*

2875   It is a socialist idea that making profits is a vice. I consider the real vice is making losses.—*Winston Churchill.*

2876   Never shrink from doing anything your business calls you to do.—The man who is above his business, may one day find his business above him.—*Drew.*

2877   Call on a business man only at business times, and on business; transact your business, and go about your business, in order to give him time to finish his business.—*Wellington.*

2878   To my mind the best investment a young man starting out in business could possibly make is to give all his time, all his energies to work, just plain, hard work.—*C. M. Schwab.*

CHARACTER

2879   The end of a dissolute life is, most commonly, a desperate death.—*Bion.*

2880   It is hardly respectable to be good nowadays.—*Edith Sitwell.*

2881   We boil at different degrees.—*Emerson.*

2882   Condemn the fault, and not the actor of it?—*Shakespeare.*

2883   Be such a man, and live such a life, that if every man were such as you, and every life a life like yours, this earth would be God's Paradise.—*Phillips Brooks.*

2884   Make it thy business to know thyself, which is the most difficult lesson in the world.—*Cervantes.*

2885   I would to God thou and I knew where a commodity of good names were to be bought.—*Shakespeare.*

2886   He was ever precise in promise-keeping.—*Shakespeare.*

2887   Smooth runs the water where the brook is deep.—*Shakespeare.*

2888   To reform a man, you must begin with his grandmother.—*Victor Hugo.*

2889 He has a face like a benediction.—*Cervantes.*

2890 What the heart has once owned and had, it shall never lose.—*H. W. Beecher.*

2891 The holiest of all holidays are those kept by ourselves in silence and apart, the secret anniversaries of the heart, when the full tide of feeling overflows.—*Longfellow.*

2892 Circumstances form the character; but like petrifying waters they harden while they form.—*L. E. Landon.*

2893 Envy's memory is nothing but a row of hooks to hang up grudges on. Some people's sensibility is a mere bundle of aversions; and you hear them display and parade it, not in recounting the things they are attached to, but in telling you how many things and persons "they cannot bear."—*John Foster.*

2894 The meek are not those who are never at all angry, for such are insensible; but those who, feeling anger, control it, and are angry only when they ought to be. Meekness excludes revenge, irritability, morbid sensitiveness, but not self-defence, or a quiet and steady maintenance of right.—*Theophylact.*

2895 The hardest trial of the heart is, whether it can bear a rival's failure without triumph.—*Aikin.*

2896   Our deeds still travel with us from afar,
         And what we have been makes us what we are.
                                             George Eliot

2897 When anyone has offended me, I try to raise my soul so high that the offence cannot reach it.—*Descartes.*

2898 Secret, and self-contained, and solitary as an oyster.—*Charles Dickens.*

2899 Be and continue poor, young man, while others around you grow rich by fraud and disloyalty; be without place or power, while others beg their way upward; bear the pain of disappointed hopes, while others gain the accomplishment of theirs by flattery; forego the gracious pressure of the hand for which others cringe and crawl. Wrap yourself in your own virtue, and seek a friend and your daily bread. If you have in such a course grown gray with unblenched honor, bless God, and die.—*Heinzelmann.*

2900 Talents are best nurtured in solitude; character is best formed in the stormy billows of the world.—*Goethe.*

2901 Our character is but the stamp on our souls of the free choices of good and evil we have made through life.—*Geikie.*

2902 In the destiny of every moral being there is an object more worthy of God than happiness.—It is character.—And the grand aim of man's creation is the development of a grand character—and grand character is, by its very nature, the product of probationary discipline.—*Austin Phelps.*

2903   Leaves seem light, useless, idle, wavering, and changeable—they even dance; yet God has made them part of the oak.—So he has given us a lesson, not to deny stout-heartedness within, because we see lightsomeness without.—*Leigh Hunt.*

CHILDREN

2904   Children are the anchors that hold a mother to life.—*Sophocles.*

2905   How sharper than a serpent's tooth it is to have a thankless child!—*Shakespeare.*

2906   If I could get to the highest place in Athens, I would lift up my voice and say: "What mean ye, fellow citizens, that ye turn every stone to scrape wealth together, and take so little care of your children, to whom ye must one day relinquish all?"—*Socrates.*

2907   Childhood has no forebodings; but then it is soothed by no memories of outlived sorrow.—*George Eliot.*

2908   The first duty to children is to make them happy.—If you have not made them so, you have wronged them.—No other good they may get can make up for that.—*Buxton.*

2909   The training of children is a profession, where we must know how to lose time in order to gain it.—*Rousseau.*

CHOICE

2910   There's small choice in rotten apples.—*Shakespeare.*

2911   The question is this: Is man an ape or an angel? I, my lord, I am on the side of the angels.—*Disraeli.*

CIVILIZATION

2912   3 Fish.: "Master, I marvel how the fishes live in the sea." 1 Fish.: "Why, as men do a-land: the great ones eat up the little ones."—*Shakespeare.*

2913   Better fifty years of Europe than a cycle of Cathay.—*Tennyson.*

2914   Yet I doubt not through the ages one increasing purpose runs,
And the thoughts of men are widened with the process of the suns.

Tennyson

2915   The history of the world is the record of man in quest of his daily bread and butter.—*Hendrik Willem Van Loon.*

2916   A conviction that what is called fashionable life was compound of frivolity, of fraud and vice.—*Disraeli.*

2917 Ring in the nobler modes of life with sweeter manners, purer laws.—
Tennyson.

2918   Ring out old shapes of foul disease,
                       Ring out the narrowing lust of gold;
                       Ring out the thousand wars of old,
                       Ring in the thousand years of peace!

                                                     Tennyson

2919 The true test of civilization is, not the census, nor the size of cities, nor
the crops, but the kind of man that the country turns out.—*Emerson.*

2920 No true civilization can be expected permanently to continue which is
not based on the great principles of Christianity.—*Tryon Edwards.*

COMMON SENSE

2921 Good health and good sense are two of life's greatest blessings.—*Publius
Syrus.*

2922 Common sense does not ask an impossible chessboard, but takes the
one before it and plays the game.—*Wendell Phillips.*

CONCEIT

2923 He who is always his own counsellor will often have a fool for his
client.—*Hunter.*

2924 He was like a cock who thought the sun had risen to hear him crow.—
George Eliot.

2925 I am not in the roll of common men.—*Shakespeare.*

2926 An egotist is a man who talks so much about himself that he gives me
no time to talk about myself.—*H. L. Wayland.*

2927 Conceit in weakest bodies strongest works.—*Shakespeare.*

2928 Affectation is certain deformity.—By forming themselves on fantastic
models the young begin with being ridiculous, and often end in being vicious.
—*Blair.*

2929 A dogmatical spirit inclines a man to be censorious of his neighbors.—
Every one of his opinions appears to him written as with sunbeams, and he
grows angry that his neighbors do not see it in the same light.—He is tempted
to disdain his correspondents as men of low and dark understanding because
they do not believe what he does.—*Watts.*

2930 Truly, this world can get on without us, if we would but think so.—
Longfellow.

CONDUCT

2931 Speak with contempt of no man.—Everyone hath a tender sense of reputation.—And every man hath a sting, which he may, if provoked too far, dart out at one time or another.—*Burton.*

2932 We are growing serious, and, let me tell you, that's the very next step to being dull.—*Joseph Addison.*

2933 Sometimes we may learn more from a man's errors, than from his virtues.—*Longfellow.*

2934 In private life I never knew anyone interfere with other people's disputes but that he heartily repented of it.—*Carlyle.*

2935 It is not enough that you form, and even follow the most excellent rules for conducting yourself in the world; you must, also, know when to deviate from them, and where lies the exception.—*Greville.*

2936 A bone to the dog is not charity. Charity is the bone shared with the dog, when you are just as hungry as the dog.—*Jack London.*

CONSCIENCE

2937 The consciousness of clean linen is, in and of itself, a source of moral strength, second only to that of a clean conscience.—*Edwards.*

2938 A guilty conscience never feels secure.—*Publius Syrus.*

2939 Guilty consciences always make people cowards.—*Pilpay.*

2940 A peace above all earthly dignities, a still and quiet conscience.—*Shakespeare.*

2941 Conscience is merely your own judgment of the right or wrong of our actions, and so can never be a safe guide unless enlightened by the word of God.—*Tryon Edwards.*

2942 There is no class of men so difficult to be managed in a state as those whose intentions are honest, but whose consciences are bewitched.—*Napoleon.*

2943 It is astonishing how soon the whole conscience begins to unravel if a single stitch drops.—One single sin indulged in makes a hole you could put your head through.—*C. Buxton.*

CONSOLATION

2944 Charm ache with air, and agony with words.—*Shakespeare.*

2945 Patch grief with proverbs.—*Shakespeare.*

2946 Consolation, indiscreetly pressed upon us when we are suffering under affliction, only serves to increase our pain and to render our grief more poignant.—*Rousseau.*

CONTENTMENT

2947 Poor and content is rich and rich enough.—*Shakespeare.*

2948 The despotism of custom is on the wane.—We are not content to know that things are; we ask whether they ought to be.—*J. S. Mill.*

2949 One should be either sad or joyful. Contentment is a warm sty for eaters and sleepers.—*Eugene O'Neill.*

2950 Since we cannot get what we like, let us like what we can get.—*Spanish Proverb.*

CONVERSATION

2951 His words, like so many nimble and airy servitors, trip about him at command.—*John Milton.*

2952 Let thy speech be better than silence, or be silent.—*Dionysius the Elder.*

2953 Gratiano speaks an infinite deal of nothing; his reasons are as two grains of wheat hid in two bushels of chaff; you shall seek all day ere you find them, and when you have them they are not worth the search.—*Shakespeare.*

2954 Know how to listen, and you will profit even from those who talk badly.—*Plutarch.*

2955 Men of few words are the best men.—*Shakespeare.*

2956 Language is the dress of thought.—*Samuel Johnson.*

2957   And when you stick on conversation's burrs,
          Don't strew your pathway with those dreadful urs.
                                        Oliver Wendell Holmes.

2958 A kind of excellent dumb discourse.—*Shakespeare.*

COURAGE

2959 We should do by our cunning as we do by our courage,—always have it ready to defend ourselves, never to offend others.—*Greville.*

2960 Cowards do not count in battle; they are there, but not in it.—*Euripides.*

2961 Courage is grace under pressure.—*Ernest Hemingway.*

2962 No man is worth his salt who is not ready at all times to risk his body . . . to risk his well-being . . . to risk his life . . . in a great cause.—*Theodore Roosevelt.*

L

2963   For courage mounteth with occasion.—*Shakespeare.*

2964   The better part of valour is discretion.—*Shakespeare.*

2965   I will utter what I believe to-day, if it should contradict all I said yesterday.—*Wendell Phillips.*

2966   No man can answer for his own valor or courage, till he has been in danger.—*La Rochefoucauld.*

2967   The brave man is not he who feels no fear, for that were stupid and irrational; but he whose noble soul subdues its fear, and bravely dares the danger nature shrinks from.—*Joanna Baillie.*

2968   At the bottom of a good deal of the bravery that appears in the world there lurks a miserable cowardice.—Men will face powder and steel because they cannot face public opinion.—*E. H. Chapin.*

CREATE

2969   Originality is nothing but judicious imitation.—The most original writers borrowed one from another. The instruction we find in books is like fire. We fetch it from our neighbor's, kindle it at home, communicate it to others, and it becomes the property of all.—*Voltaire.*

2970   It is better to create than to be learned; creating is the true essence of life.—*Niebuhr.*

2971   If you would create something, you must be something.—*Goethe.*

CRIME

2972   Punishment is lame, but it comes.—*Herbert.*

2973   Those who are themselves incapable of great crimes, are ever backward to suspect others.—*La Rochefoucauld.*

2974   The devil knoweth his own, and is a particularly bad paymaster.—*F. M. Crawford.*

2975   The consequences of our crimes long survive their commission, and, like the ghosts of the murdered, forever haunt the steps of the malefactor.—*Walter Scott.*

2976
>   Nor florid prose, nor honied lines of rhyme,
>   Can blazon evil deeds, or consecrate a crime.
>   *Lord Byron*

CRITICISM

2977   Sarcasm is the language of the devil; for which reason I have long since as good as renounced it.—*Carlyle.*

2978   The pleasure of criticism takes from us that of being deeply moved by very beautiful things.—*Bruyère*.

2979   If we had no failings ourselves, we should not take so much pleasure in finding out those of others.—*La Rochefoucauld*.

2980   There is an unfortunate disposition in man to attend much more to the faults of his companions that offend him, than to their perfections which please him.—*Greville*.

2981   Endeavor to be always patient of the faults and imperfections of others; for thou hast many faults and imperfections of thine own that require forbearance. If thou art not able to make thyself that which thou wishest, how canst thou expect to mold another in conformity to thy will?—*Thomas à Kempis*.

2982   For I am nothing, if not critical.—*Shakespeare*.

2983   Animals are such agreeable friends—they ask no questions, they pass no criticisms.—*George Eliot*.

CURIOSITY

2984   Where necessity ends, desire and curiosity begin; no sooner are we supplied with everything nature can demand, than we sit down to contrive artificial appetites.—*Johnson*.

2985   The curiosity of an honorable mind willingly rests where the love of truth does not urge it further onward and the love of its neighbor bids it stop.—In other words, it willingly stops at the point where the interests of truth do not beckon it onward, and charity cries "Halt."—*Coleridge*.

DEATH

2986   At my fingers' ends.—*Shakespeare*.

2987   Out of the jaws of death.—*Shakespeare*.

2988   He that dies pays all debts.—*Shakespeare*.

2989   When death, the great reconciler, has come, it is never our tenderness that we repent of, but our severity.—*George Eliot*.

2990   Did any man at his death, ever regret his conflicts with himself, his victories over appetite, his scorn of impure pleasure, or his sufferings for righteousness' sake?—*Channing*.

2991   But oh for the touch of a vanished hand,
                And the sound of a voice that is still!
                              Tennyson

2992 Each in his narrow cell forever laid, the rude forefathers of the hamlet sleep.—*Thomas Gray.*

2993 Let's talk of graves, of worms, and epitaphs.—*Shakespeare.*

2994 A man can die but once.—*Shakespeare.*

2995 Cowards die many times before their deaths; the valiant never taste of death but once.—*Shakespeare.*

2996 Dear as remembered kisses after death.—*Tennyson.*

2997 Thy ignominy sleep with thee in the grave, but not remember'd in thy epitaph!—*Shakespeare.*

2998 Vicissitude of fortune which spares neither man nor the proudest of his works, but buries empires and cities in a common grave.—*Gibbon.*

2999 Why fear death? It is the most beautiful adventure in life.—*Charles Frohman.*

3000 Man wants but little, nor that little long. How soon must he resign his very dust, which frugal nature lent him for an hour.—*Young.*

3001 The boast of heraldry, the pomp of pow'r, and all that beauty, all that wealth e'er gave, await alike the inevitable hour; the paths of glory lead but to the grave.—*Gray.*

3002 Fear death?—to feel the fog in my throat, the mist in my face.—*Robert Browning.*

3003 It is an infamy to die and not be missed.—*Carlos Wilcox.*

3004 In every parting, there is an image of death.—*George Eliot.*

3005 Who knows but life be that which men call death, and death what men call life?—*Euripides.*

3006 I know of but one remedy against the fear of death that is effectual and that will stand the test either of a sick-bed or of a sound mind—that is, a good life, a clear conscience, an honest heart, and a well-ordered conversation; to carry the thoughts of dying men about us, and so to live before we die as we shall wish we had when we come to it.—*Norris.*

3007 Death has nothing terrible which life has not made so. A faithful Christian life in this world is the best preparation for the next.—*Tryon Edwards.*

3008 A dislike of death is no proof of the want of religion. The instincts of nature shrink from it, for no creature can like its own dissolution.—But though death is not desired, the result of it may be, for dying to the Christian is the way to life eternal.—*W. Jay.*

3009 Time for him had merged itself into eternity; he was, as we say, no more.—*Thomas Carlyle.*

3010 The grave buries every error, covers every defect, extinguishes every resentment.—From its peaceful bosom spring none but fond regrets and tender recollections.—Who can look down upon the grave of an enemy, and not feel a compunctious throb that he should have warred with the poor handful of dust that lies moldering before him.—*Washington Irving.*

DECEPTION

3011 Half the work that is done in this world is to make things appear what they are not.—*E. R. Beadle.*

3012 The very essence of assumed gravity is design, and consequently deceit; a taught trick to gain credit with the world for more sense and knowledge than a man is worth.—*Sterne.*

3013 The cunning livery of hell.—*Shakespeare.*

3014 It is a shameful and unseemly thing to think one thing and speak another, but how odious to write one thing and think another.—*Seneca.*

3015 It goes far toward making a man faithful to let him understand that you think him so; and he that does but suspect I will deceive him, gives me a sort of right to do it.—*Seneca.*

DECISION

3016 Decision of character will often give to an inferior mind command over a superior.—*W. Wirt.*

3017 Tomorrow I will live, the fool does say: today itself's too late; the wise lived yesterday.—*Martial.*

DETERMINATION

3018 I'll not budge an inch.—*Shakespeare.*

3019 The best lightning-rod for your protection is your own spine.—*Emerson.*

3020 Man has his will,—but woman has her way.—*Oliver Wendell Holmes.*

3021 He who is firm and resolute in will moulds the world to himself.—*Goethe.*

3022 Either I will find a way, or I will make one.—*Sir P. Sidney.*

3023 Energy will do anything that can be done in the world; and no talents, no circumstances, no opportunities will make a two-legged animal a man without it.—*Goethe.*

3024 The truest wisdom, in general, is a resolute determination.—*Napoleon.*

3025 Toil, feel, think, hope; you will be sure to dream enough before you die, without arranging for it.—*J. Sterling.*

DOING

3026 Do not then be afraid of defeat.—You are never so near to victory as when defeated in a good cause.—*H. W. Beecher.*

3027 To do two things at once is to do neither.—*Publius Syrus.*

3028 None are so busy as the fool and knave.—*John Dryden.*

3029 If to do were as easy as to know what were good to do, chapels had been churches, and poor men's cottages princes' palaces.—*Shakespeare.*

3030 Try to put well in practice what you already know; and in so doing, you will, in good time, discover the hidden things which you now inquire about. Practice what you know, and it will help to make clear what now you do not know.—*Rembrandt.*

3031 Our grand business is not to see what lies dimly in the distance, but to do what lies clearly at hand.—*Carlyle.*

3032 Doing is the great thing. For if resolutely, people do what is right, in time they come to like doing it.—*Ruskin.*

DUTY

3033 He on whom Heaven confers a sceptre knows not the weight till he bears it.—*Corneille.*

3034 I do perceive here a divided duty.—*Shakespeare.*

3035 Every duty which we omit, obscures some truth which we should have known.—*Ruskin.*

3036 We live in a world which is full of misery and ignorance, and the plain duty of each and all of us is to try to make the little corner he can influence somewhat less miserable and somewhat less ignorant than it was before he entered it.—*Huxley.*

3037 An ambassador is an honest man sent to lie and intrigue abroad for the benefit of his country.—*Sir H. Wotton.*

3038
> Not once or twice in our rough-island story
> The path of duty was the way to glory.
> *Tennyson*

ECONOMY

3039 Employment gives health, sobriety, and morals.—Constant employment and well-paid labor produce, in a country like ours, general prosperity, content, and cheerfulness.—*Daniel Webster.*

3040 Socrates said, "Those who want fewest things are nearest to the gods."—*Diogenes Laertius.*

3041 He seldom lives frugally who lives by chance. Hope is always liberal, and they that trust her promises make little scruple of revelling today on the profits of tomorrow.—*Johnson.*

3042 A sound economy is a sound understanding brought into action. It is calculation realized; it is the doctrine of proportion reduced to practice; it is foreseeing contingencies and providing against them; it is expecting contingencies and being prepared for them.—*Hannah More.*

3043 Nothing is cheap which is superfluous, for what one does not need, is dear at a penny.—*Plutarch.*

3044 There are but two ways of paying a debt; increase of industry in raising income, or increase of thrift in laying out.—*Carlyle.*

EDUCATION

3045 There is a time in every man's education when he arrives at the conviction that envy is ignorance; that imitation is suicide; that he must take himself for better, for worse, as his portion; that though the wide universe is full of good, no kernel of nourishing corn comes to him but through his toil bestowed on that plot of ground which is given him to till. The power which resides in him is new in nature, and none but he knows what that is which he can do, nor does he know until he has tried.—*Emerson.*

3046 Aristotle said that education was an ornament in prosperity and a refuge in adversity.—*Diogenes Laertius.*

3047 The great end of education is, to discipline rather than to furnish the mind; to train it to the use of its own powers, rather than fill it with the accumulations of others.—*Tryon Edwards.*

3048 He is to be educated not because he is to make shoes, nails, and pins, but because he is a man.—*Channing.*

3049 Culture is "To know the best that has been said and thought in the world."—*Matthew Arnold.*

3050 A mixture of misery and education is highly explosive.—*Herbert Samuel.*

3051   Out of monuments, names, words, proverbs, traditions, private records and evidences, fragments of stories, passages of books and the like, we do save and recover somewhat from the deluge of time.—*Bacon.*

3052   The real object of education is to give children resources that will endure as long as life endures; habits that time will ameliorate, not destroy; occupations that will render sickness tolerable, solitude pleasant, age venerable, life more dignified and useful, and death less terrible.—*Sidney Smith.*

3053   Education is the knowledge of how to use the whole of oneself. Many men use one or two faculties out of the score with which they are endowed. A man is educated who knows how to make a tool of every faculty—how to open it, how to keep it sharp, and how to apply it to all practical purposes.—*H. W. Beecher.*

3054   All who have meditated on the art of governing mankind have been convinced that the fate of empires depends on the education of youth.—*Aristotle.*

3055   Do not ask if a man has been through college; ask if a college has been through him—if he is a walking university.—*E. H. Chapin.*

ELOQUENCE

3056   Eloquence is the child of knowledge.—*Disraeli.*

3057   The manner of speaking is full as important as the matter, as more people have ears to be tickled than understandings to judge.—*Chesterfield.*

ENEMY

3058   Observe thyself as thy greatest enemy would do, so shalt thou be thy greatest friend.—*Jeremy Taylor.*

3059   He makes no friend who never made a foe.—*Tennyson.*

3060   Fools may our scorn, not envy raise, for envy is a kind of praise.—*Gay.*

3061   The envious praise only that which they can surpass; that which surpasses them they censure.—*Colton.*

3062   If we could read the secret history of our enemies, we should find in each man's life sorrow and suffering enough to disarm all hostility.—*Longfellow.*

3063   It is much safer to reconcile an enemy than to conquer him; victory may deprive him of his poison, but reconciliation of his will.—*Feltham.*

3064   However rich or powerful a man may be, it is the height of folly to make personal enemies; for one unguarded moment may yield you to the revenge of the most despicable of mankind.—*Lyttleton.*

3065 If you want enemies, excel others; if friends, let others excel you.—*Colton.*

ENTHUSIASM

3066 Violent zeal even for truth has a hundred to one odds to be either petulancy, ambition, or pride.—*Swift.*

3067 Every production of genius must be the production of enthusiasm.—*Disraeli.*

3068 Every man is enthusiastic at times. One man has enthusiasm for thirty minutes—another man has it for thirty days, but it is the man who has it for thirty years who makes a success in life.—*Edward B. Butler.*

EQUALITY

3069 Your levelers wish to level *down* as far as themselves; but they cannot bear leveling *up* to themselves.—*Samuel Johnson.*

3070 Two stars keep not their motion in one sphere.—*Shakespeare.*

3071 As men, we are all equal in the presence of death.—*Publius Syrus.*

EVIL

3072 The rankest compound of villainous smell that ever offended nostril.—*Shakespeare.*

3073 He will give the devil his due.—*Shakespeare.*

3074 There's daggers in men's smiles.—*Shakespeare.*

3075 The devil can cite Scripture for his purpose.—*Shakespeare.*

3076 The world is grown so bad, that wrens make prey where eagles dare not perch.—*Shakespeare.*

3077 All the perfumes of Arabia will not sweeten this little hand.—*Shakespeare.*

3078 There is some soul of goodness in things evil, would men observingly distil it out.—*Shakespeare.*

3079 There is this good in real evils,—they deliver us, while they last, from the petty despotism of all that were imaginary.—*Colton.*

3080 There are thousands hacking at the branches of evil to one who is striking at the root.—*Thoreau.*

EXAMPLE

3081 I am a part of all that I have met.—*Tennyson.*

L*

3082 My advice is, to consult the lives of other men as we would a looking-glass, and from thence fetch examples for our own imitation.—*Terence.*

3083 If you would convince a man that he does wrong, do right. Men will believe what they see. Let them see.—*Thoreau.*

3084 Man is an imitative creature, and whoever is foremost leads the herd.—*Schiller.*

3085 People seldom improve when they have no other model but themselves to copy after.—*Goldsmith.*

3086 No man was ever great by imitation.—*Samuel Johnson.*

3087 No man is so insignificant as to be sure his example can do no hurt.—*Lord Clarendon.*

3088 We are all of us more or less echoes, repeating involuntarily the virtues, the defects, the movements, and the characters of those among whom we live.—*Joubert.*

EXPERIENCE

3089 I had rather have a fool to make me merry than experience to make me sad.—*Shakespeare.*

3090 You take all the experience and judgment of men over 50 out of the world and there wouldn't be enough left to run it.—*Henry Ford.*

3091 I know the past, and thence will assay to glean a warning for the future, so that man may profit by his errors, and derive experience from his folly.—*Shelley.*

3092 There is no merit where there is no trial; and till experience stamps the mark of strength, cowards may pass for heroes, and faith for falsehood.—*A. Hill.*

3093 No man was ever endowed with a judgment so correct and judicious, but that circumstances, time, and experience, would teach him something new, and apprise him that of those things with which he thought himself the best acquainted, he knew nothing; and that those ideas which in theory appeared the most advantageous were found, when brought into practice, to be altogether impracticable.—*Terence.*

EYES

3094 The balls of sight are so formed, that one man's eyes are spectacles to another, to read his heart with.—*Johnson.*

3095 Eyes will not see when the heart wishes them to be blind.—Desire conceals truth, as darkness does the earth.—*Seneca.*

FAITH

3096   For they conquer who believe they can.—*Virgil*.

3097
>   Howe'er it be, it seems to me,
>   'T is only noble to be good.
>   Kind hearts are more than coronets,
>   And simple faith than Norman blood.
>   *Tennyson*

3098   Here I stand; I can do no otherwise. God help me. Amen!—*Martin Luther*.

3099   It is cynicism and fear that freeze life; it is faith that thaws it out, releases it, sets it free.—*Harry Emerson Fosdick*.

3100   When faith is lost, and honor dies, the man is dead.—*Whittier*.

3101   Fanatic faith, once wedded fast to some dear falsehood, hugs it to the last.—*Moore*.

3102   Goodness thinks no ill where no ill seems.—*Milton*.

3103   Strike from mankind the principle of faith, and men would have no more history than a flock of sheep.—*Bulwer*.

3104   All the scholastic scaffolding falls, as a ruined edifice, before one single word—faith.—*Napoleon*.

3105   Faith in order, which is the basis of science, cannot reasonably be separated from faith in an ordainer, which is the basis of religion.—*Asa Gray*.

FALSEHOOD

3106   A lie never lives to be old.—*Sophocles*.

3107   Lie not, neither to thyself, nor man, nor God.—It is for cowards to lie.—*Herbert*.

3108   The practice of politics in the East may be defined by one word—dissimulation.—*Disraeli*.

3109   The most terrible of lies is not that which is uttered but that which is lived.—*W. G. Clarke*.

3110   Never chase a lie; if you let it alone, it will soon run itself to death.—You can work out a good character faster than calumny can destroy it.—*E. Nott*.

3111   A liar should have a good memory.—*Quintilian*.

FAME

3112 Toil, says the proverb, is the sire of fame.—*Euripides.*

3113 Those who despise fame seldom deserve it.—We are apt to undervalue the purchase we cannot reach, to conceal our poverty the better.—It is a spark that kindles upon the best fuel, and burns brightest in the bravest breast.—*Jeremy Collier.*

3114 To judge of the real importance of an individual, we should think of the effect his death would produce.—*Levis.*

3115 How men long for celebrity!—Some would willingly sacrifice their lives for fame, and not a few would rather be known by their crimes than not known at all.—*Sinclair.*

3116 Our admiration of a famous man lessens upon our nearer acquaintance with him; and we seldom hear of a celebrated person without a catalogue of some of his weaknesses and infirmities.—*Addison.*

FAMILY

3117 As are families, so is society. If well ordered, well instructed, and well governed, they are the springs from which go forth the streams of national greatness and prosperity—of civil order and public happiness.—*Thayer.*

3118 Who serves his country well has no need of ancestors.—*François M. Voltaire.*

3119 It is a wise father that knows his own child.—*Shakespeare.*

3120 A man cannot leave a better legacy to the world than a well-educated family.—*Thomas Scott.*

3121 It is indeed a desirable thing to be well descended, but the glory belongs to our ancestors.—*Plutarch.*

3122 Every man is his own ancestor, and every man is his own heir. He devises his own future, and he inherits his own past.—*H. F. Hedge.*

3123 Mere family never made a man great.—Thought and deed, not pedigree, are the passports to enduring fame.—*Skobeleff.*

FAULT

3124 When a man is wrong and won't admit it, he always get angry.—*Haliburton.*

3125 Faultily faultless, icily regular, splendidly null.—*Tennyson.*

3126 The absent are never without fault, nor the present without excuse.—*Franklin.*

3127 Men do not suspect faults which they do not commit.—*Samuel Johnson.*

3128   But friend, to me
                He is all fault who hath no fault at all.
                For who loves me must have a touch of earth.
                                    Tennyson

FEAR

3129 No one loves the man whom he fears.—*Aristotle.*

3130 One of the greatest artifices the devil uses to engage men in vice and debauchery, is to fasten names of contempt on certain virtues, and thus fill weak souls with a foolish fear of passing for scrupulous, should they desire to put them in practice.—*Pascal.*

3131 The two great movers of the human mind are the desire of good, and the fear of evil.—*Johnson.*

3132   They are slaves who fear to speak
                For the fallen and the weak.
                                    Lowell

3133   They are slaves who dare not be
                In the right with two or three.
                                    Lowell

3134 Uneasy lies the head that wears a crown.—*Shakespeare.*

FLATTERY

3135 If we would not flatter ourselves, the flattery of others could not harm us.— *La Rochefoucauld.*

3136 When our vices quit us, we flatter ourselves with the belief that it is we who quit them.—*La Rochefoucauld.*

FOOD

3137 He hath eaten me out of house and home.—*Shakespeare.*

3138 And men sit down to that nourishment which is called supper.—*Shakespeare.*

3139 One meal a day is enough for a lion, and it ought to be for a man.—*G. Fordyce.*

3140 They are as sick that surfeit with too much, as they that starve with nothing.—*Shakespeare.*

3141 Food for powder, food for powder; they'll fill a pit as well as better.—*Shakespeare.*

Fools

3142 As if anything were so common as ignorance! The multitude of fools is a protection to the wise.—*Cicero.*

3143 Fortune, to show us her power, and abate our presumption, seeing she could not make fools wise, has made them fortunate.—*Montaigne.*

3144 Ridicule is the first and last argument of fools.—*C. Simmons.*

3145 A fool flatters himself; the wise man flatters the fool.—*Bulwer.*

3146 In all companies there are more fools than wise men, and the greater part always gets the better of the wiser.—*Rabelais.*

3147 Young men think old men fools, and old men know young men to be so.—*Metcalf.*

Forgiveness

3148 It is easier for the generous to forgive, than for the offender to ask forgiveness.—*Thomson.*

3149 They who forgive most, shall be most forgiven.—*Bailey.*

3150 Nothing in this lost and ruined world bears the meek impress of the Son of God so surely as forgiveness.—*Alice Cary.*

Fortune

3151 Fortune is not on the side of the faint-hearted.—*Sophocles.*

3152 Fortune is like glass, the brighter the glitter, the more easily broken.—*Publius Syrus.*

3153 In human life there is constant change of fortune; and it is unreasonable to expect an exemption from the common fate.—Life itself decays, and all things are daily changing.—*Plutarch.*

3154
There is a tide in the affairs of men
Which taken at the flood, leads on to fortune:
Omitted, all the voyage of their life
Is bound in shallows and in miseries.
Shakespeare

Frankness

3155 There are few, very few, that will own themselves in a mistake.—*Swift.*

3156 I can promise to be candid, though I may not be impartial.—*Goethe.*

FRIENDSHIP

3157 A man's best friends are his ten fingers.—*Robert Collyer.*

3158 What you dislike in another, take care to correct in yourself.—*Sprat.*

3159 Reprove thy friend privately; commend him publicly.—*Solon.*

3160 The greatest comfort of my old age, and that which gives me the highest satisfaction, is the pleasing remembrance of the many benefits and friendly offices I have done to others.—*Cato.*

3161 We gain nothing by being with such as ourselves: we encourage each other in mediocrity.—I am always longing to be with men more excellent than myself.—*Lamb.*

3162 If a man does not make new acquaintances as he advances through life, he will soon find himself left alone; one should keep his friendships in constant repair.—*Johnson.*

3163 I love a hand that meets my own with a grasp that causes some sensation.—*F. S. Osgood.*

3164 Thou mayest be sure that he that will in private tell thee of thy faults, is thy friend, for he adventures thy dislike, and doth hazard thy hatred; there are few men that can endure it, every man for the most part delighting in self-praise, which is one of the most universal follies that bewitcheth mankind.—*Sir W. Raleigh.*

3165 We take care of our health, we lay up money, we make our roof tight and our clothing sufficient, but who provides wisely that he shall not be wanting in the best property of all—friends?—*Emerson.*

3166 It is one of the severest tests of friendship to tell your friend his faults. —So to love a man that you cannot bear to see a stain upon him, and to speak painful truth through loving words, that is friendship.—*H. W. Beecher.*

GENIUS

3167 The true genius is a mind of large general powers, accidentally determined to some particular direction.—*Samuel Johnson.*

3168 Doing easily what others find difficult is talent; doing what is impossible for talent is genius.—*Henri-Frederic Amiel.*

3169 All the means of action—the shapeless masses—the materials—lie everywhere about us.—What we need is the celestial fire to change the flint into the transparent crystal, bright and clear.—That fire is genius.—*Longfellow.*

3170 Every man who observes vigilantly, and resolves steadfastly, grows unconsciously into genius.—*Bulwer.*

3171   Times of general calamity and confusion have ever been productive of the greatest minds. The purest ore is produced from the hottest furnace, and the brightest thunderbolt is elicited from the darkest storm.—*Colton.*

3172   There is no great genius without a tincture of madness.—*Seneca.*

3173   Men give me credit for some genius. All the genius I have lies in this: When I have a subject in hand, I study it profoundly. Day and night it is before me. My mind becomes pervaded with it. Then the effort which I have made is what people are pleased to call the fruit of genius. It is the fruit of labor and thought.—*Alexander Hamilton.*

GENTLEMEN

3174   Good manners are made up of petty sacrifices.—*Emerson.*

3175   Men of courage, men of sense, and men of letters are frequent: but a true gentleman is what one seldom sees.—*Steele.*

3176   Good-breeding shows itself most, where to an ordinary eye it appears the least.—*Addison.*

GIVING

3177   Give what you have. To some one it may be better than you dare to think.—*Longfellow.*

3178   There was a man, though some did count him mad,
             The more he cast away the more he had.
                                     John Bunyan

3179   Shall we call ourselves benevolent, when the gifts we bestow do not cost us a single privation?—*Degerando.*

3180   He who is not liberal with what he has, does not deceive himself when he thinks he would be liberal if he had more.—*W. S. Plumer.*

3181   We should give as we would receive, cheerfully, quickly, and without hesitation, for there is no grace in a benefit that sticks to the fingers.—*Seneca.*

GOD

3182   A mighty fortress is our God,
             A bulwark never failing;
             Our helper He amid the flood
             Of mortal ills prevailing.
                                     Martin Luther

3183   Though the mills of God grind slowly, yet they grind exceeding small;
       Though with patience He stands waiting, with exactness grinds He all.
                                     Friedrich Von Logau

3184   That is best which God sends; it was his will; it is mine.—*O. Meredith.*

3185   There's a divinity that shapes our ends, rough-hew them how we will.
—*Shakespeare.*

3186   The world is God's epistle to mankind—his thoughts are flashing upon us from every direction.—*Plato.*

3187   God hangs the greatest weights upon the smallest wires.—*Bacon.*

3188   God tempers the wind to the shorn lamb.—*Sterne.*

3189   One on God's side is a majority.—*Wendell Phillips.*

3190   Anything that makes religion a second object makes it no object.—He who offers to God a second place offers him no place.—*Ruskin.*

3191   How often we look upon God as our last and feeblest resource! We go to Him because we have nowhere else to go. And then we learn that the storms of life have driven us, not upon the rocks, but into the desired haven.
—*Geo. Macdonald.*

3192   Two men please God—who serves Him with all his heart because he knows Him; who seeks Him with all his heart because he knows Him not.—
Panin.

Gossip

3193   Many hope the tree may be felled that they may gather chips by the fall.—*Fuller.*

3194   We cannot control the evil tongues of others; but a good life enables us to disregard them.—*Cato.*

3195   Done to death by slanderous tongues.—*Shakespeare.*

3196   And there's a lust in man no charm can tame
             Of loudly publishing our neighbour's shame;
             On eagles' wings immortal scandals fly,
             While virtuous actions are but born and die.
                              Stephen Harvey

Government

3197   I carry my sovereignty under my hat.—*William A. Prendergast.*

3198   Did the mass of men know the actual selfishness and injustice of their rulers, not a government would stand a year.—The world would foment with revolution.—*Theodore Parker.*

3199   Ay, every inch a king.—*Shakespeare.*

3200 Democracy is based upon the conviction that there are extraordinary possibilities in ordinary people.—*Harry Emerson Fosdick.*

3201 Is it not a noble farce, wherein kings, republics, and emperors have for so many ages played their parts, and to which the whole vast universe serves for a theatre?—*Michel de Montaigne.*

3202 As I sat opposite the Treasury Bench, the Ministers reminded me of those marine landscapes not unusual on the coasts of South America. You behold a range of exhausted volcanoes.—*Disraeli.*

3203 Freedom of religion, freedom of the press, and freedom of person under the protection of the habeas corpus, these are principles that have guided our steps through an age of revolution and reformation.—*Jefferson.*

3204 A State to prosper, must be built on foundations of a moral character; and this character is the principal element of its strength and the only guaranty of its permanence and prosperity.—*J. Currie.*

3205 Obedience is what makes government, and not the names by which it is called.—*Edmund Burke.*

3206 The greater the power the more dangerous the abuse.—*Edmund Burke.*

3207 What is the best government?—That which teaches us to govern ourselves.—*Goethe.*

3208 Every wanton and causeless restraint of the will of the subject, whether practised by a monarch, a nobility, or a popular assembly, is a degree of tyranny. —*Blackstone.*

3209 The three great ends for a statesman are, security to possessors, facility to acquirers, and liberty and hope to the people.—*Blackstone.*

3210 The four pillars of government . . . religion, justice, counsel and treasure.—*Francis Bacon.*

3211 In that fierce light which beats upon a throne.—*Tennyson.*

3212 A man must first govern himself ere he is fit to govern a family; and his family ere he be fit to bear the government of the commonwealth.—*Sir W. Raleigh.*

3213 It is to self-government, the great principle of popular representation and administration, the system that lets in all to participate in its counsels, that we owe what we are, and what we hope to be.—*Daniel Webster.*

3214 Our rulers will best promote the improvement of the nation by strictly confining themselves to their own legitimate duties, by leaving capital to find its most lucrative course, commodities their fair price, industry and intelligence their natural reward, idleness and folly their natural punishment, by maintaining peace, by defending property and by observing strict economy in every department of the state. Let the Government do this—the people will assuredly do the rest.—*Thomas Babington Macaulay.*

GRATITUDE

3215 Ingratitude, thou marble-hearted fiend!—*Shakespeare.*

3216 Most men remember obligations, but not often to be grateful; the proud are made sour by the remembrance and the vain silent.—*Simms.*

3217 There neither is, or ever was, any person remarkably ungrateful, who was not also insufferably proud; nor any one proud, who was not equally ungrateful.—*South.*

3218 It is generally true that all that is required to make men unmindful of what they owe to God for any blessing, is, that they should receive that blessing often and regularly.—*Whately.*

3219 He who receives a benefit should never forget it; he who bestows should never remember it.—*Charron.*

GREATNESS

3220 The way of a superior man is threefold; virtuous, he is free from anxieties; wise, he is free from perplexities; bold, he is free from fear.—*Confucius.*

3221 From the sublime to the ridiculous there is but one step.—*Napoleon.*

3222 The mightiest powers by deepest calms are fed.—*B. W. Procter.*

3223 No man is so great as mankind.—*Theodore Parker.*

3224 Let him that would move the world, first move himself.—*Socrates.*

3225 Every one stamps his own value on himself.—The price we challenge for ourselves is given us.—Man is made great or little by his own will.—*Schiller.*

3226 In the heraldry of heaven goodness precedes greatness, and so on earth it is more powerful.—The lowly and lovely may often do more good in their limited sphere than the gifted.—*Bp. Horne.*

3227 All great men are in some degree inspired.—*Cicero.*

3228 Lives of great men all remind us, we can make our lives sublime.—*Longfellow.*

3229 It is not wealth, nor ancestry, but honorable conduct and a noble disposition that make men great.—*Ovid.*

3230 A nation's greatness resides not in her material resources, but in her will, faith, intelligence, and moral forces.—*J. M. Hoppin.*

3231 A great mind may change its objects, but it cannot relinquish them; it must have something to pursue; variety is its relaxation, and amusement its repose.—*Colton.*

3232 Speaking generally, no man appears great to his contemporaries, for the same reason that no man is great to his servants—both know too much of him.—*Colton.*

3233 The greatest man in history was the poorest.—*Emerson.*

3234 A great many men—some comparatively small men now—if put in the right position, would be Luthers and Columbuses.—*E. H. Chapin.*

3235 I would much rather that posterity should inquire why no statues were erected to me, than why they were.—*Cato.*

GRIEF

3236 If you have tears, prepare to shed them now.—*Shakespeare.*

3237 My grief lies onward and my joy behind.—*Shakespeare.*

HABIT

3238 How use doth breed a habit in man!—*Shakespeare.*

3239 When we have practiced good actions awhile, they become easy; when they are easy, we take pleasure in them; when they please us, we do them frequently; and then, by frequency of act, they grow into a habit.—*Tillotson.*

3240 Sow an act, and you reap a habit; sow a habit, and you reap a character; sow a character, and you reap a destiny.—*G. D. Boardman.*

HAPPINESS

3241 How bitter a thing it is to look into happiness through another man's eyes!—*Shakespeare.*

3242 Silence is the perfectest herald of joy: I were but little happy, if I could say how much.—*Shakespeare.*

3243 The most unhappy of all men is he who believes himself to be so.—*Hume.*

3244   How sweet a thing it is to wear a crown,
         Within whose circuit is Elysium
         And all that poets feign of bliss and joy!
                                        Shakespeare

3245 Only the spirit of rebellion craves for happiness in this life. What right have we human beings to happiness?—*Henrik Ibsen.*

3246 The mind that is cheerful at present will have no solicitude for the future, and will meet the bitter occurrences of life with a smile.—*Horace.*

3247 We take greater pains to persuade others that we are happy, than in endeavoring to be so ourselves.—*Goldsmith.*

3248 The fountain of content must spring up in the mind; and he who has so little knowledge of human nature as to seek happiness by changing anything but his own disposition, will waste his life in fruitless efforts, and multiply the griefs which he purposes to remove.—*Johnson.*

3249 Happiness is a sunbeam which may pass through a thousand bosoms without losing a particle of its original ray; nay, when it strikes on a kindred heart, like the converged light on a mirror, it reflects itself with redoubled brightness.—It is not perfected till it is shared.—*Jane Porter.*

HARDSHIP

3250 There are some defeats more triumphant than victories.—*Michel de Montaigne.*

3251 Fire is the test of gold; adversity of strong men.—*Seneca.*

3252 Difficulties are things that show what men are.—*Epictetus.*

3253 Nature is upheld by antagonism. Passions, resistance, danger, are educators. We acquire the strength we have overcome.—*Emerson.*

HEALTH

3254 God heals, and the doctor takes the fee.—*Franklin.*

3255 Health is the soul that animates all the enjoyments of life, which fade and are tasteless without it.—*Sir W. Temple.*

3256 Life is not to live, but to be well.—*Martial.*

3257 He who has health, has hope; and he who has hope, has everything.—*Arabian Proverb.*

HEAVEN

3258 God has two dwellings: one in heaven, and the other in a meek and thankful heart.—*Izaak Walton.*

3259 Men are all groping for infinity—every effort to prove there is no God is in itself an effort to reach for God.—*Bishop Charles Edward Locke.*

3260 Earth hath no sorrow that heaven cannot heal.—*Moore.*

3261   Men might go to heaven with half the labour they put forth to go to hell, if they would but venture their industry in the right way.—*Ben Jonson.*

3262   There's none but fears a future state; and when the most obdurate swear they do not, their trembling hearts belie their boasting tongues.—*Dryden.*

HOME

3263   The strength of a nation, especially of a republican nation, is in the intelligent and well-ordered homes of the people.—*Mrs. Sigourney.*

3264   To most men their early home is no more than a memory of their early years. The image is never marred. There's no disappointment in memory, and one's exaggerations are always on the good side.—*George Eliot.*

HONESTY

3265   No legacy is so rich as honesty.—*Shakespeare.*

3266   Make yourself an honest man, and then you may be sure that there is one rascal less in the world.—*Carlyle.*

3267   Money dishonestly acquired is never worth its cost, while a good conscience never costs as much as it is worth.—*J. P. Senn.*

3268   An honest tale speeds best, being plainly told.—*Shakespeare.*

HONOR

3269   Let us make an honourable retreat.—*Shakespeare.*

3270   For Brutus is an honourable man;
                 So are they all, all honourable men.
                                Shakespeare

3271   Great honours are great burdens.—*Ben Jonson.*

3272   Our own heart, and not other men's opinion, forms our true honour.—*Coleridge.*

3273   If honor be your clothing, the suit will last a lifetime; but if clothing be your honor, it will soon be worn threadbare.—*Arnot.*

3274   What is becoming in behavior is honorable, and what is honorable is becoming.—*Cicero.*

HOPE

3275   I laugh, for hope hath happy place with me;
                 If my bark sinks, 'tis to another sea.
                           William Ellery Channing

3276   Your heart's desires be with you!—*Shakespeare.*

3277 You believe easily that which you hope for earnestly.—*Terence.*

3278 Hope is the only good that is common to all men; those who have nothing else possess hope still.—*Thales.*

3279 He who loses hope, may then part with anything.—*Congreve.*

HUMOR

3280 Great wits are sure to madness near allied, and thin partitions do their bounds divide.—Dryden.

3281 There's the humour of it.—*Shakespeare.*

3282 Honest good humor is the oil and wine of a merry meeting, and there is no jovial companionship equal to that where the jokes are rather small and the laughter abundant.—*Washington Irving.*

3283 Where judgment has wit to express it, there is the best orator.—*Penn.*

3284 Wit loses its respect with the good, when seen in company with malice; and to smile at the jest which places a thorn in another's breast, is to become a principal in the mischief.—*Sheridan.*

3285 The little foolery that wise men have makes a great show.—*Shakespeare.*

IGNORANCE

3286 Against stupidity the very gods themselves contend in vain.—*Schiller.*

3287 An ass may bray a good while before he shakes the stars down.—*George Eliot.*

3288 A man who is ignorant of foreign languages is ignorant of his own.—*Goethe.*

3289 Mystery is but another name for our ignorance; if we were omniscient, all would be perfectly plain.—*Tryon Edwards.*

3290 The more we study the more we discover our ignorance.—*Shelley.*

3291 The common curse of mankind,—folly and ignorance.—*Shakespeare.*

INSULT

3292 The way to procure insults is to submit to them—A man meets with no more respect than he exacts.—*Hazlitt.*

3293
>   Of all the griefs that harass the distressed,
>   Sure the most bitter is a scornful jest;
>   Fate never wounds more deep the generous heart,
>   Than when a blockhead's insult points the dart.
>   *Samuel Johnson*

INTENTIONS

3294   Good intentions are very mortal and perishable things; like very mellow and choice fruit they are difficult to keep.—*C. Simmons.*

3295   In the works of man as in those of nature, it is the intention which is chiefly worth studying.—*Goethe.*

JEALOUSY

3296   In jealousy there is more of self-love, than of love to another.—*La Rochefoucauld.*

3297   All jealousy must be strangled in its birth, or time will soon make it strong enough to overcome the truth.—*Davenant.*

JUDGMENT

3298   Some to the fascination of a name surrender judgment hoodwinked.—*Cowper.*

3299   We always like those who admire us, but we do not always like those whom we admire.—*La Rochefoucauld.*

3300   Young in limbs, in judgment old.—*Shakespeare.*

3301   I never knew so young a body with so old a head.—*Shakespeare.*

JUSTICE

3302   As to be perfectly just is an attribute of the divine nature, to be so to the utmost of our abilities is the glory of man.—*Addison.*

.3303   Man is unjust, but God is just; and finally justice triumphs.—*Longfellow.*

3304   How much easier it is to be generous than just! Men are sometimes bountiful who are not honest.—*Junius.*

3305   The law is made to protect the innocent by punishing the guilty.—*Daniel Webster.*

3306   Justice and power must be brought together, so that whatever is just may be powerful, and whatever is powerful may be just.—*Pascal.*

KINDNESS

3307   Rich gifts wax poor when givers prove unkind.—*Shakespeare.*

3308   I expect to pass through life but once.—If therefore, there be any kindness I can show, or any good thing I can do to any fellow-being, let me do it now, and not defer or neglect it, as I shall not pass this way again.—*Penn.*

3309 To cultivate kindness is a valuable part of the business of life.—*Johnson.*

3310 This was the most unkindest cut of all.—*Shakespeare.*

KNOWLEDGE

3311 It is manifest that all government of action is to be gotten by knowledge, and knowledge, best, by gathering many knowledges, which is reading.—*Sir P. Sidney.*

3312 To despise theory is to have the excessively vain pretension to do without knowing what one does, and to speak without knowing what one says.—*Fontenelle.*

3313 If you have knowledge, let others light their candles by it.—*Margaret Fuller.*

3314 If a little knowledge is dangerous, where is the man who has so much as to be out of danger?—*Thomas Henry Huxley.*

3315 New ideas can be good or bad, just the same as old ones.—*Franklin D. Roosevelt.*

3316 Common sense is the knack of seeing things as they are, and doing things as they ought to be done.—*C. E. Stowe.*

3317 Socrates said that there was one only good, namely, knowledge; and one only evil, namely, ignorance.—*Diogenes Laertius.*

3318 Ignorance never settles a question.—*Disraeli.*

3319 Great objects form great minds.—*Emmons.*

3320 Who are a little wise, the best fools be.—*John Donne.*

3321 Have the courage to be ignorant of a great number of things, in order to avoid the calamity of being ignorant of everything.—*Sydney Smith.*

3322 Command large fields, but cultivate small ones.—*Virgil.*

3323 Study rather to fill your mind than your coffers; knowing that gold and silver were originally mingled with dirt, until avarice or ambition parted them.—*Seneca.*

3324 It is with disease of the mind, as with those of the body; we are half dead before we understand our disorder, and half cured when we do.—*Colton.*

3325 We know accurately only when we know little; with knowledge doubt increases.—*Goethe.*

3326 Whoso neglects learning in his youth, loses the past and is dead for the future.—*Euripides.*

3327   Wearing all that weight
                       Of learning lightly like a flower.
                                       Tennyson

3328 Lack of confidence and lack of information sleep in the same bed, locked in the closest kind of embrace. When a man has confidence he gets along in business, but without confidence he might just as well not enter business at all. For confidence is the son of vision, and is sired by information. —*Cornelius Vanderbilt, Jr.*

3329 He who has no inclination to learn more will be very apt to think that he knows enough.—*Powell.*

3330 I attribute the little I know to my not having been ashamed to ask for information, and to my rule of conversing with all descriptions of men on those topics that form their own peculiar professions and pursuits.—*Locke.*

3331 Knowledge is of two kinds. We know a subject ourselves, or we know where we can find information upon it.—*Samuel Johnson.*

3332 Beside the pleasure derived from acquired knowledge, there lurks in the mind of man, and tinged with a shade of sadness, an unsatisfactory longing for something beyond the present—a striving toward regions yet unknown and unopened.—*Humboldt.*

3333 Every branch of knowledge which a good man possesses, he may apply to some good purpose.—*C. Buchanan.*

3334 The more extensive a man's knowledge of what has been done, the greater will be his power of knowing what to do.—*Disraeli.*

3335 Nothing in this life, after health and virtue, is more estimable than knowledge,—nor is there anything so easily attained, or so cheaply purchased, —the labor, only sitting still, and the expense but time, which, if we do not spend, we cannot save.—*Sterne.*

3336 All wish to possess knowledge, but few, comparatively speaking, are willing to pay the price.—*Juvenal.*

3337 To be proud of learning, is the greatest ignorance.—*Jeremy Taylor.*

LABOR

3338 If you divorce capital from labor, capital is hoarded, and labor starves. —*Daniel Webster.*

3339 Whatever there is of greatness in the United States, or indeed in any other country, is due to labor. The laborer is the author of all greatness and wealth. Without labor there would be no government, and no leading class, and nothing to preserve.—*U. S. Grant.*

LANGUAGE

3340 Words should be employed as the means, not as the end; language is the instrument, conviction is the work.—*Sir J. Reynolds.*

3341 The knowledge of words is the gate of scholarship.—*Wilson.*

3342 It makes a great difference in the force of a sentence whether a man be behind it or no.—*Emerson.*

LAUGHTER

3343 Laff every time you pheel tickled, and laff once in awhile enyhow.—*Josh Billings.*

3344 They laugh that win.—*Shakespeare.*

3345 I am persuaded that every time a man smiles, but much more often when he laughs, it adds something to his fragment of life.—*Sterne.*

3346 Men show their character in nothing more clearly than by what they think laughable.—*Goethe.*

3347 If we consider the frequent reliefs we receive from laughter, and how often it breaks the gloom which is apt to depress the mind, one would take care not to grow too wise for so great a pleasure of life.—*Addison.*

LAW

3348 The law hath not been dead, though it hath slept.—*Shakespeare.*

3349 No people were ever better than their laws, though many have been worse.—*Priestley.*

3350 It is a very easy thing to devise good laws; the difficulty is to make them effective. The great mistake is that of looking upon men as virtuous, or thinking that they can be made so by laws; and consequently the greatest art of a politician is to render vices serviceable to the cause of virtue.—*Bolingbroke.*

3351 Good laws make it easier to do right and harder to do wrong.—*Gladstone.*

3352 We should never create by law what can be accomplished by morality.—*Montesquieu.*

3353 Laws are the very bulwarks of liberty; they define every man's rights, and defend the individual liberties of all men.—*J. G. Holland.*

LIBERTY

3354 Eternal vigilance is the price of liberty.—*Jefferson.*

3355 The true danger is, when liberty is nibbled away, for expedients, and by parts.—*Burke.*

3356 I know not what course others may take; but as for me, give me liberty or give me death!—*Patrick Henry.*

3357 Liberty and union, now and forever, one and inseparable.—*Daniel Webster.*

3358 Free will is not the liberty to do whatever one likes, but the power of doing whatever one sees ought to be done, even in the very face of otherwise overwhelming impulse. There lies freedom, indeed.—*G. Macdonald.*

3359 It is a strange desire, to seek power, and to lose liberty.—*Francis Bacon.*

3360 Liberty is the right to do what the laws allow; and if a citizen could do what they forbid, it would be no longer liberty, because others would have the same powers.—*Montesquieu.*

3361 O Liberty, how many crimes are committed in thy name!—*Mad. Roland.*

3362 The people never give up their liberties but under some delusion.—*Burke.*

LIBRARY

3363 A great library contains the diary of the human race.—The great consulting room of a wise man is a library.—*G. Dawson.*

3364 The true university of these days is a collection of books.—*Carlyle.*

3365 We enter our studies, and enjoy a society which we alone can bring together. We raise no jealousy by conversing with one in preference to another; we give no offense to the most illustrious by questioning him as long as we will, and leaving him as abruptly. Diversity of opinion raises no tumult in our presence; each interlocutor stands before us, speaks or is silent, and we adjourn or decide the business at our leisure.—*Landor.*

LIFE

3366 The smallest worm will turn, being trodden on.—*Shakespeare.*

3367 I have had my day and my philosophies.—*Tennyson.*

3368 The web of our life is of a mingled yarn, good and ill together.—*Shakespeare.*

3369 Press not a falling man too far!—*Shakespeare.*

3370 The pleasantest things in the world are pleasant thoughts, and the great art in life is to have as many of them as possible.—*C. N. Bovee.*

3371 The shell must break before the bird can fly.—*Tennyson.*

3372 There is more to life than increasing its speed.—*Mahatma Gandhi.*

3373 Life is a quarry, out of which we are to mold and chisel and complete a character.—*Goethe.*

3374 Though we seem grieved at the shortness of life in general, we are wishing every period of it at an end. The minor longs to be at age, then to be a man of business; then to make up an estate, then to arrive at honors, then to retire.—*Addison.*

3375 If I could get the ear of every young man but for one word, it would be this; make the most and best of yourself—There is no tragedy like a wasted life—a life failing of its true end, and turned to a false end.—*T. T. Munger.*

3376 Life is the childhood of our immortality.—*Goethe.*

3377 Hope writes the poetry of the boy, but memory that of the man. Man looks forward with smiles, but backward with sighs. Such is the wise providence of God. The cup of life is sweetest at the brim, the flavor is impaired as we drink deeper, and the dregs are made bitter that we may not struggle when it is taken from our lips.—*A. Monod.*

3378 Life resembles the banquet of Damocles; the sword is ever suspended. —*Voltaire.*

3379
Of all the words of tongue and pen,
The saddest are, "It might have been,"
More sad are these we daily see
"It is, but it hadn't ought to be!"
Bret Harte

3380 The vocation of every man and woman is to serve other people.— *Count Lyoff Nikolayevitch Tolstoi.*

3381 The measure of a man's life is the well spending of it, and not the length.—*Plutarch.*

3382
My life is like the summer rose
That opens to the morning sky,
But ere the shades of evening close
Is scattered on the ground—to die.
Richard Henry Wilde

3383 It matter not how long you live, but how well.—*Publius Syrus.*

3384   Roaming in thought over the Universe, I saw the little that is Good steadily hastening towards immortality, and the vast that is evil I saw hastening to merge itself and become lost and dead.—*Walt Whitman.*

3385   One life; a little gleam of time between two eternities; no second chance for us forever more.—*Carlyle.*

3386   As no true work since the world began was ever wasted, so no true life since the world began has ever failed.—*Emerson.*

3387   Why all this toil for the triumphs of an hour?—*Young.*

3388   While we are reasoning concerning life, life is gone; and death, though perhaps they receive him differently, yet treats alike the fool and the philosopher.—*Hume.*

3389   We never live; we are always in the expectation of living.—*Voltaire.*

3390   You know how little while we have to stay, and, once departed, may return no more.—*Fitzgerald.*

3391   The Wine of Life keeps oozing drop by drop, the Leaves of Life keep falling one by one.—*Fitzgerald.*

3392   A Book of Verses underneath the Bough,
A Jug of Wine, a Loaf of Bread—and Thou
Beside me singing in the Wilderness—
Oh, Wilderness were Paradise enow!

Fitzgerald

3393   Oh threats of Hell and Hopes of Paradise!
One thing at least is certain—*This* life flies;
One thing is certain, and the rest is Lies;
The Flower that once has blown for ever dies.

Fitzgerald

3394   The Moving Finger writes; and, having writ,
Moves on: nor all your Piety nor Wit
Shall lure it back to cancel half a Line,
Nor all your Tears wash out a Word of it.

Fitzgerald

LITERATURE

3395   In science, read, by preference, the newest works; in literature, the oldest. The classic literature is always modern.—*Bulwer.*

3396   The decline of literature indicates the decline of a nation; the two keep pace in their downward tendency.—*Goethe.*

3397 Nothing lives in literature but that which has in it the vitality of creative art; and it would be safe advice to the young to read nothing but what
is old.—*E. P. Whipple.*

3398 Literature is the immortality of speech.—*Schlegel.*

Love

3399   To do him any wrong was to beget
           A kindness from him for his heart was rich—
           Of such fine mould that if you sowed therein
           The seed of Hate, it blossomed Charity.

Tennyson

3400 The course of true love never did run smooth.—*Shakespeare.*

3401 To be rich in admiration and free from envy; to rejoice greatly in the
good of others; to love with such generosity of heart that your love is still a
dear possession in absence or unkindness—these are the gifts of fortune which
money cannot buy and without which money can buy nothing. He who has
such a treasury of riches, being happy and valiant himself, in his own nature,
will enjoy the universe as if it were his own estate; and help the man to whom
he lends a hand to enjoy it with him.—*Robert Louis Stevenson.*

3402 Self-love, my liege, is not so vile a sin as self-neglecting.—*Shakespeare.*

3403   And on her lover's arm she leant,
           And round her waist she felt it fold,
           And far across the hills they went
           In that new world which is the old.

Tennyson

3404 Then, must you speak of one that loved not wisely but too well; of one
not easily jealous, but being wrong perplex'd in the extreme.—*Shakespeare.*

3405 There's beggary in the love that can be reckon'd.—*Shakespeare.*

3406 Men have died from time to time, and worms have eaten them,—but
not for love.—*Shakespeare.*

3407 No man at one time can be wise and love.—*Robert Herrick.*

3408 'T is better to have loved and lost than never to have loved at all.—
Tennyson.

3409   Let me not to the marriage of true minds
           Admit impediments: love is not love
           Which alters when it alteration finds.

Shakespeare

3410
> Drink to me only with thine eyes,
> And I will pledge with mine;
> Or leave a kiss but in the cup,
> And I'll not look for wine.

Ben Jonson

3411 I do not love thee, Sabidius, nor can I say why; this only I can say, I do not love thee.—*Martial.*

3412 Never to judge rashly; never to interpret the actions of others in an ill-sense, but to compassionate their infirmities, bear their burdens, excuse their weaknesses, and make up for their defects—to hate their imperfections, but love themselves, this is the true spirit of charity.—*Caussin.*

3413 Next to God, thy parents.—*Penn.*

3414 The conqueror is regarded with awe; the wise man commands our respect; but it is only the benevolent man that wins our affection.—*Howells.*

3415 Courtship consists in a number of quiet attentions, not so pointed as to alarm, nor so vague as not to be understood.—*Sterne.*

3416 In charity there is no excess.—*Francis Bacon.*

3417 I am not one of those who do not believe in love at first sight, but I believe in taking a second look.—*H. Vincent.*

3418 Man's love is of man's life a part; it is woman's whole existence.—*Byron.*

3419 There is nothing half so sweet in life as love's young dream.—*Moore.*

3420 It is astonishing how little one feels poverty when one loves.—*Bulwer.*

LUXURY

3421 Luxury makes a man so soft, that it is hard to please him, and easy to trouble him; so that his pleasures at last become his burden. Luxury is a nice master, hard to be pleased.—*Mackenzie.*

3422 Avarice and luxury, those pests which have ever been the ruin of every great state.—*Livy.*

3423 On the soft bed of luxury most kingdoms have expired.—*Young.*

3424 War destroys men, but luxury destroys mankind; at once corrupts the body and the mind.—*Crown.*

MAJORITY

3425 The voice of the majority is no proof of justice.—*Schiller.*

3426   It never troubles the wolf how many the sheep may be.—*Virgil*.

3427   We go by the major vote, and if the majority are insane, the sane must go to the hospital.—*H. Mann*.

3428   A man in the right, with God on his side, is in the majority though he be alone.—*H. W. Beecher*.

MANKIND

3429   He that is good for making excuses, is seldom good for anything else.—*Franklin*.

3430   Man proposes, but God disposes.—*Thomas à Kempis*.

3431   What a piece of work is a man! in form and moving how express and admirable! in action how like an angel! in apprehension how like a god!—*Shakespeare*.

3432   Lord, what fools these mortals be!—*Shakespeare*.

3433   A man of my kidney.—*Shakespeare*.

3434   His life was gentle, and the elements so mix'd in him, that Nature might stand up and say to all the world, "This was a man!"—*Shakespeare*.

3435   It takes a clever man to turn cynic and a wise man to be clever enough not to.—*Fannie Hurst*.

3436   He was a man, take him for all in all, I shall not look upon his like again.—*Shakespeare*.

3437   In counsel it is good to see dangers; but in execution, not to see them unless they be very great.—*Bacon*.

3438   The tendency is to be broadminded about other people's security.—*Aristide Briand*.

3439   There is no man so good, who, were he to submit all his thoughts and actions to the law, would not deserve hanging ten times in his life.—*Montaigne*.

3440   So far is it from being true that men are naturally equal, that no two people can be half an hour together but one shall acquire an evident superiority over the other.—*Johnson*.

3441   I do not mean to expose my ideas to ingenious ridicule by maintaining that everything happens to every man for the best; but I will contend, that he who makes the best use of it, fulfills the part of a wise and good man.—*Cumberland*.

M

3442 There is no less misery in being cheated than in that kind of wisdom which perceives, or thinks it perceives, that all mankind are cheats.—*E. H. Chapin.*

3443 In my youth I thought of writing a satire on mankind, but now in my age I think I should write an apology for them.—*Walpole.*

3444 I never could believe that Providence had sent a few men into the world, ready booted and spurred to ride, and millions ready saddled and bridled to be ridden.—*Richard Rumbold.*

3445 Man is not the creature of circumstances. Circumstances are the creatures of men.—*Disraeli.*

3446 Youth is a blunder; manhood is a struggle; old age a regret.—*Disraeli.*

3447 Passion often makes fools of the ablest men, and able men of the most foolish.—*La Rochefoucauld.*

3448 Nothing is so uncertain as the minds of the multitude.—*Leiz.*

3449 The multitude is always in the wrong.—*Roscommon.*

3450   The Devil was sick,—the Devil a monk would be;
      The Devil was well,—the Devil a monk was he.
                              Francis Rabelais

3451 Were we to take as much pains to be what we ought to be, as we do to disguise what we really are, we might appear like ourselves without being at the trouble of any disguise whatever.—*La Rochefoucauld.*

3452 I can make a lord, but only the Almighty can make a gentleman.—*James I.*

3453 I do not know what comfort other people find in considering the weakness of great men, but 'tis always a mortification to me to observe that there is no perfection in humanity.—*S. Montague.*

3454 Not armies, not nations, have advanced the race; but here and there, in the course of ages, an individual has stood up and cast his shadow over the world.—*E. H. Chapin.*

3455 The proper study of mankind is man.—*Pope.*

3456 Man's inhumanity to man makes countless thousands mourn.—*Burns.*

3457 Man! thou pendulum betwixt a smile and tear.—*Byron.*

3458 We have all sufficient strength to endure the misfortunes of others.—*La Rochefoucauld.*

3459 In the adversity of our best friends we often find something that is not exactly displeasing.—*La Rochefoucauld.*

MARRIAGE

3460 I chose my wife, as she did her wedding gown, for qualities that would wear well.—*Goldsmith.*

3461 Men should keep their eyes wide open before marriage, and half shut afterward.—*Mad. Scuderi.*

3462 The sanctity of marriage and the family relation make the corner-stone of our American society and civilization.—*Garfield.*

MASTER

3463 If thou art a master, sometimes be blind; if a servant, sometimes be deaf.—*Fuller.*

3464 Men, at some time, are masters of their fates.—*Shakespeare.*

MAXIMS

3465 Maxims are the condensed good sense of nations.—*Sir J. Mackintosh.*

3466 All maxims have their antagonist maxims; proverbs should be sold in pairs, a single one being but a half truth.—*W. Matthews.*

3467 The two maxims of any great man at court are, always to keep his countenance, and never to keep his word.—*Swift.*

MEDICINE

3468 The best of all medicines are resting and fasting.—*Franklin.*

3469 Over the door of a library in Thebes is the inscription, "Medicine for the soul."—*Diodorus Siculus.*

MEDIOCRITY

3470 Mediocrity is not allowed to poets, either by the gods or men.—*Horace.*

3471 Nothing in the world is more haughty than a man of moderate capacity when once raised to power.—*Wessenburg.*

3472 There are certain things in which mediocrity is not to be endured, such as poetry, music, painting, public speaking.—*Bruyère.*

MEDITATION

3473 Meditation is the nurse of thought, and thought the food of meditation.—*C. Simmons.*

3474 It is not the number of books you read, nor the variety of sermons you hear, nor the amount of religious conversation in which you mix, but it is the frequency and earnestness with which you meditate on these things till the truth in them becomes your own and part of your being, that ensures your growth.—*F. W. Robertson.*

MEMORY

3475   Memory, the warder of the brain.—*Shakespeare.*

3476   Memory tempers prosperity, mitigates adversity, controls youth, and delights old age.—*Lactantius.*

3477   Memory is the receptacle and sheath of all knowledge.—*Cicero.*

3478   The memory is a treasurer to whom we must give funds, if we would draw the assistance we need.—*Rowe.*

3479   Everyone complains of his memory; nobody of his judgment.—*La Rochefoucauld.*

3480   Memory seldom fails when its office is to show us the tombs of our buried hopes.—*Lady Blessington.*

3481   The true art of memory is the art of attention.—*Johnson.*

MERCY

3482   Among the attributes of God, although they are all equal, mercy shines with even more brilliancy than justice.—*Cervantes.*

3483   We hand folks over to God's mercy, and show none ourselves.—*George Eliot.*

3484   Teach me to feel another's woe, to hide the fault I see; that mercy I to others show, that mercy show to me.—*Pope.*

METHOD

3485   Though this be madness, yet there is method in't.—*Shakespeare.*

3486   Method is like packing things in a box; a good packer will get in half as much again as a bad one.—*Cecil.*

3487   Every great man exhibits the talent of organization or construction, whether it be in a poem, a philosophical system, a policy, or a strategy. And without method there is no organization nor construction.—*Bulwer.*

MISER

3488   The prodigal robs his heir; the miser robs himself.—*Bruyère.*

3489   A miser grows rich by seeming poor; an extravagant man grows poor by seeming rich.—*Shenstone.*

MISFORTUNE

3490 He that is down needs fear no fall.—*Bunyan*.

3491 Little minds are tamed and subdued by misfortune; but great minds rise above it.—*Washington Irving*.

MISTAKE

3492 The sight of a drunkard is a better sermon against that vice than the best that was ever preached on that subject.—*Saville*.

3493 A man should never be ashamed to own he has been in the wrong, which is but saying in other words that he is wiser today than he was yesterday.—*Pope*.

3494 Any man may make a mistake, but none but a fool will continue in it.—*Cicero*.

3495 No man ever became great or good except through many and great mistakes.—*Gladstone*.

3496 The only people who make no mistakes are dead people. I saw a man last week who has not made a mistake for four thousand years. He was a mummy in the Egyptian department of the British Museum.—*H. L. Wayland*.

MOB

3497 Human affairs are not so happily arranged that the best things please the most men.—It is the proof of a bad cause when it is applauded by the mob.—*Seneca*.

3498 A mob is a society of bodies, voluntarily bereaving themselves of reason, and traversing its work. The mob is man, voluntarily descending to the nature of the beast. Its fit hour of activity is night; its actions are insane, like its whole constitution.—*Emerson*.

3499 We are all of us imaginative in some form or other, for images are the brood of desire.—*George Eliot*.

MODERATION

3500 Moderation is the inseparable companion of wisdom, but with it genius has not even a nodding acquaintance.—*Colton*.

3501 Everything that exceeds the bounds of moderation, has an unstable foundation.—*Seneca*.

MODESTY

3502 Bashfulness is an ornament to youth, but a reproach to old age.—*Aristotle*.

3503 It is no great thing to be humble when you are brought low; but to be humble when you are praised is a great and rare attainment.—*St. Bernard.*

3504 A false modesty is the meanest species of pride.—*Gibbon.*

3505 Modesty is a shining light; it prepares the mind to receive knowledge, and the heart for truth.—*Guizot.*

3506 Modesty seldom resides in a breast that is not enriched with nobler virtues.—*Goldsmith.*

3507 The greatest ornament of an illustrious life is modesty and humility, which go a great way in the character even of the most exalted princes.—*Napoleon.*

MONEY

3508 But the jingling of the guinea helps the hurt that Honour feels.—*Tennyson.*

3509 No man but a blockhead ever wrote except for money.—*Samuel Johnson.*

3510 All love has something of blindness in it, but the love of money especially.—*South.*

3511 Men are seldom more innocently employed than when they are honestly making money.—*Johnson.*

3512 The covetous man never has money; the prodigal will have none shortly.—*Ben Jonson.*

3513 To despise money is to dethrone a king.—*Chamfort.*

3514 Ready money is Aladdin's lamp.—*Byron.*

MONUMENT

3515 No man who needs a monument ever ought to have one.—*Hawthorne.*

3516 Tombs are the clothes of the dead; a grave is but a plain suit; a rich monument is an embroidered one.—*Fuller.*

MORNING

3517 The morning hour has gold in its mouth.—*Franklin.*

3518 Now from night's gloom the glorious day breaks forth, and seems to kindle from the setting stars.—*D. K. Lee.*

MOTHER

3519 The mother's heart is the child's schoolroom.—*H. W. Beecher.*

3520 Let France have good mothers, and she will have good sons.—*Napoleon.*

3521 My mother's influence in molding my character was conspicuous. She forced me to learn daily long chapters of the Bible by heart. To that discipline and patient, accurate resolve I owe not only much of my general power of taking pains, but the best part of my taste for literature.—*Ruskin.*

3522 A mother is a mother still, the holiest thing alive.—*Samuel Coleridge.*

3523 All that I am, or hope to be, I owe to my angel mother.—*Lincoln.*

3524 I would desire for a friend the son who never resisted the tears of his mother.—*Lacretelle.*

3525 A father may turn his back on his child; brothers and sisters may become inveterate enemies; husbands may desert their wives and wives their husbands. But a mother's love endures through all; in good repute, in bad repute, in the face of the world's condemnation, a mother still loves on, and still hopes that her child may turn from his evil ways, and repent; still she remembers the infant smiles that once filled her bosom with rapture, the merry laugh, the joyful shout of his childhood, the opening promise of his youth; and she can never be brought to think him all unworthy.—*Washington Irving.*

MUSIC

3526 There is something marvelous in music. I might almost say it is, in itself, a marvel. Its position is somewhere between the region of thought and that of phenomena; a glimmering medium between mind and matter, related to both and yet differing from either. Spiritual, and yet requiring rhythm; material, and yet independent of space.—*H. Heine.*

3527 Music is the art of the prophets, the only art that can calm the agitations of the soul; it is one of the most magnificent and delightful presents God has given us.—*Luther.*

3528 Music is well said to be the speech of angels.—*Carlyle.*

NATION

3529 Socrates said he was not an Athenian or a Greek, but a citizen of the world.—*Plutarch.*

3530 The primary duty of organized society is to enlarge the lives and increase the standards of living of all the people.—*Herbert Hoover.*

3531 Our purpose is to build in this nation a human society, not an economic system.—*Herbert Hoover.*

3532   Praise the Power that hath made and preserved us a nation,
    Then conquer we must, for our cause it is just,
    And this be our motto, "In God is our trust."

Francis S. Key

3533   A good newspaper and Bible in every house, a good schoolhouse in every district, and a church in every neighborhood, all appreciated as they deserve, are the chief support of virtue, morality, civil liberty, and religion.—*Franklin*.

3534   Patriotism is the last refuge of a scoundrel.—*Samuel Johnson*.

3535   Individuals may form communities, but it is institutions alone that can create a nation.—*Disraeli*.

3536   Territory is but the body of a nation.—The people who inhabit its hills and valleys are its soul, its spirit, its life.—*Garfield*.

3537   No nation can be destroyed while it possesses a good home life.—*J. G. Holland*.

3538   At twenty, everyone is republican.—*Lamartine*.

3539   Not that I loved Caesar less, but that I loved Rome more.—*Shakespeare*.

3540   A horse! A horse! my kingdom for a horse!—*Shakespeare*.

3541   The noblest motive is the public good.—*Virgil*.

3542   After what I owe to God, nothing should be more dear or more sacred than the love and respect I owe to my country.—*De Thou*.

3543   Republics come to an end by luxurious habits; monarchies by poverty. —*Montesquieu*.

3544   Taxes are the sinews of the state.—*Cicero*.

NATURE

3545   To him who in the love of nature holds communion with her visible forms, she speaks a various language.—*W. Cullen Bryant*.

3546   One touch of nature makes the whole world kin.—*Shakespeare*.

3547   To hold, as't were, the mirror up to nature.—*Shakespeare*.

3548   Nature is the living, visible garment of God.—*Goethe*.

3549   Nature is the most thrifty thing in the world; she never wastes anything; she undergoes change, but there's no annihilation—the essence remains. —*T. Binney*.

NECESSITY

3550   Necessity knows no law except to conquer.—*Publius Syrus*.

3551   Necessity reforms the poor, and satiety the rich.—*Tacitus*.

3552   Necessity is the argument of tyrants: it is the creed of slaves.—*William Pitt.*

3553   A people never fairly begins to prosper till necessity is treading on its heels. The growing want of room is one of the sources of civilization. Population is power, but it must be a population that, in growing, is made daily apprehensive of the morrow.—*Simms.*

3554   The argument of necessity is not only the tyrant's plea, but the patriot's defense, and the safety of the state.—*James Wilson.*

NIGHT

3555   The death-bed of a day, how beautiful!—*Bailey.*

3556   I must become a borrower of the night for a dark hour or twain.—*Shakespeare.*

3557   Ye stars, that are the poetry of heaven!—*Byron.*

3558   The stars hang bright above, silent, as if they watched the sleeping earth.—*Coleridge.*

3559   The curfew tolls the knell of parting day,
        The lowing herd winds slowly o'er the lea,
        The ploughman homeward plods his weary way,
        And leaves the world to darkness and to me.
                                        Thomas Gray

3560   The day is done, and darkness falls from the wings of night.—*Longfellow.*

3561   In her starry shade of dim and solitary loveliness, I learn the language of another world.—*Byron.*

3562   Wisdom mounts her zenith with the stars.—*Mrs. Barbauld.*

NOBILITY

3563   Tears are the noble language of the eye.—*Robert Herrick.*

3564   The original of all men is the same and virtue is the only nobility.—*Seneca.*

3565   Virtue is the first title of nobility.—*Molière.*

3566   If a man be endued with a generous mind, this is the best kind of nobility.—*Plato.*

3567   It is better to be nobly remembered, than nobly born.—*Ruskin.*

3568   It seems to me 'tis only noble to be good.—*Tennyson.*

M*

OBEDIENCE

3569 No man doth safely rule but he that hath learned gladly to obey.—*Thomas à Kempis.*

3570 Let the child's first lesson be obedience, and the second may be what thou wilt.—*Fuller.*

3571 Wicked men obey from fear; good men, from love.—*Aristotle.*

OBLIVION

3572
Full many a gem of purest ray serene,
The dark, unfathomed caves of ocean bear:
Full many a flower is born to blush unseen,
And waste its sweetness on the desert air.

Thomas Gray

3573 Oblivion is the flower that grows best on graves.—*George Sand.*

3574 Fame is a vapor; popularity an accident; riches take wings; the only certainty is oblivion.—*Horace Greeley.*

OPEN-MINDED

3575 It is well for people who think to change their minds occasionally in order to keep them clean. For those who do not think, it is best at least to rearrange their prejudices once in a while.—*Luther Burbank.*

3576 The great menace to the life of an industry is industrial self-complacency.—*David Sarnoff.*

3577 It is always the minorities that hold the key of progress; it is always through those who are unafraid to be different that advance comes to human society.—*Raymond B. Fosdick.*

3578 "Can any good come out of Nazareth?"—This is always the question of the wiseacres and knowing ones.—But the good, the new, comes from exactly that quarter whence it is not looked for, and is always something different from what is expected.—Everything new is received with contempt, for it begins in obscurity. It becomes a power unobserved.—*Feuerbach.*

OPINION

3579 Emulation, in the sense of a laudable ambition, is founded on humility, for it implies that we have a low opinion of our present, and think it necessary to advance and make improvement.—*Bp. Hall.*

3580 I have bought golden opinions from all sorts of people.—*Shakespeare.*

3581 There is no such thing as modern art. There is art—and there is advertising.—*Albert Sterner.*

3582 Nothing is less sincere than our mode of asking and giving advice. He who asks seems to have deference for the opinion of his friend, while he only aims to get approval of his own and make his friend responsible for his action. And he who gives repays the confidence supposed to be placed in him by a seemingly disinterested zeal, while he seldom means anything by his advice but his own interest or reputation.—*La Rochefoucauld*.

3583 Predominant opinions are generally the opinions of the generation that is vanishing.—*Disraeli*.

3584 The eyes of other people are the eyes that ruin us. If all but myself were blind, I should want neither fine clothes, fine houses, nor fine furniture.—*Franklin*.

3585 The men of the past had convictions, while we moderns have only opinions.—*H. Heine*.

3586 The history of human opinion is scarcely anything more than the history of human errors.—*Voltaire*.

OPPORTUNITY

3587 Art is long, life short; judgment difficult, opportunity transient.—*Goethe*.

3588 You should hammer your iron when it is glowing hot.—*Publius Syrus*.

3589 Next to knowing when to seize an opportunity, the most important thing in life is to know when to forego an advantage.—*Disraeli*.

3590 Great opportunities come to all, but many do not know they have met them. The only preparation to take advantage of them, is simple fidelity to what each day brings.—*A. E. Dunning*.

PAIN

3591 Pain is the deepest thing we have in our nature, and union through pain and suffering has always seemed more real and holy than any other.—*Hallam*.

3592 He jests at scars that never felt a wound. But, soft! what light through yonder window breaks? It is the east, and Juliet is the sun.—*Shakespeare*.

PATIENCE

3593 If I have ever made any valuable discoveries, it has been owing more to patient attention, than to any other talent.—*Sir Isaac Newton*.

3594 How poor are they that have not patience!—*Shakespeare*.

3595 It's easy finding reasons why other folks should be patient.—*George Eliot*.

3596 The two powers which in my opinion constitute a wise man are those of bearing and forbearing.—*Epictetus.*

3597 They also serve who only stand and wait.—*Milton.*

3598 Patience is bitter, but its fruit is sweet.—*Rousseau.*

3599 There are times when God asks nothing of his children except silence, patience, and tears.—*C. S. Robinson.*

3600 Patience is power; with time and patience the mulberry leaf becomes silk.—*Chinese Proverb.*

3601 Steady, patient, persevering thinking will generally surmount every obstacle in the search after truth.—*Emmons.*

PEACE

3602 God's in His heaven—all's right with the world!—*Robert Browning.*

3603 Peace hath her victories no less renown'd than war.—*John Milton.*

3604 Peace is such a precious jewel that I would give anything for it but truth.—*M. Henry.*

3605 Five great enemies to peace inhabit with us: viz., avarice, ambition, envy, anger, and pride. If those enemies were to be banished, we should infallibly enjoy perpetual peace.—*Petrarch.*

3606 There is but one way to tranquillity of mind and happiness, and that is to account no external things thine own, but to commit all to God.—*Epictetus.*

PERFECTION

3607 It is a bad plan that admits of no modification.—*Publius Syrus.*

3608 Bachelors' wives and old maids' children are always perfect.—*Chamfort.*

3609 Even the worthy Homer sometimes nods.—*Horace.*

3610 It takes a long time to bring excellence to maturity.—*Publius Syrus.*

3611 It is only imperfection that complains of what is imperfect.—The more perfect we are, the more gentle and quiet we become toward the defects of others.—*Fenelon.*

PERSISTENCE

3612 Every noble work is at first impossible.—*Carlyle.*

3613 The falling drops at last will wear the stone.—*Lucretius.*

3614   And many strokes, though with a little axe, hew down and fell the hardest-timbered oak.—*Shakespeare.*

3615   Knock and the door will open to you. For it is always the one who asks who receives and the one who searches who finds, and the one who knocks to whom the door opens.—*Goodspeed's* Translation of the New Testament.

PHILOSOPHY

3616   Three things too much, and three too little are pernicious to man; to speak much, and know little; to spend much, and have little; to presume much, and be worth little.—*Cervantes.*

3617   There are more things in heaven and earth, Horatio, than are dreamt of in your philosophy.—*Shakespeare.*

3618   It was through the feeling of wonder that men now and at first began to philosophize.—*Aristotle.*

3619   There is nothing so ridiculous that has not at some time been said by some philosopher.—*Oliver Goldsmith.*

3620   The greatest object in the universe, says a certain philosopher, is a good man struggling with adversity; yet there is a still greater, which is the good man that comes to relieve it.—*Oliver Goldsmith.*

3621   The discovery of what is true, and the practice of that which is good, are the two most important objects of philosophy.—*Voltaire.*

3622   Philosophy is the art of living.—*Plutarch.*

3623   The first business of a philosopher is, to part with self-conceit.—*Epictetus.*

3624   Philosophy, when superficially studied, excites doubt; when thoroughly explored, it dispels it.—*Bacon.*

PLEASURE

3625   The generous heart should scorn a pleasure which gives others pain.—*Thomson.*

3626   When I play with my cat, who knows whether I do not make her more sport than she makes me?—*Michel de Montaigne.*

3627   If all the year were playing holidays, to sport would be as tedious as to work.—*Shakespeare.*

3628   I drink to the general joy o' the whole table.—*Shakespeare.*

3629 No man is a hypocrite in his pleasures.—*Johnson*.

3630 With pleasure drugged, he almost longed for woe.—*Byron*.

3631 Consider pleasures as they depart, not as they come.—*Aristotle*.

3632 He who can at all times sacrifice pleasure to duty approaches sublimity.
—*Lavater*.

POETRY

3633 A poet must needs be before his own age, to be even with posterity.—
J. R. Lowell.

3634 Poets utter great and wise things which they do not themselves understand.—*Plato*.

3635 One merit of poetry few persons will deny; it says more, and in fewer words, than prose.—*Voltaire*.

POLITENESS

3636 As charity covers a multitude of sins before God, so does politeness before men.—*Gréville*.

3637 A polite man is one who listens with interest to things he knows all about, when they are told him by a person who knows nothing about them.—*De Morny*.

POLITICS

3638 The universe is not rich enough to buy the vote of an honest man.—*Gregory*.

3639 A statesman makes the occasion, but the occasion makes the politician.
—*G. S. Hillard*.

3640 Politics is the art of being wise for others—policy of being wise for self.
—*Bulwer*.

3641 There is no gambling like politics.—*Disraeli*.

3642 Nothing is politically right which is morally wrong.—*Daniel O'Connell*.

3643 There is an infinity of political errors which, being once adopted, become principles.—*Abbé Raynal*.

3644 Every political question is becoming a social question, and every social question is becoming a religious question.—*R. T. Ely*.

POVERTY

3645 Meager were his looks, sharp misery had worn him to the bones.—*Shakespeare*.

3646 Let not ambition mock their useful toil, their homely joys and destiny obscure; nor grandeur hear with a disdainful smile, the short and simple annals of the poor.—*Thomas Gray.*

3647 Poverty is the wicked man's tempter, the good man's perdition, the proud man's curse, the melancholy man's halter.—*Bulwer.*

3648 Of all the advantages which come to any young man, I believe it to be demonstrably true that poverty is the greatest.—*J. G. Holland.*

3649 Poverty is uncomfortable, as I can testify: but nine times out of ten the best thing that can happen to a young man is to be tossed overboard and compelled to sink or swim for himself.—*Garfield.*

3650 He is not poor that has little, but he that desires much.—*Daniel.*

POWER

3651 But yesterday the word of Caesar might have stood against the world; now lies he there and none so poor to do him reverence.—*Shakespeare.*

3652 Power will intoxicate the best hearts, as wine the strongest heads. No man is wise enough, nor good enough, to be trusted with unlimited power.—*Colton.*

3653 Self-reverence, self-knowledge, self-control,—these three alone lead life to sovereign power.—*Tennyson.*

PRAISE

3654 Sweet is the scene where genial friendship plays the pleasing game of interchanging praise.—*Oliver Wendell Holmes.*

3655 Praising what is lost makes the remembrance dear.—*Shakespeare.*

3656 Praise undeserved is satire in disguise.—*Broadhurst.*

3657 Those who are greedy of praise prove that they are poor in merit.—*Plutarch.*

3658 Damn with faint praise.—*Pope.*

3659 As the Greek said, many men know how to flatter; few know to praise.—*Wendell Phillips.*

PRAYER

3660 I pray thee, O God, that I may be beautiful within.—*Socrates.*

3661 Her eyes are homes of silent prayer.—*Tennyson.*

3662 Our prayers should be for blessings in general, for God knows best what is good for us.—*Socrates.*

3663   Holiness is religious principle put into action.—It is faith gone to work. —It is love coined into conduct; devotion helping human suffering, and going up in intercession to the great source of all good.—*F. D. Huntington.*

3664   A strict belief in fate is the worst kind of slavery; on the other hand there is comfort in the thought that God will be moved by our prayers.— *Epicurus.*

3665   Ring in the valiant man and free, the larger heart, the kindlier hand! Ring out the darkness of the land, ring in the Christ that is to be!—*Tennyson.*

3666   Certain thoughts are prayers. There are moments when, whatever be the attitude of the body, the soul is on its knees.—*Victor Hugo.*

3667   Let not him who prays, suffer his tongue to outstrip his heart; nor presume to carry a message to the throne of grace, while that stays behind.— *South.*

3668   A prayer in its simplest definition is merely a wish turned God-ward.— *Phillips Brooks.*

3669   The Lord's Prayer contains the sum total of religion and morals.— *Wellington.*

3670   The Lord's Prayer is not, as some fancy, the easiest, the most natural of all devout utterances. It may be committed to memory quickly, but it is slowly learned by heart.—*Maurice.*

PREJUDICE

3671   To be prejudiced is always to be weak.—*Samuel Johnson.*

3672   Never try to reason the prejudice out of a man.—It was not reasoned into him and cannot be reasoned out.—*Sydney Smith.*

3673   Prejudice is the reason of fools.—*Voltaire.*

3674   Ignorance is less remote from the truth than prejudice.—*Diderot.*

3675   Prejudice is the child of ignorance.—*Hazlitt.*

3676   When the judgment is weak, the prejudice is strong.—*O'Hara.*

3677   Even when we fancy we have grown wiser, it is only, it may be, that new prejudices have displaced old ones.—*Bovee.*

3678   Prejudices are what rule the vulgar crowd.—*Voltaire.*

3679   Prejudice squints when it looks, and lies when it talks.—*Duchess de Abrantes.*

PRETENSE

3680 Where there is much pretension, much has been borrowed; nature never pretends.—*Lavater.*

3681 Everyone must see daily instances of people who complain from a mere habit of complaining; and make their friends uneasy, and strangers merry, by murmuring at evils that do not exist, and repining at grievances which they do not really feel.—*Graves.*

PRIDE

3682 Prouder than rustling in unpaid-for silk.—*Shakespeare.*

3683 To be vain of one's rank or place, is to show that one is below it.—Stanislaus.

3684 Pride is seldom delicate; it will please itself with very mean advantages.—*Johnson.*

3685 Of all marvellous things, perhaps there is nothing that angels behold with such supreme astonishment as a proud man.—*Colton.*

3686 Haughty people seem to me to have like the dwarfs, the statures of a child and the face of a man.—*Joubert.*

PRINCIPLES

3687 He who merely knows right principles is not equal to him who loves them.—*Confucius.*

3688 Expedients are for the hour; principles for the ages.—*H. W. Beecher.*

PROGRESS

3689 Progress—the onward stride of God.—*Victor Hugo.*

3690 I find the great thing in this world is not so much where we stand, as in what direction we are moving.—*Oliver Wendell Holmes.*

PROMISE

3691 The vow that binds too strictly snaps itself.—*Tennyson.*

3692 Apt to promise is apt to forget.—*Thomas Fuller.*

3693 Promise is debt.—*Chaucer.*

PROSPERITY

3694 Treason doth never prosper; for if it prosper, none dare call it treason.—*Sir J. Harrington.*

3695 Prosperity tries the fortunate, adversity the great.—*Pliny the Younger.*

3696 All sunshine makes the desert.—*Arab Proverb.*

3697 Everything in the world may be endured, except continual prosperity. —*Goethe.*

PRUDENCE

3698 The one prudence in life is concentration; the one evil is dissipation.— *Emerson.*

3699 Rashness is the characteristic of ardent youth, and prudence that of mellowed age.—*Cicero.*

PURPOSE

3700 Of what use are forms, seeing at times they are empty?—Of the same use as barrels, which, at times, are empty too.—*Hare.*

3701 He who wishes to fulfill his mission in the world must be a man of one idea, that is of one great overmastering purpose, overshadowing all his aims, and guiding and controlling his entire life.

QUOTATIONS

3702 Next to the originator of a good sentence is the first quoter of it.— *Emerson.*

3703 I quote others only the better to express myself.—*Montaigne.*

3704 The wisdom of the wise and the experience of ages may be preserved by quotation.—*Disraeli.*

3705 A great man quotes bravely, and will not draw on his invention when his memory serves him with a word as good.—What he quotes he fills with his own voice and humor, and the whole cyclopedia of his table-talk is presently believed to be his own.—*Emerson.*

3706 By necessity, by proclivity, and by delight, we quote.—We quote not only books and proverbs, but arts, sciences, religions, customs, and laws; nay, we quote temples and houses, tables and chairs by imitation.—*Emerson.*

READING

3707 Deep versed in books, and shallow in himself.—*Milton.*

3708 Read not to contradict and confute; nor to believe and take for granted; nor to find talk and discourse: but to weigh and consider.—*Francis Bacon.*

3709 Books are men of higher stature, and the only men that speak aloud for future times to hear.—*Elizabeth Browning.*

3710 You may glean knowledge by reading, but you must separate the chaff from the wheat by thinking. Much reading, like a too great repletion, stops up through a course of diverse, sometimes contrary opinions, the access of a nearer, newer, and quicker invention of your own.—*Osborn.*

3711 There is no book so bad but something valuable may be derived from it.—*Pliny.*

3712 Some books are to be tasted; others swallowed; and some few to be chewed and digested.—*Bacon.*

3713 When a book raises your spirit, and inspires you with noble and manly thoughts, seek for no other test of its excellence.—It is good, and made by a good workman.—*Bruyère.*

3714 Reading maketh a full man; conference a ready man; and writing an exact man; and, therefore, if a man write little, he had need have a great memory; if he confer little, he had need have a present wit; and if he read little, he had need have much cunning, to seem to know that he doth not.—*Bacon.*

3715 We should accustom the mind to keep the best company by introducing it only to the best books.—*Sydney Smith.*

3716 To read without reflecting, is like eating without digesting.—*Burke.*

3717 That is a good book which is opened with expectation, and closed with delight and profit.—*A. B. Alcott.*

REASON

3718 Blot out vain pomp; check impulse; quench appetite; keep reason under its own control.—*Marcus Aurelius Antoninus.*

3719 We may take Fancy for a companion, but must follow Reason as our guide.—*Samuel Johnson.*

3720 O judgment! thou art fled to brutish beasts, and men have lost their reason.—*Shakespeare.*

3721 Neither rhyme nor reason.—*Shakespeare.*

3722 When passion is on the throne, reason is out of doors.—*M. Henry.*

3723 Never reason from what you do not know. If you do, you will soon believe what is utterly against reason.—*Ramsay.*

3724 To reason correctly from a false principle, is the perfection of sophistry.—*Emmons.*

3725 Neither great poverty nor great riches will hear reason.—*Fielding.*

RELIGION

3726　What greater calamity can fall upon a nation than the loss of worship. —*Carlyle.*

3727　You are Christians of the best edition, all picked and culled.—*Cervantes.*

3728　A strong and faithful pulpit is no mean safeguard of a nation's life.— *John.*

3729　Christianity is the companion of liberty in all its conflicts, the cradle of its infancy, and the divine source of its claims.—*De Tocqueville.*

3730　A little philosophy inclineth man's mind to atheism; but depth in philosophy bringeth men's minds about to religion.—*Francis Bacon.*

3731　Morality without religion has no roots. It becomes a thing of custom, changeable, transient, and optional.—*H. W. Beecher.*

3732　The blood of the martyrs is the seed of the church.—*Jerome.*

3733　Seems it strange that thou shouldst live forever? Is it less strange that thou shouldst live at all?—This is a miracle; and that no more.—*Young.*

3734　I have immortal longings in me.—*Shakespeare.*

3735　The best theology is rather a divine life than a divine knowledge.— *Jeremy Taylor.*

3736　Carry the cross patiently, and with perfect submission; and in the end it shall carry you.—*Thomas à Kempis.*

3737　An agnostic is a man who doesn't know whether there is a God or not, doesn't know whether he has a soul or not, doesn't know whether there is a future life or not, doesn't believe that anyone else knows any more about these matters than he does, and thinks it a waste of time to try to find out.—*Dana.*

3738　No sciences are better attested than the religion of the Bible.—*Sir Isaac Newton.*

3739　The longer you read the Bible, the more you will like it; it will grow sweeter and sweeter; and the more you get into the spirit of it, the more you will get into the spirit of Christ.—*Romaine.*

3740　Do you know a book that you are willing to put under your head for a pillow when you lie dying? That is the book you want to study while you are living. There is but one such book in the world. The Bible.—*Joseph Cook.*

3741　The whole hope of human progress is suspended on the ever-growing influence of the Bible.—*William H. Seward.*

3742 Men will wrangle for religion; write for it; fight for it; die for it; anything but live for it.—*Colton.*

3743 If religious books are not widely circulated among the masses in this country, and the people do not become religious, I do not know what is to become of us as a nation.—*Daniel Webster.*

3744 Religion cannot pass away. The burning of a little straw may hide the stars of the sky, but the stars are there, and will reappear.—*Carlyle.*

3745 Culture of intellect, without religion in the heart, is only civilized barbarism and disguised animalism.—*Bunsen.*

3746 Religion is the best armor in the world, but the worst cloak.—*John Newton.*

3747 The nature of Christ's existence is mysterious, I admit; but this mystery meets the wants of man.—Reject it and the world is an inexplicable riddle; believe it, and the history of our race is satisfactorily explained.—*Napoleon.*

3748 One truly Christian life will do more to prove the divine origin of Christianity than many lectures. It is of much greater importance to develop Christian character, than to exhibit Christian evidences.—*J. M. Gibson.*

3749 He who shall introduce into public affairs the principles of primitive Christianity, will revolutionize the world.—*Franklin.*

3750 Christianity requires two things from every man who believes in it: first, to acquire property by just and righteous means, and second, to look not only on his own things, but also on the things of others.—*H. J. Van Dyke.*

3751 There's not much practical Christianity in the man who lives on better terms with angels and seraphs, than with his children, servants and neighbors. —*H. W. Beecher.*

3752 A Christian church is a body or collection of persons, voluntarily associated together, professing to believe what Christ teaches, to do what Christ enjoins, to imitate his example, cherish his spirit, and make known his gospel to others.—*R. F. Sample.*

REMORSE

3753 Remorse is the echo of a lost virtue.—*Bulwer.*

3754 Remorse is beholding heaven and feeling hell.—*Moore.*

3755 Believe me, every heart has its secret sorrows, which the world knows not; and oftentimes we call a man cold when he is only sad.—*Longfellow.*

3756 Of all the sad words of tongue or pen, the saddest are these: "It might have been."—*Whittier.*

REPENTANCE

3757   Of all acts of man repentance is the most divine.—The greatest of all faults is to be conscious of none.—*Carlyle*.

3758   To do so no more is the truest repentance.—*Luther*.

3759   There is one case of death-bed repentance recorded, that of the penitent thief, that none should despair; and only one that none should presume.—*Augustine*.

REPUTATION

3760   Reputation, reputation, reputation! Oh, I have lost my reputation! I have lost the immortal part of myself, and what remains is bestial.—*Shakespeare*.

3761   The way to gain a good reputation, is, to endeavor to be what you desire to appear.—*Socrates*.

3762   One may be better than his reputation, but never better than his principles.—*Latena*.

3763   Good name in man and woman, dear my lord, is the immediate jewel of their souls: Who steals my purse steals trash; 't is something, nothing; 'Twas mine, 'tis his, and has been slave to thousands: Robs me of that which not enriches him and makes me poor indeed.—*Shakespeare*.

REVOLUTION

3764   Revolution is the larva of civilization.—*Victor Hugo*.

3765   Revolutions begin in the best heads, and run steadily down to the populace.—*Metternich*.

3766   Too long denial of guaranteed right is sure to lead to revolution—bloody revolution, where suffering must fall upon the innocent as well as the guilty.—*U. S. Grant*.

3767   Revolutions are not made, they come. A revolution is as natural a growth as an oak. It comes out of the past. Its foundations are laid far back.—*Wendell Phillips*.

REWARD

3768   Recompense injury with justice and unkindness with kindness.—*Confucius*.

3769   The evening of a well-spent life brings its lamps with it.—*Joubert*.

3770   He who wishes to secure the good of others has already secured his own.—*Confucius*.

RICHES

3771 We have seen better days.—*Shakespeare.*

3772 Most of the luxuries and many of the so-called comforts of life are not only not indispensable, but positive hindrances to the elevation of mankind.—*Thoreau.*

3773 Can one desire too much of a good thing?—*Shakespeare.*

3774 There are two things needed in these days; first, for rich men to find out how poor men live; and second, for poor men to know how rich men work.—*E. Atkinson.*

3775 Riches are apt to betray a man into arrogance.—*Addison.*

3776 I am happy in having learned to distinguish between ownership and possession. Books, pictures, and all the beauty of the world belong to those who love and understand them. All of these things that I am entitled to, I have—I own them by divine right. So I care not a bit who possesses them. I used to care very much and consequently was very unhappy.—*James Howard Keller.*

3777 My riches consist not in the extent of my possessions, but in the fewness of my wants.—*J. Brotherton.*

3778 The pride of dying rich raises the loudest laugh in hell.—*John Foster.*

3779 To have what we want is riches, but to be able to do without is power.—*G. Macdonald.*

3780 Public sentiment will come to be, that the man who dies rich dies disgraced.—*Andrew Carnegie.*

RIGHT

3781 I would rather be right than be president.—*Henry Clay.*

3782 Let us have faith that right makes might, and in that faith, let us to the end, dare to do our duty, as we understand it.—*Lincoln.*

3783 All men are endowed by their Creator with inalienable rights; among these are life, liberty, and the pursuit of happiness.—*Jefferson.*

SABBATH

3784 He who ordained the Sabbath loves the poor.—*J. R. Lowell.*

3785 The longer I live the more highly do I estimate the Christian Sabbath, and the more grateful do I feel to those who impress its importance on the community.—*Daniel Webster.*

3786 A corruption of morals usually follows a profanation of the Sabbath.—*Blackstone.*

SECRET

3787 A truly wise man should have no keeper of his secret but himself.—*Guizot.*

3788 Three may keep a secret, if two of them are dead.—*Franklin.*

SELF-CONTROL

3789 By taking revenge, a man is but even with his enemy; but in passing over it, he is superior.—*Bacon.*

3790 Shame may restrain what law does not prohibit.—*Seneca.*

3791 A panic is the stampede of our self-possession.—*Rivarol.*

3792 Heat not a furnace for your foe so hot.—*Shakespeare.*

3793 He who reigns within himself and rules his passions, desires and fears is more than a king.—*Milton.*

SILENCE

3794 Blessed is the man who, having nothing to say, abstains from giving in words evidence of the fact.—*George Eliot.*

3795 Deep vengeance is the daughter of deep silence.—*Alfieri.*

3796 Speech is great, but silence is greater.—*Carlyle.*

3797 Silence never shows itself to so great an advantage as when it is made the reply to calumny and defamation.—*Addison.*

3798 'Tis not my talent to conceal my thoughts, or carry smiles and sunshine in my face, when discontent sits heavy at my heart.—*Addison.*

3799 Learn to hold thy tongue; five words cost Zacharias forty weeks of silence.—*Fuller.*

3800 Speaking much is a sign of vanity, for he that is lavish in words is a niggard in deed.—*Sir W. Raleigh.*

SIMPLICITY

3801 The fashion wears out more apparel than the man.—*Shakespeare.*

3802 Simplicity, of all things, is the hardest to be copied.—*Steele.*

3803 Nothing is more simple than greatness; indeed, to be simple is to be great.—*Emerson.*

3804 The greatest truths are the simplest; and so are the greatest men.—*Hare.*

SIN

3805 Selfishness is the greatest curse of the human race.—*Wm. E. Gladstone.*

3806 I am a man more sinn'd against than sinning.—*Shakespeare.*

3807 Some rise by sin, and some by virtue fall.—*Shakespeare.*

3808 No man ever became extremely wicked all at once.—*Juvenal.*

3809 Of Man's first disobedience, and the fruit of that forbidden tree whose mortal taste brought death into the world, and all our woe.—*John Milton.*

3810 Sin is essentially a departure from God.—*Luther.*

3811 How immense appear to us the sins that we have not committed.—*Mad. Necker.*

3812 Sins are like circles in the water when a stone is thrown into it; one produces another.—When anger was in Cain's heart, murder was not far off.—*Philip Henry.*

SINCERITY

3813 Without earnestness no man is ever great or does really great things. He may be the cleverest of men; he may be brilliant, entertaining, popular; but he will want weight.—*Bayne.*

3814 Sincerity and truth are the basis of every virtue.—*Confucius.*

SLANDER

3815 Slander is a vice that strikes a double blow, wounding both him that commits, and him against whom it is committed.—*Saurin.*

3816 Slander is the revenge of a coward, and dissimulation his defense.—*Johnson.*

3817 We cannot control the evil tongues of others, but a good life enables us to despise them.—*Cato.*

SLEEP

3818 Sleep that knits up the ravell'd sleave of care, the death of each day's life, sore labour's bath, balm of hurt minds, great nature's second course, chief nourisher in life's feast.—*Shakespeare.*

3819 O sleep, O gentle sleep, nature's soft nurse! how have I frightened thee, that thou no more wilt weigh my eyelids down and steep my senses in forgetfulness?—*Shakespeare.*

SOCIETY

3820   The best cure for worry, depression, melancholy, brooding, is to go deliberately forth and try to lift with one's sympathy the gloom of somebody else.—*Arnold Bennett.*

3821   God has made no one absolute.—The rich depend on the poor, as well as the poor on the rich.—The world is but a magnificent building; all the stones are gradually cemented together.—No one subsists by himself alone. —*Feltham.*

3822   Society is composed of two great classes: those who have more dinners than appetite, and those who have more appetite than dinners.—*Chamfort.*

3823   Society is now one polished horde, formed of two mighty tribes, the bores and bored.—*Byron.*

3824   No man can possibly improve in any company for which he has not respect enough to be under some degree of restraint.—*Chesterfield.*

SOLITUDE

3825   No one is so utterly desolate, but some heart, though unknown, responds unto his own.—*Longfellow.*

3826   Eating the bitter bread of banishment.—*Shakespeare.*

3827   I never found the companion that was so companionable as solitude. —*Thoreau.*

3828   A wise man is never less alone than when he is alone.—*Swift.*

3829   Conversation enriches the understanding, but solitude is the school of genius.—*Gibbon.*

3830   If from society we learn to live, it is solitude should teach us how to die.—*Byron.*

3831   It is easy, in the world, to live after the world's opinion; it is easy, in solitude, to live after your own; but the great man is he who, in the midst of the crowd, keeps with perfect sweetness the independence of solitude.— *Emerson.*

SORROW

3832   The deeper the sorrow the less tongue it hath.—*Talmud.*

3833   When sorrows come, they come not single spies, but in battalions.— *Shakespeare.*

3834   Good night, good night! parting is such sweet sorrow, that I shall say good night till it be morrow.—*Shakespeare.*

3835 Men can counsel and speak comfort to that grief which they themselves not feel.—*Shakespeare*.

3836 Joys are our wings; sorrows our spurs.—*Richter*.

3837 Tearless grief bleeds inwardly.—*Bovee*.

3838 Tears are often the telescope by which men see far into heaven.—*H. W. Beecher*.

3839 Everyone can master a grief but he that has it.—*Shakespeare*.

SOUL

3840 Sensuality is the grave of the soul.—*Channing*.

3841 It is the mind that makes the man, and our vigour is in our immortal soul.—*Ovid*.

3842 Great truths are portions of the soul of man; great souls are portions of eternity.—*Lowell*.

3843 Two souls with but a single thought, two hearts that beat as one.—*Von Münch Bellinghausen*.

3844
Build thee more stately mansions, O, my soul,
As the swift seasons roll!
Leave thy low-vaulted past!
Let each new temple, nobler than the last
Shut thee from heaven with a dome more vast,
'Till thou at length art free,
Leaving thine outgrown shell by life's unresting sea!
Oliver Wendell Holmes

3845 Whatever that be which thinks, which understands, which wills, which acts, it is something celestial and divine, and on that account must necessarily be eternal.—*Cicero*.

3846 I am fully convinced that the soul is indestructible, and that its activity will continue through eternity. It is like the sun, which, to our eyes, seems to set in night; but it has in reality only gone to diffuse its light elsewhere.—*Goethe*.

SPEECH

3847 Charm us, orator, till the lion look no larger than the cat.—*Tennyson*.

3848 Speech is a faculty given to man to conceal his thoughts.—*Talleyrand*.

3849 Speeches cannot be made long enough for the speakers, nor short enough for the hearers.—*Perry*.

3850 Repartee is perfect, when it effects its purpose with a double edge. Repartee is the highest order of wit, as it bespeaks the coolest yet quickest exercise of genius at a moment when the passions are roused.—*Colton.*

3851 Rhetoric is nothing but reason well dressed, and argument put in order.—*Jeremy Collier.*

3852 "I have heard many great orators," said Louis XIV to Massilon, "and have been highly pleased with them; but whenever I hear you, I go away displeased with myself." This is the highest encomium that could be bestowed on a preacher.—*C. Simmons.*

3853 With words we govern men.—*Disraeli.*

3854 What too many orators want in depth, they give you in length.—*Montesquieu.*

3855 The language of the heart which comes from the heart and goes to the heart—is always simple, graceful, and full of power, but no art of rhetoric can teach it. It is at once the easiest and most difficult language,—difficult, since it needs a heart to speak it; easy, because its periods though rounded and full of harmony, are still unstudied.—*Bovee.*

SPRING

3856 Winter, lingering, chills the lap of May.—*Goldsmith.*

3857 In the spring a livelier iris changes on the burnished dove; in the spring a young man's fancy lightly turns to thoughts of love.—*Tennyson.*

SUCCESS

3858 Nothing succeeds so well as success.—*Talleyrand.*

3859 Benjamin Franklin's secret of success: "I will speak ill of no man, and speak all the good I know of everybody."

3860 Many shining actions owe their success to chance, though the general or statesman runs away with the applause.—*Home.*

3861 To succeed in the world, it is much more necessary to possess the penetration to discern who is a fool, than to discover who is a clever man.—*Talleyrand.*

3862 The way to be nothing is to do nothing.—*Howe.*

TACT

3863 It is a very hard undertaking to seek to please everybody.—*Publius Syrus.*

3864 Tact comes as much from goodness of heart as from fineness of taste.—*Endymion.*

3865 It is a sad thing when men have neither the wit to speak well, nor judgment to hold their tongues.—*Bruyère.*

TEMPTATION

3866 No man is matriculated to the art of life till he has been well tempted. —*George Eliot.*

3867 Every temptation is great or small according as the man is.—*Jeremy Taylor.*

3868 Better shun the bait than struggle in the snare.—*Dryden.*

3869 Some temptations come to the industrious, but all temptations attack the idle.—*Spurgeon.*

THOUGHT

3870 True, I talk of dreams, which are the children of an idle brain, begot of nothing but vain fantasy.—*Shakespeare.*

3871 Thy wish was father, Harry, to that thought.—*Shakespeare.*

3872 Give thy thoughts no tongue.—*Shakespeare.*

3873 There is nothing either good or bad, but thinking makes it so.— *Shakespeare.*

3874 Think wrongly, if you please; but in all cases think for yourself.— *Lessing.*

3875 Thinking is the hardest work there is, which is the probable reason why so few engage in it.—*Henry Ford.*

3876 Sit in reverie, and watch the changing color of the waves that break upon the idle seashore of the mind.—*Longfellow.*

3877 Every thought which genius and piety throw into the world alters the world.—*Emerson.*

3878 Freethinkers are generally those who never think at all.—*Sterne.*

3879 They only babble who practise not reflection.—I shall think; and thought is silence.—*Sheridan.*

3880 Some persons do first, think afterward, and then repent forever.— *Secker.*

3881 A picture is an intermediate something between a thought and a thing.—*Coleridge.*

3882 The most important thought I ever had was that of my individual responsibility to God.—*Daniel Webster.*

3883 Thinking is the talking of the soul with itself.—*Plato.*

3884 It is not strange that remembered ideas should often take advantage of the crowd of thoughts and smuggle themselves in as original.—Honest thinkers are always stealing unconsciously from each other.—Our minds are full of waifs and estrays which we think our own.—Innocent plagiarism turns up everywhere.—*O. W. Holmes.*

3885 Thought is the property of those only who can entertain it.—*Emerson.*

3886 The men of action are, after all, only the unconscious instruments of the men of thought.—*Heine.*

TIME

3887 The inaudible and noiseless foot of Time.—*Shakespeare.*

3888 We burn daylight.—*Shakespeare.*

3889 You cannot give an instance of any man who is permitted to lay out his own time, contriving not to have tedious hours.—*Johnson.*

3890 It is hoped that, with all modern improvements, a way will be discovered of getting rid of bores; for it is too bad that a poor wretch can be punished for stealing your handkerchief or gloves, and that no punishment can be inflicted on those who steal your time, and with it your temper and patience, as well as the bright thoughts that might have entered your mind, if they had not been frightened away by the bore.—*Byron.*

3891 O, call back yesterday, bid time return!—*Shakespeare.*

3892 Ring out the old, ring in the new, ring, happy bells, across the snow!—*Tennyson.*

3893 Come what come may, time and the hour runs through the roughest day.—*Shakespeare.*

3894 For ever and a day.—*Shakespeare.*

3895 In the posteriors of this day, which the rude multitude call the afternoon.—*Shakespeare.*

3896 For men may come and men may go, but I go on forever.—*Tennyson.*

3897 The great rule of moral conduct is, next to God, to respect time.—*Lavater.*

3898 Time will discover everything to posterity; it is a babbler, and speaks even when no question is put.—*Euripides.*

3899 If hours did not hang heavy, what would become of scandal?—*Bancroft.*

3900 Dost thou love life?—Then do not squander time, for that is the stuff life is made of.—*Franklin.*

3901 No hand can make the clock strike for me the hours that are passed.—*Byron.*

3902 Never put off till tomorrow that which you can do today.—*Franklin.*

3903 Tomorrow is the day when idlers work, and fools reform, and mortal men lay hold on heaven.—*Young.*

3904 Every man's life lies within the present; for the past is spent and done with, and the future is uncertain.—*Marcus Antoninus.*

3905 Live this day as if it were the last.—*Kerr.*

3906 Thou wilt find rest from vain fancies if thou doest every act in life as though it were thy last.—*Marcus Aurelius Antoninus.*

3907 Time is a sort of river of passing events, and strong is its current; no sooner is a thing brought to sight than it is swept by and another takes its place, and this too will be swept away.—*Marcus Aurelius Antoninus.*

3908 The whole life of man is but a point of time; let us enjoy it, therefore, while it lasts, and not spend it to no purpose.—*Plutarch.*

3909 Dionysius the Elder, being asked whether he was at leisure, he replied, "God forbid that it should ever befall me!"—*Plutarch.*

3910 Time hath often cured the wound which reason failed to heal.—*Seneca.*

3911 As if you could kill time without injuring eternity!—*Thoreau.*

3912 Nothing lies on our hands with such uneasiness as time. Wretched and thoughtless creatures! In the only place where covetousness were a virtue we turn prodigals.—*Addison.*

3913 All my possessions for a moment of time.—*Queen Elizabeth's last words.*

TOLERANCE

3914 He who never leaves his own country is full of prejudices.—*Goldoni.*

3915 Intolerance has been the curse of every age and state.—*S. Davies.*

3916   Tolerance comes with age; I see no fault committed that I myself could not have committed at some time or other.—*Goethe.*

TRADITION

3917   A precedent embalms a principle.—*Disraeli.*

3918   But to my mind, though I am native here and to the manner born, it is a custom more honoured in the breach than the observance.—*Shakespeare.*

3919   Tradition is an important help to history, but its statements should be carefully scrutinized before we rely on them.—*Addison.*

TRAGEDY

3920   The worst is not so long as we can say, "This is the worst."—*Shakespeare.*

3921   A perfect tragedy is the noblest production of human nature.—*Joseph Addison.*

3922   Never morning wore to evening, but some heart did break.—*Tennyson.*

TRAVEL

3923   Usually speaking, the worst bred person in company is a young traveller just returned from abroad.—*Swift.*

3924   The travelled mind is the catholic mind, educated out of exclusiveness and egotism.—*A. B. Alcott.*

TRIFLES

3925   Small to greater matters must give way.—*Shakespeare.*

3926   Good taste rejects excessive nicety; it treats little things as little things, and is not hurt by them.—*Fenelon.*

3927   Trifles make perfection, but perfection itself is no trifle.—*Michael Angelo.*

3928   Men are led by trifles.—*Napoleon.*

3929   He that despiseth small things, shall fall by little and little.—*Ecclesiasticus.*

3930   Most of the critical things in life, which become the starting points of human destiny, are little things.—*R. Smith.*

3931   It is the little rift within the lute that by and by will make the music mute, and ever widening slowly silence all.—*Tennyson.*

TROUBLES

3932   This world has cares enough to plague us; but he who meditates on others' woe, shall, in that meditation, lose his own.—*Cumberland*.

3933   Troubles are often the tools by which God fashions us for better things.—*H. W. Beecher*.

TRUTH

3934   Logic is the art of convincing us of some truth.—*Bruyère*.

3935   Those who exaggerate in their statements belittle themselves.—*C. Simmons*.

3936   Truth is truth to the end of reckoning.—*Shakespeare*.

3937   The truth is always the strongest argument.—*Sophocles*.

3938   A man should never be ashamed to own he has been in the wrong, which is but saying, in other words, that he is wiser today than he was yesterday.—*Pope*.

3939   The telling of a falsehood is like the cut of a sabre; for though the wound may heal, the scar of it will remain.—*Saadi*.

3940   Truth sits upon the lips of dying men.—*Matthew Arnold*.

3941   In the mountains of truth, you never climb in vain. Either you already reach a higher point today, or you exercise your strength in order to be able to climb higher tomorrow.—*Friedrich Wilhelm Nietzsche*.

3942   The criterion of a scholar's utility is the number and value of the truths he has circulated, and the minds he has awakened.—*Coleridge*.

3943
>   Truth, crushed to earth, shall rise again:
>   The eternal years of God are hers;
>   But Error, wounded, writhes with pain,
>   And dies among his worshippers.
>   *W. Cullen Bryant*

3944   To die for the truth is not to die merely for one's faith, or one's country; it is to die for the world.
   Their blood is shed in confirmation of the noblest claim—the claim to feed upon immortal truth, to walk with God, and be divinely free.
>   *Cowper*

3945   Truth is the foundation of all knowledge and the cement of all societies.—*Dryden*.

N

3946   If the world goes against truth, then Athanasius goes against the world.—*Athanasius.*

3947   He who seeks truth should be of no country.—*Voltaire.*

VANITY

3948   It is our own vanity that makes the vanity of others intolerable to us.—*La Rochefoucauld.*

3949   Vanity is the fruit of ignorance.—*Ross.*

3950   There is no arena in which vanity displays itself under such a variety of forms as in conversation.—*Pascal.*

3951   There's none so homely but loves a looking-glass.—*South.*

VENGEANCE

3952   The fire you kindle for your enemy often burns yourself more than him.—*Chinese Proverb.*

3953   No man ever did a designed injury to another, but at the same time he did a greater to himself.—*Home.*

VIRTUE

3954   Virtue is bold, and goodness never fearful.—*Shakespeare.*

3955   Of all virtues magnanimity is the rarest; there are a hundred persons of merit for one who willingly acknowledges it in another.—*Hazlitt.*

3956   The less a man thinks or knows about his virtues, the better we like him.—*Emerson.*

3957   There is but one virtue—the eternal sacrifice of self.—*George Sand.*

3958   True humility, the highest virtue, mother of them all.—*Tennyson.*

3959   Confidence in another man's virtue, is no slight evidence of one's own.—*Montaigne.*

3960   He that is good will infallibly become better, and he that is bad will as certainly become worse; for vice, virtue, and time are three things that never stand still.—*Colton.*

3961   I cannot praise a fugitive and cloistered virtue, unexercised and unbreathed, that never sallies out and sees her adversary. The virtue that knows not the utmost that vice promises to her followers, and rejects it, is but a blank virtue, not a pure.—*Milton*

WAR

3962 Take my word for it, if you had seen but one day of war, you would pray to Almighty God, that you might never see such a thing again.—*Wellington.*

3963 In disarming Peter, Christ disarmed every soldier.—*Tertullian.*

3964 One murder makes a villain; millions a hero.—*Bp. Porteus.*

3965 Who overcomes force, hath overcome but half his foe.—*John Milton.*

3966 War loves to seek its victims in the young.—*Sophocles.*

3967 War! that mad game the world so loves to play.—*Swift.*

3968 There never was a good war, or a bad peace.—*Franklin.*

3969 War is the business of barbarians.—*Napoleon.*

3970 I am of opinion that, unless you could bray Christianity in a mortar, and mould it into a new paste, there is no possibility of a holy war.—*Bacon.*

3971
Someone had blundered:
Theirs not to make reply,
Theirs not to reason why,
Theirs but to do and die.

Tennyson

3972
Cannon to right of them,
Cannon to left of them,
Cannon in front of them.

. . . .

Into the jaws of death,
Into the mouth of hell
Rode the six hundred.

Tennyson

WEALTH

3973 Rich people should consider that they are only trustees for what they possess, and should show their wealth to be more in doing good than merely in having it.—They should not reserve their benevolence for purposes after they are dead, for those who give not of their property till they die show that they would not then if they could keep it any longer.—*Bp. Hall.*

3974 Farewell! thou art too dear for my possessing.—*Shakespeare.*

3975 All that glisters is not gold.—*Shakespeare.*

3976   Rank and riches are chains of gold, but still chains.—*Ruffini*.

3977   Supine amidst our flowing store, we slept securely, and we dreamt of more.—*John Dryden*.

3978   He is richest who is content with the least, for content is the wealth of nature.—*Socrates*.

3979   The gratification of wealth is not found in mere possession or in lavish expenditures, but in its wise application.—*Cervantes*.

3980   Wealth may be an excellent thing, for it means power, leisure, and liberty.—*J. R. Lowell*.

3981   There is no society, however free and democratic, where wealth will not create an aristocracy.—*Bulwer*.

3982   Wealth consists not in having great possessions but in having few wants.—*Epicurus*.

WILL

3983   If weakness may excuse, what murderer, what traitor, parricide, incestuous, sacrilegious, but may plead it? All wickedness is weakness; that plea, therefore, with God or man will gain thee no remission.—*Milton*.

3984   At twenty years of age the will reigns; at thirty, the wit; and at forty, the judgment.—*Gratian*.

3985   He who has a firm will molds the world to himself.—*Goethe*.

3986   People do not lack strength; they lack will.—*Victor Hugo*.

3987   To deny the freedom of the will is to make morality impossible.--*Froude*.

WIND

3988   The gentle wind, a sweet and passionate wooer, kisses the blushing leaf.—*Longfellow*.

3989   God tempers the wind to the shorn lamb.—*Sterne*.

WISDOM

3990   Never reason from what you do not know.—*Ramsay*.

3991   Knowledge comes, but wisdom lingers.—*Tennyson*.

3992   A child can ask a thousand questions that the wisest man cannot answer.—*J. Abbott*.

3993 Judge of a man by his questions rather than by his answers.—*Voltaire.*

3994 The years teach much which the days never know.—*Emerson.*

3995 Wise men argue causes; fools decide them.—*Anacharsis.*

3996 The fool doth think he is wise, but the wise man knows himself to be a fool.—*Shakespeare.*

3997 When he that speaks, and he to whom he speaks, neither of them understand what is meant, that is metaphysics.—*Voltaire.*

3998 He draweth out the thread of his verbosity finer than the staple of his argument.—*Shakespeare.*

3999 He is truly wise who gains wisdom from another's mishap.—*Publius Syrus.*

4000 People generally quarrel because they cannot argue.—*G. K. Chesterton.*

4001 If a man will begin with certainties, he shall end in doubts; but if he will be content to begin with doubts, he shall end in certainties.—*Francis Bacon.*

4002 A fool may have his coat embroidered with gold, but it is a fool's coat still.—*Rivarol.*

4003 This dead of midnight is the noon of thought, and wisdom mounts her zenith with the stars.—*Mrs. Barbauld.*

4004 A well cultivated mind is made up of all the minds of preceding ages; it is only the one single mind educated by all previous time.—*Fontenelle.*

4005 Few minds wear out; more rust out.—*Bovee.*

4006 Common-sense in an uncommon degree is what the world calls wisdom. —*Coleridge.*

4007 The Delphic oracle said I was the wisest of all the Greeks. It is because that I alone, of all the Greeks, know that I know nothing.—*Socrates.*

4008 No man can be wise on an empty stomach.—*George Eliot.*

4009 The first consideration a wise man fixeth upon is the great end of his creation; what it is, and wherein it consists; the next is of the most proper means to that end.—*Walker.*

4010 Perfect wisdom hath four parts, viz., wisdom, the principle of doing things aright; justice, the principle of doing things equally in public and private; fortitude, the principle of not flying danger, but meeting it; and temperance, the principle of subduing desires and living moderately.—*Plato.*

WIT

4011   To leave this keen encounter of our wits.—*Shakespeare.*

4012   There's a skirmish of wit between them.—*Shakespeare.*

4013   I am not only witty in myself, but the cause that wit is in other men.— *Shakespeare.*

WOMAN

4014   The sum of all that makes a just man happy consists in the well choosing of his wife.—*Massinger.*

4015   For a wife take the daughter of a good mother.—*Fuller.*

4016   I have no other but a woman's reason: I think him so, because I think him so.—*Shakespeare.*

4017   Frailty, thy name is woman!—*Shakespeare.*

4018   Her voice was ever soft, gentle, and low,—an excellent thing in woman. —*Shakespeare.*

4019   A lion among ladies is a most dreadful thing.—*Shakespeare.*

4020   Woman apparently is doing everything possible to destroy in herself those very qualifications which render her beautiful, namely, modesty, purity, and chastity. It is a blindness which can only be explained by the fascination of that vanity of which the Scriptures speak with such severity.—*Pope Pius XI.*

4021   No one knows like a woman how to say things which are at once gentle and deep.—*Victor Hugo.*

4022   All the reasonings of men are not worth one sentiment of women.— *Voltaire.*

4023   Men have sight; women insight.—*Victor Hugo.*

WORK

4024   Rest is the sweet sauce of labor.—*Plutarch.*

4025   God gives every bird its food, but he does not throw it into the nest.— *J. G. Holland.*

4026   So many worlds, so much to do, so little done, such things to be.— *Tennyson.*

4027   Things don't turn up in this world until somebody turns them up.—*Garfield.*

4028   In all departments of activity, to have one thing to do, and then to do it, is the secret of success.—*Edwards.*

4029   It is a sober truth that people who live only to amuse themselves, work harder at the task than most people do in earning their daily bread.—*H. More.*

4030   Few things are impracticable in themselves: and it is for want of application, rather than of means, that men fail of success.—*La Rochefoucauld.*

4031   Nothing is really work unless you would rather be doing something else.—*Sir James M. Barrie.*

4032   Light is the task where many share the toil.—*Homer.*

4033   Every man is, or hopes to be, an Idler.—*Samuel Johnson.*

4034   Few men are lacking in capacity, but they fail because they are lacking in application.—*Calvin Coolidge.*

4035   Temptation rarely comes in working hours. It is in their leisure time that men are made or marred.—*W. M. Taylor.*

4036   Laziness grows on people; it begins in cobwebs and ends in iron chains. The more business a man has to do the more he is able to accomplish, for he learns to economize his time.—*Sir M. Hale.*

4037   If you have great talents, industry will improve them; if moderate abilities, industry will supply their deficiencies. Nothing is denied to well-directed labor; nothing is ever to be attained without it.—*Sir Joshua Reynolds.*

4038   Every industrious man, in every lawful calling, is a useful man.—And one principal reason why men are so often useless is, that they neglect their own profession or calling, and divide and shift their attention among a multiplicity of objects and pursuits.—*Emmons.*

4039   He who has battled with poverty and hard toil will be found stronger and more expert than he who could stay at home from the battle, concealed among the provision wagons, or unwatchfully abiding by the stuff.—*Carlyle.*

4040   There is only one thing which will really train the human mind, and that is the voluntary use of the mind by the man himself. You may aid him, you may guide him, you may suggest to him, and, above all you may inspire him; but the only thing worth having is that which he gets by his own exertions: and what he gets is proportionate to the effort he puts into it.—*A. Lawrence Lowell.*

WRITING

4041   The wise men of old have sent most of their morality down the stream of time in the light skiff of apothegm or epigram.—*E. P. Whipple.*

4042   The two most engaging powers of an author, are, to make new things familiar, and familiar things new.—*Johnson.*

4043   Classical quotation is the parole of literary men all over the world.—*Samuel Johnson.*

4044   A man will turn over half a library to make one book.—*Samuel Johnson.*

4045   The pen is the tongue of the mind.—*Miguel de Cervantes.*

4046   The press is the foe of rhetoric, but the friend of reason.—*Colton.*

4047   There are only two powers in the world, the sword and the pen; and in the end the former is always conquered by the latter.—*Napoleon.*

4048   Plagiarists have, at least, the merit of preservation.—*Disraeli.*

YOUTH

4049   So wise so young, they say, do never live long.—*Shakespeare.*

4050   He wears the rose of youth upon him.—*Shakespeare.*

4051   We have some salt of our youth in us.—*Shakespeare.*

4052   The excesses of our youth are drafts upon our old age, payable with interest about thirty years after date.—*Colton.*

4053   Girls we love for what they are; young men for what they promise to be.—*Goethe.*

INDEX

All numbers in this index refer to numbers placed in numerical order at the left-hand margins of the pages. The 4,000 items of source material are completely indexed so that it is possible quickly to find all the items throughout the book which relate to a particular idea. To illustrate, under the classification, *marriage*, in the index, one can immediately locate the numbers of all quotations, epigrams, humorous stories, definitions and other items relating to this subject. In addition, almost every one of the 4,000 items has been classified in the index under several headings so the reader who is seeking a quotation, epigram, or humorous story to illustrate even a particular word or a relatively restricted idea may find it by using the index.

A

AAA, 1679
Abase, 2723
Abhorrence, 2769
Abide, 2788
Ability, 1306, 1657, 1819, 2438, 2816, 2818, 3045, 3047, 4037
Abomination, 2646
Abraham, 2350
Absence, 2082, 3126, 3401
Absent, 2778
Absent-minded, 167, 272, 469, 1242, 1987
Abundance, 2712-2713, 3140
Abuse, 3206
Accept, 2456
Acceptance, 3708
Accident, 460, 568, 600, 648, 698, 754, 823, 1399, 1643, 1707, 1738; insurance, 1399
Accomplishment, 2430, 2819, 2831
Accounting, 298, 479, 2063
Accumulate, 2573
Accuracy, 2083, 3325
Achates, 2434
Ache, 2944
Achievement, 22, 77, 1694, 2819-2831
Achilles, 2351-2352
Acknowledgment, 2362
Acoustics, 445
Acquaintances, 1411
Acquainted, 395, 665
Acquiescence, 2800
Acrobat, 527, 529; definition of, 1752
Action, 2832-2833, 3311, 3886
Actions, 2941, 3196, 3439, 3860, 3906
Activity, 2832-2833, 3028, 4028
Actor, 871, 949, 1042, 1331, 1498
Actress, 976
Adam, 550, 589, 1190, 1270; definition of, 1753
Adams, President John, 1984
Addison, Joseph, 1983, 2932, 3116, 3176, 3302, 3347, 3374, 3797-3798, 3912, 3919, 3921
Address, 852, 2008
Adenoids, 1805
Admetus, 2438
Administration, 3213

Admirable, 3431
Admiral, 1702
Admiration, 3116, 3299, 3401
Adonis, 2353
Adultery, 2541
Advance, 2084
Advancement, 3577, 3579
Advantage, 3589-3590, 3648, 3684
Adventure, 2358, 2368, 2845, 2999
Adversity, 1569, 2085, 2619, 2834-2843, 3046, 3250-3253, 3441, 3458-3459, 3476, 3490-3491, 3620, 3695
Advertisement, 1414, 1512
Advertising, 75, 161, 208, 783, 1107, 1202, 1342, 1663, 1757, 1843, 1950, 3581
Advice, 776, 832, 1365, 1651, 2021, 3582; definition of, 1754
Aegis, 2422
Aeneid, 2360, 2434
Affectation, 2928, 3680-3681
Affection, 3414
Affliction, 2562, 2571, 2946
Afraid, 1188
Afternoon, 1556, 3895
Agamemnon, 2352
Age, 153, 192, 200, 217, 285, 397, 400, 532, 564, 566, 690, 699, 712, 732, 866, 884, 916, 952, 1016, 1426, 1457, 1687, 1946, 1951, 2557, 2659, 2844-2856, 2899, 3052, 3090, 3160, 3300-3301, 3633, 3916
Agent, 1950
Ages, 2914, 3201, 3203, 3688, 3704, 3915
Aggressive, 1609
Agitations, 3527
Agnostic, 3737
Agony, 2272, 2944
Agree, 1070, 1716, 1927, 2014
Ahead, 1659
Aid, 4040
Aims, 3701
Air, 382, 836, 2703
Air-condition, 175
Airplane, 723, 911, 1184, 1852, 2383
Aisle seats, 1352
Alarm, 973
Alarmist, 1722
Alaska, 1165

O

Album, 1524
Alcott, Louisa M., 2098
Alertness, 3170
Alexander the Great, 1991
Alibi, 842, 977; definition of, 1755
Alimony, 697, 1168; definition of, 1756
Aliquando bonus dormitat Homerus, 2518
All-expense tour, 1757
Allen, Fred, 1829
Alley, 1295
Alliteration, use of, 136-138
Alms, 1065, 2765
Alone, 2525, 2667
Alpha, 2356, 2815
Alphabet, 329, 1005, 1073, 1679
Alteration, 3409
Alternative, 2486
Amateur, 938, 950, 1405, 1646; athlete, definition of, 1758; carpenter, 1759; golfer, definition of, 1760
Amazon, 2359
Ambassadors, 3037, 3467
Ambidextrous, 1008
Ambition, 593, 609, 668, 1960, 2087, 2221, 2413, 2419, 2856-2863, 3066, 3323, 3579, 3605, 3646
Ambrosia, 2361
Amende honorable, 2362
America, 1489, 1593, 3462; in the early nineteenth century, 2030
American, 618, 1168, 1435, 1590, 1740, 2038
Ammunition, 271
Amphibious, 1021
Amplifier, 1408, 1488
Amusement, 732, 3231, 4029
Amusing definitions, 1752-1963
Anaesthetic, 711, 993
Ancestors, 197, 730, 1175, 1480, 1910, 2992, 3118, 3121-3123, 3567
Anchor, 819
Ancient, 2088
Andersen, Hans Christian, 2108, 2252, 2308
Angels, 209, 422, 1020, 2093, 2255, 2911, 3431, 3523, 3528, 3685, 3751
Anger, 292, 460, 1520, 2445, 2602, 2606, 2681, 2808, 2881, 2894, 2929, 2931, 3124, 3605, 3812
Anglin, Margaret, 2049
Angry, 292, 460, 2681
Anguish, 2104
Animal, 1137, 1275, 1315, 1382, 1475, 1867, 1903, 2292, 2450, 2983
Anniversary, 305, 1029, 2891
Anonymous, 897
Answer, 290, 328, 622, 897, 1901, 2602, 3993
Ant, 806, 2592, 2632
Antagonism, 3253
Antagonist, 2491
Anticipation, 1143, 2864-2866
Antique, 1446, 1662, 2122; collector's song, definition of, 1761
Antoninus, Marcus Aurelius, 3904, 3906-3907
Antony, Marc, 1861
Antonyms, use of, 120
Anvil, 1515
Anxieties, 3220
Apartment, 175, 355, 1453; house bonds, definition of, 1762
Apollo, 2365, 2378, 2438, 2440
Apology, 2362, 3443

Apparel, 3801
Appearance, 690, 692, 1023, 2756, 2870, 2889, 3011, 3451, 3761
Appendicitis and tonsillitis, definition of, 1763
Appendix, 1805
Appetite, 2087, 2990, 3718
Applause, 1668, 3860
Apple, 154, 182, 550, 2367, 2622
Applesauce, 1481, 1695
Application, 101, 3333, 3979, 4030, 4034
Appointment, 760
Appreciation, 313, 1151, 2409, 2867-2868, 3177
Apprehension, 2864-2866
Appropriate, 444
Appropriations, 1641
Approval, 2868, 3582
April, 2194
Apron, 481
Apron-strings, 1432
Arabs, 2140
Arc, Joan of, 95, 814
Archaic, 828
Archer, 1824
Architect, 589, 805
Arctic, 340
Argonauts, 2368
Argue, 1372, 2391
Argument, 864, 1243, 1246, 2001, 2491, 3851, 3937, 3998, 4000
Argus-eyed, 2369
Aristocracy, 3981
Aristotle, 2391, 2501, 3046, 3054, 3129, 3502, 3571, 3618, 3631
Arithmetic, 237, 479, 482, 528, 1194, 1679
Ark, Noah's, 814, 884
Armageddon, 2372
Armor, 1623, 3746
Army, 186, 271, 284, 309, 485, 570, 597, 618, 634, 716, 724, 745, 764, 767, 771, 889, 1062, 1066, 1123, 1125, 1132, 1152, 1866, 2089, 2154, 2411
Arnold, Matthew, 3049, 3940
Arrogance, 3775
Arrow, 2351, 2357
Art, 471, 1435, 1437, 1620, 1651, 3397, 3527, 3581, 3587, 3622, 3706, 3776, 3881
Artist, 471, 2424
Artistic, 2090
Ashes, 1361
Ask, 2684, 2695, 3615
Askelon, 2552
Aspiration, 2857-2863
Aspirin, 1086
Ass, 2492, 2645
Asset, 1343, 2005
Assistance, 1220, 2509
Assumption, 1934, 2391
Asthma, 1551
Astonishment, 3685
Astronomy, 440
Atheism, 354, 3730
Atherton, Gertrude, 1974
Athlete, 1266, 1316, 1758, 1760
Atom, 1455
Attainment, 2819-2831, 3302, 3535, 4037
Attention, 327, 2450, 3481, 3593, 4038
Attorneys (see Lawyers)
Attraction, 2090
Attractive, 834
Audience, 1606, 2010

Augeas, 2404
August, 1667
Author, 191, 372, 425, 578, 1051, 2969, 4041-4048
Authority, 2422, 2702
Autograph, 890
Automobile, 159, 163, 246, 267, 273, 275, 322, 326, 331, 339, 351, 356, 374, 426, 475, 490, 497, 500, 525, 545-546, 548, 560, 639, 655, 670, 673, 679, 698, 704, 709, 714, 728, 735, 765, 786, 821-823, 853, 855, 888, 890, 896, 909, 914, 940, 968, 1110, 1139, 1168, 1170, 1208, 1248-1250, 1317, 1342, 1404, 1485, 1513, 1582, 1639, 1656, 1683, 1764, 1781, 1850, 1905, 1947
  definition of, 1764
Autumn, 2086, 2091, 2110, 2242
Avarice, 2479, 2803, 3323, 3422, 3605
Avenge, 2771
Aversion, 2893, 3671-3679
Aviation, 982, 1184
Awake, 777
Awkward, 1036, 1132, 2051
Axe, 2666

B

Baal, 2554
Baby, 344, 365, 372, 379, 384, 413, 646, 797, 1131, 1487, 2511
Babylon, 2652
Bacchus, 2381
Bachelor, 159, 380, 523, 626, 630, 927, 1037, 1765, 2200, 3608; definition of, 1765; of Arts, 1587
Back, 1659
Bacon, 1823; Francis, 1983, 2844-2845, 3051, 3187, 3210, 3359, 3416, 3437, 3624, 3708, 3712, 3714, 3730, 3789, 3970, 4001
Bad, 3711; habit, 1672; man, 1664; sign, 1514
Bagatelle, 2382
Baggage, 661
Bait, 3868
Balance, 987, 2656
Bald, 468, 614, 2167
Balfour, Earl Arthur James, 2008
Balloon, 1618
Balzac, Honore de, 2225, 2249, 2278, 2284, 2293, 2309, 2315
Banana, 1962, 2168; oil, 1803
Bancroft, George, 1968
Band, 491
Banishment, 3826
Bank, 1007, 1104, 1189, 1718; check, 199, 214; notes, 2101; officer, 1957
Banker, 551, 580; responsibility of, 82
Banking, 509, 739
Bankroll, 1507
Bankrupt, 214, 221, 325, 431, 1882
Banquo, 2148
Baptist, 334
Bar, 665
Barbarians, 3969
Barbarism, 3745
Barber, 187, 255, 468, 750, 831, 944, 1034, 1381, 1572
Bargain, 275; sale, 1766
Bark, 540, 1745, 2267
Barkis, 2386
Barnum, 1319

Barrel, 1197
Barren, 1532
Barrie, Sir James Matthew, 4031
Baseball, 755, 798, 1168, 1712, 1954, 2304
Bashful, 2052, 3502
Bath, 312, 594, 603, 720, 818, 945
Bathing, 424, 860
Bathtub, 549, 603
Battle, 2286, 2352, 2360, 2372, 2569, 2639, 2960
Bay, 2292
Bayonet, 2157
Beach, 637, 2059
Beans, 1064, 1499
Bear, 226
Bearing, 3596
Beast, 2189, 2310, 2414, 3760
Beatitudes, 2668-2677
Beautiful, 188, 308, 1374, 1471, 2053-2054, 2113, 2255, 2367, 2432
Beauty, 1767, 1824, 1975, 2017, 2414, 2416, 2633, 2869-2871, 2978, 2999, 3001, 3555, 3660, 3776; definition of, 1767; parlor, 1431
Bed, 1349, 1583, 1669, 1955
Bedroom, 644
Bee, 398, 1011, 2149
Beersheba, 2495
Beg, 329, 349, 366, 648, 2391
Beggar, 2389
Begin, 2356, 2524, 2824
Beginner's luck, 1768
Beguile, 1661
Behavior, 1780, 2870, 3274
Behind, 899
Belial, 2468
Belief, 2734-2735, 2759, 2785, 2965, 3096-3105, 3243, 3277
Bell, 2096, 2228, 2394, 2407, 3892
Belligerent, 2505
Belling, 2394
Bellows, 1515, 2241
Belshazzar, 2395
Benefits, 3160, 3181
Benevolence, 3177-3181, 3414, 3973
Bennett, James Gordon, 2013
Bent, 1055, 2055
Bernhardt, Sarah, 2048
Berries, 1293
Best, 2678; seller, 1578
Bestow, 2784, 3177-3181
Bet, 369, 433, 1997
Betrayal, 3775
Better, 1311; half, 1472
Bible, 476, 1169, 2350, 2356, 2372, 2384, 2395-2396, 2498, 2506, 2509, 2520, 3521, 3533, 3738-3741, 4020
Bicycle, 850
Big, 169, 893; game hunter, 1769
Bigamy, 920, 1067
Bigot, 289
Bigotry, 1067
Bill, 842, 861, 970, 1156, 1261, 1286, 1733, 1919, 1921, 2009
Billboard, 396, 655
Billiards, 598
Biography, use of in speeches, 93
Biologist, 1219
Bird, 1565, 1901, 2169, 2280, 2291, 2590, 3371
Birth, 3567; control, 1966
Birthday, 397, 408, 794

Birthright, 2520
Bishop, 145, 210
Biting, 752
Bitterness, 3241, 3246, 3293, 3598, 3826
Black, 2056
Blame, 959, 2498
Bleed, 3837
Blessed, 2559, 2574, 2668-2677, 2765; event, 1770
Blessedness, 3794
Blessings, 2921, 3218, 3662
Blindness, 95, 127, 1731, 2715, 3095, 3463, 3510, 3584, 4020
Bliss, 1487, 3244
Block, 1771
Blonde, 2053
Blondes, 207, 630
Blood, 787, 1427, 2530; pressure, 1211
Blotter, 1772
Bluff, 871
Blunder, 2517, 2824, 3155, 3493-3496
Board, 1576; mortar, 844
Boarding house, 1412; school, 1773
Boast, 197, 432, 438, 490, 505, 1175, 1206, 2613, 2623, 2627, 3262
Boaster, 1314
Boat, 678
Boccaccio, Giovanni, 1983
Body, 911, 2277, 2778, 3324, 3424, 3666
Body of the speech: writing, 40; five rules for preparing: begin with subject audience agrees on, 53; do not argue, but explain, 54; know the subject, 41; state briefly points to be discussed, 57; use facts, figures and illustrations, 45
Bok, Edward, 2007
Bold, 559, 2628, 3220, 3954
Bolt, 573
Bonanza, 2399
Bonaparte, Napoleon (see Napoleon)
Bonds, 1466, 1679, 1762
Bone, 935
Books, 1578, 1978, 2643, 2843, 3051, 3311, 3364, 3392, 3395-3398, 3474, 3706-3717, 3740, 3743, 3776, 4044
Bookworm, 1015
Boom, 1017
Booth, telephone, 804
Borah, William E., 2014
Bore, 156, 222, 287, 722, 1210, 1394, 1704, 1928, 2447, 3823, 3890
Born, 2234
Borrow, 1031, 1179, 2572, 2684, 3680
Borrower, 2616, 3556
Boss, 409, 452, 481, 588, 597, 602, 875, 905, 1963
Boswell, James, 1990
Bottom, 1734
Bottoms up, 1774
Bough, 3392
Bountifulness, 3304
Bourgeois, 2522
Bow, 1626, 2357
Box, 2393
Boxer, 517
Boy, 169, 348, 532, 721, 731, 1490, 1679, 1780, 1789, 2436
Boycott, 1818
Bradstreet, 850

Brag, 231, 417, 490, 492, 1175, 1206, 1295, 3262
Braggart, 1689
Brains, 252, 280, 284, 391, 394, 418, 1256, 1373, 1703, 1867, 2831, 3475, 3870
Brake, 2012
Brandeis, Louis D., 2001
Brandy, 761
Bravery, 533, 2959-2968, 2995, 3113
Bread, 892, 1584, 2526, 2534, 2545, 2639, 2641, 2667, 2696, 3392; lines, 1337
Breakfast, 664
Breeding, 3923
Brethren, 2731
Brevity, 2872-2873
Brick, 460
Bride, 338, 365, 454, 462, 487, 569, 611, 848, 999, 1014, 1059, 1142, 1421, 1424, 1948, 2155
Bridegroom, 330, 400, 487, 611, 1059, 1142, 1424
Bridesmaids, 1424
Bridge, 1082, 1278, 1280, 1469, 2054, 2492; definition of, 1775
Brief, 293, 472
Bright, 2092
Brilliant, 2114, 3813
Broadmindedness, 1369, 1657, 3438
Broke, 709, 1435, 1677
Broker, 923
Broncho, 2181
Brooding, 3820
Brook, 2078, 2118, 2283, 2575
Brooks, Phillips, 2883, 3668
Brother, 1163, 1183, 2528, 2587, 2681
Browning, Elizabeth B., 2177, 2272; Robert, 2270, 2857, 3002, 3602
Bryant, William Cullen, 2283, 2294, 3545, 3943
Bubble, 2514
Bucket, 2656
Budget, 185, 653, 838, 1031, 1290
Buffalo, 1135, 1557
Buffer state, 1776
Build, 2701, 2585
Buildings, 805, 1671
Bull, 2051, 2491; Ole, 2013
Bulwer (see Lytton, Edward Bulwer)
Buncombe, 2403
Bungalow, 1004
Bunk, 1669, 2403
Bunyan, John, 3178, 3490
Buoyant, 712
Burbank, Luther, 3575
Burden, 2580, 3271, 3412, 3421
Burglar, 342, 519, 880, 1035
Burke, Edmund, 1990, 3205-3206, 3355, 3362, 3716
Burn, 2067, 2626, 2755
Burns, Robert, 3456
Burnt-offering, 981
Bury, 2704
Bus, 414, 723
Bushel, 2680
Business, 55, 84, 431, 446, 640, 820, 922, 994, 1212, 1289, 1501, 1777, 1915, 2617, 2874-2878, 3328, 3374, 4036
Businessman, 72, 1493, 1579
Busy, 412, 702, 1778, 1887
Butcher, 255, 2009
Butter, 608, 1881, 2579

Butterfly, 876
Button, 324
Buyer, 2613
Byron, Lord George Gordon, 1991, 2127, 2134, 2265, 2976, 3418, 3457, 3514, 3557, 3561, 3630, 3823, 3830, 3890, 3901

C

CCC, 1679
Caddy, 378, 477, 638, 696, 840, 1071
Cadence, 133-138
Cadmean, 2397
Caesar, 2722; definition of, 1779; Julius, 134, 2437; render unto, 2722
Cake, 611, 828, 882, 2132
Calamity, 3171, 3490-3491, 3726, 3999
Calendar, 824
Caliber, 1619
California, 266, 490, 850, 1948
Call, 2576, 2721
Calm, 2093, 3222
Calumny, 3110, 3193-3196, 3797, 3899
Calvin, John, 1985
Camel, 2719, 2724
Camera, 189, 925, 1524
Camp, 1213
Campaign, 1536, 1589
Campaigner, 1359
Cancel, 294
Candid, 537, 3155-3156
Candidates, 170, 1536, 2513
Candle, 2680
Candor, 908
Candy, 236, 651
Cannibal, 499, 748
Canoe, 1780
Can-opener, 1857, 1887, 1948
Cap, 2407
Capable, 427
Capacity, 4034
Capital, 780, 1326, 3214, 3338
Capitalist, 1366
Car, 1249-1250, 1342, 1404, 1416, 1420, 1434, 1485, 1582, 1639, 1656
Cards, 1865, 2044
Care, 2273
Career, 425
Careful, 869, 1643, 1781
Careless, 868, 1183, 1190
Cares, 3818, 3932-3933
Cargo, 1368
Carlos of Portugal, 2035
Carlyle, Thomas, 2934, 2977, 3009, 3031, 3044, 3266, 3364, 3385, 3528, 3612, 3726, 3744, 3757, 3796, 4039
Carnal, 2767
Carnegie, Andrew, 3780
Carpenter, 1759, 1773
Carriage, 1977
Carving, 1105
Cash, 1147
Cash surrender value, 1756
Cashier, 987
Cassandra, 2365
Cat, 251, 1087, 1166, 1188, 1592, 2076, 2394, 2502, 3626
Catacomb, 2224
Caterpillar, 876
Cathay, 2913

Cathedral, 274
Cato, the Censor, 3160, 3194, 3235, 3817
Cause, 2681, 2962, 3026, 3497, 3532
Caustic, 179
Cautious, 473, 1177, 1343, 2060
Caviar, 2409
Celebrate, 856, 2482
Celebrity, 3112-3116, 3574
Celestial, 3845
Cellophane, 919
Cement, 844
Cemetery, 232, 671, 1018, 2029, 2031-2032, 2081, 2481
Censor, 2816, 3061
Census, 2919
Centaur, 2408
Centenarian, 1782
Cerberus, 2420
Certainty, 3393, 3574, 4001
Cervantes, Miguel de, 2884, 2889, 3482, 3616, 3727, 3979, 4045
Chaff, 2071, 3710
Chain, 2109, 3976
Chairman, 212, 287, 672, 803
Challenge, 475, 2829
Chamber of commerce, 1017
Chance, 930, 1069, 2639, 3041, 3151-3154, 3860
Change, 2377, 2780, 2834, 2998, 3153, 3409, 3549
Changeless, 2094
Chaos, 589
Character, 35-36, 183, 1299, 1520, 1703, 1984-1985, 2145, 2879-2903, 2937-2943, 3016, 3110, 3204, 3240, 3309, 3346, 3373, 3507, 3521, 3748
Charge, 758, 778, 1173
Charity, 1487, 1668, 2032, 2410, 2630, 2684-2685, 2697, 2730-2731, 2765, 2768, 2772, 2781, 2784-2786, 2788, 2801, 2804, 2936, 3399, 3412, 3416, 3636
Charles I., 1976
Charles V., 1980
Charm, 2414, 3847
Charybdis, 2423
Chasten, 2807
Chastity, 4020
Chatterton, Thomas, 1991
Chaucer, Geoffrey, 1983, 2096, 3693
Chauffeur, 580, 930
Chauvinist, 2505
Cheap, 862, 2520, 3335
Cheat, 433, 455, 1072, 1099, 2410, 3442
Check, 403, 661, 1007, 1925
Cheek, 2683
Cheerful, 2603, 2768, 2838, 3181, 3246
Cheer-leader, 1061, 1218, 1855
Cheers, 1558
Cheese, 518, 608, 1696, 1863
Chef, 190, 1058
Chemistry, 207, 276
Chess, 200, 898
Chest, 2371
Chesterfield, Lord, 1975
Chew, 3712
Chewing gum, 983, 2302
Chic dresser, 1684
Chickens, 158, 254, 277, 295, 470, 503, 700, 775, 809, 826, 867, 906, 911, 957, 1089, 1367, 2193
Chief, 2506

Child, 1432, 1896, 2093, 2097, 2240, 2244-2245, 2284, 2615, 2787
Childhood, 609, 614, 857, 932, 935, 953, 2095
Children, 77, 84, 361, 443, 784, 876, 999, 1006, 1012, 1041, 1138, 1157, 1214-1215, 1407, 1453, 1486, 1686, 1978, 2042, 2418, 2586, 2674, 2735-2736, 2796, 2904-2909, 3052, 3119, 3519-3521, 3525, 3570, 3608, 3751, 3992
Chilly, 1649
Chimney, 1973
Chinese, 793, 893
Chiropodist, 537; definition of, 1784
Chivalry, 429
Choate, Joseph, 2011; Rufus, 2037
Choice, 316, 366, 1094, 2035, 2425, 2486, 2491, 2614, 2910-2911
Chosen, 2721
Christ, Jesus, 95, 2350, 2356, 2481, 2658, 2703-2704, 2709, 2730-2731, 2736, 2749-2750, 2752
Christen, 797
Christian, 1596
Christianity, 1729, 1741, 2920, 3007-3008, 3726-3752, 3970
Christmas, 225, 362, 901, 1261, 1292-1294; Carol, 2478
Church, 22, 302, 334, 652, 833, 1065, 1095, 1144, 1318, 1640, 3029, 3533, 3752
Churchill, Winston S., 85, 137, 1974, 2875
Churchyard, 2274
Cicero, 3142, 3227, 3274, 3477, 3494, 3544, 3699, 3845; essentials of public speaking outlined by, 1
Cigar, 240, 1837, 1972
Cigarettes, 1361
Cincinnatus, 2411
Cipher, 1546
Circe, 2414
Circle, 1380, 2483
Circumstances, 2892, 3023, 3093, 3445
Circus, 1078, 2151, 2278
Citizen, 1290, 3360, 3529
City, 666, 1018, 1093, 1671, 2679, 2919, 2998
Civilization, 125, 1642, 2069, 2912-2920, 3054, 3103, 3186, 3223, 3291, 3363, 3424, 3429-3459, 3462, 3553, 3764, 3772, 3805
Civilized, 1529, 1725
Claim, 707
Classes, 3339, 3822; of society, 1352
Classics, 3395, 4043
Clauses, use in groups, 133-135
Claws, 2170
Clay, 2127, 2657
Clay, Henry, 2004, 2010
Clean, 603, 626, 709, 2937
Cleanliness, 2725
Clear, 1045, 1053, 2096
Clemens, Samuel, 1964, 1994, 2018
Clever, 1910, 2363, 2377, 3435, 3813, 3861
Cliché, 2523
Cliff, 703
Climber, 2060
Clippers, 831
Clock, 337, 708, 725, 973, 1886, 3901; alarm, 1889
Clod, 2142
Close, 1050
Cloth, 2111, 2459, 2705
Clothe, 2618
Cloud, 2211, 2217, 2623
Club, 2405; secretary, 1785

Coach, 1316, 1827
Coal, 149, 2056, 2626
Coat, 324, 1903-1904
Cobb, Irving S., 2121, 2139, 2193
Cobs, 1580
Code of conduct for employees of Carson, Pirie, Scott & Company, Chicago, 2027
Coed, 1088, 1790, 1810
Coffee, 429, 777, 1237
Coincidence, 356
Colchis, 2368
Cold, 244, 335, 340, 506, 541, 1115, 1171, 1177, 1649, 1754, 3755; feet, 1786
Coleridge, Samuel Taylor, 2195, 2985, 3272, 3522, 3558, 3881, 3942, 4006
Collar-button, 261, 1242
Collateral, 551
Collect, 1195, 1919, 2126
Collection, 1195
Collector, 616, 900, 1806
College, 417, 434, 557, 590, 734, 779, 837, 1088, 1103, 1148, 1185, 1217, 1223, 1330, 1346, 1348, 1389, 1543, 1584, 1587, 1621, 1642, 1679, 1737, 1904, 1912, 3055; definition of, 1787; English department, 1788; football team, 1789; graduates, 1348; mixer, 1790; professor, 1309; senior, 1791
Collision, 436, 1317, 1707
Color, 262, 291, 1139; scheme, 1424
Colt, 2307
Colton, Charles Caleb, 3061, 3065, 3079, 3171, 3231-3232, 3324, 3652, 3685, 3742, 3850, 3960, 4046, 4052
Comet, 2062
Comfort, 822, 2570, 2669, 2836, 2944-2946, 3433, 3664, 3772, 3835
Comfortable, 1216
Comforter, 2498
Comic strips, 1458
Comma, 1788, 2049
Commencement de la fin, 2524
Commend, 2750, 3159, 3654-3659
Commendable, 1642
Commence, 350
Commission, 729
Commodities, 3214
Common sense, 12, 2921-2922, 3316, 3465, 4006
Commonplace, 2925, 3470-3472
Communion, 3545
Communism, 50, 1366
Communities, 3535, 3785
Companionable, 2076
Companions, 2980-2981, 2983, 3157-3166, 3282, 3715, 3719, 3827
Company, 1363, 1493, 1495
Comparison, 903, 936
Compassion, 2742, 2811, 3412
Compel, 2449
Compensation, 568
Competence, 565, 2816-2818
Competition, 591, 706, 1112, 1250, 1357, 1573, 2433
Complaint, 892, 1843, 1935, 3479, 3681
Compliment, 955, 1555, 2041, 3654-3659
Compositions, 1675
Compromise, 2410
Compunctions, 3010
Conceit, 227, 432, 533, 2493, 2624-2625, 2770, 2781, 2923-2930, 3623, 3924
Concentration, 3698

Concert, 870
Concertina, 2139
Concerto, 1998
Concise, 157, 2872-2873
Conclusion, 982, 1667, 1934; of the speech: climax, 60-62; seven methods of concluding: ask for some form of action, 79; compliment the audience, 73; describe a great event, 76; develop a grand climax, 70; outline points, 63; tell a humorous story, 83; use a quotation, 64; writing, 59
Concrete, 844
Condescend, 2770
Condolence, 2944-2946
Conduct, 2931-2936, 3229, 3897
Conductor, street car, 1936
Conference, 997, 3714
Confession, 1268
Confidence, 401, 3328, 3959
Conflict, 630, 2990
Conformity, 2981
Confucius, 2312, 3220, 3687, 3768, 3770, 3814
Confuse, 1130, 2477
Congenial, 1665
Congratulations, 416
Congregate, 1195
Congregation, 1095, 1195
Congressman, 924
Connections, 1744
Conquer, 3063, 3550
Conqueror, 3414
Conscience, 36, 183, 1608, 1908, 1917, 2247, 2937-2943, 3006, 3267; definition of, 1792
Conscientious, 756
Conscious, 3757
Consecration, 2976
Consequences, 1786, 2354, 2649, 2975
Conservation, 1193
Consider, 2574, 2592, 2692
Considerate, 357
Consolation, 1525, 2944-2946
Conspicuous, 783
Constitution, 1267, 2379
Construction, 3487
Contagious, 2097
Contaminate, 2779
Contemporaries, 3232
Contempt, 2931, 3130, 3578
Content, 1275, 2739, 2803
Contentious, 2626
Contentment, 1233, 1496, 2800, 2947-2950, 3978
Contingencies, 3042
Continuous, 494
Contractor, 1150
Contradict, 670, 2660, 2965, 3708
Contrast, 927; use of, 123
Contributions, 210, 886, 1095, 1283, 1318, 1379
Control, 2894, 2967, 3194, 3718
Convenient, 796, 858
Convention, 1798
Conversation, 181, 625, 1231, 1910, 2951-2958, 3006, 3330, 3474, 3829, 3950
Conviction, 1254, 1627, 3340, 3585
Cook, 427
Cooking, 376, 380, 626, 632, 663, 848, 981, 1014, 1022, 1077, 1843, 1933
Coolidge, Calvin, 2067, 4034
Cooperation, 322, 628
Copying, 718, 3802
Copyright laws, 1340

Cordelia, 2417
Cork, 2298
Corn, 705, 935, 965, 1153, 1580, 1840, 2547
Corpuscle, 753
Correct, 561, 585, 1165, 1182
Corrupt, 2468, 2688, 2700, 2711, 3424, 3786
Cortez, Hernando, 1976
Cosmetic, 772, 1258, 1676, 1810
Cosmopolitan, 2062
Cost accounting, 1043; of living, 1415
Cottages, 3029
Cotton, 1147, 1530
Cough, 311
Counsel, 2578, 2923, 3437, 3835
Counsellor, 2595
Countenance, 2603, 3467
Counterfeit, 1794
Countless, 2099
Country, 666, 909, 1320, 1456, 1530
Coup d'état, 2435; de grace, 2431
Courage, 1199, 1238, 1254, 2364, 2959-2968, 2995, 3175, 3321
Court, 228, 269, 421, 2037, 2100
Courteous, 1016
Courtesy, 1636
Courtship, 346
Covenant, 2371, 2655
Cover charge, 829
Covet, 2544, 3512, 3912
Cow, 393, 399, 471, 685, 707, 743, 983, 1039, 1043, 1077, 1085, 1133, 1153, 1194, 1275, 1287, 1549, 1793
Cowardice, 1096, 2939, 2995, 3092, 3107, 3816
Cowboy, 2181
Cowhide, 1793
Cowper, William, 3298, 3944
Crab, 420, 510, 2135
Cradle-sheet, 2294
Cramp, 145, 355
Crazy, 446, 1325
Cream, 858, 1043
Create, 2828, 2969-2971, 3397, 3535
Creation, 825, 1540, 4009
Creator, 2642
Creature, 2802
Credit, 250, 560, 569, 852, 947, 1072, 1147
Creditor, 727, 1673
Crew, 1774
Crib, 2645
Crime, 1750, 2482, 2972-2976, 3115, 3361
Crisp, 2101
Critic, 1331, 1808, 2102
Criticism, 1988, 2021, 2071, 2366, 2868, 2977-2983
Croak, 1828
Crockett, David, 1995
Crocodiles, 1052
Croesus, 2421
Crook, 1234, 1751, 1828, 1911
Crooked dough, 1794
Crop, 795, 965, 2919
Croquette, 1403
Cross, 3736; bar, 1469; examination, 781, 1134
Crow, 2456
Crowd, 474, 1588, 1891
Crowded, 662, 1510
Crown, 954, 2597, 2605
Crucifixion, 2290, 2749-2750
Crumble, 2050
Crust, 610, 632, 1492, 1695

Cry, 1939, 2104
Cud, 983
Cultivation, 3322
Culture, 3049
Cunning, 2105, 2588, 2959, 3714
Cup-bearer, 2436
Cupid, 513
Curb, 1888
Cure, 850, 1630, 1867
Curiosity, 1138, 2984-2985
Curious, 905, 1140
Curse, 2630
Custom, 2948, 3706, 3917-3919
Cycles, 1380
Cyclone, 2069, 2144
Cynic, 1518
Cynicism, 2080, 3099, 3435

D

Dad, 1217, 1330, 1346, 1940
Damage, 660, 1133, 1719
Damn, 3658
Damocles, 2439, 3378
Dampness, 549
Danaides, 2392
Danaus, 2392
Dance, 537, 818, 1036, 1531, 1895
Dandelion, 490
Danger, 1560, 1795, 2423, 2439, 2962, 2966, 3253, 3314, 3437
Dangerous surgical operation, 1795
Dante, Alighieri, 1983
Daring, 2967
Dark ages, 2444
Darkness, 2106, 2385, 2754, 3095, 3556-3560, 3572
Darrow, Clarence, 1966
Dates, 1790
Daughter, 203, 524, 636, 1279, 1978, 2384, 2663, 2763, 4015
David, 2553
Dawn, 2117, 2128, 2201
Day, 1230, 2095, 2134, 2138, 2152, 2185, 2235, 2556-2557, 2627, 2774, 3518, 3555, 3559-3560, 3818, 3893, 3895, 3905, 3922
Daylight, 3888
Days, 2583
Deacon, 1596
Dead, 671, 677, 875, 1093, 1255, 1667, 2107, 2111, 2638, 2704, 2751
Deadly, 1733
Deaf, 488, 1381, 3463; and dumb couple, 1796
Deal, 881
Death, 195, 307, 405, 1156, 1184, 1276, 1615, 1628, 2082, 2084, 2161, 2202, 2225, 2236, 2269, 2290, 2387, 2431, 2446, 2570, 2655, 2750, 2767, 2814, 2821, 2879, 2986-3010, 3052, 3071, 3100, 3114, 3195, 3356, 3377, 3382, 3388, 3393, 3406, 3496, 3549, 3651, 3740, 3759, 3778, 3788, 3809, 3818, 3830, 3940, 3943-3944, 3971-3972, 4049
Debate, 418, 2621
Debt, 169, 250, 640, 1004, 1033, 1826, 2988, 3044, 3693
Debtor, 727
Decay, 2215
Deceit, 341, 2633, 2795
December, 1010
Deception, 2375, 2377, 2725, 3011-3015

Decision, 130, 3016-3017, 3995
Decisive, 2431, 2435, 2437
Decline, 2444, 3396
Decorated, 533
Deed, 2731
Deeds, 2700, 2754, 2896, 2976, 3123, 3800
Deep, 2131, 2576
Deer, 463
Defamation, 3797
Defeat, 869, 1302, 2286, 3026
Defeated politician, 1797
Defendant, 1134, 1854
Defense savings stamps, 1718
Deference, 3582
Deficiencies, 4037
Definition, 503, 573, 627, 642, 661, 703-704, 706, 727, 734, 780, 859, 920, 961, 1021, 1153
Definitions, humorous, 1752-1963
De Foe, Daniel, 1983
Deformity, 2928
Degree, 737, 1587
Delay, 282, 917, 1678
Delayed, 917
Delegate at large, 1798
Deliberation, 2845
Delicate, 2108
Delicatessen, 462, 1431, 1799
Delights, 2866, 3717
Deliverance, 2571, 3079
Deluge, 2354
Delusion, 3362
Democracy, 71, 2022, 3200, 3981
Democrat, 584
Demosthenes, 123
Denomination, 1718
Dentist, 261, 555, 581, 607, 760, 846, 895, 1809; definition of, 1800
Department store, 1180
Dependent, 835
Depew, Chauncey M., 2006, 2041
Deported, 518
Depression, 1017, 1670, 1682, 1706, 1801, 3820; definition of, 1801
Depth, 2887, 3832, 3854
Desert, 3696
Deserter, 437
Design, 3012
Desire, 1634, 1711, 1739, 2984, 3000, 3040, 3095, 3276, 3499, 3650, 3773, 3793
Desolate, 2081, 3825
Despair, 2469, 3759
Desperation, 1571
Dessert, 521
Destiny, 1023, 2521, 2607, 3240, 3646, 3930
Destroy, 2474, 2502, 2599, 2604, 2666, 2698
Detail, 782, 909, 1988
Detective, 963, 1952
Determination, 676, 3018-3025
Detour, 1231, 1802
Deviation, 2935
Devil, 741, 2410, 2974, 2977, 3073, 3075, 3450
Devotion, 3663
Devour, 2737
Diagnose, 674-675, 1128
Diamond, 314, 346
Diary, 3363
Dickens, Charles, 2101, 2262, 2266, 2281, 2322, 2478, 2504, 2507, 2898
Dictators, 65, 800
Didoes, 2427

Die, 2234, 2557, 2654, 2775, 2789, 2797
Diet, 943, 1341, 1358, 1374, 1475, 1748, 3468
Difference, 666, 775, 1016, 1094, 1102
Different, 576, 579, 677, 815-816, 2003
Difficult, 529, 785, 2401, 2412, 2515, 2598, 2748, 2837, 3168, 3250-3253, 3863
Dig, 2640
Digest, 633, 3712, 3716
Dignity, 2113, 2940
Dilemma, 2491
Diligence, 2617, 2768
Dillingham, Charles, 1997
Dining, 1678
Dinner, 151, 157, 270, 462, 467, 470, 484, 544, 1279, 1367, 1442, 1883, 1900
Diogenes, Laertius, 716, 2080, 2508, 3040, 3046, 3317
Diploma, 978, 1348
Diplomat, definition, 1803
Diplomatic, 383, 566, 866, 961, 1172, 1971, 2000, 3037, 3467
Direction, 782, 3690
Directness, 1231
Dirty, 860
Disadvantage, 762
Disappointment, 2188, 2355, 2899, 3264
Disaster, 2834-2843
Discipline, 2902, 3047, 3521
Disconcerting, 1606
Discontent, 3798
Discord, 2367
Discourage, 84, 2469
Discovery, 2462, 3593, 3621
Discretion, 830, 2964; definition of, 1804
Discussion, 1243, 1246, 1400, 2071, 2501
Disdain, 2929, 3646
Disease, 1328, 2918, 3324
Disengaged, 2043
Disgrace, 2485, 2997, 3003, 3780
Disguise, 3451
Dishes, 1351, 1883
Dishonest, 1750
Dishonesty, 3267
Dishonor, 2997
Dish-washing, 1076
Dislike, 1012, 1989, 3164
Disloyalty, 2899
Disobedience, 3809
Disorder, 2109, 2448, 2476
Displeased, 3852
Dispositions, 3229, 3248
Disputes, 2929, 2934
Disqualified, 812
Disraeli, Benjamin, 1965, 2911, 2916, 3056, 3067, 3108, 3202, 3318, 3334, 3445-3446, 3535, 3583, 3589, 3641, 3704, 3853, 3917, 4048
Disregard, 3194
Dissimulation, 3108
Dissipation, 3698
Distance, 3031
Distinction, 2429-2430
Distressed, 799
Disturb, 708
Ditch, 2715
Diversity, 3365
Divert, 2450
Dividends, 1842
Divineness, 3735, 3757, 3845
Divinity, 3182-3192

Divorce, 587, 697, 976, 1604, 1629, 1686, 2718
Doctor, 49, 165, 176, 194-195, 283, 361, 411, 428, 456, 467, 504, 549, 586, 589, 644, 650, 674-676, 737, 758, 861, 966, 1128, 1156, 1176, 1192, 1328, 1397, 1491, 1598, 1732, 1778, 1944, 1979, 3254; definition of, 1805
Doctrine, 1598, 2793
Dog, 355, 523, 540, 677, 726, 811, 918, 948, 1087, 1111, 1667, 2248, 2420, 2638, 2812; definition of, 1806
Dogmatic, 2929
Dogmeat, 2229
Doing, 3026-3032, 3862, 3880, 4024-4040
Doldrums, 2447
Dollar, 1318, 1378
Domestic service, 1746
Donations, 1379
Donkey, 570, 1241, 2440
Donnybrook Fair, 2448
Doorman, 1702
Doubt, 166, 1300, 3325, 3624, 4001
Doubtful, 1054
Dough, 1492, 1807
Doughnut, 836, 1869
Douglas, Stephen A., 2004
Dove, 2577
Down payment, 1423, 1445
Doyle, Sir A. Conan, 2135
Dragon, 2397-2398
Dragoon, 2449
Drakes, 2451
Drama, 239, 913
Dramatic critic, 1808
Draw, 1809
Drawer, 2145
Dream, 388, 1739, 2124, 2260, 2663, 2763, 2856, 3025, 3419, 3870
Dregs, 3377
Dress, 698, 1540, 1879, 1999
Drill, 1132, 1153
Drink, 512, 933, 2494, 2612, 2654, 2744, 2789
Driven, 2110
Driver, 322, 326, 331, 351, 356, 374, 475, 525, 639, 655, 657, 673, 679, 765, 821, 823, 896, 914, 995, 1044, 1170, 1208, 1317, 1452, 1640, 1643, 1723, 1764, 1781, 1905
Drought, 583
Drowning, 1114, 1160
Drowsy, 2618
Drug store, 1576
Druggist, 467
Drugs, 411, 1504
Drum, 225, 2154
Drunkard, 3492
Dryden, John, 3028, 3262, 3280, 3868, 3945, 3977
Duck, 270, 368, 1442, 1858
Ducks, 2451
Duel, 1893
Duet, 964
Dulcinea, 2452
Dull, 1344, 1915, 2932
Dumb, 415, 528, 839, 1353, 1479, 1494, 1796, 1810, 2131
Dummy, 1345
Dust, 1660, 2527, 2562, 2656
Duty, 2908, 3033-3038, 3214, 3632, 3782
Dwarfs, 3686
Dwell, 2650
Dyspepsia, 1155

E

Ear, 894, 1091, 1291, 1861, 1892, 2440, 2733, 2776
Earnestness, 3813
Earnings, 1506
Earth, 1270, 1467, 1945, 2529, 2548, 2556, 2634, 2670, 2678, 2738, 2783, 2883, 3558, 3617
Easy, 873, 967, 3168, 3239; payments, 1391, 1444
Eat, 147, 151, 157-158, 186, 270, 376, 429, 484, 486, 536, 649, 669, 751, 881, 1063, 1090, 1181, 1565, 1799, 1847, 2035, 2395, 2456, 2534, 2654, 2744, 2789, 3716
Ebb, 2232
Echo, 1392
Economic condition, 1286; question, 1470; theory, 1337
Economics, 1585, 1859, 2024
Economist, 509, 1690; definition of, 1811
Economy, 454, 496, 500, 663, 838, 964, 1159, 1470, 1777, 2025, 3039-3044, 3214, 4036
Edified, 2781
Edison, Thomas, 105, 1737
Editor, 204, 1429, 1482
Education, 28, 37, 77, 152, 162, 214, 237, 282, 285, 301, 328, 386, 417, 434, 450, 476, 575, 998, 1005, 1088, 1103, 1141, 1187, 1222-1223, 1239, 1337, 1348, 1462, 1587, 1679, 1730, 3045-3055, 3120, 3253, 3290, 3924; definition of, 1812
Educator, 1812
Edward, King, 2035
Effectiveness, 3350
Effeminate, 1743
Efficiency, 294, 416, 466, 944, 1180
Effort, 2443, 2868, 3173, 4040
Egg, 254, 451, 457, 503, 520, 751, 826, 867, 912, 1089, 1100, 1412, 1822, 1886, 2237, 2282
Ego, 1224
Egotism, 1503, 2923-2930, 3623, 3924
Egotist, 308, 1371, 1573-1574, 1618, 1689
Egypt, 2534
Einstein, Albert, 2015
El Dorado, 2457
Election, 170, 441, 741, 869, 872, 878, 1464, 1527, 1617, 1813, 2495
Electrician, 1001, 1011; definition of, 1814
Electricity, 32, 1592
Elegance, 3584
Elegy, Gray's, 1992
Elephant, 196, 561, 598, 651, 705, 1078, 1374, 1616, 1689, 1943; definition of, 1815
Elevator, 247, 1161, 1924
Eliminated, 563
Eliot, George, 2261, 2864, 2896, 2907, 2924, 2983, 2989, 3004, 3264, 3287, 3483, 3499, 3595, 3794, 3866, 4008
Eloquence, 85, 2226, 3056-3057
Elysium, 2387, 3244
Embarrassing, 144
Emerson, Ralph Waldo, 2824, 2833, 2859, 2874, 2881, 2919, 3019, 3045, 3165, 3174, 3233, 3253, 3342, 3386, 3498, 3702, 3705-3706, 3803, 3831, 3877, 3885, 3956, 3994
Emissary, 2386
Emotion, 2226
Emperors, 3201

Empires, 2998, 3054, 3422-3423
Employee, 198
Employment, 702, 1000, 3039, 3511
Emptiness, 3700
Emulation, 3579
End, 961, 2203, 2206, 2356, 2524, 2643, 2815
Endeavor, 3247, 3761
Endurance, 2364, 3525, 3612-3615, 3697
Endure, 2807
Enemy, 1062, 2620, 2685, 2772, 3058-3065, 3525, 3605, 3789, 3952
Energy, 2878, 3023
Engagement, 314, 464, 512-513, 564, 807, 1705
Engineer, 714, 1076, 1523
England, 1591, 3038
English, 1720, 1788
Englishman, 1253
Enjoyment, 3908, 4031
Ennui, 2159
Enough, 1063
Enterprise, 252
Enthusiasm, 3066-3068
Envy, 430, 2785, 2893, 3045, 3060-3061, 3116, 3605
Epictetus, 2819, 2828, 3252, 3596, 3606, 3623
Epicurean, 125
Epicurus, 2837, 3664, 3982
Epigram, 4041
Epitaph, 354, 671, 754, 2029, 2031-2032, 2041, 2993, 2997
Equality, 74, 115, 3069-3071, 3440, 3687
Error, 247, 365, 553, 612, 852, 941, 1164, 1816-1817, 1832, 1952, 2732, 2933, 3010, 3091, 3586, 3643, 3943; definition of, 1816
Erskine, Lord Henry, 1987
Erudition, 918
Esau, 2520, 2531
Escape, 1899
Eskimo, 1457
Essay, 1068
Estates, 1449, 1477, 2472, 3374
Eternity, 456, 3009, 3390, 3842, 3845-3846, 3894, 3911
Etiquette, 348, 1237, 1364, 1401
Eureka, 2462
Euripides, 2960, 3005, 3112, 3326, 3898
Europe, 2913
Eve, 550, 589, 1483
Evening, 2111, 2268
Everett, Edward, 2021
Everlasting, 2634, 2813
Evidence, 2806
Evil, 721, 1729, 2365, 2372, 2401, 2410, 2458, 2473, 2558, 2570, 2642, 2676, 2693, 2754, 2769, 2803, 2901, 2976, 3072-3080, 3130-3131, 3194, 3317, 3368, 3384, 3525, 3571, 3681, 3698, 3859, 3873, 3960, 3983
Evolution, 593, 968, 1540, 1874
Ewe, 567
Ex Cathedra, 2463
Exactness, 3183
Exaggeration, 3264, 3935
Exalt, 2601, 2723, 2857, 3066-3068
Exam, 1810
Examination, 779
Example, 244, 940, 3081-3088; definition of, 1818
Excel, 2433
Excellence, 2867, 3610, 3713
Exception, 872

Excess, 3416, 4052
Exchange, 384, 2497
Excitement, 789
Excuse, 1755, 2746, 3126, 3429
Executive, 1819, 3437; ability, 1819; college, 13
Exercise, 1266, 1324
Exertion, 4040
Exhaustion, 1502, 2272, 3202
Existence, 3418, 3747
Expand, 2232
Expectation, 2864-2866, 3389, 3717
Expedients, 3688
Expenses, 258, 985, 1272
Expensive, 534, 547, 621, 667, 791, 1027, 1158, 1214, 1713, 2409, 3043, 3335-3336
Experience, 527, 650, 978, 1264, 1304, 1339, 1391, 1714, 1923, 3089-3093, 3704
Experienced, 2057
Expert, 1872, 4039
Explanation, 627, 753
Exploring, 335, 1577, 1976
Exposure, 925
Expression, 2067, 3283, 3703
Extensiveness, 3334
Extravagance, 838, 915, 1185, 1502, 1603, 2354, 2747, 3489
Extreme, 1582, 2297
Eye, 256, 557, 941, 1163, 1397, 1659, 1833, 1880, 1913, 2114, 2115, 2117-2118, 2156, 2162, 2369, 2546, 2567, 2630, 2649, 2682, 2719, 2776, 3094-3095, 3410, 3461, 3563, 3584, 3661, 3846
Eyesight, 1954

F

F H A, 1679
Face, 292, 327, 2072-2074, 2120-2123, 2128, 2132, 2209, 2374-2375, 2526, 2648, 2889, 3686, 3798
Facilities, 1735
Faculties, 3848
Fade, 2256, 2659
Fail, 2786
Failings, 2979, 2981
Failure, 575, 1212, 1229, 1236, 1304, 1599, 1744, 1970, 2004, 2809, 2895, 3375, 3386, 4030, 4034
Faint, 2619, 2792
Faint-heartedness, 3151
Fair, 338, 2108, 2127-2128
Faith, 974, 1464, 1487, 1607, 1668, 2655, 2788, 2805-2806, 2809, 2814, 3092, 3096-3105, 3230, 3663, 3782
Faithful, 1820, 2425, 2434, 2727, 3007, 3015, 3728
Fall, 2604, 2640, 2715, 3409
Fallen, 2552, 2651-2652
False, 1598, 2543, 2623, 2676, 2699, 3375
Falsehood, 130, 3011-3015, 3037, 3092, 3101, 3106-3111, 3939
Fame, 1255, 3112-3116, 3574
Familiarity, 4042
Family, 596, 704, 708, 730, 825, 857, 1027, 1121, 1149, 1416, 1420, 2022, 2366, 3117-3123, 3212, 3463; wash, 1561
Famous, 360, 578, 1654
Fanaticism, 3101
Fancy, 3719, 3857

Fantastic, 2514, 2516
Fantasy, 3870
Fare, 1518, 1537
Farewell, 579
Farmer, 146, 158, 164, 189-190, 277, 319, 396, 398-399, 457, 503, 571, 685, 705, 743, 965, 983, 1030, 1039, 1046, 1100, 1133, 1189, 1241, 1275, 1549, 1821
Farming (see Farmer)
Farsighted, 1822
Fascinating, 2432
Fascination, 3298
Fashion, 717, 2657, 2780, 2916, 3801
Fast, 404, 542; liver, 1474
Fasting, 3468
Fat, 127, 150, 223, 802, 893, 934, 1565, 1622, 2011
Fate, 2826, 3054, 3153, 3184, 3464, 3646, 3664, 3930
Father, 77, 84, 174, 182, 201, 203, 220, 225, 243, 282, 301, 413, 419, 461, 463, 499, 587, 604, 695, 708, 816, 871, 916, 977, 980, 1019, 1023, 1121, 1163, 1199, 1261, 1330, 1307, 1591, 2392, 2506, 2594, 2749-2750, 3119, 3751; definition of, 1823; -in-law, 1154; of the Navy, 1971; Time, 1056
Fattening, 1240
Fault, 2826, 2980-2981, 3116, 3124-3128, 3158, 3164, 3166, 3484, 3757, 3916
Faultless, 2130
Faun, 2160
Favor, 1589, 2373, 2633, 2639
Favoritism, 2764
Fear, 1589, 2558, 2589, 2854, 2967, 2999, 3002, 3006, 3026, 3099, 3129-3134, 3220, 3262, 3571, 3793
Fearlessness, 3577
Feast, 2395
Feeble-minded, 1721
Feebleness, 3191
Feelings, 2131, 2891, 3592, 3835
Feet, 242, 323, 917, 1032, 1786, 2034, 2294
Fellow, 1273, 1333, 1335, 1515, 1574, 1927
Female, 1733; archer, 1823
Fence, 252, 1570, 2296
Fenders, 1518, 1664
Festival, 1144
Fidelity, 3590
Field, 2142, 2692; Eugene, 2258, 2297
Fight, 576, 2359-2360, 2364, 2448, 2502, 2549, 2805
Fighter, 1566
Figs, 2828
Figures, 2137
Filled, 2671
Finance, 369, 2514
Financial difficulties, 1204
Financier, 1742
Find, 2641, 2695, 2714, 3615
Finger-printing, 1486
Fingers, 2170, 3157
Finish, 2805
Fire, 177, 660, 972, 1541, 1611, 1719, 2133, 2156, 2186, 2393, 2626; department, 1719
Fired, 905
Fireman, 660, 1145, 1611
Fireplace, 2064
Firmament, 2222
Firmness, 3021
First, 2720

Fish, 42, 310, 394, 1009, 1021, 1295, 1343, 2076, 2183, 2207, 2465, 2912
Fishermen, 1450, 1602
Fishing, 278, 447, 514, 631, 635, 678, 752, 1169
Fiske, Minnie Maddern, 2049
Fit, 894
Fitzgerald, Edward, 3390-3394
Five-day-week, 1447
Flabby, 2136
Flagpole, 2055, 2060
Flail, 2071
Flame, 1611
Flatter, 188, 317, 383, 1644, 1661, 2439
Flattery, 683, 955, 1206, 2899, 3135-3136, 3145, 3659
Flavor, 312, 3377
Flaw, 1825
Flea, 1689
Flesh, 2465, 2643, 2790
Flesh-pots, 2396, 2534
Flirt, 192, 230
Float, 2211
Floating debt, 1826
Flood, 571, 721
Floor, 1583
Florida, 1948
Flourish, 2583
Flow, 2533, 2635
Flower, 620, 793, 1201, 1322, 2583, 3393, 3572-3573
Flute, 1164
Fly, 2090, 2577; -paper, 483
Foe, 2222, 2708, 3058-3065
Fog, 1574, 3002
Folks, 1305, 1371, 1717
Follow, 2704
Folly, 2865, 3091, 3164, 3214, 3291
Food, 186, 389, 520-521, 586, 606, 700, 881, 892, 988, 1003, 1006, 1047, 1058, 1181, 1238, 1279, 1881, 1933, 1955, 2361, 2428, 2446, 2803, 2915, 3137-3141, 4025
Fool, 374, 802, 1263, 1265, 1300, 1310, 1323, 1360, 1372, 1465, 1543, 1614, 2470-2471, 2599, 2609, 2923, 3017, 3028, 3060, 3089, 3142-3147, 3320, 3388, 3432, 3447, 3494, 3673, 3861, 3903, 3995-3996, 4002; proof, 1247
Foolish, 2451, 2777
Foot, 1784, 1920, 2546
Football, 318, 350, 789, 877, 938, 1218, 1264, 1389, 1789, 1827
Forbearance, 2979-2981, 3596
Forbidden, 3809
Force, 2449, 3342, 3965
Ford, Henry, 2003, 2848, 3090, 3875
Forebodings, 2907
Forefathers, 1480, 2992, 3118, 3121, 3123, 3567
Forego, 3589
Forehead, 2141
Foreigner, 1720
Forestry, 1143
Forever, 3894, 3896
Forget, 179, 532, 742, 845, 883, 986, 2390, 2588, 3692, 3819
Forgiveness, 2749, 2794, 3148-3150
Forgotten, 2142
Fork, 279
Forlorn, 2091
Form, 2657, 3700

Formal, 818
Fortitude, 2903, 4010
Fortress, 3182
Fortunate, 3695
Fortune, 1449, 1477, 2143, 2399, 2496, 2834-2843, 2998, 3143, 3151-3154, 3401
Fosdick, Harry Emerson, 3099, 3200; how he prepares his sermons, 7
Foul, 1280
Foundations, 3501, 3767
Founders, 1480
Fountain, 2164, 2383, 2442; pen, 966, 1186
Fourth estate, 2472
Fowls, 911
Fox, 2703; George, 1985
Fragrance, 2145
Frailty, 4017
Frank, Glenn, 95, 110, 114, 127, 138
Frankenstein, 2474
Franklin, Benjamin, 1592, 1971, 1973, 1993, 2004, 2033, 2172, 3126, 3254, 3429, 3468, 3517, 3533, 3584, 3749, 3788, 3902, 3968
Frankness, 537, 544, 683, 908, 2299, 3155-3156
Fraternity, 659, 1679, 1791
Fraud, 2899, 2916
Frederick the Great, 2000
Free, 1173, 2146, 2757; will, 3358
Freedom, 3203, 3844, 3944
Freethinkers, 3878
French bread, 1492
Frequency, 3239
Fresh, 493, 892, 912, 975, 1009, 2258
Freshman, 357, 363, 434, 436, 719, 1182, 1691, 1768
Friction, 1636
Friend, 167, 286, 543, 741, 1265, 1496, 1532, 1569, 1655, 2147, 2222, 2350, 2389, 2394, 2434, 2607, 2665, 2697, 2745, 2761, 2899, 2985, 2980-2981, 2983, 3058-3059, 3065, 3128, 3157-3166, 3459, 3524, 3582, 3654
Friendship (see Friend)
Frightened, 2148, 2245
Frivolous, 2194, 2916
Frock, 1540
Frog, 1068; definition of, 1828
Frugality, 3000, 3039-3044
Fruit, 2143, 2215, 2700, 2711, 2828, 2850, 2910, 3598
Fruitless, 2149, 3248
Fullness, 2783
Fulton, Robert, 2045
Fun, 1079, 1567
Function, 919
Funds, insufficient, 842
Funeral, 78, 875
Funny, 672
Fur, 424, 891, 1137, 1227, 1903
Furnace, 1440, 1851, 3792
Furniture, 658, 686, 1446, 3584
Furrow, 2309
Futile, 2150
Future, 360, 1136, 1228, 1433, 1466, 1521, 1659, 3091, 3122, 3246, 3326, 3709, 3737, 3904

G

Gabriel, 548
Gain, 2717, 2797, 3012
Galileo Galilei, 1983

Gallant, 712, 740
Galsworthy, John, 2187
Gamble, 512, 815, 1645, 3641
Game, 433, 455, 1145, 1356, 1775
Ganymede, 2436
Garage, 1386
Garbage, 1002
Garden, 295, 620, 1201, 1562
Gargle, 851
Garment, 2705
Garrick, David, 1990
Garrulous, 839
Gas, 833
Gasoline, 497, 888, 1893
Gate, 1570, 2698
Gather, 2573
Gaul, 1779
Gay, 2377, 2475
Geese, 2355
Generalities, 1589, 1644
Generation, 1531, 1722, 2634, 3583
Generosity, 286, 569, 610, 854, 878, 901, 1057,
    1156, 1241, 2478, 3148, 3304, 3401, 3566,
    3625
Genius, 51, 1026, 1638, 1981, 2152, 3067,
    3167-3173, 3500, 3829, 3850, 3877
Gentle, 707, 946, 3434, 3611, 3988
Gentleman, 1459, 1829, 3174-3176, 3452
Genuine, 2477
Geography, 1165
Geology, 1140
Geometry, 2492
George the Third, 1993
George, David Lloyd, 1693
German stories, 2040
Gestures, 142
Gettysburg, Battle of, 1970
Ghastly, 2153
Ghost, 492, 1101, 2148, 2281, 2975
Giant, 2529
Gibbon, Edward, 1968, 2817, 2998, 3504, 3829
Gift, 313, 426, 465, 794, 1167, 1666, 1918,
    2020, 2360, 2380, 2408, 2420, 2610, 2623,
    3177-3181, 3307
Gifted, 3226
Gilead, 2384
Giraffe, 917
Girl, 772, 1108, 1351, 1365, 1461, 1487, 1490,
    1494, 1519, 1632, 1657, 1679, 1708, 1718,
    1743, 1824, 2052, 4053
Giving, 2559, 2684, 2713, 2729, 2765, 2768,
    3177-3181, 3973
Glaciers, 1140
Glad, 2097, 2594, 2620, 2677
Gladstone, William Ewart, 3351, 3495, 3805
Glamor, 602
Glasses, 1291, 1973
Glee club, 1405
Glitter, 2216
Globe, 1219
Gloomy, 2376, 2385, 3347, 3820
Glory, 1961, 2605, 2692, 2837, 2861, 3001,
    3038, 3302
Gloves, 506
Gnat, 2724
Go-between, 2386
Goat, 160
God, 2198, 2240, 2521, 2535, 2554, 2558, 2561,
    2673-2674, 2691, 2718, 2722, 2752, 2764,
    2776-2777, 2802, 2813, 2871, 2902-2903,

2941, 3098, 3105, 3182-3192, 3218, 3254,
    3258-3259, 3289, 3303, 3377, 3413, 3428,
    3430, 3452, 3482-3483, 3527, 3532, 3542,
    3548, 3599, 3602, 3606, 3636, 3660, 3662,
    3664-3665, 3668, 3689, 3737, 3739, 3747,
    3752, 3783, 3810, 3821, 3882, 3897, 3933,
    3943-3944, 3989, 4025
Goethe, Johann Wolfgang von, 2200, 2288,
    2830, 2900, 2971, 3021, 3023, 3156, 3207,
    3288, 3295, 3325, 3346, 3373, 3376, 3396,
    3548, 3587, 3697, 3846, 3916, 3985, 4053
Golconda, 2479
Gold, 1377, 1575, 1830, 2199, 2457, 2462,
    2622, 2918, 3323, 3517, 3975-3976, 4002;
    digger, 1830
Golden Fleece, 2368, 2496
Goldsmith, Oliver, 2082, 3085, 3247, 3460,
    3506, 3619-3620, 3856
Golf, 161, 205, 378, 402, 477, 479, 629, 638,
    650, 693, 773, 785, 812, 840, 849, 1071,
    1121, 1129, 1149, 1176, 1266, 1356, 1450,
    1564, 1613, 1697, 1760, 1831, 1916, 1957
Golgotha, 2481
Gong, 2133
Good breeding, 3174-3176
Good luck, 1418
Good manners, 1401
Good morning, 1674
Good times, 1308
Good works, 974
Goodness, 863, 1311, 2255, 2372, 2525, 2753,
    2769, 2804, 2843, 2864, 2880, 2901, 3029,
    3078-3079, 3102, 3130-3131, 3194, 3226,
    3278, 3308, 3317, 3368, 3384, 3401, 3439,
    3441, 3495, 3568, 3571, 3578, 3620, 3652,
    3663, 3770, 3817, 3859, 3864, 3873, 3954,
    3960, 3973, 4015
Goose, 515, 1858
Gopher hole, 990
Gordian knot, 2455
Gorge, 990
Gossip, 817, 1260, 1393, 1413, 2159, 2607,
    2665, 3110, 3193-3196, 3797, 3899
Gourmand, 2035
Gout, 2293
Governess, 1012
Government, 705-706, 1272, 1290, 1473, 1641,
    1672, 1688, 2073, 2435, 2464, 2485, 2512,
    3054, 3117, 3197-3214, 3339
Gown, 1540
Gracchi, 2418
Grace, 1279
Graces, 1364, 2160, 2961, 3181, 3855
Grades, 264, 449
Graduate, 978, 1223, 1365, 1497, 1621, 1679
Grafting, 1473, 1894
Grammar, 249, 478, 483, 602, 615, 1832
Grand Canyon, 990
Grandchildren, 694, 1308
Grandeur, 3646
Grandfather, 884
Grandmother, 478, 677, 732, 952, 1591
Grandson, 312
Grant, Ulysses S., 2004, 3339, 3766
Grapefruit, 490, 1002, 1833
Grasp, 2161
Grass, 471, 2134
Gratitude, 313, 3215-3219
Grave, 793, 1615, 2166, 2275, 2992-2993, 2997-

2998, 3001, 3010, 3516, 3840
Gray, Thomas, 1992, 2992, 3001, 3559, 3572, 3646
Great, 1255, 1502, 2610, 2661, 2677, 2912, 3086, 3117, 3220-3235, 3339, 3436, 3453, 3487, 3491, 3495, 3695, 3705, 3803-3804, 3813, 3831
Greed, 81, 2276, 2446, 2478, 3323, 3657
Greeks, 1040, 2360, 2480
Greeley, Horace, 3574
Green, Colonel Edward H. R., 2006
Green, Hetty, 2006
Green light, 1947
Greeting, 1674
Grey, 2162
Gridiron, 1316
Grief, 2163, 2370, 2636, 2658, 2945-2946, 3236-3237, 3248, 3293, 3835, 3837, 3839
Grievances, 2602, 3681
Grind, 1915, 2648
Grindstone, 1701
Griselda, 2510
Groan, 382
Groove, 1615
Growth, 3474
Grudges, 2893
Grumbling, 1703
Guess, 1519
Guest, 249, 963, 1367, 1486, 1834, 2210
Guidance, 4040
Guide, 274, 511, 776, 1140, 1908, 2724
Guilt, 421, 926, 1092, 1931, 2178, 2841, 2938-2939, 3305, 3766
Gullible, 2724, 2795
Guns, 1210, 1619, 1664
Gush, 2164
Gust, 2165

H

Habeas Corpus, 3203
Habit, 543, 1307, 1734, 3052, 3238-3240
Hackney, 2523
Hades, 2385, 2388, 2390, 2392, 2420, 2428
Hair, 401, 468, 498, 614, 736, 750, 866, 944, 953, 1401, 2847
Half-fare, 1041
Ham, 368, 1003, 1047, 1498, 1924
Hamburger, 606; definition of, 1835
Hamilton, Alexander, 3173
Hamlet, 2281, 2409
Hammer, 1515, 1906
Hammerstein, Oscar, 2039
Hammock, 1143
Hand, 1351, 2093, 2168, 2531, 2546, 2588, 2637, 2686, 3157, 3163
Handicap, 693, 1638
Handsome, 763, 2353, 2436
Handwriting, 989; on the wall, 2395
Hanging, 3439
Happiness, 69, 308, 1267, 1295-1296, 1303, 1338, 1421, 1656, 1728, 2169, 2370, 2387, 2689, 2834, 2902, 2908, 3117, 3237, 3241-3249, 3401, 3606, 3783
Hara-kiri, 2485
Harass, 2449
Hard, 2100, 2171-2172, 2239
Hard-boiled, 2282
Harding, Warren G., 2014
Hardship, 2396, 2834-2843, 3250-3253

Hardware, 44
Hardy, Thomas, 2298, 2319
Harmless, 2289
Harmony, 1636, 3855
Harness manufacturer, 1836
Harp, 1020
Harpy, 2446
Harte, Bret, 1999, 3379
Harvard, 799, 1658, 1825
Harvest, 2706
Hash, 1069, 1181
Haste, 2629
Hat, 444, 590, 834, 862, 894, 1106, 1172, 1288, 1684, 2139, 2186
Hate, 2600, 2893, 3164, 3399, 3513, 3817
Haughtiness, 2604, 3471, 3682-3686
Havana tobacco, 1837
Haven, 3191
Hawthorne, Nathaniel, 1969, 2145, 2227, 3515
Hay, 865; fever, 1397; John, 1999
Haydn, Franz Joseph, 1981
Hazlitt, William, 3292, 3675, 3955
Head, 533, 954, 1066, 1091, 1171, 1298, 1503, 1532, 1539, 1600, 1618, 1699, 1771, 2133, 2173-2174, 2605, 2703; waiter, 1678
Headache, 1630, 1650
Headline, 1911
Healing, 2740, 3254, 3260, 3910
Health, 155, 449, 1414, 2921, 3039, 3254-3257, 3335
Hear, 2733, 2808
Hearers, 3849
Heart, 1280, 1373, 2176, 2219, 2551, 2579, 2603, 2620, 2673, 2689, 2712, 2759, 2776, 2847, 2871, 2890-2891, 2895, 2903, 3094-3095, 3097, 3192, 3215, 3249, 3258, 3262, 3272, 3276, 3293, 3399, 3401, 3505, 3519, 3652, 3665, 3667, 3745, 3755, 3798, 3825, 3843, 3855, 3864, 3922
Heat, 175, 244, 1087, 1648, 1851
Heater, 1639
Heave, 2177
Heaven, 209, 354, 405, 548, 646, 1020, 1296, 2094, 2190, 2387, 2461, 2651, 2668, 2675, 2677, 2719, 2748, 2820, 3033, 3258-3262, 3557, 3602, 3617, 3754, 3838, 3844, 3903
Heckling, 25
Hector, 2366
Heel, 1334, 1395, 1784, 2351
Heep, Uriah, 2213
Heine, Heinrich, 3526, 3585, 3886
Heira, 1477, 3122, 3488
Helen of Troy, 2416
Hell, 2186, 2276, 3013, 3261, 3393, 3754, 3778, 3972
Helmet, 1066
Help, 2509, 2581, 2734, 3182
Helpless, 715
Hemingway, Ernest, 2961
Hen, 1315
Henry, Patrick, 2004, 3356
Herald, 2415
Heraldry, 3001, 3226
Herbert, George, 1986
Hercules, 2400-2401, 2404-2405, 2408
Heredity, 2888, 3117-3123
Hermes, 2414
Herod, 2511
Heroes, 1495, 3964
Heroine, 239

Herring, 2107
Hesitate, 2292, 3181
Hiccough, 311
Hide, 2680; and seek, 1838
Hides, 1494
Hieroglyphics, 2484
High-hat, 948
High-horse, 1333
High-life, 1258, 1673
High school, 1679
Hike, 246, 1839
Hill, 2211, 2679
Hill-billy stories, 162, 234, 450, 453, 491, 1032, 1187
Hindrances, 3772
Hinge, 700
Hint, 577, 1666
Hippocrene, 2383, 2442
Hiss, 913, 2179-2180
History, 304, 511, 1269, 1274, 1489, 1926, 2915, 3038, 3103, 3233, 3747, 3919
Hitch-hiker, 1336, 1839
Hoax, 2519
Hobbies, 1325, 1761
Hobo, 1692
Hobson's choice, 2486
Hoc opus hic labor est, 2412
Hockey, 1775
Hold, 2182
Holding company, 1287
Hole, 836
Holidays, 3627
Holiness, 2891, 3591, 3663, 3970
Hollow, 2116
Holly, 1293
Hollywood, 1425
Holmes, Oliver Wendell, 2124, 2191, 2215, 2268, 2330, 2597, 3020, 3654, 3690, 3844, 3884
Home, 387, 539, 704, 711, 731, 1131, 1258, 1288, 1407, 1420, 1441, 1495, 3263-3264, 3537, 3584; definition of, 1840
Homeliness, 3951
Homer, 2489, 2518, 4032
Honesty, 390, 435, 441, 516, 591, 716, 770, 863, 1097, 1357, 1803, 2039, 2508, 2799, 3006, 3037, 3265-3268, 3304, 3511, 3638, 3884
Honey, 2533
Honeymoon, 325, 813
Honor, 837, 2362, 2539, 2557, 2899, 2985, 3100, 3269-3274, 3374, 3508
Hook, 2647
Hoover, Herbert, 48, 3530-3531
Hope, 407, 614, 930, 1487, 1668, 1923, 2185, 2233, 2393, 2470, 2624, 2664, 2788, 2806, 2856, 3025, 3041, 3209, 3257, 3275-3279, 3377, 3393, 3480
Horace, 2840, 3246, 3470, 3609
Horn, 267, 735, 743, 853, 927, 1371, 1542, 1574, 2491
Horse, 181, 527, 546, 590, 680, 684, 743, 865, 968, 1127, 1332, 1764, 1836, 1977, 2360, 2383, 2389, 2467, 2480, 2486, 3540; race, 987; sense, 1653, 1764
Horticulture, 1201
Hospital, 327, 711, 885, 1207, 1681; definition of, 1841
Hostess, 467
Hot, 389, 1649

Hotel, 164, 199, 247, 547, 644-645, 659, 796, 874, 1124, 1196
Houdini, 1997
Hour, 543, 1785, 2083, 3387, 3556, 3899, 3901
House, 178, 856, 1825, 2665, 2701, 2760
House-broken, 971, 1029
Household, 2708
Housewife, 1561
Housework, 315, 1732, 1746
Howells, William Dean, 3414
Howl, 372, 607
Hugo, Victor, 1991, 2142, 2180, 2198, 2241, 2259, 2295, 2313, 2326, 2888, 3666, 3689, 3764, 3986, 4021, 4023
Human, 1665, 1842; dynamos, 1474; nature, 1028, 3248, 3921; definition of, 1842
Humanity, 1064, 1478, 3453, 3531, 3586, 3805
Humble, 994, 2213, 2723, 2745, 2770, 3503
Humid, 2114
Humility, 2190, 3507, 3579, 3958
Humor, 1269, 1419, 3280-3285; in advertising, 1843; in speeches, 87-92
Humorist, 1444
Hunger, 689, 2087, 2174, 2191-2192, 2671, 2936, 4008
Hunt, 2508
Hunter, 226, 368, 423, 766, 1271, 1442, 1769
Hurry, 939, 966, 1145, 1452
Hurrying, 1560
Hurt, 848, 2735, 3508
Husband, 14, 165, 200, 224, 240, 245, 337, 341, 351, 361, 391, 395, 403, 448, 501, 508, 569, 619, 633, 681, 711, 726, 734, 739, 854, 901, 929, 971, 1015-1016, 1022, 1099, 1137, 1278, 1332, 1376, 1392, 1409, 1446, 1511, 1730, 1868, 1875, 1959, 2370, 2392, 2597; definition of, 1844
Hustings, 2490
Hybrid, 1153
Hydra-headed, 2401
Hypnotism, 1118
Hypocrite, 1487, 2507, 2725, 3629
Hysterical, 2193

I

I owe it all to . . . , 1845
Ibex, 1595
Ibsen, Henrik, 3245
Icarian, 2426
Ice, 355; cream, 300, 608, 1006
Icicle, 2074
Idea, 1385, 1488, 1532, 1699, 1710, 1749, 1768, 2846, 3093, 3315, 3701, 3884
Ideal, 2454
Identification, 172, 184, 623, 713
Idiot, 171, 184
Idleness, 2159, 2195, 2262, 2419, 3214, 3869-3870, 3903, 3908, 4033, 4036
Ignominy, 2997
Ignorance, 201, 205, 753, 774, 1171, 1360, 2196, 2749, 3036, 3045, 3142, 3286-3291, 3317, 3318, 3321, 3337, 3674-3675, 3949
Iliad, 2415, 2473, 2489, 2518
Ill, 1921, 2473
Ill-fortune, 1703
Illegal, 1240
Illusion, 2470
Illusive, 2260
Illustration, 1122, 1818

Image, 2082, 2536, 3499
Imaginary, 2458, 2519
Imagination, 95, 98, 127, 471
Imitation, 2969, 3045, 3081-3088, 3706
Immerse, 720
Immigrant, 1068, 1740
Immorality, 1240, 2197, 2468, 2879
Immortality, 2813-2814, 2821, 3376, 3384, 3397, 3734, 3841
Immortals, 2821
Immovable, 630
Impediments, 3409
Impending, 2439
Imperfections, 2981, 3412, 3611
Impersonal, 2198
Impertinence, 2493
Important, 540, 3114
Imported, 518
Imposing, 2199
Impossibilities, 2829, 3612
Impossible, 1124, 2404-2405, 2516, 2690
Impostor, 2477
Impractical, 2454, 4030
Improvement, 1192, 1247, 1478, 3579
Improving, 575
Impulse, 3358, 3718
In the money, 1846
Incapability, 2973
Incense, 2646
Inch, 1784
Inclination, 3329
Income, 258, 359, 508, 526, 1221, 1672, 1683, 3044; tax, 1257, 1443, 1688
Incubator, 826
Indecision, 2554
Independent, 409-410
Indestructible, 3846
Index, 1595
Indian, 1061, 1281
Indifferent, 735
Indigestion, 1847
Indispensability, 3772
Indolent, 2200
Indulgence, 2943
Industriousness, 3028, 3044, 3214, 3261, 3869, 4037-4038
Industry, 2023, 3576
Inert, 2059
Inevitable, 2521
Inexperience, 1241
Infamy, 3003
Infant, 2294
Inferiority, 3016; complex, 1164, 1856
Infinity, 3259
Inflexible, 2301
Influence, 893, 2373, 3036, 3521
Information, 230, 343, 914, 1138, 1196, 1678, 3328, 3330-3331
Ingenuity, 279
Ingratitude, 3215-3219
Inherit, 2670
Inheritance, 1937
Inhumanity, 3456
Iniquity, 2785
Initial payment, 1433
Initiative, 100
Injure, 2498, 3953
Injurious, 3616
Injustice, 3198
Ink, 1772

Inn, 1004, 1696
Innocence, 2244, 2629, 3305, 3766
Inquisitive, 419, 1025
Insanity, 33, 47, 58, 144, 3427, 3498
Insects, 806
Inseparable, 2304
Insight, 95, 127, 4023
Insignificance, 3087
Insincere, 2507, 2699
Insipid, 2500
Insomnia, 1554, 1630, 1848
Inspector, customs, 2057
Inspiration, 1571, 1969, 1990, 2442, 2829, 3227, 3713, 4040
Installment, 314, 330, 545, 601, 658, 686, 900, 968, 1460; collector, 1629; payment, 1447; purchase, 1423, 1444-1446, 1616
Instinct, 3008
Institutions, 3535
Instructions, 293, 318, 599, 880, 2969
Insulated, 1011
Insult, 3292-3293
Insurance, 177, 215, 338, 511, 637, 729, 928, 946, 1399, 1611, 1679, 1862
Intellect, 2201, 3745
Intellectual, 1605
Intelligence, 144, 654, 678, 690, 918, 1735, 3214, 3230, 3263; test, 1430
Intelligent, 1726
Intentions, 2942, 3294-3295
Interest, 1390, 1878, 2026
Interference, 2934
Interminable, 2033
Internationalism, 3529, 3947
Intersection, 1947
Intolerance, 3914-3915
Intoxicated, 233, 643, 782, 1052, 1109, 1146, 2187, 3652
Intrigue, 3037
Introduction, 1753; of the speech: eight methods of preparing, 8; announce subject directly, 9; ask a question, 27; excite attention and arouse curiosity, 15; show importance of subject to audience, 31; tell humorous story, 21; tell story of human interest, 10; use a quotation, 34; use some form of exhibit, 26; apologizing in the introduction, 38-39
Intrusion, 1354
Invention, 94, 104-105, 1408, 2045, 3705, 3710
Inventive, 1650
Investment, 2878
Invoice, 792, 842
Involuntary, 886
Ireland, 1849
Irish stories, 383, 605, 634, 967, 1007, 2037
Irishman, 1699
Iron, 573
Irons, 1541
Irresistible, 630
Irresolution, 56
Irrevocable, 2202
Irving, Washington, 2083, 3010, 3282, 3491, 3525
Ism, 1329
Itch, 1897

J

Jack, 1850
Jackanapes, 2493

Jackson, Andrew, 2004
Jacob, 2520, 2531
Jail, 1173, 1443, 1882
James I., 1591
Janitor, 175, 1648; definition of, 1851
Janus, 2374-2375
Jason, 2368, 2496
Jaw, 1207
Jazz, 203
Jealousy, 3296-3297, 3365, 3404
Jefferson, Thomas, 2025, 3203, 3354, 3783
Jerusalem, 2588, 2661
Jest, 3592
Jester, 2407
Jeweler, 612
Jewelry, 316, 2085
Jewels, 2418
Jingo, 2505
Job, 410, 616, 969, 1365, 1508, 2498
Johnson, Samuel, 1704, 1990, 2956, 2984, 3041,
    3069, 3086, 3094, 3127, 3131, 3162, 3167,
    3248, 3293, 3309, 3331, 3440, 3481, 3509,
    3511, 3534, 3629, 3671, 3684, 3719, 3816,
    3889, 4033, 4042-4044
Jokes, 1236, 1270, 3282
Jonson, Ben, 2860, 3261, 3271, 3410, 3512
Joy, 1284, 2620, 2869-2870, 2949, 3237, 3242,
    3244, 3255, 3628, 3836
Judge, 168, 172, 228, 345, 383, 437, 489, 624,
    648, 846, 2532, 2694, 2756, 2825
Judgment, 1652, 1817, 2440, 2681, 2724, 3090
    3093, 3283, 3298-3301, 3479, 3587, 3676,
    3720, 3865, 3984; Day, 1230
Jujitsu, 342
Juleps, 1575
July, 1685
Jump, 982, 1852
June, 1685, 2130; definition of, 1853
Juno, 2367, 2370, 2400, 2461
Jury, 654, 958, 996; definition of, 1854
Justice, 1443, 1731, 2198, 3210, 3302-3306,
    3425, 3482, 3750, 3768, 4010

K

Kangaroo, 1855
Keeper, 2528
Kibitzer, 1856
Kick, 984, 1051, 1082, 1183
Kidney, 3433
Kilkenny cats, 2502
Kill, 1676, 1890, 2392, 2540
Kindness, 707, 2504, 2792, 2801, 3307-3310,
    3399, 3665, 3768
King, 2251, 2503, 2617, 3199, 3201
Kingdoms, 3422-3423, 3540
Kipling, Rudyard, 1996, 2007, 2111
Kiss, 220, 559, 681, 770, 950, 1487, 2048, 2996,
    3410, 3998
Kitchen, 1001
Kitchenette, 1857, 1887
Knee action, 822
Knees, 1600
Knife, 279
Knight-errant, 2503
Knock, 1098, 2695
Knowledge, 97, 654, 769, 774, 814, 1148, 1196,
    1199, 1544, 2463, 2494, 2568, 2608, 2686,
    2884, 3012, 3030, 3049, 3053, 3093, 3120,

3311, 3337, 3341, 3477, 3505, 3616, 3710,
    3723, 3735, 3945, 3990-3991

L

La Fayette, Marquis D., 1977
La Rochefoucauld, Francois, Duc de, 2966,
    2973, 2979, 3135-3136, 3296, 3299, 3447,
    3451, 3458-3459, 3479, 3582, 3948, 4030
Labor, 298, 780, 1326, 1447, 2400, 2706, 2709,
    3039, 3173, 3335, 3338-3339, 4024-4040
Laborer, 2741, 3339
Ladder, 1621
Lady, 1282, 1555, 1611; of the Lake, 1978
Lamb, 695, 701, 759, 2650, 3989; Charles,
    1983, 2044, 3161
Lame duck, 1858
Lamp, 2115, 2119
Land, 1821, 2533-2534
Landlady, 881
Landlord, 180, 502, 1845
Landlubber, 931
Language, 297, 486, 1045, 1720, 2040, 2956,
    2977, 3288, 3340-3342, 3545, 3561, 3563,
    3847
Languid, 2204
Lark, 2289
Last, 2720
Late, 198, 219, 337, 917, 1191
Latin, 406
Laugh, 386, 574, 1345, 1369, 1382, 1419, 2116,
    2153, 2489, 3275, 3282, 3343-3347, 3778
Laundry, 173, 635, 1448, 1859
Laurel, 1362, 2429-2430
Lavish, 2406, 3800
Law, 572, 1215, 1322, 1724, 2087, 2917, 3305,
    3348-3353, 3360, 3439, 3550, 3706, 3790;
    of diminishing returns, 1859
Lawn, 265; mower, 1822, 1964
Lawyer, 172, 200, 450, 591, 713, 1449, 1710,
    1966, 2037
Laziness, 1134, 3869, 3903, 4036
Lead, 2698, 2715
Leadership, 96-106, 117, 1479, 1984, 2506
Lean years ahead, 1860
Leaning Tower of Pisa, 1150
Learning, 148, 162, 2766, 2970, 3175, 3326-
    3328, 3337, 3670, 3830
Leather, 439
Leaven, 2779
Leaves, 2110, 2129, 2242, 2659, 2903, 3391
Lecture, 722, 1577, 1700, 1874, 2018, 3748
Lecturer, 1314, 1436
Left-overs, 988
Leg, 866
Legacies, 3120, 3265
Legislature, 1382
Leisure, 1354, 3909, 3980, 4035
Lemon, 490
Lend, 2611; me your ears, 1861
Length, 3381, 3383, 3854
Leopard, 1494, 1769, 2650
Lesson, 808, 880, 2884, 3569-3570
Lethe, 2390
Letter, 897, 1119, 2020
Liar, 713, 875, 1450, 1601, 2480
Liberal, 1211, 3041, 3177-3181
Liberalism, 17, 19, 66, 1283

Liberty, 46, 65, 1656, 1930, 2379, 3209, 3353-
    3362, 3533, 3729, 3783, 3980
  Loan, 1971
Library, 1647, 1902, 3363-3365, 3469, 4044
Lie, 953, 1041, 1483, 1669, 1765, 2205, 3037,
    3106-3111, 3393, 3679, 3939
Life, 128, 338, 347, 455, 928, 1199, 1276,
    1451, 1537, 1613-1614, 1628, 1656, 1862,
    1885, 2206, 2259, 2560, 2761, 2810, 2814,
    2834-2843, 2852, 2854, 2999, 3005-3007,
    3256, 3366-3394, 3419, 3587, 3733, 3844,
    3866, 3900, 3905-3906
Lifeless, 2207
Light, 1631, 2125, 2187, 2190, 2208, 2679-
    2680, 2754-2755, 3846
Lilies, 2692
Limburger cheese business, 1863
Limit, 145, 2495
Limitations, 993, 1638
Lincoln, Abraham, 46, 1710, 1970, 2034, 2038,
    2043, 3523, 3782
Linger, 2210
Lion, 695, 2628, 2638
Liquor, 2381
Listen, 992, 2954, 3637
Listless, 2447
Liszt, Franz, 2019
Literature, 476, 578, 3395-3398, 3521; use of
    in speeches, 93
Little, 531
Live, 1221, 1556, 2587, 2650, 2667, 2775,
    2797
Living, 1239, 1623, 1646, 2638, 2751; wage,
    1396
Loaf, 1169
Loan, 286, 705, 965, 1179, 1189, 1285, 1677
Lobster, 1009, 2170
Lodge, 800
Logic, 447, 3934
Long trail, 978
Longfellow, Henry Wadsworth, 2140, 2184,
    2271, 2280, 2825, 2839, 2858, 2891, 2930,
    2933, 3062, 3169, 3177, 3228, 3303, 3560,
    3755, 3825, 3876, 3988
Longing, 2396, 3332, 3734
Lord, 2559, 2571, 2580, 2584, 2586, 2591,
    2611, 2734, 2771, 2783, 2796, 2807
Lord's Prayer, 3669-3670
Loss, 571, 706, 1953, 2875, 2890, 3279, 3408
Lost, 561, 1697
Lothario, 2475
Lotus-eater, 2419
Loud, 291, 872, 2415, 2489
Lounge, smoking, 1928
Louse, 463
Love, 174, 202, 353, 377, 458, 523, 526, 553,
    740, 937, 1008, 1088, 1103, 1428, 1487, 1573,
    1611, 1695, 1873, 2082, 2591, 2644, 2685,
    2761, 2807, 2811, 3128-3129, 3166, 3296,
    3399-3420, 3510, 3525, 3539, 3542, 3571,
    3663, 3857; at first sight, 1864
Lowell, James Russell, 130, 2273, 2838, 3132-
    3133, 3603, 3784, 3842, 3980
Lowly, 3226
Loyola, St. Ignatius, 1985
Lucifer, 2488, 2651
Luck, 287, 388, 815, 1074, 1653, 1768; defini-
    tion of, 1865
Lump, 1048

Lust, 2813, 2918, 3196
Luther, Martin, 3098, 3182, 3527, 3758, 3810
Luxury, 3421-3424, 3543, 3772
Lynch, 615
Lytton, Edward Bulwer, 2004, 2097, 2243, 2277,
    2320, 2847, 3103, 3145, 3170, 3395, 3420,
    3487, 3640, 3647, 3753, 3981

M

Macaulay, Lord Thomas Babington, 1983, 3214
Macbeth, 2148
Macedonian cry, 2509
Machiavellian, 2512
Machinery, 911
Mad, 1277, 1520, 3172, 3178, 3280, 3485
Magazine, 542, 1429, 1800
Magic, 663, 1079, 1161, 2414, 3514
Magna Charta, 1175
Magnanimity, 3955
Magnetic, 947
Maid (see Servant)
Mail, 845, 847, 1733
Majestic, 2214
Major general, 1866
Majority, 3189, 3425-3428, 3497, 3678
Malaprop, Mrs., 2517
Malice, 3284
Mammon, 2691
Man, 382, 531, 1038, 1219, 1221, 1223, 1225-
    1226, 1229, 1238, 1244, 1249, 1257, 1259,
    1295, 1299, 1304, 1376, 1382, 1388, 1398,
    1410-1411, 1416, 1422, 1440-1442, 1449,
    1454, 1456, 1472, 1485, 1487, 1495, 1505,
    1511, 1515, 1520, 1528, 1535, 1542, 1559,
    1614, 1650, 1654, 1687, 1724, 1912, 1917,
    1926, 1932, 1938, 2061, 2068, 2095, 2102,
    2259, 2286, 2525, 2530, 2545, 2551, 2553,
    2560-2563, 2581, 2583, 2586, 2589, 2610,
    2624, 2626, 2631, 2667, 2696, 2705, 2717,
    2719, 2787, 2791, 2857, 2912-2920, 3000,
    3020, 3048, 3054, 3064, 3103, 3164, 3186,
    3223, 3245, 3291, 3363, 3369, 3418, 3424,
    3429-3459, 3461, 3553, 3564, 3616, 3618,
    3764, 3772, 3805, 3838, 3841-3842, 3853,
    3866-3867, 3896, 4014, 4022-4023, 4033,
    4038; definition of, 1867; of few words,
    1868
Management, 1104
Mankind (see Man)
Manners, 851, 1237, 1248, 2917, 3174-3176,
    3452, 3636, 3923
Mansions, 2760, 3844
Manufacturer, harness, 1836
Manuscript, 1909
Marble, 2288, 2301
Marconi, Guglielmo, 2022
Mare's Nest, 2519
Marksmanship, 771
Marriage, 218, 224, 245, 302, 305, 308, 324,
    332, 341, 352, 371-372, 380, 388, 400, 422,
    427, 437, 465-466, 519, 530, 539, 543, 556,
    563, 579-580, 587, 600, 667-668, 697, 699,
    768, 789-790, 792, 807, 810-811, 813, 845,
    871, 912, 920, 927, 933, 941, 946, 958, 971,
    976, 999, 1010, 1016, 1025, 1029, 1037, 1075,
    1081, 1096, 1118, 1126, 1130, 1142, 1157,
    1174, 1198, 1204, 1277, 1365, 1388, 1409,
    1421, 1430, 1461, 1472, 1487, 1490, 1568,
    1629, 1685-1686, 1705, 1745-1746, 1765,

1796, 1857, 1870, 1923, 1959, 1963, 2217, 2718, 2746, 3460-3462
Martyr, 1917
Masquerade, 876
Masses, 3743
Master, 2645, 2690, 2826, 3463-3464
Mastery, 2826, 3322, 3839
Match, 262, 371, 1682
Maternity, 456
Mathematics, 336, 746
Matrimony (see Marriage)
Mature, 2787, 3610
Maxims, 3465-3467
May, 1010, 3856
Mayflower, 1910
Mayor, 170, 334
McClellan, General George B., 2043
McCormick, Cyrus, 104
Meal, 795, 981, 3139
Mean, 1307, 1381, 3684
Meaningless, 2465
Measure, 3381
Meat, 259, 496, 731, 1403, 2147, 2632
Medicine, 20, 49, 467, 650, 861, 1192, 1598, 1795, 1841, 1953, 3468-3469
Mediocrity, 3161, 3470-3472
Meditation, 3473-3474, 3932
Meek, 1945, 2670, 2861, 2894, 3258
Melancholy, 1106, 2219, 3647, 3820
Memories, 742, 2891, 2907, 3264
Memory, 1205, 1965, 3111, 3377, 3475-3481, 3521, 3670, 3705, 3714
Men (see Man also), 1210, 1282, 1289, 1499, 1508, 1510, 1619, 1681, 1750, 2215-2216, 2273, 2550, 2599, 2617, 2625, 2639, 2663, 2676, 2697, 2738, 2754, 2763
Merciless, 2221
Mercury, 2377
Mercy, 2222, 2278, 2431, 2572, 2672, 2768, 2772, 3148-3150, 3482-3484
Merit, 2816, 3092, 3657, 3955, 4048
Merry, 2603, 2744, 3343-3347
Mess, 406, 414, 2520
Messenger, 566
Metaphysics, 3997
Method, 3485-3487
Michelangelo, 3927
Microscope expert, 1872
Midas-eared, 2440
Middle-aged, 1324
Middleclass, 2522
Mighty, 1566, 2552, 2606
Mileage, 1485
Milk, 248, 393, 399, 486, 577, 608, 685, 858, 1039, 1043, 1085, 1194, 1287, 1549, 2533
Mill, John Stuart, 1983
Millinery, 834, 862, 1106, 1172
Million dollars, 969, 1555
Millionaire, 388, 801, 1830
Mills of God, 2521
Millstone, 2735
Milton, John, 2095, 2214, 2323, 2832, 2951, 3102, 3597, 3603, 3707, 3793, 3809, 3961, 3965, 3983
Mind, 1225-1226, 1256, 1298, 1341, 1411, 1532, 1605, 1747, 1884, 1922, 2631, 2821, 2831, 2856, 2985, 3016, 3047, 3131, 3167, 3171, 3231, 3246, 3248, 3319, 3324, 3332, 3347, 3409, 3424, 3448, 3475, 3505, 3526, 3566, 3575, 3606, 3715, 3818, 3841, 3870, 3876,

3924, 3942, 4004-4005, 4040, 4045; reader, 391, 1119
Minerva, 2367, 2380, 2422
Minister (see Preacher)
Mink coat, 1079
Minnows, 2433
Minorities, 3577
Minotaur, 2413
Mint, 1575
Miracle, 3733
Mirror, 1418, 1522, 1626, 2155, 2299
Mirth, 3343-3347
Mischievous, 721, 761, 2427
Miser, 477, 1505, 1557, 3488-3489
Misery, 1634, 3036, 3050, 3154, 3442, 3645, 3647
Misfortune, 1057, 1665, 2834-2843, 3250-3253, 3441, 3458-3459, 3490-3491, 3620, 3695, 3726, 3999
Misplaced, 2042
Misrepresent, 1370
Missed, 1047
Mission, 3701
Mississippi Bubble, 2514
Missouri, 656
Mist, 2111, 2256, 3002
Mistake, 557, 612, 959, 1816, 1952, 2043, 3155, 3492-3496
Misunderstand, 146, 241, 488
Mixed, 486, 554
Mixer, 1790
Mob, 3497-3499
Model, 240, 1740, 3081-3088
Moderation, 3500-3501
Modern, 332, 524, 701, 916, 925, 1662, 1873, 2122, 3581
Modest, 530, 730, 2112, 3093, 3502-3507, 4024
Modification, 3607
Momentum, 1167
Monarchies, 3543
Monastery, 1597, 2058
Money, 176, 185, 210, 232, 250, 263, 282, 298, 329, 345, 369, 425, 480, 509, 551, 572, 601, 734, 838, 900, 1035, 1081, 1211, 1292-1293, 1296, 1309, 1315, 1318, 1375, 1378, 1496, 1505, 1509, 1511-1512, 1527, 1543, 1567, 1584, 1604, 1684, 1690, 1713, 1717, 1801, 1807, 1811, 1814, 1830, 1846, 1873, 1891, 1912, 1937, 1941, 2026, 2399, 2451, 2480, 2918, 3267, 3401, 3508-3514
Monkey, 213, 299, 825, 1874, 2493
Monologue, 1875, 2295
Monotony, 2223
Monster, 1597, 2401, 2474
Montaigne, Miguel de, 3143, 3201, 3250, 3439, 3626, 3703, 3959
Monument, 3051, 3515-3516
Moon, 145, 1126, 2108, 2235
Moral, 808, 1608
Morality, 1620, 2937-2943, 3039, 3204, 3230, 3533, 3669, 3731, 3786, 3987, 4041
Morning, 2095, 2162, 2233, 2254, 2256, 2258, 2651, 3517-3518
Morse, Samuel F. B., 1979
Mortar board, 844
Mortgage, 178, 387, 560, 886, 1168, 1512, 1821, 1945
Mosquitoes, 1623
Moth, 424, 2187, 2688

Mother, 77, 225, 236, 243, 301-302, 338, 419, 461, 463, 499, 595, 816, 916, 932, 951-952, 1131, 1163, 1432, 1490, 1499, 1861, 1986, 2240, 2351, 2904, 3519-3525; -in-law, 155, 725, 875, 1024, 1158, 1770, 1820
Motionless, 2224
Motive, 3541
Motorist (see Automobile and Driver)
Mountaineer, 234, 776
Mourn, 2669, 2991, 3456
Mouse, 196, 2394
Mouth, 1163, 1516
Moving pictures, 189, 574, 1168, 1207, 1406, 1581
Mozart, Wolfgang Amadeus, 1981, 1998
Muddy, 1549
Muddled, 781
Mudguard, 1888
Mugwump, 2513
Mule, 146, 596, 656, 984, 1667
Multitude, 1563, 3448-3449
Mummy, 2224, 3496
Munchausen, Baron, 2516
Murder, 2178, 2530, 2540, 3812, 3964
Murmur, 2131, 2228
Muscles, 1373
Muscular, 2229
Muses, 2383, 2494
Music, 203, 209, 367, 370, 404, 491, 625, 1151, 1967, 1981, 1998, 2019, 3472, 3526-3528, 3931
Musician, 365
Mussolini, Benito, 1876
Mustache, 1974
Mute, 2230-2231
Mutton, 2223
Muzzle, 2547
Mystery, 258, 2484, 3289, 3747; definition of, 1877

N

Nabob, wealthy as a, 2487
Nag, 466
Nails, 1906
Naive person, 1878
Naked, 379
Namby pamby, 2500
Name, 235, 517, 623, 744, 1201, 2239, 2614, 2885, 3763
Naples, 1184
Napoleon, 112, 1982, 1991, 2002, 2016, 2045, 2216, 2435, 2942, 3024, 3104, 3221, 3507, 3520, 3747, 3929, 3969, 4047
Napping, 2518
Nation, 507, 1285, 1502, 2232, 2601, 2656, 3117, 3204, 3214, 3230, 3263, 3339, 3396, 3465, 3529-3544, 3554, 3726, 3728, 3743, 3915
Nationality, 1264
Nature, 223, 867, 1291, 2466, 3295, 3434, 3545-3549, 3680, 3978; human, 1665, 1842
Navigation, 2817-2818, 2837
Nazareth, 2753, 3578
Necessity, 2984, 3550-3554
Neck, 539, 1550
Necktie, 474, 1289, 1994
Nectar, 2361
Need, 1603, 3550-3554
Neglect, 2235, 3035, 3326, 3402, 4038

Negro stories, 181, 210, 215, 232, 253, 277, 292, 298, 307, 345, 362, 387, 406, 421-422, 428, 442, 460, 492, 515, 533, 548, 551, 563, 572, 580, 585, 619, 635, 640, 642, 669, 671, 754, 791, 798, 800, 835, 847, 883, 902, 906, 926, 931, 945, 956-957, 962, 984, 1002, 1010, 1021, 1097, 1123, 1144, 1173, 1179, 1865
Neighbor, 521, 541, 921, 1031, 1355, 1422, 1460, 1673, 1701, 2621, 2929, 2985, 3196, 3751
Nerve, 430, 1523, 1779
Nervous, 464, 1564, 1578; in speaking, 141
Nessus, shirt of, 2408
Nest, 330, 2280, 2519
Net, 2590
Neurologist, 1416
New, 710, 772, 988, 3578; customers, 922; deal, 1439; era, 1579; year, 3892
New York, 1720, 1879
News, 1482, 1501
Newsboys, 860
Newspaper, 43, 204, 208, 365, 472, 554, 710, 994, 1028, 1114, 1911, 2013, 2021, 2472, 3533
Newton, Sir Isaac, 1983, 1991, 3593
Niagara Falls, 11, 494
Nicaragua canal, 80
Nickel, 1318, 1557
Nietzsche, Friedrich, 89
Night, 2138, 2152, 2265, 2385, 2653, 2758, 2774, 3498, 3518, 3555-3562, 3846, 3922; club, 333
Nobleness, 2917, 3097, 3506, 3541, 3563-3568, 3612, 3713, 3844, 3921, 3944
Noise, 853, 1647, 2150
Nome, 1165
Nonsense, 703, 2403
Noose, 1854
Normal times, 1585
North, 495
Nose, 1397, 1701, 1896
Note, 572
Nothing, 2465, 2613, 2827, 3862
Nourishment, 1224, 3138
Novel, 1209
November, 2086
Nurse, 327, 443, 1192, 2284
Nut, 573, 1699, 1748

O

Obedience, 971, 3205, 3569-3571
Objection, 667, 1154, 2845
Objectives, 3231, 3319
Oblation, 2646
Obligation, 2499, 2773, 3033-3038, 3216
Obliging, 363, 574
Oblivion, 3572-3574
Obscurity, 2953, 3234, 3578
Observation, 763, 3058
Obstacles, 2492, 3601
Obstinate, 459, 811, 1115, 2236
Occasionally, 976
Occupations, 3052
Ocean, 931, 985, 1377, 1594, 1838, 2195
Oculist, 1880
Odyssey, 2358, 2414, 2419
Offense, 2897, 2959, 2980, 3365
Office, 556, 592, 800, 1060, 1574
Offspring, 1477, 1480

Oil, 1383, 1394, 2119; cans, 1547
Old age, 2844-2856, 3202, 3446, 3476, 3502, 3769, 4052
Old maids, 3608
Oleomargarine, 1881
Olive tree, 2380
Olympian anger, 2445
Olympus, 2217, 2445
Omega, 2356
Omit, 882
Omnipotent, 2815
O'Neill, Eugene, 2949
On the rocks, 1882
Open, 895
Open-minded, 1245, 1747, 1884, 3575-3578
Opera, 372, 1168, 1680
Operation, 589, 1795
Opinion, 958, 1179, 1219, 1490, 1635, 2554, 2694, 2929, 3272, 3365, 3579, 3710, 3831
Opportunity, 46, 77, 319, 929, 1338, 1709, 1885, 2237, 3023, 3587-3590
Opposites, 3466
Optimist, 661, 1017, 1301, 1433, 1538, 1891; definition of, 1886
Optometrist, 256
Oracle, 2373
Orator, 39, 3283, 3847, 3852, 3854
Oratory, 642-643
Order, 3105, 3117, 3851
Orders, 293, 318, 1162
Ordinary, 3470-3472
Organ, 22
Organization, 3487
Orgy, 2381
Original, 980, 3564
Originality, 2969, 3884
Originator, 3702
Orphan, 499
Ostrich, 633
Ouija board, 1688
Ourselves, 2825-2826, 2896, 2979-2981, 3058, 3085, 3093, 3107, 3135-3136, 3158, 3224-3225, 3247, 3331, 3451, 3483, 3703, 3760
Outdoors, 2068
Outfitted, 1163
Overalls, 1709
Overbearing, 231
Overcoat, 291
Overworked, 452, 1887
Ovid, 3229, 3841
Owe, 2773
Owner, 2645, 2890, 3776
Ox, 2547, 2593, 2645
Oxford University, 1996
Oyster, 493, 2059

P

Packing, 3486
Pactolian flood, 2441
Paderewski, Ignace, 991
Pain, 323, 1550, 2177, 2238, 2870, 2946, 3591-3592, 3625
Painless, 607
Painter, 824, 1970-1980
Painting, 599, 3472
Palaces, 3029
Palladium of our liberty, 2379
Palm, 1897
Pan, 1316, 1823, 2175, 2440; pipes of, 2466

Pancake, 859
Pandora, 2393
Panic, 1670, 3791
Pant, 2241
Pants, 609, 1282, 2066
Parable, 1169
Parachute, 733, 767, 982
Paradise, 2470, 2883, 3392-3393
Paraphrasing, 1055
Parchment, 2072, 2123
Pardon, 2240
Parents, 77, 264, 734, 1215, 1531, 2007, 2796, 3413
Paris, 2351, 2366-2367
Parking, 320, 896; space, 1888
Parliament, 2472, 2490
Parrot, 746
Parting, 3004, 3834
Partnership, 962
Party, 179, 216, 288, 408, 689, 915, 1063, 1349, 1425
Pass, 2006
Passenger, 1838
Passions, 3253, 3447, 3722, 3793, 3850
Past, 1136, 1659, 3091, 3122, 3326, 3585, 3767, 3844, 3901, 3904
Pastor (see Preacher)
Patent Medicine, 1414
Pathetic, 2242
Patience, 278, 1553, 1968, 2510, 3521, 3593-3601
Patient, 176, 194, 327, 1192, 1778, 1809, 2243, 2510, 2981
Patriarch, 2506
Patriotism, 2411, 3037, 3118, 3534, 3539, 3542, 3554
Paul, Saint, 128
Pawnbroker, 923, 1845
Pawnshop, 1033
Pay, 854, 1500; check, 1685; envelope, 1461; roll, 938, 1232
Payment, 314, 1542, 1907, 3044
Peace, 304, 1619, 2370, 2380, 2609, 2660, 2738, 2798, 2940, 3214, 3602-3606, 3968
Peacemakers, 2674
Peanuts, 651, 1238, 2304
Pearl, 2714
Pecksniffian, 2507
Pedagogy, 998
Pedestrian, 273, 453, 822, 1044, 1317, 1322, 1402, 1742
Pedigree, 948, 3118, 3121-3123
Pegasus, 2383
Pen, 1898, 4045, 4047
Pencil, 966; sharpener, 1871
Pendulum, 2297
Penelope, 2425
Penitence, 2163
Penitentiary, 1234
Penn, William, 3283, 3308, 3413
Pennsylvania, University of, 1973
Pension, 593
People, 1220, 1286, 1310, 1320, 1417, 1465, 1478, 1492, 1665, 1717, 2632, 3200, 3209, 3214, 3349, 3362, 3530, 3536, 3553, 3580, 3584, 3765, 3780
Perceive, 2764
Perfection, 171, 240, 443, 448, 498, 894, 933, 1038, 2454, 2980, 3453, 3607-3608, 3929; definition of, 1889

Perfume, 2361, 3077
Peril, Yellow, 1962
Peripatetic, 2501
Perished, 2145
Permanence, 379, 2920, 3204
Perpetual, 352, 2078
Persecute, 2675-2677
Perseverance, 459, 801, 2848, 3593-3601
Pershing, General John J., 1988
Persistence, 2181, 3612-3615
Person, 1339, 1344
Personal, 652, 1092, 1930
Personality, 947, 1024
Personnel, 602
Pessimism, 754
Pessimist, 1235, 1433, 1538, 1890
Pet, 251
Petition, 2483
Petrified, 960
Pettiness, 3174
Petunias, 1201
Pharmacist, 1086
Philanthropist, 480
Philosopher, 3388
Philosophy, 1159, 1693, 2842, 3367, 3616-3624, 3730
Photographer, 925
Phrases, use of colorful, 124; use in groups of two or three, 133-135
Physician, 1324, 2740
Physiology, 223
Piano, 268, 370, 404, 964, 991, 1164, 1892, 1950, 2019; mover, 1164; tuner, 252
Pickpocket, 1891
Pickwickian, 2504
Picnic, 473, 2212
Picture, 1406, 1581, 2212, 2622
Pie, 632, 649, 1695
Piecework, 1500
Pierian spring, 2494
Piety, 3394
Pike's Peak, 1663
Pilate, 2762
Pile Ossa upon Pelion, 2515
Pilgrims, 1594
Pill, 1921
Pillar, 2301
Pioneer, 522
Pit, 2640
Pity, 1275, 1339, 2611
Plagiarism, 1251, 3884, 4048
Plan, 2693
Plato, 3186, 3566, 3634, 3883, 4010
Play, 1491
Playing by note, 1892
Plays, use of in speeches, 93
Plead, 2245
Pleasant, 2587, 3370
Please, 2980, 3863
Pleasure, 1908, 2866, 2978-2979, 2990, 3160, 3239, 3255, 3332, 3421, 3459, 3625-3632
Ploughshares, 2647
Plumber, 756
Plutarch, 2954, 3043, 3121, 3153, 3381, 3529, 3622, 3657, 3908-3909, 4024
Poe, Edgar Allan, 1991
Poetry, 512, 3472, 3487, 3557, 3633-3635
Poets, 1294, 3470, 3633-3635
Poignant, 2247
Poison, 428, 2174; ivy, 1362

Poker, 2064
Police, 163, 228, 272, 475, 821, 1139, 1849, 1932, 1952, 2075
Policy, 1693, 3487, 3640
Polish, 1344
Polished, 691, 2239
Polite, 273, 566, 995, 1124, 1141, 3636-3637
Political plum, 1894
Politician, 204, 441, 589, 741, 1359, 1383, 1400, 1454, 1476, 1500, 1617, 1783, 1797, 1858, 1894, 1922, 3350; definition of, 1893
Politics, 1359, 1464, 1470, 1481, 1588-1589, 1730, 1797, 1974, 2014, 2467, 2485, 2490, 2495, 2512-2513, 3108, 3638-3644
Polka, 1895
Pollock, Channing, 11, 24, 116, 2102
Polls, 1527
Polygamy, 206
Pomp, 3718
Pomposity, 2036
Pond, 2204
Pons asinorum, 2492
Poor, 688, 1214, 2142, 2574, 2611, 2616, 2630, 2648, 2668, 3405; house, 949, 1443; loser, 1358
Pope, Alexander, 2494, 3484, 3493, 3658, 3938
Popular, 870, 3574, 3813
Population, 52, 3553, 3765
Pork, 1481
Porter, 1104, 1523
Portrait, 2036
Positive, 810, 2929
Possessions, 3776-3777, 3913, 3973-3974, 3979, 3982
Possibilities, 3042, 3200
Post office, 717
Posterity, 1480, 2010, 3235, 3633, 3898
Postman, 2166
Postpone, 1633
Potatoes, 162, 482
Pottage, 2520
Poverty, 558, 964, 1035, 1227, 2389, 2863, 2899, 2947, 3029, 3113, 3405, 3420, 3489, 3543, 3551, 3594, 3645-3650, 3763, 3774, 3784, 3821-3822, 4039
Power, 552, 2406, 2422, 2435, 2463, 2488, 3001, 3045, 3167, 3206, 3222, 3226, 3306, 3334, 3359-3360, 3471, 3553, 3578, 3600, 3651-3653, 3855, 3980
Powers, 4042, 4047
Practice, 1050, 1263, 3030, 3621
Praise, 1503, 2007, 2727, 2799, 3060-3061, 3503, 3654-3659, 3852
Prance, 2307
Prayers, 296, 507, 997, 1688, 2228, 3660-3670
Preach, 2509, 2733, 2740, 3492
Preacher, 156, 158, 210, 238, 296, 334, 347, 405, 445, 507, 515, 640, 652, 761, 833, 886, 902, 957, 974, 1035, 1115, 1167, 1176, 1195, 2248, 3852
Precedent, 3917
Preciseness, 2886
Precocious, 925, 1896
Prejudice, 996, 1360, 1627, 1884, 3575, 3671-3679, 3914
Preliminary, 1203
Premonition, 1897
Preparation, 1143, 2046, 2760, 2776, 2834, 3042, 3590
Preparedness, 2046

Presbyterian, 1718
Present, 2143, 2778, 3904
Preservation, 1113, 3704, 4048
President, 1456, 3781
Press, 3203, 4046
Presumption, 3616, 3759
Pretense, 2467, 2928, 3680-3681
Pretty, 1716, 2249
Pretzel, 1794
Prey, 2188
Price, 468, 1713, 2565, 2714, 3214, 3335-3336
Pride, 23-24, 77, 503, 1715, 2488, 2604, 3066,
    3216-3217, 3337, 3504, 3605, 3647, 3682-
    3686, 3778
Prim, 2250
Prince, 2532
Principles, 854, 1299, 2920, 3203, 3643, 3687,
    3688, 3762, 3917
Priority, 2499
Prison, 856 ; warden, 1898
Privation, 3179
Privilege, 1487, 2251
Prize fighter, 1895
Problem, 254, 980, 1019, 2515
Procrastination, 1633
Prodigal, 3488, 3512, 3912
Productiveness, 3171
Profanity, 1899, 2537, 3786
Profession, 589, 3330, 4038
Professor, 152, 272, 276, 305, 336, 375, 469,
    573, 672, 720, 722, 749, 769, 779, 837, 844,
    998, 1122, 1148, 1182, 1242, 1309, 1353,
    1467, 1669,
Profit, 1228, 2717, 2784, 2875, 2954, 3041,
    3091, 3717
Profitless, 2471
Progress, 581, 605, 968, 1020, 1233, 1609,
    2023, 2030, 2447, 2780, 3577, 3689-3690
Promise, 1536, 4053
Promises, 2886, 3691-3693
Promptness, 2033
Pronunciation, 235, 744, 788
Proof, 904, 1109, 1547 ; reader, 959
Propeller, 1184
Property, 3165, 3885, 3973
Prophesy, 2365, 2663, 2763
Prophets, 1228, 2677, 3527
Proposal, 1075, 1198
Prose, 1625, 2976, 3635
Prosperity, 1434-1435, 1784, 1900, 2835, 3039,
    3046, 3117, 3204, 3214, 3476, 3553, 3694-
    3697
Protean artist, 2424
Protection, 887, 921, 3019
Proverb, 540, 1901, 2945, 3465-3466
Providence, 3444
Provider, 619, 1296
Prudence, 3698-3699
Prunes, 1144, 2285
Psychiatrist, 1325
Psychology, 627, 1738
Public, 1736, 3541; affairs, 3749; debt, 1555;
    library building, 1902; opinion, 2968;
    speaking, 3472; before the audience, 141-
    142; essentials of, outlined by Cicero, 1; how
    to make your speech sparkle, 85-138, 140;
    in a nutshell, 139; what it requires, 143;
    utility, 1287
Publius Syrus, 2921, 2938, 3071, 3152, 3383,
    3550, 3588, 3607, 3610, 3863, 3999

Puffed, 2252
Pulpit, 3728
Pun, 621
Punctual, 198, 415, 973, 1060, 1125, 1191,
    1437, 2254
Punctuation, 415
Punishment, 706, 2428, 2521, 2591, 2972
Pupin, Michael, life of, 94
Pure, 128, 2141, 2255, 2477, 2561, 2673, 2767,
    2799, 4020
Purple, born to the, 2402
Purpose, 2914, 3333, 3700-3701, 3908
Purring, 1166
Pursue, 1656, 2628
Pursuit, 3231, 3330, 4038
Puzzle, 297, 514, 567
Pygmalion, 2231

Q

Quagmire, 2469
Quarrel, 1070, 1796, 2453, 4000
Quest, 2496, 2915
Question, 290, 328, 515, 622, 1245, 1400, 1445,
    1486, 2391, 2653, 2983, 3993 ; use of, 121-
    122
Quick, 885
Quid pro quo, 2497
Quiet, 346, 1387, 2058, 2637, 3611
Quiz, 863, 1165
Quotations, 3702-3706, 4043 ; Biblical, use of,
    126-128 ; from literature, 129-132

R

Rabbit, 939, 1079, 1384, 1653 ; definition of,
    1903
Rabelais, François, 3146, 3450
Raccoon coats, 1904
Race, 2639
Radiator, 490, 497
Radical, 1438
Radio, 288, 370, 658, 1020, 1107, 1177, 1213,
    1279, 1355, 1932
Railroad, 293, 320, 702, 744, 747, 1135, 1262,
    1514, 1580, 1643, 1781, 2006, 2012
Rain, 248, 266, 303, 469, 502, 740, 1046, 1085,
    1561, 1660, 2623
Raincoat, 357
Raleigh, Sir Walter, 2131, 3164, 3212, 3800
Rank, 3683, 3976
Raphael, Sanzao, 1991
Rapid, 629, 2065
Rascals, 2507, 3266
Rattled, 2144
Razor, 255, 910, 1034, 1049, 1865, 1871
Reading, 584, 1187, 3311, 3707-3717
Real estate, 1018
Reap, 2662, 2728, 2791-2792
Reason, 242, 545, 1052, 1081, 2625, 3498,
    3672-3673, 3718-3725, 3851, 3910, 3990,
    4016, 4046
Reasoning, 4022
Rebellion, spirit of, 3245
Rebukes, 3159
Receive, 2695, 2728-2729, 2765, 3181, 3615
Recession, 1670
Recipe, 611, 882
Reckless, 356, 1905 ; driver, 1905-1906
Recognition, 485

Recognize, 188
Recompense, 3768
Reconciliation, 2989, 3063
Record, 1476, 3051
Recruit, 597, 634
Recuperate, 419
Red, 2257; herring, 2450, 2465
Reduce, 150, 802, 943, 1090, 1417, 1632
Reducing machine, 1907
References, 1000
Reflection, 691, 3473-3474, 3716, 3879
Reform, 933, 1439, 1736, 2888, 3203, 3903
Reformer, 1422, 1908
Refrigerator, 1001
Refuge, 3046
Refugee, 437
Refused, 2585
Regiment, 2157
Regret, 2990, 3010, 3757-3759
Regularity, 2154
Reincarnation, 1181
Reiteration, importance of, 107-112
Rejection, 1429, 1909
Rejoice, 2482, 2620, 2677, 3401
Relapse, 1003
Relaxation, 3231
Relief, 956
Religion, 19, 125, 640, 814, 1607, 1741, 3007-3008, 3105, 3190, 3203, 3210, 3474, 3533, 3644, 3669, 3706, 3726-3752, 3877
Remarks, 1200, 1203
Remarque, Eric, 2040
Remedy, 2384
Remember, 986, 2642, 3219, 3567
Remembrance, 2991, 2996-2997, 3010, 3160, 3216, 3655
Reminder, 595
Remorse, 601, 3753-3756
Repartee, 672, 741, 2017, 3850; definition of, 1910
Repentance, 2845, 2934, 3757-3759, 3880
Repetition, 849, 2401, 2687, 3088
Replies, 1202
Reporter, 472
Representation, 3213
Representatives, House of, 924
Reproach, 3159, 3502
Republican, 591
Republics, 3201, 3543
Reputation, 1268, 1345, 1634, 2931, 3582, 3760-3763
Rescue, 613
Research, 1251, 2023
Resemblance, 596
Resentment, 3010
Reserve, 2196
Resistance, 3253
Resolution, 3018-3025, 3170
Resort, 1526, 1941, 1955
Resources, 1502, 1725, 3052, 3191, 3230
Respect, 866, 1982, 3292, 3414, 3542, 3824, 3897
Respectability, 2880
Responsibility, 67, 679, 959, 3033-3038, 3882
Rest, 281, 889, 1010, 2538, 2577, 2703, 2744, 3468, 4024
Restaurant, 147, 157, 270, 392, 420, 439, 486, 536, 606, 684, 775, 829, 1003, 1077, 1504, 1822

Restless, 903, 2218
Restraint, 3208, 3789-3793, 3824
Restrict, 145
Results, 1102, 2975
Retailer, 294, 451, 457, 696, 1147
Retaliation, 1504
Retire, 1937, 3374
Retraction, 1911
Retreat, 3269
Retribution, 2474
Return, 2166, 2641, 2812
Returns, 1859
Revenge, 2894, 3064, 3789, 3816, 3952-3953
Revile, 2676
Revolution, 3198, 3203, 3764-3767
Reward, 613, 2677, 2729, 2791, 3768-3770
Rhetoric, 3851, 3855, 4046
Rheumatism, 549, 945
Rhyme, 2976, 3721
Ricardo, David, 1983
Rich (or Riches), 131, 231, 402, 936, 1604, 1862, 1912, 1961, 2145, 2406, 2421, 2479, 2487, 2557, 2573, 2614, 2616, 2629, 2639, 2719, 2748, 2804, 2899, 2947, 3401, 3574, 3771, 3780, 3973-3982
Riddle, 495
Ridicule, 3144
Ridiculous, 2471, 2517, 2928, 3221, 3619
Riding, 527, 680, 865, 1127
Rifle, 745, 771
Right, 1456, 1487, 1566, 2894, 2941, 2948, 3032, 3083, 3133, 3351, 3428, 3642, 3687, 3781-3783; of way, 1322
Righteous, 2567, 2571-2572, 2580, 2601, 2605, 2675, 2764, 2990
Rights, 3353, 3766, 3783
Riley, James Whitcomb, 2117, 2128, 2254
Ring, 314
Riotous, 2448
Ripeness, 2850
Risk, 2394, 2962
Rival, 878, 2895
River, 2262, 2385, 2404, 2437
Road, 322, 1434; hogs, 1534; manners, 1248
Roast of beef, 1367
Rob, 924, 1104, 2263, 2499, 2737, 3488
Rock, 960, 1140, 2061, 2287, 2423
Rockne, Knute, 117
Rod, 2570, 2600
Rolling-pin, 1458
Romance, 1202
Romantic, 903
Romeo, 458
Room-mate, 1657
Roosevelt, Franklin D., 71, 74, 135; Theodore, 2962
Root, 2666
Rose, 2130, 3382
Rosetta stone, 2484
Rough, 1613, 1802; it, 1213, 1484, 1639
Round Robin, 2483
Round-up, 1835
Rounder, 1913
Rousseau, Jean Jacques, 2909, 2946, 3598
Royal, 2402
Rubber band, 1507
Rubicon, crossing the, 2437
Rug-beater, 1815
Ruin, 2050, 2259

Rule, 1520, 2606, 2616, 2768, 3569, 3678, 3793
Ruler, 2506, 3198, 3214
Rules of conduct, 2027, 2935
Rumble seat, 1679, 1752
Rumor, 2464, 2726, 3193-3196
Rundown, 1681, 1914
Rushed, 922
Ruskin, John, 2084, 2228, 3032, 3035, 3190, 3521, 3567
Rust, 1612, 2688, 4005

S

Sabbath, 3784-3786
Sack, 2172
Sacred, 2371, 3542
Sacrifice, 81, 1706, 2413, 2761, 2784, 3174, 3632, 3957
Sadness, 2949, 3089, 3332, 3755-3756
Safe, 473, 926
Safety, 331, 389, 645, 869, 896, 921, 2595, 3554
Sagacity, 435
Sailor, 641, 687, 819, 2033
St. Helena, 1982
Salary, 306, 390, 445, 600, 616, 738, 790, 969, 1099, 1112, 1506, 1777, 1877, 1951, 1957
Sale, 827, 1766
Salesman, 153, 401, 545, 729, 762, 1162, 1901
Salesmanship, 215, 317, 451, 457, 493, 647, 696, 827, 855, 1186
Saliva, 1201
Salt, 306, 2678, 4051
Sample, 294
Sands, 2099, 2701
Sandwich, 473, 1047, 1084, 1262
Sanity, 3427
Santa Claus, 1586
Sarcasm, 212, 1060, 2463, 2977
Sarnoff, David, 3576
Satan, 636, 2105, 2488, 2716
Satiety, 3551
Satire, 3443, 3656
Satisfaction, 609, 1455, 2947-2950
Saturn, 2376, 2482
Saturnalia of crime, 2482
Saunter, 2262
Sausage, 259
Save (and Savings), 243, 1506, 1567, 3335
Savonarola, Girolamo, 2004
Saxophone, 921, 1727, 1950
Scales, 967, 1178
Scandal, 1393, 2263, 3110, 3193-3196, 3797, 3899
Scarce, 1501
Scared, 277, 296, 321
Scarlet Letter, 1969
Scars, 3592, 3939
Scent, 936, 1806, 2145
Scheme, 550, 2363, 2514
Schiller, Johann Christoph Friedrich von, 1983, 2178, 2222, 2275, 3084, 3225, 3286, 3425
Scholarship, 1117, 3175, 3341, 3942
School, 162, 201, 214, 264, 282, 301, 360, 449, 573, 575, 682, 718, 857, 862, 978, 1019, 2257, 3533; correspondence, 847
Schubert, Franz, 1967
Schwab, Charles, 103, 1972, 2868, 2878
Science, 189, 307, 573, 720, 960, 1327, 1748, 3105, 3395, 3706, 3738

Scientific opinion, 1467
Scientist, 1086, 1535, 1631
Scissors grinding, 1915
Scold, 2453
Scorn, 3113, 3293, 3625
Scotch stories, 151, 161, 238, 353, 445, 663, 879, 915, 990, 1159, 1916
Scotchman, 1697, 1918; definition of, 1916
Scott, Sir Walter, 1978, 2305, 2975
Scrambled, 365
Scripture, 3075
Scrooge, Ebenezer, 2478
Scrupulousness, 3130
Sculptor, 632, 2266
Scylla, 2423
Sea, 1498, 2179, 2287, 2303, 2584, 2635, 2818, 2912
Seal skin coat, 1384
Sealed, 2264
Search, 2496, 3615
Season, 412, 3844
Seat, 1042, 1410, 1510, 1581
Second helping, 1090
Secret, 2464, 2621, 3755, 3787-3788
Secretary, 898, 1785
Securities exchange, 1624
Security, 131, 202, 2865, 2938, 3438
Seeds, 1143, 3732
Seek, 2695, 2751, 3192
Self-complacency, 3576; -conceit, 3623; -contained, 2898; -control, 1636, 2683, 3653, 3789-3793; -defense, 2894; -denial, 1703; -esteem, 2923-2930; -government, 3207, 3213; -knowledge, 3653; -love, 3296, 3402; -made man, 227, 1508, 1917; -pity, 1307; -possession, 3791; -praise, 3164
Selfishness, 2354, 2874, 3198, 3805
Senate, 924
Senior, 1791
Sensation, 3163
Sense, 496, 1604, 1708, 1792, 2921-2922, 3178; of humor, 1918
Sensible, 1708
Sensitiveness, 662, 2466, 2894
Sensuality, 3840
Sentences, 3342, 3702; in groups of two or three, 133-135; interspersing short with long, 113-115; short, crisp, 116-117
Sentiment, 3780, 4022
Sentry, 618, 1123
September, 1667
Sepulchres, 2725
Serene, 2265
Sergeant, 597, 634, 724, 910, 1066, 1132
Seriousness, 2932
Sermon, 209, 347, 515, 833, 886, 902, 2047, 2843, 3474, 3492; on the Mount, illustration of reiteration, 108-109
Servant, 193, 220, 253, 299, 359, 524, 1002, 1883, 1982, 2616, 2723, 2727, 3232, 3463, 3751
Serve, 1105, 2438, 2690-2691, 3597
Service, 193, 283, 298, 736, 1110, 1173, 1729, 3118, 3380
Settlement work, 1919
Severity, 2989
Sew, 324
Sewing machine, 673
Shadow, 2084, 2556

Shakespeare, William, 191, 1983, 2085, 2109, 2138, 2146, 2822-2823, 2826-2827, 2842-2843, 2846, 2849-2851, 2853, 2855, 2862-2863, 2872-2873, 2882, 2885-2887, 2905, 2910, 2912, 2925, 2927, 2940, 2944-2945, 2947, 2953, 2955, 2958, 2963-2964, 2982, 2986-2988, 2993-2995, 2997, 3013, 3018, 3029, 3034, 3070, 3072-3078, 3089, 3119, 3134, 3137-3138, 3140-3141, 3154, 3185, 3195, 3199, 3215, 3236-3238, 3241-3242, 3244, 3265, 3268-3270, 3276, 3281, 3285, 3291, 3300-3301, 3307, 3310, 3344, 3348, 3366, 3368-3369, 3400, 3402, 3404-3406, 3409, 3431-3434, 3436, 3464, 3475, 3485, 3539-3540, 3546-3547, 3556, 3580, 3592, 3594, 3614, 3617, 3627-3628, 3645, 3651, 3655, 3682, 3720-3721, 3734, 3760, 3763, 3771, 3773, 3792, 3801, 3806-3807, 3818-3819, 3826, 3833-3835, 3839, 3870-3873, 3887-3888, 3891, 3893-3895, 3918, 3920, 3925, 3936, 3954, 3974-3975, 3996, 3998, 4011-4013, 4016-4019, 4049-4051
Shallow, 2175, 3707
Shame, 3014, 3196, 3303, 3493, 3790
Sharing, 2739, 2936, 3249, 4032
Shave, 187, 255, 787, 910, 1034
Shaw, George Bernard, 25, 95, 2042, 2332
Sheep, 567, 1554, 1848, 2699, 3426
Shell, 1335, 2135, 2182, 3371, 3844
Shelley, Percy Bysshe, 2210, 3091, 3290
Sheridan, Richard Brinsley, 3284, 3879
Sheriff, 221
Shine, 2268, 2755
Ship, 2177, 2252, 2287, 2309, 2584
Shirt, 173, 1448, 2408
Shoehorn, 1920
Shoes, 242, 582, 647, 1539, 1682
Shoot, 309, 353, 423
Shopping, 631, 951
Shopworn, 1553
Short, 803, 2296
Shortcake, 1144
Short-circuit, 1011
Short-wave set, 1321
Shot, 234, 766, 904; gun, 1097
Shriveled, 2285
Shun, 2270
Shutter, 2144
Shyness, 3502
Sick, 20, 176, 196, 850, 879, 903, 1192, 1763, 1914, 3052, 3140, 3324; definition of, 1921
Siesta, 1324
Sift, 2271
Sigh, 2272-2273, 3377
Sight, 2582, 2590, 3094-3095
Sightseeing, 164
Sign, 260, 450, 510, 547, 783, 1514
Signal, 525, 657, 1208
Silence, 1300, 1387, 1658, 2015, 2247, 2274-2275, 2952, 3242, 3558, 3599, 3794-3800, 3879, 3931; definition of, 1922
Silk, 1530, 3600
Silver, 2622, 3323
Similes, use of, 118
Simmer, 1013
Simon Pure, 2477
Simplicity, 2025, 2768, 3801-3804, 3855
Sin, 640, 2384, 2811, 2943, 3402, 3805-3812
Sincerity, 2725, 3582, 3813-3814
Singer, 229, 430, 541, 847, 870, 887
Singing, 1405, 1427, 1535

Sinon, 2480
Siren, 2432
Sisters, 1490
Sisyphus, a task of, 2388
Sit, 257
Sixes and sevens, 2476
Size, 2919
Skating, 719
Skepticism, 125, 199, 2734
Skill, 2503, 2639, 2816-2817, 2837
Skin, 748, 843, 919, 2560
Skinned, 1137
Slack, 412
Slander, 3193-3196, 3797, 3815-3817
Slaughter, 2593
Slavery, 3132-3133, 3444, 3552, 3664, 3763
Sleep, 156, 385, 413, 501, 504, 671, 889, 973, 1060, 1080, 1216, 1355, 1416, 1583, 1648, 1654, 1848, 1929, 2369, 2618, 2992, 3818-3819
Sleeplessness, 3819
Slide rule, 1688
Slogan, 339; definition of, 1924
Slot machine, 1645
Slough of Despond, 2469
Slow, 492, 555, 592, 1738, 2606, 2808
Sluggard, 2592, 2625
Small, 1098; boy, 1487; town, 1925; voice, 2555
Smart, 1650, 1726, 1927, 1931, 2596
Smile, 292, 1657, 2376, 3074, 3246, 3345, 3377, 3457, 3798
Smoke, 240, 933, 1782, 1972
Smoking lounge, 1928
Smooth, 1048
Snake, 16, 2180
Snare, 3868
Snobbish, 1701, 1715
Snore, 385, 1080, 1929-1930, 2077
Snow, 2091-2092, 2098, 2205, 2271
Soap, 1949
Sob, 2277
Social knowledge, 1364
Social tact, 1363
Socialism, 2875
Society, 1546, 1680, 2278, 3117, 3365, 3462, 3530, 3577, 3644, 3820-3824, 3945, 3981
Socrates, 128, 2906, 3040, 3224, 3317, 3660, 3662, 3761, 3978, 4007
Soft, 2253, 2279-2281, 3421
Solace, 1559, 2660
Soldier, 186, 570, 764, 1926
Solicitous, 217, 3246
Solitary, 1749, 3561, 3821
Solitude, 1441, 2149, 2898, 2900, 3052, 3162, 3559, 3825-3831
Solomon, 832, 2213, 2692
Solve, 2455
Son, 174, 182, 217, 1199, 1788, 1904, 1913, 2468, 2594, 2600, 2651, 2663, 2763, 3520, 3524
Song, 367, 1721, 3392
Sophisticated, 494, 1676, 1931
Sophistry, 3724
Sophocles, 2852, 2904, 3106, 3151, 3937, 3966
Sopranos, 1321
Sorrow, 2658, 2891, 2907, 2945-2946, 2991, 3062, 3236-3237, 3260, 3755, 3832-3839

INDEX

409

Soul, 1268, 2115, 2178, 2277, 2446, 2717, 2897, 2901, 3469, 3527, 3660, 3666, 3737, 3763, 3840-3846, 3883
Sound, 1246; effects man, 1932
Soup, 186, 389, 394, 851, 1073, 1840
South, 495, 2253; Robert, 3510, 3667, 3951
Southey, Robert, 2092, 2110
Sovereignty, 3197, 3653
Sow, 2398, 2662, 2728, 2791, 2812
Spaghetti, 1933
Spark, 2308, 2562
Sparkle, 2283
Speak, 1300, 2463, 2808, 3859
Speaker, 212, 222, 287, 381, 642, 672, 803, 929, 1038, 1203, 1205, 1252, 1394, 1408, 1436, 1900, 1948, 3849, 3852, 3854
Speaker's voice, 1488
Spectacles, 1291, 1428
Speech, 929, 1205, 1668, 1700, 1995, 2008, 2010, 2046-2047, 2065, 2109, 2165, 2490, 2951-2958, 3014, 3056-3057, 3398, 3528, 3616, 3796, 3800, 3847-3855, 3865, 3950; preparation of, 1-84; before the audience, 141-142; body of, 40; conclusion, 59; how to make your speech sparkle, 85-138, 140; in a nutshell, 139; introduction, 8; steps in preparing, 5; what a speech requires, 143
Speed, 163, 655, 701, 747, 786, 890, 939, 1170, 1342, 1631, 1956, 3372
Spellbound, 2284
Spelling, 162, 289, 358, 538, 989, 1053, 1120, 1155, 1942
Spencer, Herbert, 1983
Spend, 653, 1185, 1533, 1567, 3335, 3616
Spendthrift, 349, 1227
Spin, 2692
Spinach, 535, 953, 1593
Spine, 3019
Spirit, 2604, 2606, 2668, 2778, 2824, 3713
Spitting, 1050
Splendor, 2251
Spoil, 1468, 2779
Sponge, 521, 2136
Sport, 1069, 1602, 1646
Sports, 1356
Spring, 1294, 2169, 2233, 2249, 2494, 3856-3857
Squander, 2451, 3900
Squirrel, 290, 1271
Stable, 2404
Stagger, 2286
Stagnation, 1609, 2444
Stalking horse, 2467
Stamp, Sir Josiah, 1812, 2047
Stand, 2172, 2288, 2617, 2782
Star, 145, 166, 440, 2088, 2114, 2197, 2251, 2268, 2549, 2859, 3070, 3287, 3518, 3557-3558, 3562, 3744, 4003; chamber, 2464
Starvation, 48, 1907, 3140, 3338
Stateliness, 2461, 3844
Statesman, 18, 68, 1617, 1742, 3037, 3209, 3467, 3639, 3860
Statistician, 1698, 2137; definition of, 1934
Statistics, 152-153, 166, 211, 237, 751, 1194, 2024
Statue, 2100, 2122, 2288, 2379, 3235
Status quo, 406
Steal, 277, 519, 601, 624, 659, 681, 808, 874, 2405, 2542, 2688, 3763, 3884, 3890
Stealthy, 2287

Steamboat, 931, 985, 2045, 2212
Steam-roller, 2066
Stenographer, 592
Stentorian voice, 2415
Sterne, Laurence, 3012, 3188, 3335, 3415, 3878, 3989
Stevenson, Robert Louis, 51, 2245, 3401
Stew, 759, 1058
Still, 2280
Sting, 398
Stingy, 1557-1558
Stock market, 1459, 1624
Stockbroker, 923
Stockings, 262
Stoicism, 125
Stomach, 1847, 2174
Stone, 2141, 2388, 2484, 2585, 2696, 3613
Storm, 819, 1142, 2295, 2460
Story, 461, 1101, 1209, 1712, 1902, 2284, 2516
Stout, 693, 934, 943, 955, 1078, 1565, 1622; -heartedness, 2903
Stove, 1973, 2067
Straight, 928
Straightforwardness, 1244
Strain, 2459
Stranger, 1095, 2596, 2730
Strap, 595; hanger, 1935
Strategy, 271, 627, 738, 1172, 3487
Stream, 2054, 2264
Streamlined, 911, 1650, 1683
Street, 885, 1707, 1888
Streetcar, 662, 1410; conductor, 1936
Strength, 957, 2357, 2359, 2400, 2405, 2443, 2619, 2927, 2937, 3092, 3253, 3458, 3728, 3986, 4039
Strict, 434
Strive, 3332
Strong, 1863, 2550
Struggle, 2290
Strut, 1521
Stubby, 2296
Stuck, 2267
Student, 219, 244, 263, 375, 440, 459, 463, 538, 672, 682, 749, 769, 828, 863, 919, 980, 1021, 1064, 1102, 1117, 1120, 1122, 1544, 1669, 1818, 1996
Study, 2492, 2643, 3173, 3290, 3323, 3365
Stupid, 1532, 1638
Stygian darkness, 2385
Style, 891, 1002
Styx River, 2351, 2385
Sublime, 3221, 3228, 3632
Submarine, 641
Submission, 3292, 3736
Substitute, 358, 1144, 1653
Subtraction, 1194
Subways, 1510
Success, 176, 237, 390, 435, 605, 692, 801, 820, 848, 942, 1511, 1572, 1599, 1694, 1728, 1744, 1970, 2015, 2045, 2786, 2819-2831, 2858, 3068, 3112-3116, 3858-3862, 4028, 4030; definition of, 1937
Successful man, 1938
Successful wife's motto, 1939
Succor, 2709
Sucker, 1319, 1463
Sudden, 516, 2828
Suffer, 2481, 2785, 2946, 3062, 3591-3592, 3766
Sufficient, 2693
Suffocate, 804

Sugar daddy, 1940
Suggestion, 4040
Suicide, 1720, 1890, 2485
Suit, 357, 1284
Suitor, 1570
Sulking Achilles, 2352
Summer, 364, 1013, 1027, 2117, 2128, 2632; resort, 1941
Sun, 145, 2176, 2225, 2283, 2794, 2914, 2924, 3696, 3846; -dial, 2083
Sunday, 238, 1513, 2538; school, 636, 954
Superfluousness, 3043, 3140
Superiority, 2835, 3016, 3220, 3440, 3789
Superstitions, 1514, 1653
Supper, 3138
Surety, 2596
Surgeon, 589, 1578
Surprise, 426, 2248, 2393
Survival, 1622, 1635, 1905, 2912, 2975
Suspense, 516, 733, 2459, 3378
Suspicion, 2973, 3015, 3127
Sustain, 2580
Swallow, 3712
Swans, 2355
Sway, 2291
Swear, 1257, 1899, 2537
Sweat, 1579, 2526
Swedish farmer, 1046
Sweet, 2215, 2578, 3377; Adeline, 1535
Sweetheart, 2452
Swift, 2639, 2808; Jonathan, 3066, 3155, 3467, 3828, 3923, 3967
Swim, 565, 637, 884, 1160, 1351, 3649
Swinburne, Algernon Charles, 2264
Swindle, 624, 2737
Swing, 203
Switches, 1407
Sword, 2439, 2455, 2579, 2647, 3378, 4047
Sympathy, 2039, 2498, 3484, 3820
Symphony, Schubert's C-Major, 1967
Synonym, use of, 119, 358; definition of, 1942
System, 3485-3487

T

Tabloid, 1028
Tact, 188, 408-409, 588, 690, 726, 1312-1313, 1601, 1943, 1972, 3863-3865
Taft, Robert A., how he prepares his addresses, 6; William Howard, 893
Tailor, 324, 970, 1040
Take back, 2456
Talent, 1312-1313, 1703, 2293, 2424, 2840, 2900, 3023, 3167-3173, 3226, 3593, 4037
Talk, 2500, 2926, 2951-2958, 3705, 3708, 3829, 3883
Talkative, 839, 841, 864, 907, 992, 1207
Tall, 1902, 2034
Talleyrand-Perigord, Charles Maurice de, 3848, 3858, 3861
Tantalus, the suffering of, 2428
Target, 309, 771
Task, 2392, 2400, 2404, 2412, 2438, 4032
Taste, 669, 2409, 3521, 3712, 3864, 3926
Tattoo, 687
Tax payers, 1272, 1276, 1290, 1586, 1590
Taxes, 160, 341, 531, 706, 1197, 1257, 1276, 1477, 1641, 1671, 3544
Taxi, 1518, 1545
Tea, 715, 1048

Teacher, 148, 162, 211, 219, 223, 234, 244, 263, 304, 310, 321, 328, 412, 419, 459, 463, 482-483, 506, 510, 528, 538, 561, 594, 656, 658, 660, 695, 703-705, 806, 828, 867, 919, 980, 1021, 1064, 1102
Teaching, 1122
Tears, 229, 552, 1552, 2240, 3236, 3394, 3457, 3524, 3563, 3599, 3837-3838
Technical knowledge, 12
Tediousness, 3627, 3889
Teeth, 1944, 2199, 2397-2398, 2564
Teetotaler, 879
Telegram, 293, 416, 2126
Telephone, 94, 184, 253, 343, 585, 720, 778, 992, 1519, 1679; pole, 1247
Teller, bank, 1846
Temper, 2453
Temperament, 2377
Temperance, 4010
Temperature, 1649
Tempest, 2177
Temptation, 2716, 2782, 3647, 3866-3869, 4035
Ten Commandments, 1123, 1175, 2371, 2535-2544
Tender, 2294, 2989
Tennyson, Alfred Lord, 1991, 2861, 2913-2914, 2917-2918, 2991, 2996, 3038, 3059, 3081, 3097, 3125, 3128, 3211, 3327, 3367, 3371, 3399, 3403, 3408, 3508, 3568, 3653, 3661, 3665, 3691, 3847, 3857, 3892, 3896, 3922, 3931, 3958, 3971-3972, 3991, 4026
Tenor, 2150
Tenterhooks, 2459
Tents, 2140
Term papers, 1340
Terrify, 2295, 2422
Thackeray, William Makepeace, 2036, 2867
Thankfulness, 3215-3219, 3258
Thanklessness, 2905
Theater, 191, 257, 949, 1042, 1051, 1352, 1522, 1808, 1879, 1924, 2048-2049, 3201
Theft, 277
Theology, 3735
Theory, 1248, 1398, 3093, 3312
Thief, 399, 874, 906, 1234, 2263, 2688, 3759
Thin, 802, 881, 1084, 1622
Thinking, 99, 1054, 1563, 1927
Thirst, 2575, 2671
Thirty years old, 1946
Thistle, 2279
Thomson, James, 3148, 3625
Thoreau, Henry David, 3080, 3083, 3772, 3827, 3911
Thorn, 2790
Thoroughness, 3027
Thought, 1260, 2065, 2118, 2297, 2833, 2846, 2914, 2956, 3006, 3014, 3025, 3049, 3123, 3173, 3186, 3370, 3439, 3473, 3575, 3601, 3710, 3713, 3798, 3843, 3845, 3848, 3857, 3870-3886, 3890, 4003
Thoughtful, 357
Thrift, 185, 454, 653, 658, 729, 838, 1557, 2020, 2024, 3039-3044, 3549
Throat, 187, 917
Throne, 1591, 3211
Tide, 1126, 2232, 3154
Tiger, 423
Tight, 2267
Tilt, 2458

INDEX

Time, 362-363, 377, 410, 522, 722, 937, 1350, 1395, 2070, 2828, 2853, 2855, 2909, 3009, 3051, 3090, 3093, 3335, 3394, 3600, 3887-3913, 3960, 3994, 4004, 4036, 4041
Timid, 728, 1461
Tipping, 830
Titans, 2443
Titian, 1980
Toad, 2085, 2843
Toast, 1692, 1774, 1993; master, 1547, 1948
Tobacco, 1837
Today, 3017, 3031, 3041, 3493, 3590, 3902, 3938, 3941
Toil, 1751, 2637, 2692, 3025, 3045, 3112, 3387, 3646, 4024-4040
Tolerance, 2979-2981, 3914-3916
Toll, 275
Tolstoi, Count Lyof Nikolayevitch, 3380
Tomb, 2230, 3516
Tombstone, 978
Tomorrow, 2627, 2654, 2789, 2824, 3017, 3031, 3041, 3553, 3834, 3902-3903
Tongue, 276, 1298, 1373, 2227, 3194-3195, 3667, 3799, 3817, 3832, 3865, 3872, 4045
Tonsillitis, 1550, 1763
Tonsils, 1805, 1944
Tools of effective speech, 86; fifteen tools: alliteration, 136-138; humor, 87-92; illustrations from biography, plays, literature, 93-106; intersperse short sentences with long ones, 113-115; place ideas in contrast, 123; repetition of words and phrases, 107-112; antonyms, 120; Biblical quotations, 126-128; colorful phrases, 124-125; phrases, sentences, clauses i- groups of two or three, 133-135; questions, 121-122; quotations from literature, 129-132; short, crisp sentences, 116-117; similes, 118; synonyms, 119
Toot ensemble, 1947
Tooth, 261, 555, 581, 760, 846, 895, 1901, 2546, 2682
Torment, 2481
Tossed, 2298
Touch, 843
Tough, 182, 470, 496, 731, 1032, 1049, 1089
Tourist, 260, 303, 453, 1061, 1098, 1150
Towel, 348, 1174, 1834, 1949
Town, 1229, 1482; small, 1925
Tradition, 3051, 3917-3919
Traffic, 273, 1139, 1560, 1679
Tragedy, 1948, 2473, 3920-3922
Trailer, 1561
Train, 320, 495, 522, 1133, 1146, 1250, 1327, 1514, 1523, 1683, 1932, 2615
Training, 1812, 2909, 3047
Tramp, 245, 349, 366, 586, 617, 868, 964, 1111
Tranquillity, 1693, 2738, 2800, 3606
Transfusion, 787
Transgressor, 2598
Travail, 2637, 2709
Travel, 155, 260, 310, 558, 582, 830, 931, 985, 1206, 1789, 2503, 3923-3924
Traveling man's estate, 1949
Treason, 3694
Treasure, 2689
Treasury, 1575, 3478
Tree, 374, 757, 960, 1129, 1143, 2129, 2227, 2267, 2666, 2711, 2843, 3193, 3614
Trial, 2510, 3092
Tribulation, 442

Tribute, 2722
Trifle, 2382, 2475, 3925-3931
Trigonometry, 1067
Trite, 1675
Triton among minnows, 2433
Triumph, 1421, 2462, 2895, 3387
Trojans, 2360, 2363-2364, 2367, 2473, 2480
Trombone, 491
Trouble, 784, 807, 1297, 1390, 1468, 2393, 2398, 2420, 2460, 2562-2563, 3932-3933
Trousers, 481, 1163, 1282
Troy, 2360, 2379
Truism, 1637
Trust, 624, 1843, 3532
Trustees, 3973
Truth, 65, 130, 168, 241, 534, 544, 1524, 1601, 1635, 1757, 1901, 2391, 2757, 2764, 2785, 2985, 3035, 3066, 3095, 3166, 3297, 3466, 3474, 3505, 3601, 3604, 3621, 3674, 3804, 3814, 3842, 3934-3947; -in-advertising, 1950
Truthful woman, 1951
Tuberculosis, 51
Turkey, 454, 988, 1521, 2191
Turn, 2300
Turnover, 1517, 1548
Turret-top, 1650
Turtle, 1650
Twain, Mark, 1964, 1994, 2018
Twilight, 2261
Twins, 436
Two-faced, 817
Typographical error, 1952
Tyrants, 3552, 3554

U

Ultimatum, 961
Ulysses, 2357-2358, 2363, 2425
Umbrella, 469; definition of, 1953
Umpire, 755, 798; definition of, 1954
Unanimous, 856
Unbelief, 2734
Uncertainty, 2627, 2834, 2865, 3448, 3904
Uncle, 268; Sam, 1586
Uncompromising, 2075
Unconquerable, 2302
Undecided, 799
Undergraduate, 1088
Underlings, 2826
Understanding, 95, 127, 1045, 2492, 2639, 2798, 2929, 3057, 3412, 3484, 3634, 3829, 3845
Understatement, 1319
Uneasiness, 1281, 3912
Unemployed, 1256
Unhappiness, 3241, 3243, 3776
Union, 1160, 3357
United States, 1489, 1533, 3339
Unity, 2587
Universe, 3201, 3384, 3401, 3620, 3638
University, 688, 998, 1117, 1217, 1973, 3055, 3364
Unjust, 3303
Unkindness, 3284, 3307, 3310, 3401
Unknown, 3332, 3825
Unreasonable, 996
Unscrupulous, 2410, 2475, 2512
Unselfishness, 594, 2411
Unsettled, 562
Unworthiness, 3525

Upright, 2305
Usher, 257, 2039
Utopia, 1534, 2454

V

Vacant, 1545, 1817
Vacation, 155, 281, 364, 534, 675, 1013, 1027, 1261, 1525, 1683, 1941; resort, 1955
Vacuum cleaner, 373, 483, 549, 831, 1440, 1815
Vagrant, 2306
Vain, 2581, 2590, 2633, 2646, 2687, 2795
Valedictorian, 1462
Valiancy, 3401, 3665
Valor, 830, 2964, 2966, 2995
Value, 1306, 3225, 3711
Vandenberg, Arthur H., importance of preparing a speech, 4
Vanish, 2308-2309, 2810
Vanity, 2036, 3216, 3312, 3683, 3718, 3800, 3870, 3906, 3948-3951, 4020
Variety, 295, 3231
Vegetarian, 371, 1111, 1374, 1782
Velocity, 1956
Vengeance, 2682, 2771, 3795, 3952-3953
Venus, 2353, 2367
Verbosity, 1710, 3998
Verse, 1625, 3392
Vest, 167
Vice, 2310, 2875, 2916, 3136, 3350, 3492, 3815, 3960-3961; president, 1957
Vicissitude, 2998
Victory, 1468, 2397, 3026, 3250, 3603
Viewpoint, 149, 154, 1094
Vigilance, 3354
Villain, 239, 2116, 3964
Violinist, 2013
Virgil, 2870, 3096, 3322, 3426, 3541
Virginia Military Institute, 1083
Virginians, great, 18
Virtue, 2510, 2597, 2870, 2899, 2933, 3088, 3130, 3196, 3220, 3335, 3350, 3506, 3533, 3564-3565, 3753, 3807, 3814, 3912, 3954-3961
Vision, 2663, 2763, 3328
Visitors, 1363
Vitamins, 1475
Vocabulary, 1517
Vocation, 3380
Voice, 1408, 1535, 2225, 2264, 2417, 2531, 2555, 2991, 4018
Voltaire, François Marie Arouet de, 1975, 2005, 2088, 2129, 2317, 2969, 3118, 3378, 3389, 3586, 3621, 3635, 3673, 3678, 3947, 3993, 3997, 4022
Vote, 1527, 3427, 3638
Voters, 1360
Vows, 3691
Vulnerability, 2351

W

Waffle, 859
Wages, 756, 1396, 2739
Wait, 233, 664, 3597
Waiter, 249, 389, 392, 420, 536, 684, 694, 829, 1003, 1058, 1678
Walk, 246, 344, 1417, 2158, 2281, 2501, 2599
Wall, 1906
Wander, 2211, 2358

Want ad, 1677
Wants, 902, 1528, 1603, 1711, 1739, 3777, 3982
War, 304, 899, 1529, 1776, 2002, 2437, 2505, 2579, 2726, 2918, 2960, 3424, 3603, 3962-3972
Warden, 1898
Warm, 1649, 2064
Warning, 1897, 2225
Wash, 603, 634
Washing, 628, 835, 956, 962; machine, 1440
Washington, George, 135, 1984, 1986, 1993, 2004, 2025, 2411
Waste, 232, 1603, 2747, 3375, 3386, 3549, 3572; basket, 483
Wasteful, 1193
Watch, 612, 974, 1704, 1926, 2047, 2582
Watchful, 2369
Watchman, 2653
Water, 334, 720, 914, 972, 1955, 2155, 2183, 2390, 2584, 2644, 2887, 3613; power, 1552
Waterloo, Battle of, 2002
Watermelon, 957
Waves, 2298, 2817
Wax, 2246, 2426
Way, 1610, 2548
Weak, 715, 1085, 1732, 1743, 2351, 2500, 3130, 3412, 3453, 3671, 3983
Wealth, 1377, 1496, 2026, 2389, 2406, 2421, 2479, 2487, 2899, 2906, 3001, 3064, 3178, 3229, 3323, 3339, 3489, 3574, 3638, 3694-3697, 3725, 3771-3780, 3973-3982
Wealthy, 3551, 3821-3822
Wear, 1612, 3460
Weary, 2643, 2792, 2801
Weather, 266, 303, 502, 1046, 1649; cock, 2300
Webster, Daniel, 1992, 1995, 2004, 2009, 2037, 3039, 3213, 3305, 3338, 3357, 3743, 3785, 3882; Noah, 1968; definition of, 1958
Wedding, 999, 1059, 1685, 1870
Weeds, 265
Weeping, 2219
Weighing, 967, 1178
Weight, 934, 1072, 1108, 1178, 1341, 1632, 1951, 1960, 2011, 3033, 3187, 3327, 3708, 3813
Welcome, 2126
Wesley, John, 1985
West Point, 799, 1083
Westinghouse, George, 2012
Whale, 1383
Wheat, 583
Wheel, 822-823
Whirlwind, 2662
Whiskey, 879, 1154, 1782
Whisper, 963, 997, 1713, 2220, 2227
Whistle, 788, 972
White, 2074; race, 52
Whitman, Walt, 3384
Whittier, John Greenleaf, 2091, 2093-2094, 2141, 3100, 3756
Wicked, 2468, 2511, 2572, 2628, 3072, 3080, 3571, 3647, 3711, 3808
Wide, 895, 1347
Widow, 338, 371, 2737
Wife, 165, 206, 216, 224, 240, 245, 248, 337, 341, 381, 388, 391, 395, 403, 437-438, 448, 508, 681, 738-739, 790, 810, 832, 849, 855, 880, 904, 920, 927, 929, 946, 986, 992, 1022,

1024, 1057, 1067, 1070, 1074, 1096, 1099, 1115, 1130, 1278, 1335, 1392, 1511, 1516, 1577, 1701, 1798, 1804, 1845, 1871, 1875, 1913, 1938-1939, 2425, 2746, 3460, 4014-4015; definition of, 1959
Wild, 903, 1149, 1475
Wild oats, 1116
Wildcat, 505
Will, 1347, 1610, 1652, 1921, 3018-3025, 3184, 3225, 3230, 3358, 3845, 3983, 3987
Wilson, Woodrow, 2046
Win, 117, 300, 878, 3344
Wind, 914, 2071, 2086, 2110, 2146, 2165, 2173, 2218, 2220, 2253, 2300, 2306, 2447, 2623, 2662, 2793, 2817, 3188, 3988-3989
Windmills, tilt at, 2458
Window, 1327, 2115, 2144
Windshield, 1247
Wine, 2381, 2612, 3391-3392, 3410, 3652
Wings, 911, 2426, 2577
Winter, 175, 3856
Wire, 1744, 1814
Wisdom, 768, 998, 1448, 1475, 2213, 2565, 2592, 2594, 2599, 2609, 2625, 2631, 2636, 2639, 2649, 2770, 2777, 2834, 3017, 3024, 3119, 3142, 3145-3147, 3165, 3220, 3285, 3320, 3347, 3363, 3404, 3407, 3414, 3442, 3493, 3500, 3562, 3596, 3634, 3640, 3652, 3677, 3704, 3787, 3828, 3938, 3979, 3990-4010, 4041, 4049
Wish, 407, 932, 3871
Wishbone, 535, 809
Wishing, 1350
Wit, 273, 367, 1273, 1652, 1716, 2017, 2873, 3280, 3283-3284, 3394, 3714, 3850, 3984, 4011-4013
Witch, 373
Withered, 2129, 2145
Witness, 269, 505, 670, 1134, 2037, 2543
Wizard, 1460, 1505
Woe, 2473, 3484, 3630, 3932-3933
Wolf, 1227, 2188, 2192, 2650, 2699, 3426
Woman, 382, 564, 864, 1056, 1235, 1282, 1358, 1384, 1386, 1388, 1410, 1413, 1426, 1431, 1457, 1471, 1483, 1487, 1511, 1517, 1548, 1552, 1559, 1614, 1676, 1686, 1730, 1732-1733, 1767, 1829, 1860, 1906, 1946, 1951, 2173, 2248, 2359, 2416, 2432, 2461, 2563, 2597, 3020, 3418, 4014-4023
Woman's ambition, 1960; crowning glory, 1961
Wonder, 3618
Wonderful, 254, 2589
Woolworth, Frank W., 102, 2003
Wordiness, 3998
Words, 297, 1182, 1844, 1868, 1942, 2028, 2041, 2498, 2517, 2558, 2579, 2602, 2608, 2622, 2626, 2795, 2951-2958, 3051, 3340-3342, 3379, 3635, 3702, 3705, 3756, 3794, 3799, 3847-3855

Work, 29, 101, 189, 329, 452, 580, 598, 617, 619, 635, 883, 956, 1000, 1010, 1232, 1303, 1336, 1385, 1491, 1512, 1709, 1737, 1751, 1819, 1909, 1919, 2741, 2758, 2774, 2804, 2809, 2868, 3011, 3045, 3112, 3340, 3875, 4024-4040
Workingmen's compensation, 1200
World, 1320, 1468, 1513, 1725, 1735, 2222, 2679, 2717, 2777, 2813, 2830, 2915, 2930, 2968, 3021, 3036, 3076, 3090, 3120, 3186, 3224, 3529, 3546, 3559, 3602, 3651, 3749, 3809, 3831, 3877, 3944, 3946, 3967, 3985, 4006
Worm, 182, 2993, 3366, 3406
Worry, 442, 507, 637, 653, 1136, 1390, 3820
Worship, 2642, 3726
Worst, 3920
Worthiness, 2741, 2816, 2953, 3381, 3383, 3429, 3616
Wound, 1395, 2665, 3592, 3815, 3910, 3939
Wrath, 2602, 2794, 2808
Wreck, 525, 554, 714, 765, 2423
Wrestling, 342
Wrinkles, 2123
Writers, 2969, 4041-4048
Writing, 280, 749, 989, 1113, 1187, 1969, 1983, 2463, 3014, 3509, 3714, 4041-4048
Wrong, 315, 553, 980, 1792, 2503, 2908, 2938-2939, 2941, 2943, 3083, 3351, 3379, 3399, 3404, 3449, 3642, 3938; time, 1114

X

Xanthippe, 2453

Y

Yacht, 1826
Yawn, 913, 1364, 1693
Yearn for the fleshpots, 2396
Yellow peril, 1962
Yellowstone Park, 1061
Yesterday, 3017, 3493, 3891, 3938
Yodel, 851
Youngster, 916
Youth, 524, 1487, 1497, 1677, 1991, 2042, 2124, 2413, 2642, 2851, 2928, 3054, 3147, 3300-3301, 3326, 3374-3375, 3377, 3397, 3446, 3476, 3502, 3538, 3648-3649, 3857, 3966, 3984, 4049-4053

Z

Zadig, A Mystery of Fate, 2005
Zeal, 3066
Zebra, 1153
Zero, 336, 375
Ziegfeld, Florenz, 1997
Zoo, 196, 213, 651, 1943